Private Sector and Enterprise Development

Private Sector and Enterprise Development

Fostering Growth in the Middle East and North Africa

Lois Stevenson

Visiting Research Fellow, International Development Research Centre, Cairo, Egypt

Edward Elgar
Cheltenham, UK • Northampton, MA, USA

International Development Research Centre
Ottawa • Cairo • Dakar • Montevideo • Nairobi • New Delhi • Singapore

Copublished by
Edward Elgar Publishing Limited
The Lypiatts
15 Lansdown Road
Cheltenham
Glos GL50 2JA
UK

Edward Elgar Publishing, Inc.
William Pratt House
9 Dewey Court
Northampton
Massachusetts 01060
USA

International Development Research Centre
PO Box 8500
Ottawa, ON, K1G 3H9
Canada
www.idrc.ca/info@idrc.ca
ISBN 978 1 55250 474 1 (IDRC e-book)

A catalogue record for this book
is available from the British Library

Library of Congress Number: 2010926006

MIX
Paper from
responsible sources
FSC® C018575

ISBN 978 1 84980 295 6 (cased)

Printed and bound by MPG Books Group, UK

Contents

Abbreviations

ACAA	Agreement on Conformity Assessment and Acceptance of Industrial Products
ADB	Asian Development Bank
AfDB	African Development Bank
AFEM	Association des Femmes chefs d'Enterprises du Maroc
AG	Algeria
AHDR	Arab Human Development Report
ANAPEC	Agence Nationale de Promotion de l'Emploi et des Compétences
ANDPME	Agence Nationale de Développement de la Petite et Moyenne Entreprise
ANETI	Agence Nationale pour l' Emploi et le Travail Indépendant
ANGEM	National Microcredit Management Agency
ANPME	Agence Nationale pour la Promotion de la Petite et Moyenne Entreprise
ANSEJ	Agence Nationale de Soutien à l'Emploi des Jeunes
ANVREDET	Agence Nationale de Valorisation de la Recherche et du Développement Technologique
APEC	Asia-Pacific Economic Cooperation
APS	Adult Population Survey
AUB	American University of Beirut
BDC	Business Development Center
BDS	business development services
BDSSP	Business Development Services Support Project
BEE	business enabling environment
BFPME	Banque de Financement des PME
BTI	Bertelsmann Transformation Index
CARE	Club d'Action et de Réflexion
CAS	Central Administration of Statistics
CAWTAR	Center of Arab Women for Training and Research
CCG	Caisse Centrale de Garantie
CCSBE-CCPME	Canadian Council for Small Business and Entrepreneurship

CGGI	Investment Credit Guarantee Fund
CGEM	General Confederation of Moroccan Enterprises
CIDA	Canadian International Development Agency
CIPE	Center for International Private Enterprise
CIS	Cooperative Insurance Society
CNC PME	Conseil National Consultatif pour la Promotion des Petites et Moyennes Entreprises
CREAD	Centre de Recherche en Economie Appliquée pour le Développement
CSO	Central Statistical Office
CSO	civil society organization
DAC	Development Assistance Committee
DEF	Development and Employment Fund
DfID	Department for International Development
DPPR	Development Plan for Poverty Reduction
DZD	Algerian dinar
EBF	Entrepreneurs Business Forum
EBRD	European Bank for Reconstruction and Development
EBWA	Egyptian Business Women Association
ECA	Economic Commission for Africa
ECES	Egyptian Center for Economic Studies
EFCs	Entrepreneurial Framework Conditions
EG	Egypt
EGP	Egyptian pound
EIB	European Investment Bank
EJB	Egyptian Junior Business Association
ELMPS	Egyptian Labor Market Panel Survey
ERF	Economic Research Forum
ERFKE	Education Reform for Knowledge Economy
ERP	Economic Reform Programme
ERRADA	Egyptian Regulatory Reform and Development Activity
EU	European Union
FCE	Forum des Chefs d'Entreprises
FDI	foreign direct investment
FEMISE	Forum Euroméditerranéen des Instituts Economiques
FGAR	SME Guarantee Fund
FSF	Swedish Foundation for Small Business Research
FTA	Free Trade Agreement
FTZ	Free Trade Zone
FYP	Five-Year Plan
GAFI	General Authority for Investment

GAFTA	Greater Arab Free Trade Area
GCC	Gulf Cooperation Council
GCI	Global Competitiveness Index
GDP	gross domestic product
GEM	Global Entrepreneurship Monitor
GGGI	Global Gender Gap Index
GGP	Globalization, Growth and Poverty
GIA	General Investment Authority
GNI	gross national income
GONU	Government of National Unity
GOSS	Government of Southern Sudan
GTZ	German Technical Cooperation
HCST	Higher Council for Science and Technology
HDI	Human Development Index
HI	High income
HIBA	Higher Institute of Business Administration
IADB	Inter-American Development Bank
IBIZ	International Network of Institutes for Small Business Counsellors
IBCM	Improving the Business Climate in Morocco programme
ICBG	Iraqi Company for Bank Guarantees
ICSB	International Council for Small Business
ICT	information and communication technology
IDRC	International Development Research Centre
IEF	Index of Economic Freedom
IFC	International Finance Corporation
IGEM	Enterprise Development Centre
ILO	International Labour Organization
IMC	Industrial Modernization Centre
IMF	International Monetary Fund
INS	Institute of National Statistics
IPP	intellectual property protection
IQ	Iraq
IZDIHAR	Iraq Private Sector Growth and Employment Generation
JCPPR	Jordan Centre for Public Policy Research and Dialogue
JD	Jordanian dinar
JFBPW	Jordan Forum for Business and Professional Women
JIB	Jordan Investment Board
JLGC	Jordan Loan Guarantee Corporation

JNCT	Jordan National Competitiveness Team
JO	Jordan
JUMP	Jordan Upgrading and Modernisation Programme
KAB	Know About Business
KAGDIR	Women Entrepreneurs Association of Turkey
KGF	Turkish Credit Guarantee Fund
KOSGEB	Small and Medium Enterprises Development Organization
LE	Lebanon
LMI	lower-middle income
LUMI	lower- and upper-middle income
MA	Morocco
MAD	Moroccan dirham
MAS	Palestine Economic Policy Research Institute
MAWRED	Modernizing and Activating Women's Role in Economic Development
MBA	Master of Business Administration
MCSBE	Middle East Council for Small Business and Entrepreneurship
MDGs	Millennium Development Goals
MDTF	Multi-Donor Trust Fund
MED	EU Mediterranean partner countries and territories
MEDA	Middle East and Developing Africa
MENA	Middle East and North Africa
MERO	Middle East/North Africa Regional Office
MFI	microfinance institution
MHE	Ministry of Higher Education
MICNT	Ministry of Industry, Commerce and New Technologies
MIEPME	Ministère de l'Industrie, de l'Energie et des Petites et Moyennes Entreprises
MIGA	Multilateral Investment Guarantee Agency
MIM	Ministry of Industry and Minerals
MIT	Ministry of Industry and Trade
MoET	Ministry of Economy and Trade
MPIC	Ministry of Planning and International Cooperation
MPMEA	Ministère de la Petite et Moyenne Entreprise et de l'Artisanat
MSA	Ministry of Social Affairs
MSEs	micro and small enterprises
MSME	micro, small and medium enterprise

MTEVT	Ministry of Technical Education and Vocational Training
MTI	Ministry of Trade and Industry
NAFES	National Fund for Enterprise Support
NCW	National Council for Women
NEDP	National Economic Dialogue Project
NGO	Non-governmental organization
ODA	official development assistance
OECD	Organisation for Economic Co-operation and Development
OFPPT	Office de la Formation Professionelle de la Promotion du Travail
OSS	one-stop shop
PA	Palestinian Authority
PCBS	Palestinian Central Bureau of Statistics
PCEED	Public Commission for Employment and Enterprise Development
PNA	Palestinian National Authority
PPP	public–private partnership
PPP	purchasing power parity
PRDP	Palestinian Reform and Development Plan
PRSP	Poverty Reduction Strategy Paper
PSD	private sector development
PSDTF	Private Sector Development Task Force
PSUT	Princess Sumaya University for Technology
QIZ	Qualifying Industrial Zone
QRCE	Queen Rania Center for Entrepreneurship
R&D	research and development
RIC	Regional Investment Centre
RWEL	Role of Women in Economic Life
S&T	science and technology
SBDC	Small Business Development Center
SD	Sudan
SEBC	Syrian Enterprise and Business Centre
SEVE	Association des Femme Chefs d'Entreprises
SFD	Social Fund for Development
SICAR	Venture Capital Investment Company
SMED	Small and Microenterprise Development
SMEs	micro, small and medium enterprises
SMEPol	Small, Medium and Micro Enterprise Policy
SMEPS	Small and Micro Enterprise Promotion Service
SMIs	small and medium investors

SOE	state-owned enterprise
SPC	State Planning Commission
STD	Syria Trust for Development
SY	Syria
SYEA	Syria Young Entrepreneurs Association
SYOB	Start Your Own Business
SYP	Syrian pound
TEA	Total Entrepreneurial Activity
TEKMER	Technology Development Centre
TFER	Task Force on Economic Reforms and Private Sector Capacity
TN	Tunisia
TND	Tunisian dinar
TR	Turkey
TTIC	Technology Transfer and Innovation Center
TVET	technical and vocational education and training
UNDP	United Nations Development Programme
UNECE	United Nations Economic Commission for Europe
UNIDO	United Nations Industrial Development Organization
UNPME	National Union of SMEs
US	United States
USAID	United States Agency for International Development
USD	United States dollars
VET	vocational education and training
WB&G	West Bank & Gaza Strip
WDI	World Development Indicators
WEEA	Women Economic Empowerment Association
WEF	World Economic Forum
WFB	*World Factbook*
WTO	World Trade Organization
YE	Yemen
YEA	Young Entrepreneurs Association
YR	Yememi rial
YTL	New Turkish lira

About the International Development Research Centre

To achieve self-reliance, poor communities need answers to questions like: How can we grow more and healthier food? Protect our health? Create jobs? IDRC, Canada's International Development Research Centre, supports research in developing countries to answer these questions. IDRC also encourages sharing this knowledge with policymakers, other researchers, and communities around the world. The result is innovative, lasting local solutions that aim to bring choice and change to those who need it most.

About the author

Lois Stevenson, a leading authority on the role of entrepreneurship and micro, small and medium enterprises (SMEs) in development and government policy, is a Visiting Research Fellow with Canada's International Development Research Centre (IDRC) and has been living in Egypt since 2006. She initially joined IDRC to coordinate the Small, Medium and Micro Enterprise Policy (SMEPol) Development Project, a partnership between the Canadian International Development Agency (CIDA), the IRDC and the Government of Egypt, and to carry out an assessment of the policy, research and institutional capacities for private sector and SME development in 12 Middle East and North Africa (MENA) countries. Lois organized a number of regional consultations on the private sector policy needs of MENA countries, led a project to carry out Global Entrepreneurship Monitor studies in seven MENA countries, and participated in development of the National Micro and Small Enterprise Development Strategy for the Egyptian Social Fund for Development.

Before joining IDRC Lois spent several years with the Government of Canada, holding directorate positions related to economic framework policies, innovation policy, small business policy and entrepreneurship development. She also spent ten years as a university professor, teaching and researching in the areas of entrepreneurship and small business management. She has authored (or co-authored) 12 books on entrepreneurship-related issues and more than 45 articles and papers for refereed journals and conference proceedings, including several on women entrepreneurs, young entrepreneurs and entrepreneurship policy.

She has consulted to the Organisation for Economic Co-operation and Development (OECD) on the development of benchmark indicators for entrepreneurship education policy; carried out assessments for the International Labour Organization (ILO) on policy for women's entrepreneurship in East African countries; and conducted a scientific analysis of the construction of entrepreneurship policy and its practice in 15 countries, including China, as a Visiting Researcher with the Swedish Foundation for Small Business Research (FSF). Lois is a past President of the International Council for Small Business (ICSB), a past President of the Canadian Council for Small Business and Entrepreneurship

(CCSBE-CCPME), and a founding member of the Middle East Council for Small Business and Entrepreneurship (MCSBE). She has three degrees, from Dalhousie University in Canada and the University of Bath in the United Kingdom.

Preface

Much has been written about the political, economic and social dimensions and challenges of the Middle East and North Africa (MENA) (see Noland and Pack 2007; World Bank 2007b; AfDB and OECD 2008; Muasher 2008; Richards and Waterbury 2008; World Bank 2008d; IMF 2009b). These works cover the situation in different combinations of countries in the region depending on how they chose to define it and their particular perspectives and geopolitical interests.

This book is concerned with the context for private sector development (PSD) including micro, small and medium enterprises (SMEs[1]), the PSD challenges and the relevant policy, institutional and research capacity, responses and needs in 12 MENA countries: Algeria (AG), Egypt (EG), Iraq (IQ), Jordan (JO), Lebanon (LE), Morocco (MA), Sudan (SD), Syria (SY), Tunisia (TN), Turkey (TR), the West Bank & Gaza (WB&G) and Yemen (YE), hereafter referred to as the MENA-12. The rationale for this particular selection of MENA countries is that they all fall within the geographic domain of the Middle East/North Africa Regional Office (MERO) of Canada's International Development Research Centre (IDRC).

The results shared in the book are based on a scoping study carried out by the IRDC from 2007 to 2009. Building on IDRC's growing interest in the topic of PSD over the past few years and an expanding literature on PSD strategies as a vehicle for economic growth in developing countries, the book presents a diagnostic of the PSD challenges in the MENA-12 countries, offers conceptual frameworks for PSD, SME and entrepreneurship development, and shares country-level approaches to enhancing growth of the private sector.

BACKGROUND

IDRC's focus on the broad theme of private sector development began in the fall of 2004 with the formation of a Private Sector Development Task Force (PSDTF). The purpose of the Task Force was to explore PSD as a research theme and identify possible IDRC programme niches. The PSDTF commissioned three PSD scoping studies: a scan of the PSD-related activities and research of other donors (IDRC 2004); a review of projects in the IDRC portfolio with a PSD component (IDRC 2006); and a conceptual paper on PSD frameworks and research themes (White 2008).

A number of IDRC research projects and programmes in various regions of the world could be seen to fit within a PSD support framework. One of these initiatives was a project concerned with evidence-based policy for SME development in Egypt. The Small, Medium and Micro Enterprise Policy (SMEPol) Development Project, a partnership between the IDRC, the Canadian International Development Agency (CIDA) and the government of Egypt was ongoing from 2000 to 2008. The independent evaluations of the SMEPol Project concluded that it achieved very positive results in terms of building research and policy capacity within the government, influencing the SME policy development process and fostering stakeholder consultation and engagement (Lynch 2003; ODI 2006). In addition to policy development lessons learned during the execution of the SMEPol Project, a number of policy tools, processes and stakeholder engagement approaches were developed and refined.

To further IDRC's aim of sharing proven approaches in the development of evidence-based policy and stakeholder consultation processes and building research and policy capacity, IDRC (MERO) decided to explore potential opportunities for a regional initiative embracing other MENA countries that could potentially benefit from the tools, approaches and lessons learned from the success of the SMEPol Project. A comprehensive scoping study, including an examination of the broader PSD issues, began in earnest in 2007.

The main objective of the scoping study was to examine the potential for value-added policy and research support to advance PSD and SME development efforts and to identify mechanisms for providing research and policy development support at the MENA regional level.

SCOPING STUDY APPROACH

The approach to the study required a situation analysis of the economic, social and policy context in each country and their private sector and SME development environments and challenges, taking into consideration government activity and other donor and related supports. In-depth country assessments involved study visits to Algeria, Egypt, Jordan, Morocco, Syria and Yemen, and detailed desktop reviews for Iraq, Lebanon, Sudan, Turkey, Tunisia and the West Bank & Gaza. The six countries selected for study visits were chosen because they represented diversity in population size, levels of economic development (low income, lower-middle income and upper-middle income), degrees of resource abundance and stages of transition to a market economy. Conflict and political instability would have made it difficult for country visits to Iraq, Lebanon, Sudan and the West Bank & Gaza for safety and security reasons.

The country visits were carried out between April and September 2007. Interviews were conducted with 139 representatives from 94 organizations, including government ministries and agencies, research organizations, private sector business associations, financial institutions, non-governmental development organizations, key donor organizations and other relevant PSD and SME stakeholder groups. Information gained from key informants was supplemented by a review of country documents and reports and international comparative studies and data, including government National Development Plans, policy and strategy documents, investment climate assessments and other analysis conducted by international organizations and donors. Desktop reviews were supplemented by input from officials during consultations in 2007 and 2008.

Efforts were made to examine the research capacity, the policy capacity, the institutional capacity, the capacity of the private sector to influence the policy development process, and the status of the governments' PSD policy reforms and capacities. The analysis included a mapping of current PSD reforms and SME interventions (what was being done and who was doing it); the major barriers to effective PSD and SME policy development and implementation; and the PSD and SME policy and research needs, gaps and opportunities. The situation analysis and preliminary diagnostic framework of identified gaps and needs were presented to stakeholders at a two-day regional workshop in November 2007 (IDRC 2008a) and further refined. This workshop was attended by representatives from ten of the 12 countries and interested regional donors, all of whom were given an opportunity to comment on an early draft of the regional analysis and to introduce additional themes. To as great an extent as possible, this book incorporates many of the suggested themes.

The analysis in this book also draws on PSD-related situation analyses and assessments carried out by a number of international organizations and researchers and attempts to bring together a comprehensive picture of the many factors affecting PSD in the MENA-12 countries and to provide a point-in-time snapshot of the context for PSD and SME development. It further outlines some of the major policy initiatives of the governments to support private sector activity. The policy landscape in these countries is constantly changing and this book does not pretend to make an exhaustive presentation of the PSD reform and SME development efforts in each one, but a synopsis profile of the 12 countries in Part II serves to provide a sense of the priorities and basic directions in each country.

One of the challenges in putting together the analysis for this book has been that of accessing up-to-date and comparable statistical data on the many socio-economic and PSD indicators. As far as possible, the latest available data from credible international and country data sources have been used.

OUTLINE OF THE BOOK

The book is aimed primarily at the policymaking, research and donor communities and other stakeholders involved in building capacity in PSD and SME policy development who are interested in the MENA region. It is presented in two parts.

Part I has seven chapters. Chapter 1 presents an overview of the private sector development-related discourse and a conceptual framework of the policy components of private sector and enterprise development. It includes a discussion of donor PSD approaches, priorities and trends, the impact of PSD strategies and efforts on the inclusive, pro-poor growth of developing countries, and the challenges of measuring changes in the level of PSD performance. Chapter 2 provides an introduction to the context within the MENA region, including a comparative analysis of the MENA-12 economies on key demographic and structural features. Chapters 3 and 4 describe the key social and economic growth challenges facing the MENA countries, such as employment creation, informality of enterprises and workers, education and skills, science and technology (S&T) and innovation, global integration, gender equality and development of SMEs and entrepreneurship, all of which play a role in the context for PSD reform. Chapter 4 focuses exclusively on the SME and entrepreneurship challenge and elaborates more fully on the role and importance of the SME sector in PSD, and the SME policy approaches, strategies and implementation structures in the MENA-12. Chapter 5 discusses the status of the MENA-12 countries in relationship to the market economy and the PSD environment, and categorizes the countries on their relative private sector dynamism and economic outcomes. Chapter 6 presents an assessment of the PSD priorities and deficiencies and raises related policy, research and institutional capacity issues. The views expressed in the chapter are largely those of stakeholders from each of the countries gathered during country visits and regional consultation workshops. Chapter 7 emphasizes the importance of developing strategic policies to advance the level and quality of entrepreneurship in the next phase of private sector and inclusive growth, and presents a framework to guide thinking about future policy directions and initiatives.

Part II includes brief descriptive synopses of each of the MENA-12 countries. Chapter 8 profiles the context and recent policy developments and priorities of the set of countries assessed as having the most dynamic PSD outcomes, and Chapter 9 presents profiles of the set of countries with less dynamic PSD outcomes.

NOTE

1. The acronym 'SME' will be used in this book to refer to micro, small and medium enterprises. When the reference is specifically to micro and small enterprises, the acronym 'MSEs' will be used.

Acknowledgements

Several people need to be acknowledged for their contributions to this book. First and foremost I would like to extend much gratitude to Dr Eglal Rached, Regional Director for the International Development Research Centre (IDRC) Middle East/North Africa Regional Office (MERO) and to Dr Rohinton Medhora, Vice-President Program and Partnership Branch, IDRC Ottawa for supporting this work, and to Dr Brent Herbert-Copley, former Director of Social and Economic Policy, IDRC, Ottawa, for encouraging the initiative. Secondly, special thanks go to Tamer El-Meehy, Entrust: Management & Development Consultants, who participated in fact-finding missions to Algeria, Jordan, Morocco, Syria and Yemen and drafted preliminary country reports, and to Sahar Zaki who assisted in the initial desktop reviews of private sector and small and medium enterprise developments in Iraq, Lebanon, Sudan, Tunisia, Turkey and the West Bank & Gaza, and drafted preliminary country profiles.

Dr Brent Herbert-Copley and Susan Joekes, Senior Program Specialist for IDRC's Globalization, Growth and Poverty (GGP) programme in the Middle East/North Africa Office, provided input and advice on the evolution of the research project and the structure and content of the manuscript. Susan was particularly helpful with suggestions on drafts of the book and I am greatly appreciative of her analytical contributions. Bill Carman, IDRC's Senior Communications Advisor, was extremely important to the project by facilitating discussions with Edward Elgar on the co-publishing arrangements, and is to be commended.

I would be remiss if I did not acknowledge the value of candid comments and suggestions from stakeholders who were consulted during country fact-finding missions, and their input on the validity of the preliminary diagnostic analysis of the economic and social challenges facing the MENA countries during IRDC-hosted regional workshops in 2007 and 2008.

Finally I would like to thank the editing and publishing team at Edward Elgar for their thorough and professional treatment during the process of preparing the manuscript for publication.

PART I

Context, challenges and priorities

1. Private sector development: context and framework

Before beginning the more detailed discussion of private sector and enterprise development in the MENA-12 countries, Chapter 1 lays out the landscape of private sector development (PSD), covering its many facets, the different views held by donors and international organizations about what it is, the policy areas implicated in creating a favourable environment for the emergence of a robust private sector and why this is important for growth. It presents a framework of the major components of PSD and makes the case for an integrated approach to PSD to address the growth and equity challenges in developing countries.

In 1995 the Development Assistance Committee (DAC) of the Organisation for Economic Co-operation and Development (OECD) defined the private sector as 'a basic organizing principle of economic activity where private ownership is an important factor, where markets and competition drive production and where private initiative and risk-taking set activities in motion' (OECD 1995, p. 7). The concept of private sector development is closely identified with a package of macro and liberalization reforms prompted and adopted by international financial institutions and donors in the 1980s within the framework of the 'Washington Consensus'[1] to strengthen the role and performance of the private sector in achieving sustainable growth. Consensus began to emerge in the mid-1990s that economic growth was essential to poverty reduction and that this could be best achieved through market forces, competition and private initiative (OECD 1994, 1995; Schulpen and Gibbon 2002). In fact the UK Department for International Development (DfID 2007) argues that economic growth is the single most powerful means of decreasing poverty in developing countries and that the private sector – from farmers to street traders to foreign investors – is the principal creator of growth. The point that growth takes place at the level of the productive enterprise is further reinforced by Harberger (2005) and the United States Agency for International Development (USAID 2008c).

The private sector is comprised of people organizing themselves into enterprises to carry out production of goods and services to meet market demands, and in the process creating jobs, income and wealth for the economy, and the institutions, organizations and agents that provide support to enable them to perform these functions. Sustainable growth of an economy is dependent on the ability and capacity of private individuals and enterprises to pursue market opportunities effectively, and on the presence of the appropriate enabling framework conditions. Ways of supporting the viability, expansion, productivity growth and effective governance of the private sector have been key elements of policy attention since the mid- to late 1990s in all developing countries whatever their size, structure, strategic orientation and level of development. This interest has been underpinned by the understanding that the private sector is the space where growth emerges and higher-productivity jobs are created. Over that time it has become a burning issue in government reform efforts and donor programming and of growing research and policy interest, seen as crucial to reducing global poverty (Klein and Hadjimichael 2003) and of fundamental and pervasive importance throughout the developing world.

Attention to PSD is the counterpart of a widespread withdrawal of the state from many parts of the production sector, stimulated by general acknowledgement of the inefficiency of state-owned enterprises (SOEs) and of the developmental value of allowing a vibrant market system – appropriately delineated and regulated – to flourish. However it is also acknowledged that PSD efforts must be carried out in parallel with public sector efforts because it is the public sector that influences many of the conditions for PSD to occur (ADB 2007b).

Private sector development is a concept with both broad and narrow definitions that intersects a number of policy domains. According to the OECD, PSD is: 'fundamentally about people: releasing and harnessing their productive potential and satisfying their human needs and desires; and creating pluralistic societies, which provide both human freedom and human security' (OECD 1995, p. 7). The OECD further proposes that PSD involves diverse activities ranging from microenterprise development to furthering privatization and financial sector reform. The World Bank (2002) defines PSD as a cross-cutting issue concerned with tapping private initiative for promoting growth, reducing poverty and helping people improve their quality of life. The European Commission includes within the scope of PSD, 'all interventions aiming to enhance the competitiveness of the business sector (including SMEs)' (ADE 2005, p. 8). This definition implies actions to encourage a healthy and dynamic business sector as well as specific interventions to improve the competitiveness, productivity and export capability of micro, small and medium enterprises (SMEs). White (2008) describes PSD as the process of addressing the constraints and opportunities that influence the growth of the private sector. Other related definitions are in use by individual donors and international organizations, the scope of which often reflect differences in their underlying conceptual approach to the topic.

International development organizations and donors have two major justifications for supporting PSD. Development of the private sector contributes to the growth of the economy and thereby to the reduction of poverty, and it contributes to the patterns of growth whereby poor men and women have better access to goods and services and greater opportunities to participate in the mainstream of the economy (White 2008).

The OECD, one of the first international organizations to introduce the concept of PSD within the context of donor development reform, outlined three tiers of PSD policies (OECD 1995, p. 8):

1. Macro-level policies to create fiscal stability, develop efficient financial markets and privatize parastatals. Policies in these areas would serve to build confidence in the government and the economy; foster more diverse and sustainable patterns of external finance and greater volume of resource inflows; reduce budgetary and administrative burden imposed on the public sector; and create fiscal space for expansion of key social investments in health, education and housing. The OECD suggested donor efforts to encourage policy dialogue and appropriate economic policies (such as low inflation, deregulation, fiscal and monetary stability and rational factor prices) and structural changes in areas such as competition and trade policies and the creation of a well-functioning financial system.
2. Meso-level policies to stimulate entrepreneurship, initiative and risk-taking. Donor actions at this level should assist in improving the institutional environment that frames business decisions, such as promoting the rule of law and its enforcement, reducing the scope for corruption and establishing institutions through which public and private sector dialogue can be fostered.
3. Micro-level policies to replace controls and prohibitions with incentives, promotional measures and supportive public interventions. At this level the OECD suggested donor actions to support facilitative activities, such as business training and consulting services, micro and small enterprise development, privatization, public enterprise reform and foreign direct investment.

A large number of concepts and policy themes fall within the discourse on PSD. These include:

- Privatization.
- Macroeconomic, legal, regulatory and investment frameworks conducive to business growth.
- Governance and anti-corruption.

- Physical infrastructure development.
- Foreign direct investment.
- Financial sector reform.
- Industrial and trade policy.
- Sectoral productivity and competitiveness.
- Competition policy.
- Corporate governance.
- Vocational education and training.
- Science, technology and innovation policies.
- SME development and growth.
- Entrepreneurship development.
- Support for microenterprises and actors in the informal economy.
- Financial and non-financial services for SMEs.
- Business-to-business cooperation activities, networks, supply chains and clusters.
- Institutional capacity building of intermediary organizations and structures that offer services to private sector enterprises and represent their views in dialogue with the government.

Governments, development agencies and research organizations will assume different orientations to PSD depending on their vantage point (ADE 2005). The donor discourse on PSD is grounded in market-based solutions to socio-economic problems. The departure point for formulating PSD strategies at the country level should be assessments that provide a clear understanding of the operating environment for the conduct of businesses and of where local policies and conditions hamper sound growth and development of financial markets and private enterprises (OECD 1995). Consequently donors have taken up the challenge of developing frameworks and strategies to guide their respective PSD efforts in recipient countries as well as devising instruments to assess the PSD environment at the country level. References to the investment climate and the business environment are paramount in discussions of private sector reform. While there appears to be some inconsistency and overlap in the use of these terms, the investment climate has been defined as the set of location-specific factors shaping the opportunities and incentives for firms to invest productively, create jobs and expand (World Bank 2005f), and the business environment as a subset of the investment climate consisting of the policy, legal, institutional and regulatory conditions that govern business activities (DCED 2008).

Reviewing a range of donor PSD strategy papers (UN 1997; CEC 1998; World Bank 2002, 2003; DfID 2004a, 2008; Sida 2004; CIDA 2005; ADB 2006; OECD 2006; USAID 2006; UNDP 2007a) it is obvious that specific donors will focus on a select number of priority themes in accordance with their particular mandates and priorities. For some it may be governance, privatization and infrastructure, and for others supporting growth of the microenterprise and SME sector. Snodgrass and Winkler (2004), for example, indentified that USAID is more focused on access to markets, and Migliorisi and Galmarini (2004) that the World Bank is a significant player in infrastructure, and regional banks such as the Asian Development Bank (ADB), the African Development Bank (AfDB) and the Inter-American Development Bank (IADB) are dominant in direct financial support to firms. A commonality amongst donor approaches is that they in one way or another attempt to improve the 'enabling environment' for business. This entails interventions that at the international level address trade rules, debt cancellation, access to international markets and investment; at the macro level address macroeconomic policies, physical infrastructure, human capital development and governance; at the meso level address regulatory issues around start-ups and the bureaucratic costs of SME operations, institutional infrastructure such as financial institutions, educational institutes, business associations and business development centres; and at the micro level provide financial and non-financial support to enterprises to improve their access to resources, skills, technology, technical assistance, information and markets.

Habib and White (2007) determine that the majority of donor efforts fall within the meso and micro levels of support in three major categories: (1) enabling environment; (2) access to skills, knowledge and capital; and (3) access to markets and market facilitation. However much remains unknown about the individual and interaction effects of macro, meso and micro-level policy interventions to achieve successful PSD outcomes (ADE 2005). This implies a rich area for research contributions. Lessons learned from an evaluation of the PSD strategies of the European Commission (ADE 2005) suggest that sufficient proactive government involvement, consultation with local stakeholders and capacity building of intermediary organizations to carry out policy dialogue are important success factors at the country level.

In discussions of PSD it is important to acknowledge the close link with the development of SMEs and entrepreneurship. World Bank studies find a positive and significant correlation between new business entry rates, the size of the private sector (measured as a percentage of gross domestic product, GDP) and GDP per capita, and a clear correlation between SME density and income levels of countries (World Bank 2006a; Klapper 2007). Higher-income countries have higher SME densities. Findings such as these support the centrality of SMEs and new firms to PSD and to economic growth. According to the OECD (2005a) the transformation caused by radical shifts towards economic liberalization, privatization of public enterprises and growth-led exports (reflecting changes in the investment climate and business environment) will open up new opportunities for the creation of SMEs and expand the number of entrepreneurs. It concludes that the MENA region needs more SMEs to create jobs and reduce unemployment, improve growth and productivity rates and fight poverty, but points to inadequate regulatory environments and support infrastructures and to deficiencies in the research knowledge base on SMEs and their growth prospects and the social origins of entrepreneurs.

Governments have a central role to play in creating an enabling environment for private sector growth. The World Bank (2002) stresses the importance of building an effective state, at all levels of government, that can create the setting for markets and entrepreneurship to flourish, stating that where governments are successful in creating a strong investment climate, poverty reduction is greatly facilitated. Success can be achieved through strengthened central banks and financial services, economic incentives, effective import and export facilities, reduced red tape, effective rule of law, well-functioning legal systems, efficient and effective judiciaries, fair and transparent regulatory systems, and appropriate legislation for intellectual property protection (IPP) and insolvency (UNDP and AFESD 2002). However key questions remain about whether macro-level investment climate and business environment reforms are sufficient to produce a vibrant private sector, and about which specific mix of policies, actions and interventions will produce the desired effects.

PRIVATE SECTOR DEVELOPMENT FRAMEWORK

The ultimate aim of PSD efforts is to facilitate a growing private sector in order to produce enhanced economic and social development and performance of a country. These outcomes are measured by gains in employment, trade, foreign direct investment (FDI), productivity and GDP, and reductions in poverty and inequality. The major components of PSD are captured in the framework in Figure 1.1.

The first set of framework components relates to creating market space for the private sector, which has a lot to do with deregulation and improving the investment climate. Increases in the scale and scope of private sector contribution to economic growth outcomes will occur if the government reduces its role in the economy and/or if the private sector increases its role. In the context of developing and transition countries, where the government often assumes a more active role in economic activity, actions are needed to create a larger market space for private

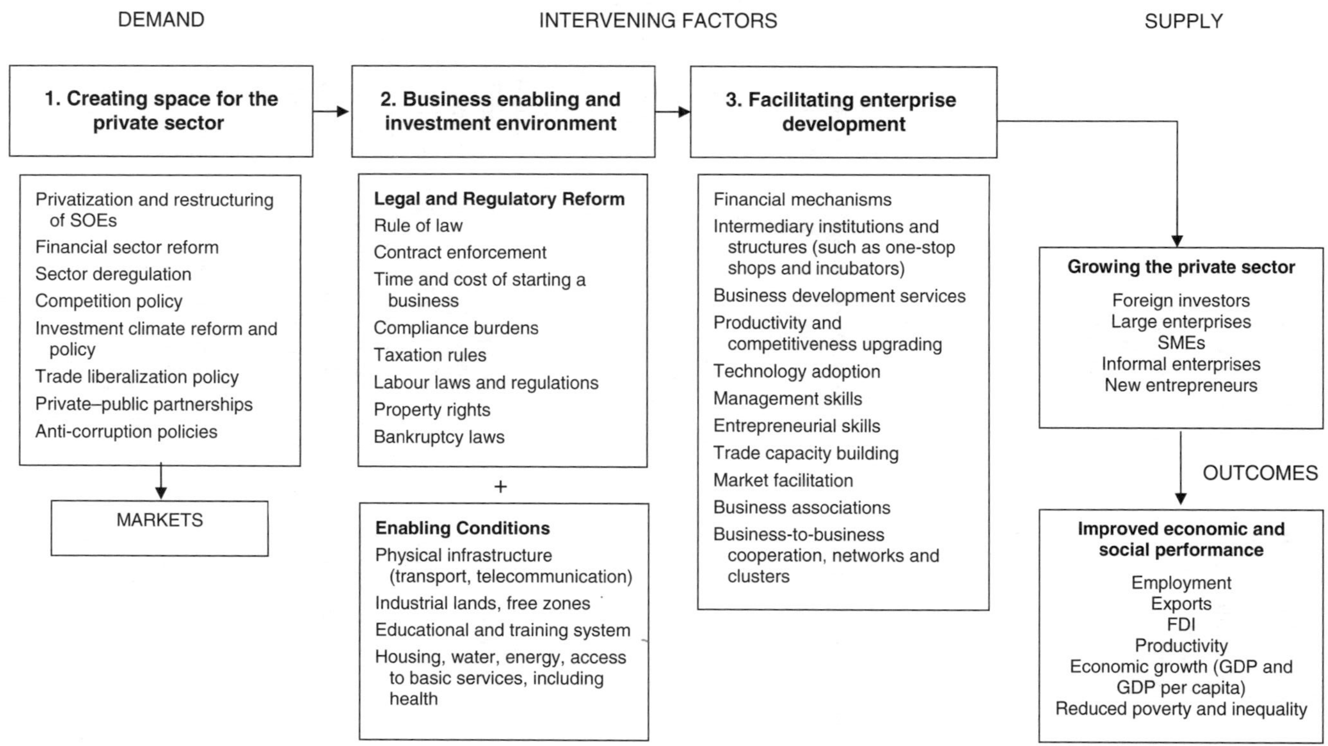

Figure 1.1 Framework of private sector development components

activity. This can be achieved through such actions as the privatization of SOEs, encouragement of public–private partnerships (PPPs), reduction of restrictions for private sector entry into key sectors of the economy previously controlled by the state, reduction of monopolistic practices, investment climate reform and the adoption of good governance practices. Opportunities for the private sector can also be created by opening up the economy to foreign investors, reducing trade restrictions and undertaking financial sector reform to build trust in the financial system and release more capital for private sector investment. These are important demand considerations.

In terms of private sector take-up and growth, there has to be an expanding supply of capable and willing private sector agents and entrepreneurs. This supply side of PSD considers the stock of existing large enterprises (both foreign and domestic-owned), SMEs, informal enterprises and new and potential entrepreneurs. Different policies and strategies will be needed to stimulate development of each of these groups. What will work to increase the supply of foreign investors will not necessarily produce a larger supply of indigenous entrepreneurs. Policies to create national champions of large domestic enterprises will not necessarily improve conditions for SMEs. Consequently tailored approaches are required.

In the intervening space between demand and supply factors, policies and interventions will be needed to create a 'business enabling and investment environment' and to 'facilitate enterprise development'. Under the heading of 'business enabling and investment environment' are included: legal and regulatory reform to set the rules of the game; reduced burdens on the private sector, such as in the time and cost of starting a business and licensing and registration complexities; and other policy areas identified in the World Bank 'ease of doing business' list of indicators (World Bank 2009b) and the indicators of economic freedom (Heritage Foundation 2010). It also includes creating other enabling conditions, such as physical infrastructure (road systems, ports and telecommunications) and industrial lands and free zones; education and training systems that will produce a supply of appropriately skilled labour; and access to housing, water, energy and other basic services that are necessary to attract investment and support the emergence of a vibrant private sector.

While improvements to the investment climate and business environment will help to attract and mobilize private investment, this alone is not sufficient to maximize the investment potential in developing countries (OECD 2006). External business conditions have a major impact on whether private enterprises emerge, grow, shrink or fail (ADB 2007a). Thus efforts must also be directed to develop and strengthen the ability of local enterprises and entrepreneurs to respond to the new opportunities offered by lowered trade barriers and a more enabling environment. This can be achieved through interventions that will improve their access to financial and non-financial resources, promote business partnerships and linkages, and improve their level of business management, entrepreneurial and innovation skills (OECD 1995). Lack of access to these provisions will pose a critical constraint on the development of private enterprises and this will impede income and employment growth.

Under the heading of 'facilitating enterprise development' are included access to intermediary institutions (such as one-stop shops, incubators, business resource centres and business associations); commercial services (such as business advice, information, consultancy and technical assistance); training and skills development opportunities to improve entrepreneurial and management skills; productivity and competitiveness upgrading services; technology; and financial mechanisms (such as microfinance, guarantee funds, leasing, venture capital, savings facilities and insurance). Access to these institutions and services will facilitate the attraction of new and the enhanced performance of existing private sector activity as well as promote entrepreneurship. These efforts must also be undertaken with a view to women's entitlements and removing barriers to women's participation in markets (OECD 2006).

A comprehensive PSD strategy would address each of the components of this framework, as they are interrelated and interdependent. Weaknesses in one area of the framework will create bottlenecks or adverse reactions in another area. For example, if the legal and regulatory reform is not done in a way that encourages the formalization of private enterprises, room is created for underperformance and corruption.

The success of PSD reforms will depend on the political will, commitment and capacity of governments to implement the right incentives and structures to produce the desired private sector response, as well on the capacity of the private sector. It is also accepted that the success of PSD reforms will be affected by the degree of macro-economic stability in the country. Sound macro-economic policies are essential to create adequate room for private initiative; however these alone are not sufficient to stimulate robust private sector development.

The challenge for governments is to develop an integrated set of policies to address weaknesses in these different levels and aspects of the economy. The set of deficiencies at any point in time will vary depending on the country context and where it is in the stage of development and transition to a market-led economy. Figure 1.2 is a simplistic portrayal of the different policy areas affecting PSD. A holistic policy approach is called for. Systematic approaches to PSD require policymakers and practitioners to see the private sector as situated within the network of institutions that

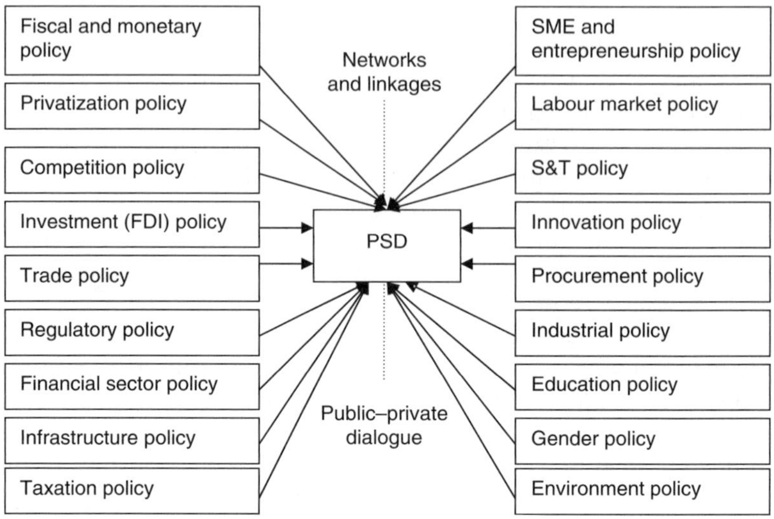

Figure 1.2 Integration of policy areas affecting private sector growth

determine the incentives and disincentives for growth and distribution (White 2008) and to promote institutional arrangements that link the key actors (for example, government agencies, regulatory authorities, business associations, civil society organizations – CSOs, and education and training institutions) and foster effective public–private dialogue.

The OECD (2005b) presents evidence that institutions are critical to the development of a market-led economy, suggesting that good institutions[2] matter more for growth than good policies. However there are still many unanswered questions about how to improve institutional performance. Accession to the WTO and regional trade entities, such as the European Union and the New Economic Partnership for Africa, have strengthened incentives for institutional improvements, but in developing countries this remains a challenge (OECD 2005b).

During the course of the International Development Research Centre (IDRC)'s consultations in 2007 and 2008 as part of its PSD assessment in the MENA-12 countries, stakeholders expressed their views that PSD policies and strategies are generally not well coordinated, and that links between the various policy areas and cooperation between responsible ministries are weak. This has to do in large part with structural divisions within government and unclear lines of responsibility, which ultimately result in weak implementation of national development plans. They also noted limited efforts to consider the interaction effects of the various policies, such as the impact of World Trade Organization (WTO) accession or

FDI policies and strategies on SME development, income inequality or gender dynamics in the economy. These issues will be discussed further in Chapter 6.

The challenge for international aid agencies and donors is to determine where and how to target aid as they consider the implications for their own PSD strategies. The majority of past donor PSD support has been in the form of direct support to enterprises, either to individual firms or through joint ventures and alliances (OECD 2004a). Technical assistance was provided through donor projects, often using non-governmental organizations (NGOs) as delivery agents, and financial assistance through banks or microfinance institutions (MFIs). These interventions have been criticized for distorting markets and crowding out private sector provision of these services, especially if subsidies were involved. Consequently there has been a recent shift in approach. More donors are now targeting the 'enabling environment' for PSD and supporting changes in institutional policies which will lead to improvements in access to markets. Much of the recent support is in partnership with governments, and not firms, with a focus on providing analytical and policy assistance to affect institutional changes that will enable the longer-term sustainability of PSD. The engagement of private and civil society stakeholders is also a feature of this approach.

PRO-POOR AND 'INCLUSIVE' GROWTH

The prevailing assumption in the 1960s was that governments in developing countries could act as the engines of development through resource allocation, state ownership of enterprises and management of the economy (White 2008). Donors accepted the view that governments could be aid-funded to stimulate investments and generate growth. However during the 1970s and 1980s developmental states failed to deliver, many in fact turning into oppressive or rent-seeking regimes divesting well-intentioned public policies to serve narrow political or economic interests. The later generation of economists and policymakers came to believe that the cost of government failures was larger than the cost of market failures, that governments interfered with development, and that constraining the role of the public sector by reducing its usage of resources and its discretion was essential for economic growth (World Bank 2005c).

The Washington Consensus sought to reduce the size and scope of the state and reinforce the role of the market as the most effective mechanism for allocating resources and promoting economic growth. The policy platform for reform had ten components:

1. Fiscal discipline.
2. Reordering of public expenditure priorities from discriminate subsidies to basic health and education.
3. Tax reform to combine a broad tax base with moderate marginal tax rates.
4. Liberalizing interest rates.
5. A competitive exchange rate.
6. Trade liberalization.
7. Liberalization of inward foreign direct investment.
8. Privatization.
9. Deregulation, with a specific focus on easing barriers to entry and exit.
10. Secure property rights.

Although reforms in the 1990s continued to focus on increasing the role of markets and decreasing the role of the state, they tended to ignore the important role of institutions (World Bank 2005c). Following the perceived failure of the Washington Consensus (which Williamson 2002 provides a defence for[3]), the policy prescription was augmented by additional areas of priority, including corporate governance, anti-corruption, flexible labour markets, adherence to WTO discipline and international financial codes and standards, social safety nets and targeted poverty reduction (Richards and Waterbury 2008).

Consensus on the crucial role of PSD in increasing the rate of growth has long been reached, but the way in which the private sector develops is now understood to have a strong bearing on the pattern of growth and whether it is inclusive of the poor. So while development and donor agencies agree on PSD as an instrument for growth and poverty reduction, not all agree on the nature of the outcomes or the way in which they can be achieved (White 2008). The fact that the benefits of growth have often been unevenly distributed among a country's population, resulting in higher levels of inequality, backed by evidence that inequality affects economic growth (World Bank 2005c), led to support of the OECD and other international and donor organizations for the concept of pro-poor growth. The OECD (2006) suggests that the way in which policies are combined to provide incentives that shape private sector activity will have a significant impact on the extent to which these lead to more and better jobs, higher incomes, better returns on goods sold, greater affordability of essential goods and services, and the extent to which poor men and women can take advantage of those opportunities. Implied here is greater access to productive assets, basic services, health, education and skills, areas where the developmental state can play a key role (World Bank 2005c).

Consequently development agencies and developing-country governments have a strong interest in fostering a policy and institutional environment that enables a robust private sector combined with delivery of strong benefits to poverty alleviation.

The pro-poor literature focuses on measuring the impact of growth on poverty reduction by tracking poverty measures. The two most commonly used are the relative and absolute measurements. Relative pro-poor growth occurs when growth produces a faster increase in the incomes of the poor than average incomes, in which case the poor are benefiting disproportionately from growth and inequality is falling. Absolute pro-poor growth occurs when the average absolute incomes of the poor are rising. Consensus is emerging that the appropriate measure of pro-poor growth is growth in the average incomes of the poor (that is, incomes of people living below the national or international poverty line) (Kraay 2004),[4] although the ideal scenario is to identify the conditions under which growth will produce both rising incomes and reduced inequalities. Kraay's results led him to suggest that a policy package focusing on the known determinants of growth in average incomes, such as the protection of property rights, stable macroeconomic policies and openness to international trade, should be at the heart of pro-poor growth strategies. Zinnes (2009) also emphasizes the importance of the protection of property rights in improving the livelihoods of the poor.

However not all international and donor agencies have bought into the pro-poor focus, debating the extent to which measures specifically targeted at the poor might actually lead to a reduced rate of economic growth. The World Bank (2005c) discusses two important questions: Is poverty reduction the goal of economic growth or a consequence? Does the distribution of resources to the poor retard growth or accelerate it? The conclusion it reaches is that poverty levels will fall with expanded per capita income, and that setting poverty reduction as the only goal of economic growth and development ignores the value of income gains for the middle class. Proponents of the pro-poor growth approach argue that there is a difference between economic growth and economic development, and that the distributional patterns of private sector-led growth have to be regarded; for example, the impacts on gender inequalities, the level of informality, opportunities for SMEs and the urban–rural divide, all subjects of debate in the PSD literature (White 2008). The World Bank (2005c) made two observations about pro-poor growth strategies. The first is that growth can be achieved using different vehicles, some of which could have a larger impact on poverty reduction than others; for example expenditures on labour-intensive agriculture versus subsidies for capital-intensive industrialization. The second is that programmes targeting poverty are not a substitute for growth in achieving reductions in the incidence of poverty. The ability of the poor to benefit from growth partly depends on whether workers can easily migrate from agriculture into emerging non-agricultural sectors, and whether these workers have the literacy and other skills needed for those new jobs (USAID 2008c). Reducing income disparities also depends on the opportunities for the poor to accumulate assets. Thus property rights, financial sector reforms and skills development are important factors in facilitating pro-poor growth.

A more recent concept of pro-poor growth is 'inclusive growth' (UNDP 2007a). To be inclusive, pro-poor growth must embrace both the pace and the pattern of growth. An inclusive growth approach focuses on production and employment rather than on direct income redistribution as the means of increasing incomes of the poor and measures the impact of growth on the utilization of the labour force and participation in productive employment (World Bank 2009f). In order for inclusive growth to occur, productivity must be improved and new employment opportunities created. Therefore enlarging the size of the economy to produce more productive employment and providing equality of access to markets, resources and an unbiased regulatory environment for businesses and individuals will have a positive impact on poverty reduction. This implies that growth in private sector activity is an essential path to poverty reduction.

White (2008) summarizes the four fundamental components of pro-poor, inclusive growth:

1. Competitive markets, with free and fair competition, low barriers to entry for new-players, effective systems for the exit of failing enterprises and the means to address market failures and equity concerns.
2. Entrepreneurship.
3. Private ownership with clear property rights for the poor.
4. Decent work conditions that are based on fair returns to labour without discrimination in terms of gender, religion or ethnicity.

The OECD (2006) emphasizes six topics important for promoting pro-poor growth and increasing the leverage of PSD on poverty reduction: (1) removing barriers to formalization; (2) implementing competition policy; (3) applying market-based approaches to business development services (BDS) and financial assistance; (4) strengthening the financial sector's contribution to pro-poor growth; (5) enhancing women's market access; and (6) constructing inclusive public–private dialogue. The OECD further stresses five interlinked and mutually reinforcing factors in its pro-poor growth framework: (1) providing incentives for entrepreneurship and investment; (2) increasing productivity through competition and innovation; (3) harnessing international linkages through trade and investment; (4) improving market access and functioning; and (5) reducing risk and vulnerability. Since these factors are brought about and influenced by policies and institutions, institutional and policy reforms are at the heart of efforts to reduce poverty through PSD. Many of the pro-poor policy actions recommended for donor action by the OECD require partnerships with governments. Thus in the pro-poor growth era, the concept of the developmental state has re-emerged, the currently accepted view being that the state plays a critical role in shaping the incentives and opportunities for PSD (DfID 2007).

MEASURING PRIVATE SECTOR DEVELOPMENT PERFORMANCE

One of the big challenges for governments and donors, once reaching agreement on the fundamental issues and policy dimensions of inclusive, private sector growth, is to define the indicators to measure and evaluate the dynamism and outcomes of PSD efforts. Unfortunately this work appears to be in its infancy. Indicators are needed at three levels: (1) macro-level indicators of private sector growth and the contribution of the private sector to improved economic and social outcomes; (2) meso-level indicators to measure an improved enabling environment and changes in government policy, institutional structures and regulatory reform that affect improved PSD performance and outcomes; and (3) micro-level indicators to measure the contribution to PSD of specific programmes, projects or initiatives. At the macro level it is possible to measure whether the private sector is growing, shrinking or stagnating (assuming country-level data are available), and at the micro level it is possible to measure the outcomes of specific projects, but it is more challenging to assess the impact of enabling factors or conditions that are critical to private sector business success. This gap has started to be addressed by various agencies and governments in recent years (ADB 2007a). The ADB reports that although international agencies, donors and governments recognize the importance of and need for developing results indicators to measure PSD strategies, this has generally not been done.

One of the major limitations is the lack of available data on the types of performance indicators that might be appropriate, especially for comparable cross-country analysis and comparison. The ADB (2007a) found no evidence that any country produces a set of statistics comprehensively covering PSD. Governments and donor agencies will work with what is available to measure PSD performance and outcomes, often making use of global survey rankings, such as the Global Competitiveness Report, the Index of Economic Freedom, the World Bank Doing Business report, the Global Entrepreneurship Monitor, the Human Development Index and others, as proxy indicators to benchmark PSD-related performance.[5] The World Bank (2005c) is critical of the use of these broad assessments because they do not easily translate into the diagnosis of specific problems or capture the particularities of institutional settings at the country level, but they nonetheless contribute to cross-country analysis. Furthermore these surveys do not necessarily cover all countries, are missing data for some indicators for some of the countries, and the indices are often constructed in complex ways making it difficult to understand precisely which policy actions are likely to make the most difference to improvements in specific outcomes.

The pro-poor, inclusive growth perspective complicates the issue even further because measurements will also be needed on provision of education and health services and basic physical infrastructure – also essential elements of the enabling environment for PSD – and on the performance of SMEs and entrepreneurial activity where indicator data in developing countries are very thin.

Most donors will have logic frameworks in place for their PSD programmes, but not always a systematic corporate approach to establishing performance indicators (ADB 2007a). The choice of indicators will depend on the definition of PSD in use. If PSD is defined in terms of 'improving the investment climate', evaluation will focus on one set of indicators. If it is to stimulate growth in the SME sector or reduce the level of informality, then a different set of indicators will be appropriate. Even then the question remains about how best to collect the measurement data and whether donors and governments are managing for the 'right' PSD results. This requires a deep understanding of the relationship hierarchy between PSD reforms and better economic and social outcomes, and of how particular policies, institutional arrangements and initiatives influence enhanced PSD outcomes and private sector performance. What is required is a simple set of appropriate indicators to measure developments in each of the areas presented in the PSD framework in Figure 1.1. This task goes beyond the objectives of this book, but the challenge of undertaking the extensive analytical research and modelling to produce PSD indicators is offered to interested stakeholders.

This concludes the description of the major components of a PSD framework and discussion of the many policy issues implicated in designing a market-led, private sector-based, pro-poor, inclusive growth strategy. The remaining chapters focus specifically on an analysis of the situation in the 12 MENA countries: Algeria, Egypt, Iraq, Jordan, Lebanon, Morocco,

Sudan, Syria, Tunisia, Turkey, the West Bank & Gaza and Yemen. Chapter 2 introduces the countries covered by the analysis and sets the context for elaboration of their economic growth and PSD challenges in Chapters 3, 4 and 5.

NOTES

1. The 'Washington Consensus' refers to policy advice developed by the Washington-based international financial institutions prescribing a development approach based on three principles: macroeconomic discipline, market economy and openness to the world (Williamson 2002). These fundamental principles were intended to replace the unsuccessful development approach in Latin American developing countries in the 1980s, which emphasized import substitution and a leading role for the state in industrialization.
2. Institutions are defined as rules and norms constraining human behaviour, including the informal rules and norms that govern personal and social behaviour and the formal rules and norms governing economic, social and political life (OECD 2005b, p. 3).
3. Williamson (2002) offers three major reasons for the disappointing results of the Washington Consensus policy prescription for Latin America in the 1990s: emerging markets suffered a series of unanticipated crises; some of the recommended reforms were neglected or not fully completed, including lack of attention to strengthening institutions to take advantage of the first generation of reforms; and the objective of the Consensus was too narrowly based on accelerating growth without worsening income, whereas it should have included provisions for income distribution as well. However Williamson stands strongly behind the three principles underpinning the policy advice.
4. The definition of poverty has recently been updated by the World Bank to refer to the percentage of the population living under US$1.25 purchasing power parity, (PPP) per day (see World Bank 2008e).
5. The ADB (2007a) offers a good review of the many international sources of PSD-related indicators in use.

2. Introduction to the MENA-12 country context

This chapter provides an overview of some of the demographic and structural features of the MENA-12 countries as a preface to a more thorough diagnostic of their economic and private sector development (PSD) challenges in successive chapters.

OVERVIEW OF COUNTRY CHARACTERISTICS

The MENA-12 countries represent a combination of republics, constitutional monarchies and parliamentary democracies. Except in Lebanon, Sudan and the West Bank & Gaza, over 90 per cent of the population in these countries is Muslim. Collectively they have an estimated population of about 360 million (larger than North America and almost three-quarters the size of the European Union), 2009 gross domestic product (GDP) of US$1.306 trillion[1] and a labour force of about 111 million.[2] The MENA-12 countries are diverse in terms of size, levels of economic development,[3] resource and labour abundance,[4] and urbanization (Table 2.1).

They range in population from around 4 million in Lebanon and the West Bank & Gaza to almost 80 million in Egypt,[5] and in GDP per capita from about US$1000 in Yemen to over US$8700 in Turkey and Lebanon (World Development Indicators, WDI[6]). Five of the countries are rich in oil resources. They also differ substantially in their urban–rural population distribution. Over 70 per cent of the population of Lebanon (87 per cent), Jordan (78 per cent) and the West Bank & Gaza (72 per cent) lives in urban areas, compared to between 54 and 69 per cent in Turkey (69 per cent), Tunisia (67 per cent), Iraq (67 per cent), Algeria (65 per cent), Morocco (56 per cent) and Syria (54 per cent) (*World Factbook*, WFB). Egypt, Sudan and Yemen are the least urbanized, with less than half of their populations living in urban areas (43, 43 and 31 per cent respectively). Considerable differences can be observed across these countries in population and GDP growth rates, income, poverty levels, literacy rates, natural resource endowments, labour force participation rates, industrial structures, economic performance, official development assistance (ODA) per capita and so on.

Table 2.1 Selected categorizations of the MENA-12 countries

Characteristic	A G	E G	I Q	J O	L E	M A	S D	S Y	T N	T R	W B	Y E
Population												
Small economy (<10M)				X	X						X	
Medium economy (10M–30M)			X					X	X			X
Large economy (>30M)	X	X				X	X			X		
GNI per capita												
Lower-income country												X
Lower-middle-income country		X	X	X		X	X	X	X		X	
Upper-middle-income country	X				X					X		
Resource and labour abundance												
Resource-rich, labour-abundant	X		X				X	X				X
Resource-poor, labour-abundant		X		X	X	X			X	X	X	
Urbanization of the population												
Largely urbanized (more than 70%)			X		X						X	
Moderately urbanized (50–69%)	X		X			X		X	X	X		
Largely non-urbanized (<50%)		X					X					X

Each of the MENA-12 countries comes from its own historical, political, economic and social background, but in all instances their governments have made the decision to move to a more liberalized and open market economy and are at various phases of making that transition. For all, major reforms are necessary to make room for a robust private sector. This entails redefining the role of government, downsizing its direct involvement in economic activity through privatization, further opening the economy to trade through liberalization reforms, creating a favourable climate for foreign direct investment (FDI), improving the competitiveness of domestic enterprises, enabling a business-friendly environment for the emergence and growth of more domestic SMEs and entrepreneurs, and fostering a stronger role for civil society. The countries differ in the extent to which they have progressed in their efforts to expand the private sector. They also differ in the capacity of their research institutes and researchers in the area of PSD and micro, small and medium enterprise (SME) development and the amount of knowledge developed about these areas.

For some of the MENA-12, such as Iraq, Lebanon, Sudan and the West Bank & Gaza, the challenges are more daunting. Long-standing conflicts have resulted in devastation of basic infrastructure, displacement of people and businesses, interruption of trade activity, outflows of private capital and skilled labour, rising public spending, high unemployment and loss of investor confidence, all adversely affecting private sector growth.

Despite their differences, which will be discussed further in this and following chapters, these countries share many similar characteristics and challenges in relation to PSD and SME development. The key similarities are summarized below.

Demography and Employment

- Compared to developed countries the MENA-12 all have a large and expanding share of the population less than 15 years of age. Because the number of new labour force entrants each year is far beyond the capacity of the current labour market to absorb them, job creation is one of the top concerns and priorities of governments.
- They all face labour force challenges, particularly large labour surpluses, high unemployment, low female labour force participation rates, outmigration of skilled workers, retrenchment in public service employment and a mismatch between the skills needed by the labour market and those produced by the education system.
- The micro and small enterprise and informal sectors have been the major absorbers of the expanding labour force.
- Unemployment rates are high and accompanied by underemployment and unpaid work in family and agricultural enterprises. The situation is most severe for women and youth, especially among the better-educated cohorts.
- The gap between the rich and the poor, although narrower than in some other parts of the developing world, appears to be increasing.
- Large investments in human capital have dramatically reduced infant mortality, raised life expectancy, expanded school enrolments and increased literacy rates since the 1990s.

Economic Management and Structure

- The MENA-12 countries have mostly emerged from a history of heavy government involvement in the economy and the state ownership of enterprises.
- They have relatively large public sectors in share of GDP, employment and investment. Job growth in the public sector has been

slowing down compared to the 1990s, but the government wage bill in some countries is often still a major component of government expenditures.

- Capital markets are largely underdeveloped and the supply of capital for private sector and SME growth is constrained, especially formal credit and risk financing.
- They all have relatively weak private sectors with few large private enterprises and a low share of formal private sector employment in total employment.
- They all have a low density of formal SMEs with extremely low proportions of women-owned enterprises. The majority of SMEs (generally 90 per cent or more of all enterprises) have fewer than five employees and are operating at a very low level of competitiveness.
- They all have a high level of informality in the private enterprise sector.
- The cost of doing business is high, with high business transactions costs (although it varies across countries).
- As a group they have underperformed countries in East and South Asia during the 1990s and 2000s, slow productivity growth being one of the main reasons. According to the World Bank (2005c) this was caused by: (1) dominance of production by the state; (2) tariff barriers among the highest in the world with high reliance on import-substitution strategies and less on opening up; and (3) domestic restrictions that impeded private investment, such as red tape, corruption, inefficient judicial systems and policy uncertainty.

Policy Development and the International Context

- These countries are all experiencing the pressures of globalization and the need to become more competitive in light of Free Trade Agreements (FTAs) with other countries and/or regions. Their domestic enterprises, accustomed to operating under protectionist regimes, are weak and under a liberalized and free trade environment have to be prepared to compete for local and regional markets with businesses from all over the world.
- Although they are pursuing reforms to liberalize their economies, facilitate the flow of trade and FDI, and improve the business enabling environment, they all lack coordination of policy for PSD to a lesser or greater degree.
- They all have relatively poor and incomplete official data and statistics on private sector activity and specifically on the SME sector.

- They have inadequate processes for formulating and developing PSD and SME policies. This includes limited consultation processes, weak advocacy efforts of private sector associations and non-governmental organizations (NGOs), and widely varying use of research and evidence-based approaches.
- They all appear to have inadequately coordinated SME policies and varying degrees of weak implementation of policies and programmes.

This chapter now begins a more detailed discussion and analysis of the similarities and differences related to economic and social outcomes, followed in Chapters 3 and 4 by an articulation of the major PSD and growth challenges.

SIZE AND GROWTH OF POPULATION AND GDP

The largest economies by population are Egypt and Turkey, both with over 75 million inhabitants, and the smallest are Lebanon and the West Bank & Gaza (Figure 2.1). Population growth in the MENA-12 is among the fastest in the world, with estimated 2009 growth rates of 2.8 per cent in Yemen, 2.7 per cent in the West Bank & Gaza, 2.5 per cent in Iraq, 2.2 per cent in Jordan and 2 per cent in Syria. The lowest growth rates are in

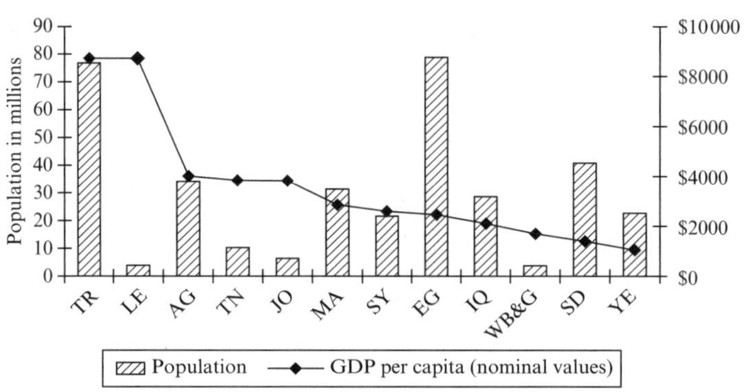

Note: Nominal GDP is the value of all final goods and services produced in the nation in a given year, converted at market exchange rates to current US dollars.

Sources: 2009 population estimates, WFB: 2009 GDP per capita data, IMF (2010): 2008 GDP per capita estimate for the WB&G, WFB.

Figure 2.1 Countries by population size and GDP per capita

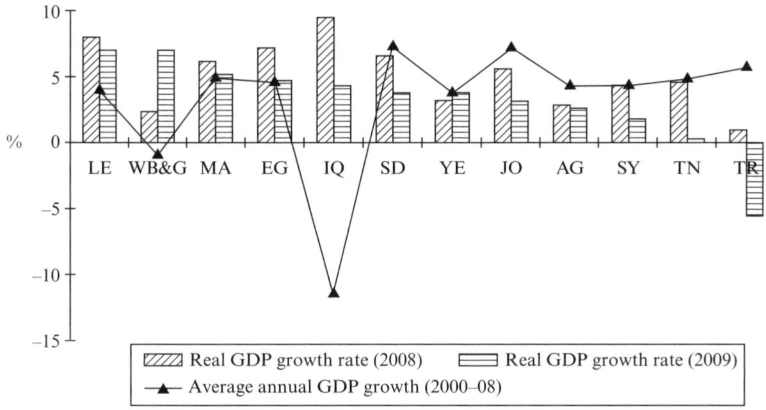

Sources: WFB for 2008 and 2009 GDP growth rates; WDI for the 2000–2008 annual average growth rate ('Private Sector at a Glance' country profiles, World Bank Group, 26 April 2010).

Figure 2.2 GDP growth rates

Tunisia (less than 1 per cent) and Algeria, Lebanon and Morocco (just over 1 per cent). Population size and growth have important implications for economic growth. On the one hand a large and/or growing population puts pressure on an economy to create employment opportunities. On the other hand it offers the potential of a growing domestic market for products and services. Smaller economies must be particularly concerned with trade openness and tapping into export markets as a source of demand and growth.

On the basis of the nominal value of GDP per capita[7] the most prosperous country is Turkey (GDP per capita of US$8723). The least prosperous is Yemen (GDP per capita of US$1061) (Figure 2.1).

Growth in real GDP across the MENA-12 has been variable. In 2008 the highest GDP growth was achieved in Iraq (9.5 per cent) followed by Lebanon (8 per cent) (Figure 2.2). The lowest growth economy was in Turkey (0.9 per cent). GDP growth in most of the countries dropped significantly in 2009, likely the effect of the global financial crisis, Turkey being the most affected. GDP growth in Yemen and the West Bank & Gaza actually increased in 2009. Compared to the average annual GDP growth rates during 2000–2008 (WDI), Iraq, the West Bank & Gaza, Egypt, Morocco and Lebanon performed better in 2008, with substantially improved performance in Iraq and Lebanon. The GDP growth rate remained at about the same level in Tunisia and Syria but declined in Algeria, Jordan, Yemen, Sudan and Turkey, with the largest decline in Turkey. Except for Iraq, Lebanon, the West Bank & Gaza, Morocco and Egypt, countries achieved 2009 GDP growth rates of below their 2000–2008 average annual growth. The average GDP growth for the 12 countries was 3.2 per cent in 2009, 5.1 per cent in 2008 and 3.3 per cent between 2000 and 2008.

The 2002 Arab Human Development Report (AHDR) projected that the MENA countries would require an annual minimum GDP growth of 5 per cent in order to reduce unemployment and provide jobs for new labour force entrants (UNDP and AFESD 2002, p. 4). Only six of the countries averaged that rate of growth in 2008 and 2009: Lebanon, Egypt, Iraq, Jordan, Morocco and Sudan.

INDUSTRIAL STRUCTURE OF THE ECONOMIES

Economic development theory suggests that the structural distribution of an economy changes with levels of development (Syrquin 1988). Low-income countries are initially more dependent on agriculture, but as the economy develops resources will shift from agriculture to industry and gradually into services. On the other hand, one cannot dismiss the essential role played by agricultural diversification and the modernization of agri-food industries as an effective driver of pro-poor growth (OECD 2007a). Although discussions of development often focus on the non-agricultural sectors, the importance of the agricultural sector should not be ignored in pro-poor growth strategies.

The industrial structure differs dramatically across the MENA-12 countries (Figure 2.3). Agriculture still plays a relatively dominant role in the Sudanese, Syrian and Moroccan economies, while it accounts for less than 10 per cent of GDP in Iraq, Algeria, Yemen, Jordan, Turkey, Lebanon and the West Bank & Gaza. Algeria and Iraq are the most heavily driven by the industry sector (accounting for over 60 per cent of their GDP[8]), while Jordan, Lebanon and the West Bank & Gaza are highly service-driven economies (accounting for over two-thirds of their GDP).

The Egyptian and Yemeni economies, with similar sector structures, approximate most closely the 2008 MENA-wide average of 11 per cent of GDP in agriculture, 43 per cent in industry and 46 per cent in services (WDI). The sector structures are very similar for Algeria and Iraq, both countries where the government still controls much of the industry sector and petroleum is a major component. Lebanon and the West Bank & Gaza are somewhat similar with low agricultural and industry sector output and large service sectors.

The MENA region is the lowest-performing region in the world in terms

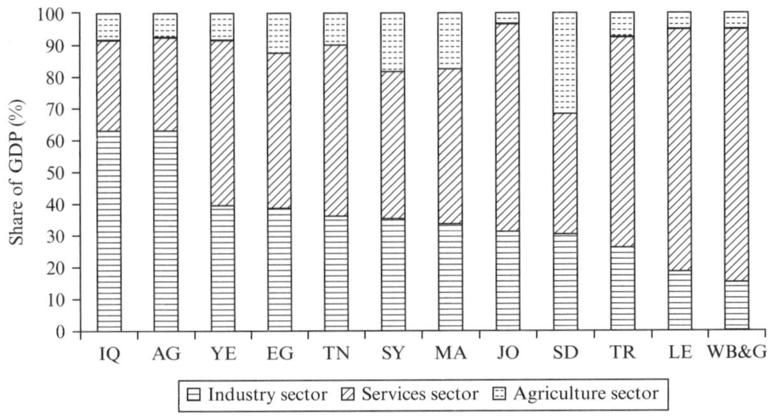

Source: WFB, 2009 estimates, 2008 for the WB&G.

Figure 2.3 Sector shares of GDP

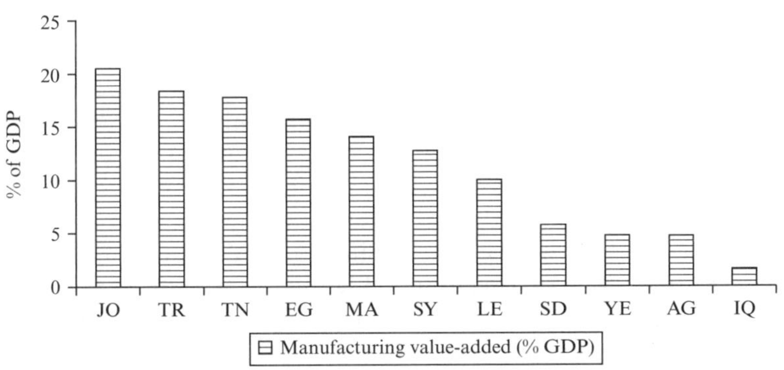

Source: WDI data for 2008; 2007 for SD; 2005 for IQ. No data for the WB&G.

Figure 2.4 Manufacturing share of GDP

of the contribution of manufacturing to GDP, averaging only 12 per cent in 2008 compared to 14 per cent for low-income countries, 22 per cent for middle-income countries and 17 per cent for high-income countries (WDI). The manufacturing contribution to GDP in the MENA-12 countries is also quite low (Figure 2.4). Manufacturing output is strongest in Jordan, Turkey and Tunisia, but Egypt, Morocco and Syria also perform above the MENA region average. Manufacturing output in the remaining five countries contributes 10 per cent or less of their GDP. Manufacturing accounts

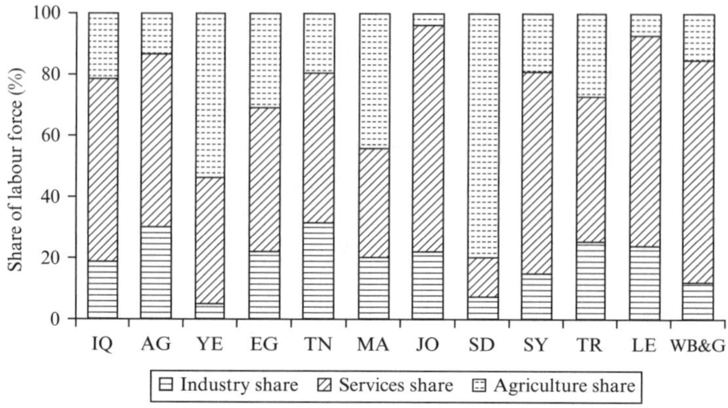

Source: WFB and country sources for latest available years, 1998–2008.

Figure 2.5 Sector share of labour force

for only a small share of the industry sector contribution to GDP in the oil-producing countries of Algeria, Iraq and Yemen, indicating a lack of diversification of industrial activity and an overdependence on the petroleum industry. This limited diversification within the manufacturing sector in MENA countries was noted by Blanc and Louis (2007), who reported that five industries account for the bulk of manufacturing employment, with dominance of the textiles and clothing and leather industries.

The MENA-12 countries are diverse with respect to the distribution of the labour force across sectors. In Sudan and Yemen the highest share of the labour force is in agriculture (Figure 2.5). Eighty per cent of the Sudanese labour force and over half of the Yemeni labour force depend on agriculture for their livelihood. This is consistent with the situation in low-income economies. Over two-thirds of the labour force in Jordan, the West Bank & Gaza, Iraq and Syria is in the service sector. Countries with the highest relative share of the labour force in the industry sector (from a quarter to one-third) are Algeria, Tunisia and Turkey.

Although the industry sector contributes over 60 per cent of GDP in Algeria and Iraq, the industry share of the labour force is much lower. This suggests that much of the industrial output is achieved without large employment implications, the dominance of low-labour-intensive oil production being one factor. Less than 7 per cent of the labour force in Sudan and Yemen is the industry sector, again implying that the industrial sectors are not large employment creators; yet the high labour force share in agriculture relative to the sector's output points to low productivity in agriculture.

Blanc and Louis (2007) suggest that changes are needed in the current structure of sector employment in order to benefit from openness and trade potential, and that jobs should be transferred from the non-tradable to the tradable sectors with competitive advantage. According to their analysis, the size of the non-tradable sectors, particularly public services, is still large compared to the tradable sectors; the agriculture and services sectors, which are absorbing most of the employment, are not sufficiently liberalized; and the manufacturing sector is relatively small (Blanc and Louis 2007).

PERFORMANCE ON HUMAN DEVELOPMENT INDICATORS

A basic level of human capacity is necessary to enable individuals to engage in productive economic activity. A nation's productivity is negatively affected if literacy rates are low or basic health is poor (Sala-i-Martin et al. 2008). The United Nations Development Programme (UNDP 2009) attempts to capture a comparative picture of the human capacity performance of countries using a number of indicators including adult literacy, poverty levels, education enrolment, life expectancy, child malnutrition and population not using an improved water source. The resulting Human Development Index (HDI) is a composite of a life expectancy index, an education index and a human poverty index.[9] Collectively these indices provide a measure of the level of human capacity in a country – education, health and well-being – important considerations when measuring pro-poor growth outcomes.

Table 2.2 presents the results of the 2009 HDI rankings and score values for the MENA-12 countries. Although all are assessed as being medium development countries, only Turkey and Jordan fall in the top half of the rankings of 182 countries with HDI values of 0.806 and 0.803 (out of a maximum value of 1). Sudan is in last place of the MENA-12 with an HDI value of 0.521. Performance variances are found across indicators and countries. The West Bank & Gaza, Jordan and Lebanon have higher adult literacy rates than Turkey, for example. Jordan has the highest performance on gross enrolment in education, but the West Bank & Gaza has the highest score on the education index. Syria and Tunisia have the highest life expectancies and the West Bank & Gaza has the best overall performance on the Human Poverty Index. Yemen and Sudan are the poorest performers on all indicators.

Although it is difficult to obtain up-to-date comparable and comprehensive data on poverty and income equality levels (Bibi and Nabli 2010),

Table 2.2 Performance of MENA countries on the Human Development Index

Country	HDI - 2007		Life expectancy at birth (yrs)	Adult literacy rate (% aged 15 and above)	Combined gross enrolment ratio in education (%)	Life expectancy index	Education index	Human poverty index (HPI-1)		Probability of not surviving to age 40 (% of cohort)	Adult illiteracy rate (% aged 15 and above)	Population not using an improved water source (%)	Children under weight for age (% under the age of 5)	Population below income poverty line		
														US$1.25 a day	US$2 a day	% under national poverty line
	Rank	Value	2007	1999–2007	2007	2007	2007	Rank	Value %	2005–10	1999–2007	2006	2000–2006	2000–2007	2000–2007	2000–2007
Turkey	79	0.806	71.7	88.7	71.1	0.779	0.828	40	8.3	5.7	11.3	3	4	2.7	9.0	27.0
Lebanon	83	0.803	71.9	89.6	78.0	0.781	0.857	33	7.6	5.5	10.4	0	4	..	..	..
Jordan	96	0.770	72.4	91.1	78.7	0.790	0.870	29	6.6	5.3	8.9	2	4	..	3.5	14.2
Tunisia	98	0.769	73.8	76.7	76.2	0.813	0.772	65	15.6	4.1	22.3	6	4	2.6	12.8	7.6
Algeria	104	0.754	73.6	75.4	73.6	0.787	0.748	71	17.5	6.4	24.6	15	4	6.8	23.6	22.6
Syria	107	0.742	74.1	83.1	65.7	0.818	0.773	56	12.6	3.9	16.9	11	10	..	..	..
West Bank & Gaza	110	0.737	73.3	93.8	78.3	0.806	0.886	24	6.0	4.3	6.2	11	3	..	..	..

Egypt	123	0.703	69.9	66.4	76.4	0.749	0.697	82	23.4	7.2	33.6	2	6	..	18.4	16.7
Morocco	130	0.654	71.0	55.6	61.0	0.767	0.5743	96	31.1	6.6	44.4	17	10	2.5	14.0	..
Yemen	140	0.575	62.5	58.9	57.4	0.624	0.574	111	35.6	15.6	41.1	34	46	17.5	46.6	41.8
Sudan	150	0.531	57.9	60.9	39.9	0.548	0.539	104	34.0	23.9	39.1	30	41	..	..	..
Iraq	..	..	67.8	74.1	60.5	0.714	0.695	75	19.4	10.0	25.9	23	8	..	..	..

Note: The HDI value is based on a maximum score of 1. The HPI-1 measures the proportion of people living below a certain threshold level in each of three dimensions of the HDI: a long and healthy life (the proportion of people who are not expected to survive to age 40); access to knowledge (the adult illiteracy rate); and a decent standard of living (unweighted average of people not using an improved water source and the proportion of children under age 5 who are underweight for their age).
Rank is out of 182 countries. The lowest-ranked country is Niger with an HDI of 0.340. Norway is the top-ranked country with an HDI of 0.971.

Source: Data from UNDP (2009).

the most recent available estimates indicate that from 7.4 per cent of the population in Tunisia to over 45 per cent in Yemen and the West Bank & Gaza lives below the national poverty line (Table 2.3). In the Gaza Strip an estimated 80 per cent of the population lives in poverty. The largest income dispersion (or inequality) is in Turkey (which has the highest GNI per capita in the MENA-12) followed by Tunisia, both countries that have been liberalizing for a long time. Income dispersion is lowest in Egypt and Algeria.

The World Bank (2005c) points out that increases in income inequality do not necessarily lead to increases in poverty. Even policies that worsen income distribution can improve poverty levels if their effects on growth are large enough; in which case, an increase in inequality can actually occur at the same time as a reduction in poverty levels. There is mounting evidence that countries with higher initial rates of inequality need higher rates of growth to reduce poverty at the same rate as those with lower initial inequality (OECD 2004a). This would suggest, for example, that higher rates of growth in GNI per capita would be needed to reduce inequalities in Turkey and Tunisia than in Egypt and Algeria. Bibi and Nabli (2010) conclude that growth-promoting policies must be accompanied by redistributive-promoting policies in order to avoid further marginalization of the poor.

Income dispersion rates in the MENA-12 have not changed much since the 1990s, although they are now somewhat higher in Egypt and Jordan than they were during that time.[10] Due to different baseline years for reporting poverty data and missing data for five of the MENA-12 countries, it is not possible to say more about how they compare. However the 2002 AHDR stated that income distribution is more equal in MENA countries than in many other regions of the world. Remittances, migrant workers, government subsidies to the poor, Islamic practices of *zakat* and *sadaqa*[11] and the presence of a large number of charitable organizations are contributing factors (UNDP and AFESD 2002).

INFLOW OF REMITTANCES

Remittances are a significant inflow of external funds into the MENA-12 countries – money sent home to families from workers who have emigrated or are working abroad. In addition to providing income for recipient families, these remittances are an important source of foreign exchange, in some cases surpassing the level of FDI inflows. Lebanon, Jordan and the West Bank & Gaza receive the highest levels of remittances, amounting to almost a quarter of GDP in Lebanon, 18 per cent in Jordan and 14 per

Table 2.3 Poverty and income inequality levels

Indicator	AG	EG	JO	LE	MA	SD	SY	TN	TR	WB&G	YE
Population below the national poverty line	25.0%	20.0%	14.2%	28.0%	9.0%	40.0%	11.9%	7.4%	20.0%	46.0%	45.2%
	2005	2005	2007	1999	2007	2004	2006	2005	2002	2007	2003
Share of household income consumption:											
Lowest 10% of population	2.8%	3.9%	3.0%		2.7%			2.3%	1.9%		2.9%
Highest 10% of population	26.8%	27.6%	30.7%	..	33.2%	..	..	31.5%	33.2%	..	30.8%
	1995	2005	2006		2007			2000	2005		2005
Income dispersion index*	9.5	7.1	10.2		12.3			13.7	17.5		10.6

Note: * A measure of income inequality calculated as a ratio of the consumption of the highest 10% of the population to the consumption of the lowest 10%.

Sources: WFB. Poverty line data for MA from KOM (2008). No available data for Iraq.

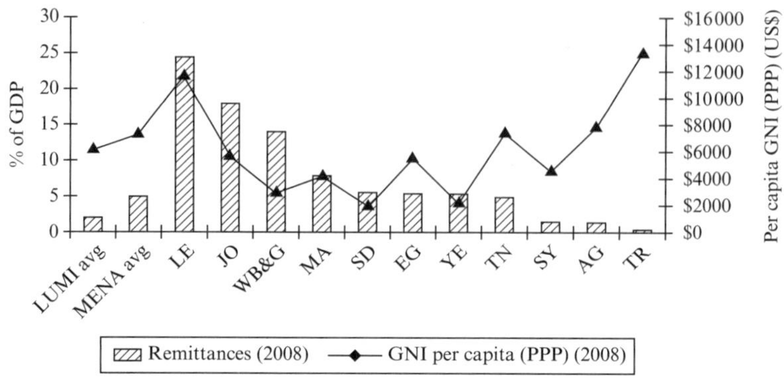

Source: WDI, 2008 data (World Bank 2010), 2007 estimate for GNI per capita in the WB&G. No data for IQ.

Figure 2.6 Level of remittances and GNI per capita

cent in the West Bank & Gaza (Figure 2.6). These are the three smallest-population countries among the MENA-12 and all have a large number of displaced persons, refugees and/or workers abroad.

OFFICIAL DEVELOPMENT ASSISTANCE

The MENA-12 countries vary widely in the level of official development assistance (ODA) they receive on an aid per capita basis and as a percentage of GNI (Table 2.4). Iraq receives the highest per capita ODA followed by the West Bank & Gaza and Lebanon, while Algeria, Yemen and Syria attract the lowest amounts. Yemen, with a GDP per capita of just over US$1000, appears to be disadvantaged in terms of attracting ODA. In fact the UNDP estimates that Yemen will need an annual ODA flow of approximately US$75 per capita in order to reach the goal of halving income poverty by 2015 (UNDP 2006a). It is noted that the oil-rich countries such as Algeria and Syria are less dependent on ODA and can be more selective about aid partnerships, especially during periods when oil revenues are high.

Table 2.4 Level of official development assistance and aid by country

Country	ODA per capita (US$)	Aid as % of GNI	Country	ODA per capita (US$)	Aid as % of GNI
Iraq	$767	..	Morocco	$39	1.4
West Bank & Gaza	$659	..	Turkey	$27	0.3
Lebanon	$257	3.7	Egypt	$17	0.8
Jordan	$126	3.3	Yemen	$13	1.3
Sudan	$58	4.8	Algeria	$9	0.2
Tunisia	$46	1.3	Syria	$7	0.3

Note: The average per capita ODA is US$42 in low-income (LI) countries, US$11 in lower- and upper-middle-income (LUMI) countries and US$73 in MENA region countries. The average aid as % of GNI is 7.4% for LI countries, 0.3% for LUMI countries and 1.9% for the MENA region.

Source: WDI, 2008 data; 2006 data for Iraq.

NOTES

1. GDP calculation is based on the exchange rate value in USD.
2. Population, GDP and labour force estimates are from the CIA *World Factbook* (WFB), available at http://www.cia.gov/library/publications/the-world-factbook/geos (accessed 4 February 2010).
3. According to the World Bank country classifications as of July 2009, using the Atlas method calculation for GNI (and based on 2008 data), the following definitions apply: lower-income countries, < US$975 GNI per capita; lower-middle-income countries, US$976–US$3855 GNI per capita; upper-middle-income countries, US$3856–US$11 905 GNI per capita; and high-income countries, US$11 906 or more.
4. Categorizations used by the World Bank (World Bank 2007b). Resource 'rich' in the case of MENA countries generally indicates the presence of oil and gas reserves.
5. WFB population estimates for July 2009.
6. These are nominal values of GDP per capita derived by converting national currencies, at market exchange rates, to current US dollars (see IMF 2010).
7. Nominal values are sourced from the International Monetary Fund database (IMF 2010). Using the purchasing power parity method of conversion produces higher absolute values for GDP per capita.
8. It should be noted that the industrial sectors in Algeria and Iraq are dominated by oil and hydrocarbon production.
9. For more information on the Human Development Index see http://hdrstats.undp.org/en/indicators.
10. In the 1990s the income dispersion index was 5.7 for Egypt (1995) and 9.1 for Jordan (1997) (UNDP and AFESD 2002, p. 91).
11. *Zakat* and *sadaqa* are Islamic practices of donating a certain percentage of individual wealth to the poor.

3. Economic growth challenges

During the first decade of the 21st century, governments in the MENA-12 economies have become increasingly engaged in creating the conditions for private sector growth. Some have achieved more progress in doing this than others, but in all cases the private sector remains underdeveloped. Given the trend towards greater liberalization and openness, a diminished role for the public sector in economic activity and employment, and the need to improve the standard of living for citizens, the impetus for accelerating further development and growth of private sector-led activity continues to be strong. In this regard the MENA-12 face a number of major economic and social pressures and challenges. Seven are identified as being the most salient:

1. the job creation and employment challenge;
2. the informal economy challenge;
3. the education, skills and knowledge challenge;
4. the science and technology (S&T) and innovation challenge;
5. the world economy integration challenge;
6. the gender challenge; and
7. the micro, small and medium enterprise (SME) and entrepreneurship challenge.

The first six of these challenges are elaborated in Chapter 3 and the SME and entrepreneurship challenge in Chapter 4. It should be noted that this set of challenges is very much interrelated, one influencing and affecting the other.

JOB CREATION AND EMPLOYMENT CHALLENGE

One of the most compelling challenges in MENA countries is employment creation. The 2002 Arab Human Development Report (AHDR) states that this task is probably more formidable in the Arab region than in any other region in the world (UNDP and AFESD 2002). The latest World Bank projections estimate that 40 million new jobs will be needed during the decade to 2020 just to absorb new job seekers (World Bank 2009c). Currently there is a large cohort of young people in the population, labour force growth that exceeds market demand and low utilization of the existing labour force, characterized by low employment rates, low female labour force participation rates and high unemployment rates. Faced with large labour surpluses, a growing supply of new labour force entrants and shrinking public sectors, the MENA region requires an expanding private sector to create employment opportunities and contribute to economic growth and poverty reduction objectives. The key to future economic growth is in enabling more people to secure productive employment and facilitating a gradual shift from low-skill, low-productivity jobs to more skill-intensive, higher-productivity jobs. The factors affecting the job creation and employment challenge are presented below.

A Large Youth Population

Compared to other regions of the world, except sub-Saharan Africa, the MENA-12 countries have a high proportion of young people in the total population. The percentage of the population under 15 years of age ranges from about 23 per cent in Tunisia to over 46 per cent in Yemen. The percentage of the population 65 or older ranges from a low of 2.5 per cent in Sudan and Yemen to a high of just over 7 per cent in Lebanon and Tunisia (Figure 3.1). The median age of the MENA-12 population is 23.6 years, spanning from less than 17 years in Yemen to just over 29 years in Lebanon and Tunisia.[1] Conflict countries have the youngest populations (Iraq, Sudan, the West Bank & Gaza and Yemen) and the highest fertility rates (an average of 4.4 births per woman[2] compared to an average of only 2.4 births per woman in the other eight MENA-12 countries).

The number of people under 15 years of age in the MENA-12 approximates 117 million,[3] an average of 32.5 per cent of the total estimated 2009 population. This demographic reality points to a growing supply of labour for years to come. Growth in the labour force is an important factor linked to economic growth if participants can be absorbed in gainful employment (UN 2007) and therefore presents both an opportunity and a challenge in the MENA-12. Silatech (2009) states that the challenge is not only to increase the number of jobs for Arab youth but also to improve the quality of those jobs.

A Labour Force Growing Faster than Labour Market Demand

The labour force is growing at a faster rate than labour market demand. With relatively young populations, the number of new labour force

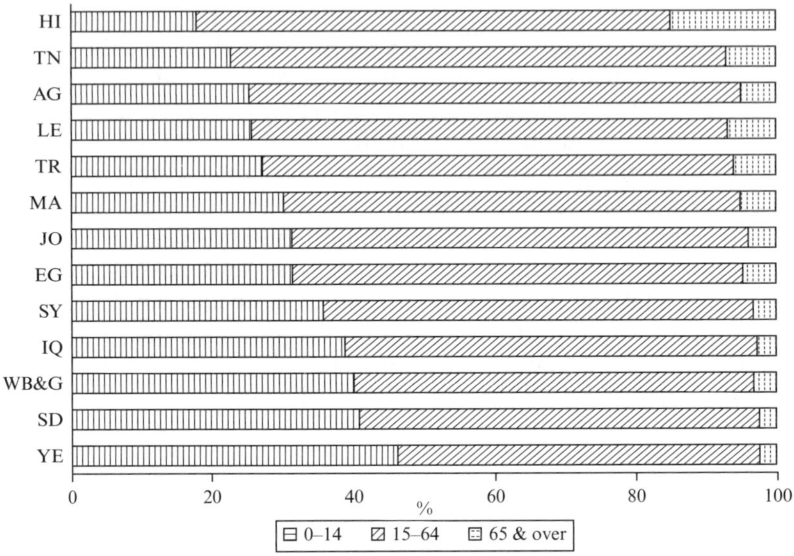

Note: The high-income (HI) country average is shown for comparison purposes.

Source: WFB, 2009 estimates.

Figure 3.1 Age distribution of the population by country

entrants each year is far beyond the capacity of current labour markets to absorb them, leading to significant annual job deficits (Table 3.1). The World Bank (2007b, p. 86) projects that the MENA-wide region would have to create 68 million new jobs to absorb new labour force entrants over the 2005–20 period, and another 20 million to eliminate unemployment.[4] An additional challenge is that the higher-valued-added sectors are not the ones creating the majority of jobs – most jobs are still low-skill and low-wage in agriculture, construction, low-skills manufacturing and the informal sector.

The public sector used to be the employer of first and last resort in the MENA-12 countries. In the absence of a dynamic private sector, government employment was the only avenue for alleviating labour market pressures and expanded rapidly in past decades. This had the effect of producing a costly public sector by international standards (World Bank 2007b). Prior to the 1990s, for example, the Syrian government required a period of mandatory public service from graduates of public universities (Huitfeldt and Kabbani 2005). Egypt also had the practice of guaranteeing government jobs for its graduates. In recent years the public sector

Table 3.1 Annual job deficit for new labour force entrants, selected countries

Country	Annual labour force growth (2005–10)* %	Annual labour force entrants**	Jobs available	Annual Job deficit
Yemen	4.3	188 000 (1)	117 000	71 000
West Bank & Gaza	3.4	54 000 (2)	..	..
Syria	3.7	196 000 (3)	140 000	56 000
Egypt	2.5	638 000 (4)	446 310	191 690
Morocco	2.2	200 000 (5)	..	..
Algeria	3.1	250 000 (6)	100 000	150 000
Tunisia	2.7	88 300 (7)	67 825 (8)	21 475
Turkey	1.7	700 000 (9)	575 000 (10)	125 000
Jordan	3.3	50 000 (11)	..	..
Lebanon	2.5	..	..	..
Iraq	3.5			

Notes:
(2) Average annual number of labour force entrants 2000–2005; an average of only 140 000 jobs were available;
(4) annual number of labour force entrants 2001–2010;
(8) average annual jobs created 2001–2005;
(7) average annual jobs created 2003–2006.

Sources:
* World Bank (2007b), p.161, based on ILO projections. TR data from IMD International (2009).
** Country sources and estimates: (1) UNDP (2006a), p. 93; (2) UNCTAD (2004), p. 7; (3) Goheer (2008), p. 12; (4) FEMISE (2009), p. 104; (5) USAID (2008b), p. 40; (6) key informant; (7) AfDB and OECD (2008d), p. 598; (8) AfDB (2007), p. 18; (9) EC (2007c); (10) UNDP (2008); (11) FEMISE (2009), p. 134.

in the region has been downsizing its employment and public expenditures as part of the reform agenda. Job growth in the public sector has slowed down compared to the 1990s, although the government wage bill to gross domestic product (GDP) has increased over the 1990 level in Egypt, Morocco, Syria and Tunisia (World Bank 2007b). Nonetheless young people still have a high preference for government jobs. Over half of 15–29-year-olds in Iraq, Syria, Jordan, Egypt and Yemen would prefer to work in the government compared to less than 20 per cent preferring work in the private sector (Silatech 2009). Sudanese youth have the highest preference for work in the private sector (32 per cent).

Governments are no longer able to employ all of the new labour market entrants and the formal private sector is not big enough or growing fast enough to absorb them. The micro and small enterprise (MSE) sector, particularly the informal sector, is noted for being a major absorber of labour surpluses, but the sector is fragile and most of the jobs created are unprotected low-skill jobs, including unpaid work in family enterprises and agriculture. Entry to the labour market for first-time job seekers, even educated youth, is increasingly through employment in the informal sector, a situation that results in a high level of underemployment. An increasing supply of jobs will have to be achieved through accelerated growth in the private sector (World Bank 2004d). This will require that governments continue to examine restrictions in their labour laws and regulations and the impact of high non-wage and social security costs on the hiring practices of enterprises, especially MSEs. Additional efforts are also needed to address the serious mismatch between the knowledge and skills of graduates and the needs of employers. These constraints, along with brain drain and the lack of eagerness of graduates to set up their own businesses, are considered to be among the most pronounced problems in the MENA region (EC 2006a; FEMISE 2008).

High Unemployment Rates

Furthermore the MENA economies are experiencing high unemployment rates. This is a huge challenge for the whole MENA region where unemployment rates are among the highest in the world and have been persistent over a long period of time (UNDP and AFESD 2002; Blanc and Louis 2007; World Bank 2007b). The official unemployment rate in the MENA-12 averages 14 per cent. It is highest in the West Bank & Gaza (26 per cent) and lowest in Lebanon and Syria (9.2 per cent) (Figure 3.2).[5]

Unemployment rates of 14 per cent or higher are reported for six of the countries. This is particularly indicative of an inefficient labour market where a large number of individuals willing to work at prevailing wage rates are unable to do so.

The unemployment situation is particularly severe among women and youth. Although women are becoming more economically active in MENA countries, more of them are ending up unemployed. The unemployment rate for women is over three times the unemployment rate for men in Egypt, Syria and Yemen, and twice the rate in Jordan. Only in Morocco, Lebanon, Turkey and the West Bank & Gaza are the unemployment rates similar for both men and women.

Youth unemployment rates are seriously high. Depending on the MENA-12 country, 15–24-year-olds make up 20–35 per cent of the labour force but represent 35–80 per cent of the unemployed. Persons under the

Sources: WFB and country data sources; various dates from 2007–2009 (2002 data for SD). No available data on male and female unemployment rates for IQ and SD.

Figure 3.2 Unemployment rates high but vary across MENA-12 countries

age of 30 account for over 70 per cent of the unemployed in Algeria, and 15–24-year-olds make up 78 per cent of the unemployed in Syria, about 65 per cent of the unemployed in Jordan, almost half of the unemployed in Lebanon and 42 per cent of the unemployed in Morocco. The unemployment rate for 20–24-year-olds is over 30 per cent in Tunisia and Lebanon and over 28 per cent in Jordan, two to three times higher than the respective national unemployment rates.

In many of the MENA-12 countries, there seems to be an unemployment penalty for educated youth (World Bank 2004d). The highest rate of unemployment for young people is often among those with university degrees, young educated women being the hardest hit (Assaad 2006; JCPPR 2006). Two reasons are given for the lower employment outcomes for young educated women: some private sector employers have a strong preference for male job seekers (supposedly to avoid the added labour costs associated with maternity leave and other allowances), and women that have gained access to education often do not want to accept the low-skilled and low-paid jobs available to them (ILO 2008b).

Several of the governments are investing heavily in youth employment schemes. The Algerian government established l'Agence Nationale de Soutien à l'Emploi des Jeunes (ANSEJ) several years ago in an effort to reduce youth unemployment rates. For the past few years ANSEJ has been delivering an enterprise creation programme targeted to university and technical institute graduates that includes training, business plan assistance and bridging to financing through a guarantee fund. Lebanese government ministries have partnered with the private sector in the launch of the Bader Young Entrepreneurs Program and the Ministry of Economy and Trade has issued a paper on encouraging youth to start businesses. The BIDAYA programme in Syria offers training and mentoring to potential young entrepreneurs and has launched several incubators that offer management training modules to help disadvantaged youth start businesses. The Moroccan Moukalatawi programme managed by l'Agence Nationale de Promotion de l'Emploi et des Compétences (ANAPEC) offers training, coaching, an 85 per cent loan guarantee and follow-up support to encourage university graduates to start MSEs. Moukalatawi 'windows' provide support to these young entrepreneurs throughout the country. The Moroccan government's initial target was to create 30 000 new enterprises through this initiative over the 2004–09 period, but due to disappointing results the programme was revised in 2009 with a reduced target of 10 000 new enterprises. The Turkish government has a credit programme for new enterprises started by young entrepreneurs, and the Tunisian government has a national campaign to support entrepreneurship among higher education students. To encourage employment of new university graduates, the Tunisian government is offering to cover the full costs of their salaries for the first two years of employment and to pay for initial training costs (US Department of State 2009). Donors, non-governmental organizations (NGOs) and young entrepreneur associations are also targeting youth with employment and enterprise creation initiatives in many of these countries.

Low Female Labour Force Participation

A related employment challenge is the low share of women in the labour force. The labour force participation rate of women in the MENA region is the lowest of any region in the world. An average of only 26 per cent of women in the 15–64 age groups are working or looking for work compared to 74 per cent of men (World Bank 2010, p. 68). Female labour force participation rates in the MENA-12 are highest in Algeria and Sudan (37 and 31 per cent respectively) and lowest in Iraq and the West Bank & Gaza (13 and 16 per cent respectively) (Figure 3.3), but in all cases they are lower than the average of 49 per cent in lower- and upper-middle-income (LUMI) countries.

Low labour force participation rates are reflected in a low share of women in the labour force. Women's absolute share of the labour force varies from a high of over 31 per cent in Algeria to a low of just over 16 per cent in Iraq and 18 per cent in the West Bank & Gaza. This compares to an average of 43.4 per cent in high-income countries, 38.8 per cent in LUMI countries and 44.5 per cent in low-income countries (World Bank 2010, p. 68). The low female labour force participation rate is accompanied by

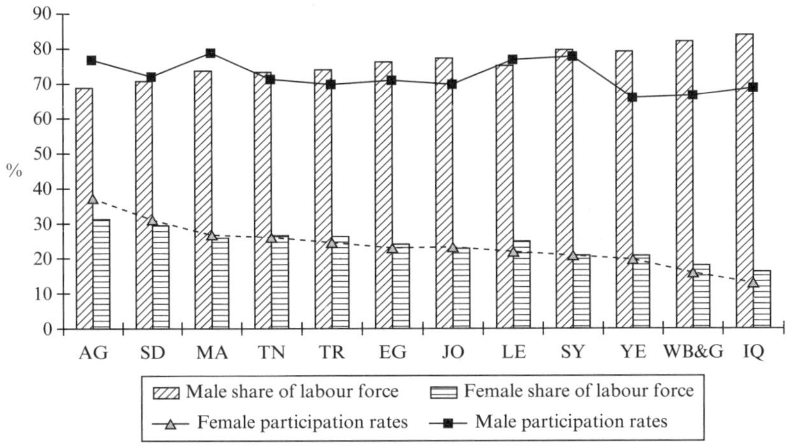

Source: WDI, 2008 data (World Bank 2010).

Figure 3.3 Male and female participation rates and share of the labour force

a higher rate of unemployment for women than for men in most of these countries (in some cases substantially higher), and a higher incidence of employment as an 'unpaid family worker'.

However, according to the World Bank (2007b), the single most important transformation affecting the MENA labour market in the past few years is the increasing presence of women workers. While still low by any international benchmarks, female labour force participation rates have increased rapidly since the early 1990s in Algeria, Jordan, Syria and Tunisia, although they have stagnated in Iraq, Lebanon, Morocco, Egypt, Sudan, Yemen and the West Bank & Gaza.

The World Bank (2004b) highlights the importance of women's labour force participation as an issue for the MENA region, pointing out that the economic well-being of a population – including consumption of food, housing, health care and other market-based goods and services – is determined by the proportion of the working population and by how much each working person earns. Thus the low participation rate of women in the labour force has a high cost to both the economy and the family. The World Bank report presents evidence that countries achieve higher levels of per capita income through the increased labour force participation of women, which in turn contributes to reduced poverty and faster economic growth, benefiting both the family and the economy.

Low Employment Rates

The average employment rate in the MENA-12 countries is only 42 per cent, ranging from a high of 49 per cent in Algeria to a low of 30 per cent in the West Bank & Gaza. Overall, well under half of the population is employed (Figure 3.4).[6] This compares to an average employment rate of 60 per cent in LUMI countries and 45 per cent in the MENA region (World Bank 2010, p. 76). Only four of the MENA-12 countries exceed the MENA region average: Algeria, Sudan, Morocco and Lebanon. Employment rates among the 15–24-year-old age group are considerably lower, averaging 26 per cent in the MENA-12 countries (from 35 per cent in Morocco to 15 per cent in the West Bank & Gaza) and 29 per cent in the MENA region, compared to 42 per cent in LUMI countries and 43 per cent in high-income countries (World Bank 2010, p. 76).

The low employment rate of women is the major contributing factor to the weak employment performance of the MENA region. Women workers average only slightly more than 20 per cent of total employment in the MENA-12, ranging from a high of over 27 per cent in Morocco and Sudan to less than 16 per cent in Algeria, Jordan and Syria (Figure 3.5). The higher rates in Morocco, Tunisia and Turkey may be partly due to women workers benefiting from growth in the textiles and garment sector in earlier years.

A high concentration of women's employment in certain subsectors of the economy indicates gender segregation in the workforce. In some

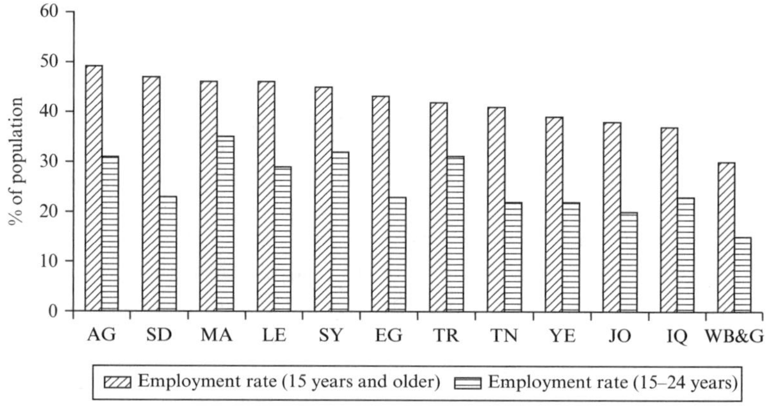

Source: WDI, 2008 data.

Figure 3.4 Employment to adult population

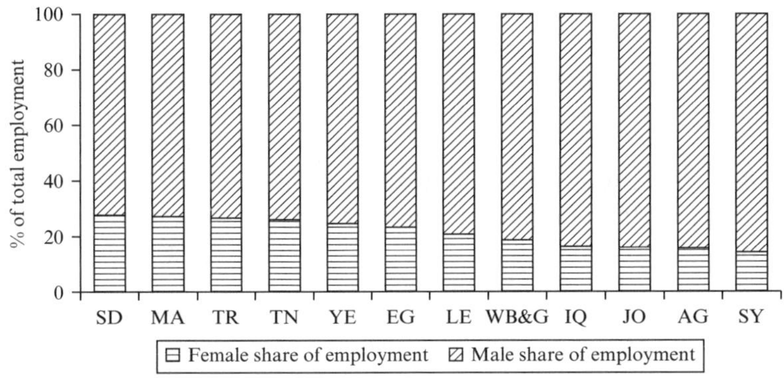

Sources: Country data sources; various years from 2005–2009 (1993 for SD).

Figure 3.5 Low shares of women in employment

countries employed women are more likely to be employed in the public sector than men, and are generally greatly underrepresented in formal private sector employment. For example, half of all employed men in Iraq work for private sector companies, but only 17 per cent of employed women; while close to half of all employed women work for the government, but only a quarter of employed men (MPDC 2005a). Women in Egypt make up only 15 per cent of all formal private sector workers. Reports of formal private sector biases against the hiring of women are prevalent throughout the region (RWEL 2008c). Women are also much more likely to be employed as unpaid family workers than men, and less likely than men to be involved in entrepreneurial and SME activity, a feature to be discussed in Chapter 4. Thus the labour force structure for women is considerably different from that for men, resulting in an untapped source of potential economic growth. This is an issue worthy of further research and policy attention.

INFORMAL ECONOMY CHALLENGE

Informality of enterprises and employment is a feature in all economies whether developing, transition or developed; what differs is the scale of the phenomenon. The informal economy plays a much stronger role in the economies of developing countries, providing employment and income to many poor households and people who cannot find employment in the formal economy (OECD 2006). However the OECD stresses that supporting informal activities is not a long-term solution to reducing poverty;

otherwise countries with large informal economies would be less poor, which is contrary to supporting evidence that countries with the highest per capita incomes have smaller informal sectors (Ayyagari et al. 2003; OECD 2006). Other studies conclude that the size of the informal sector is not only a function of the level of economic development but also strongly correlated with country-specific features. It tends to be smaller in countries with a business-friendly regulatory regime, competition-enhancing reforms, a comparatively light tax burden, security of property rights, less burdensome regulation of labour and a quality legal system (Pratap and Quintin 2006). The level of informality in a country often reflects regulatory barriers to the entry of new firms and a lack of open competition. Informality is also notably more prevalent in countries with higher income inequality (Schneider 2005), and of larger importance in economies with lower levels of human capital accumulation,[7] government expenditure and financial intermediary development (Ayyagari et al. 2003).

In order to achieve enhanced competitiveness, efforts will be needed to increase the level of formality in the private sector. This will demand more effective implementation and enforcement of policies, laws and regulations (Snodgrass and Winkler 2004) and design of appropriate business environment reforms (Zinnes 2009). Implementing policies and measures to improve conditions in the informal sector will also be an important strategy for inclusive economic growth.

A large amount of research has been done to understand better the distinctive features of informality, its causes and effects and its impact on the economy (Kuchta-Helbling 2000; Carr and Chen 2001; ADB 2004; Galal 2004; Chen 2005; USAID 2005; Chen 2007; Perry et al. 2007). Although it is commonly accepted that regulatory and administrative hurdles, lack of trust, corruption, lack of key business services and information, social practices and cultural attitudes are barriers to formalization, the OECD (2006) proposes that there is little specific research on why firms do not formalize. Certainly informality is a way for entrepreneurs to evade taxes and regulations (OECD 2006; De Paula and Scheinkman 2007), but Zinnes (2009) points out that the reasons for informality will vary across regions of the world and that evasion of taxes and regulation is not always the primary motive.

Schneider (2005), one of the few pieces of research to attempt to measure the size of the informal economy systematically on a cross-country basis,[8] concludes that informality is a complex phenomenon. People engage in informal economic activity for a variety of reasons, but Schneider concludes that the single most important factor behind high informality levels in developing countries is the burden of state regulation, such as complex tax and administrative regimes, restrictive labour laws and high social security burdens. Many entrepreneurs decide to stay informal because the costs of entry, operation and exit associated with joining the formal sector are greater than the potential benefits (Galal 2004). The decision to move to the formal sector is largely determined by the trade-off between the costs of registration and compliance with regulations, and the benefits to be derived from formality. Private enterprises are willing to forgo the benefits of better protection of property rights and to bear the cost of extra-legality (in the form of bribes, costly finance, etcetera) when it is more beneficial to remain informal. The incidence of informality appears to decrease as firm size and the value of invested capital increases, but firms of all sizes may continue to operate informally when it proves to be too costly to do otherwise. However staying informal deprives enterprises of the benefits of being able to apply for formal loans and/or acquire business development services (BDS) and supply chain contracts, thus limiting their growth potential.

There is limited consensus on the role and utility of the informal economy in poverty alleviation and national development. Although the informal sector provides livelihood options for many poor households, the working conditions in informal enterprises are often poor and the jobs insecure and low-paid. One of the big concerns of international organizations, such as the International Labour Organization (ILO), is that informal enterprises do not offer any social benefits to their workers (often because they cannot afford the high cost of social security and other insurance benefits). Bennett (2009) takes a more liberal position on the informality of enterprises, suggesting that it is a stepping stone to formality and should actually be supported. By allowing experimentation with entrepreneurship at a relatively low cost, the informal enterprise experience is critical in enabling enterprises to develop into formality over time. If informality is policed or made illegal, it would thwart these development path possibilities. On the other hand LaPorta and Shleifer (2008) find little evidence that informal firms become formal as they grow. Consequently there are still many unanswered questions about the role of informal enterprises in poverty reduction and development. Does informality cause microenterprises to be caught in a low-productivity and poverty trap or is it a stepping stone to future successful entrepreneurial activity? Would productivity significantly increase if informal firms became formal? LaPorta and Shleifer (2008) suggest that the hope of economic development lies not in the formalization of existing informal enterprises but in the creation of new registered firms run by more educated owner-managers utilizing modern practices, technology, marketing and finance.

Schneider (2005) recommends that governments aiming to decrease informal activity levels will first have to analyse the complex relationships between the official and the informal economy and the consequences of their own policy decisions, pointing out that one of the biggest challenges is undertaking efficient incentive-oriented policy measures to make work in the informal economy less attractive than work in the formal economy. Zinnes (2009) makes a similar point with respect to the formalization of enterprises. A 2004 study of the welfare impact of formalization in Egypt and a cost-benefit analysis of implementing a comprehensive reform programme demonstrated that formalization would increase GDP by 1.3 per cent each year as well as benefit enterprises, workers and the Treasury (Galal 2004). This is in line with other estimates that informality costs developing countries between one and two percentage points in annual GDP growth (Palmade 2005). Increasing the proportion of formal enterprises and jobs over the long term will provide higher-quality and better-paid jobs, broaden the tax base and improve access to formal markets, capital, land, business services and other necessary supports (OECD 2006).

The informal economy share of GDP in the MENA region increased from 21 to 31 per cent from 1990 to 2003[9] (Zinnes 2009). A high level of informality of both enterprises and employment is a common feature in the MENA-12 countries and has increased marginally from 1999 to 2006. Schneider and Buehn (2009) estimate that the informal economy accounts for just less than 20 per cent of GDP in Syria, to almost 40 per cent in Tunisia[10] (Figure 3.6). Contrary to Schneider's general finding that the size of a country's informal economy is inversely related to the level of economic development, there does not appear to be a significant relationship between the level of economic development and level of informality in the MENA-12. Thus differences across MENA countries are likely due to specific structural and institutional factors.

There is limited research on the informal sector and the effects of informality on the MENA-12 economies. One of the challenges is the lack of official data, but estimates suggest that the informal sector accounts for between 40 and 70 per cent of all private sector enterprises, and a large share of employed workers: 40–50 per cent of private sector workers in Algeria; 25–40 per cent in Lebanon, Syria, the West Bank & Gaza and Morocco; over 80 per cent in Egypt;[11] and more than half of the labour force in Turkey.

Informal workers have no social protection and the informal enterprises for which they work are not able to access formal financing, modern technologies and government contracts, and are subject to extralegal costs (a form of unofficial taxation) and harassment from government officials without protection of the law from abuse by local officials (Blanc and Louis 2007). Informality is not just an issue in the MSE sector although

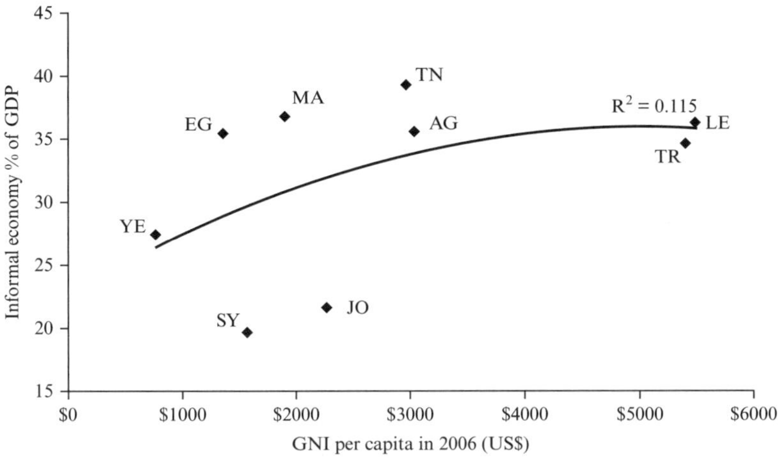

Note: The average size of the informal economy in 15 OECD countries in 2006 was 15.8% of GDP.

Sources: Schneider (2005) and Schneider and Buehn (2009). No values for IQ, SD and the WB&G.

Figure 3.6 Size of informal sector by level of economic development, MENA

it is more prevalent there. Large enterprises can also have a significant number of workers not registered for social security. Evidence that informal employment has been increasing is at least partly the result of limited job opportunities in the formal sector relative to the size of the working age population (FEMISE 2008) and overall deterioration of labour market opportunities especially for people with higher education (World Bank 2008g).

Blanc and Louis (2007) suggest that MENA governments may be willing to ignore the informality issue because it represents an inexpensive automatic mechanism for social stability and a safety valve to absorb shocks to the national economy. On the other hand a high level of informality deprives public budgets of fiscal resources and undermines the effectiveness of economic reforms.

Although most of the MENA-12 governments have not exerted much dedicated policy effort to the issue of informality reduction, recent developments are occurring in some of the countries. The Egyptian Small Enterprise Development Law (Law 141/2004) specified ceilings on the maximum time and cost required to register a micro and small enterprise and the establishment of one-stop shops (OSSs) in offices of the Social Fund for Development (SFD) in Egyptian governorates to facilitate the registration and licensing process. In spite of these measures the share of informal enterprise activity in Egypt has been increasing. The Moroccan Ministry of Finance and Privatization initiated an analysis of the informal sector situation in 2007 to inform recommendations for modernizing the sector (formalization) and increasing the tax base. The Syrian government has initiated plans to encourage MSEs to move from the informal to the formal sector through exemptions from stamp duty and reduction of real estate and registration duties (Ministry of Industry 2006). In 2008 it engaged Hernando de Soto[12] to direct a large-scale study on the informal sector in Syria and to devise policy recommendations. The Turkish government views informality as a structural weakness in the economy and has included 'reducing the informal economy' as one of the key objectives of its 'enhancing competitiveness' axes for development (SPO 2008). A study on the reasons, consequences and dimensions of the informal economy was proposed for 2008 as well as measures to decrease the financial and social burdens of informal employment and accelerate the process of transition to the formal economy.

In 2008 the Palestinian Central Bureau of Statistics (PCBS) initiated a project to conduct an Informal Sector Survey (based on establishments) and to add a module to its regular labour force surveys to capture data on informal employment and informal sector projects undertaken by household unincorporated enterprises involved in market production.[13] These surveys are intended to provide a comprehensive picture of the total size and composition of the informal sector in Palestine. The Sudanese government has also proposed to undertake a study to examine formalization barriers and then to streamline the regulatory process and develop a registry for the business assets of the economically active poor so that they can be used as security for loans (GONU 2006).

There are several research questions that could be explored around the policy challenges of facilitating the formalization process to assist MENA governments in dealing with the issue. Similar to the study proposed by the Sudanese government on the policy impediments to formalization, a regional study could examine the barriers faced by informal enterprises, the nature of their economic activities and sources of market information, and identify which ones could become a viable source of growth. It could also assess the impact of social security requirements, structures and costs on formal and informal employment across MENA countries and benchmark the results against international experience. Building on such a study, governments could more effectively design and implement financial, legal and institutional reforms to reduce barriers to becoming formal.

The Organisation for Economic Co-operation and Development (OECD 2006) supports the need for more research on why firms do not formalize and on the links between formalization and enterprise performance, suggesting that regulatory impact assessments are needed to assess the impact of new laws on the SME formalization decision.

In the meantime more work needs to be done on measuring the estimated size of the informal economy at the country level. The OECD has produced a *Handbook on Measuring the Non-observed Economy* (OECD 2002) and the United Nations Economic Commission for Europe (UNECE) has compiled an inventory of country practices in statistical measurement of the 'non-observed economy', including all informal activities (UNECE 2008b). The objective of the OECD and UNECE efforts is to ensure the exhaustiveness of national accounts in the reporting of GDP.

EDUCATION, SKILLS AND KNOWLEDGE CHALLENGE

The status of education in a country plays a key role in its economic growth and equity performance. It is linked to literacy rates, the supply of skilled labour, the level of unemployment, job opportunities, per capita income and gender equality. Barro (1998) found that an extra year of upper-level schooling for males aged 25 and over would raise a country's growth rate by 1.2 percentage points a year.[14] His results also support theories regarding the positive effect of education on an economy's ability to absorb new technologies. However increased levels of education attainment can only lead to economic growth if educated workers are engaged in jobs that capitalize on their knowledge and skills (World Bank 2008g). This has not been the case in MENA countries.

In spite of the fact that the MENA region has made significant progress in raising the level of education of the population since the 1990s, the correlation between education and economic growth in MENA countries is weak (World Bank 2008g; MBRF and UNDP 2009). Reasons given for this are plentiful, but tend to focus on the low utilization of education and skills in the labour market and the inability of the MENA region to take productive advantage of increases in its human capital. Inadequate private sector demand, and distortions caused by a premium on government jobs, have been major factors in high unemployment, underemployment and unproductive forms of employment in the public sector. Low returns to education have weakened the economic output of higher education as well its impact on poverty reduction. Closing the gap between the supply of educated people and labour demand, and reforming the education system

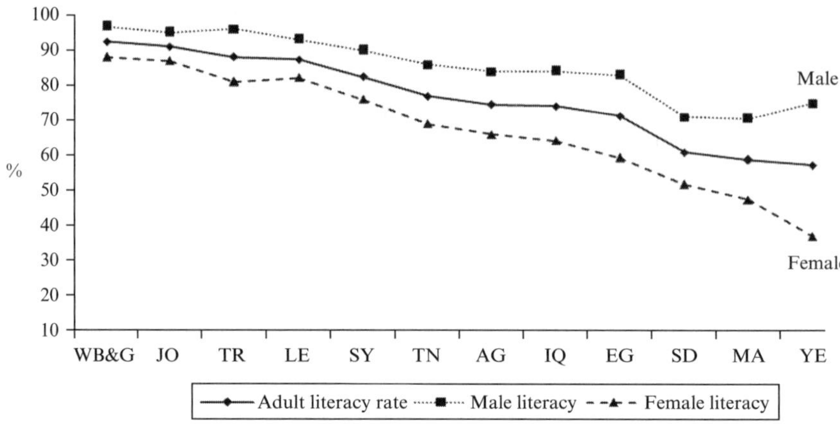

Sources: UNESCO Institute for Statistics, 2005 or closest three years, 2000 for IQ. Data for MA from KOM (2008).

Figure 3.7 Literacy rates

to respond to the requirements of a knowledge society, are among the MENA region's biggest challenges (World Bank 2008g).

The World Bank uses three indicators to measure the level of a country's human capital and its readiness for involvement in the knowledge society: (1) literary rates; (2) enrolment in secondary education; and (3) enrolment in higher education. Adult literacy rates in the MENA-12 differ dramatically, from over 90 per cent in Jordan and the West Bank & Gaza to below 60 per cent in Morocco and Yemen (Figure 3.7). Notable is the lower level of both in-country and cross-country female literacy. Although women in some parts of the region are more literate than men in other parts of the region (for example, Jordanian women are on average more literate than Yemeni men), within each country women have lower literacy rates than men. Yemen, Egypt and Morocco have the largest literacy gender gaps. The level of literacy for women does not appear to have a significant impact on their economic activity rates. For instance, literacy rates for women in the West Bank & Gaza and Jordan are the highest among the MENA-12, yet these same countries record among the lowest female labour force participation rates in the MENA region (see Figure 3.3).

The 2002 AHDR indicates that the Arab countries made tangible progress in increasing literacy rates during the 1980s and 1990s, but were still performing below international and developing-country averages (UNDP and AFESD 2002). The latest data reveal that only four of the

MENA-12 countries have male literacy rates above the 90 per cent average for LUMI countries and only three have female literacy rates higher than the LUMI country average of 80 per cent (World Bank 2009g, p. 94).

MENA countries have also made progress on education enrolment rates. The MENA-12 are compared on recent gross[15] enrolment ratios and other education input measures in Table 3.2. Most of the MENA-12 have closed the education gap at the primary education level with small remaining gender gaps, except in the cases of Iraq, Sudan and Yemen. Improvements are still necessary at the secondary education level, especially in Iraq, Sudan and Yemen. Enrolment rates in higher education vary considerably across the countries from a high of 46 per cent in Lebanon to a low of 6 per cent in Sudan. The region is at a great disadvantage when gross enrolment rates in upper secondary education remain below 55 per cent compared to around 84 per cent in advanced industrial states (MBRF and UNDP 2009). Since the mid-1970s the average investment in education of MENA countries has been about 5 per cent of GDP and 20 per cent of government budgets (World Bank 2008g, p. 3). Obviously sheer investment alone is not enough. A case in point is Morocco which still has relatively low literacy rates, high drop-out rates,[16] low tertiary enrolment rates, high unemployment among graduates and a high level of informal employment. Tunisia, Lebanon, Jordan, Turkey and Egypt have been relatively more successful in providing access to quality education for most of their population, while Yemen, Morocco and Iraq are lagging behind. However even countries with high literacy and enrolment rates, like Jordan, Lebanon and the West Bank & Gaza, produce low returns to education, reflecting their weak performance in producing quality private sector jobs.

The demand for education in MENA countries is accelerating due to the youth bulge. This has created pressure to expand the number of schools, vocational training institutes and universities to accommodate increasing enrolment demands. However issues other than education enrolment rates must also be addressed, such as the quality of available education, the qualifications held by teachers and instructors, and the state of the educational infrastructure. The World Bank (2008g) concludes that MENA countries have made only modest progress in improving the quality of education and providing incentives for reforms in the quality, focus and outcomes of the education system. The physical capacity of the education system has been expanded, but significant reforms to the content, instruction approach and governance in the education system have been much slower.

The 2002 AHDR recommended comprehensive and urgent reform to introduce new approaches that would stimulate creativity and innovation,

Table 3.2 Education indicators for the MENA-12

Country	Gross primary enrolment ratio			Gross secondary enrolment ratio			Tertiary enrolment ratio*			School life expectancy	Public expenditure in education	
	Total	M	F	Total	M	F	Total	M	F	Years	% of GDP	% of government budget
AG	108	111	104	83	80	86	21	19	24	12.8	6.4	20.0
EG	100	102	97	88	91	88	35	..	..	11.9	3.8	12.6
IQ	98	106	89	47	56	37	16	20	12	9.7	..	..
JO	96	95	97	86	85	88	40	39	41	12.8	3.5	9.5
LE	101	102	91	82	77	86	46	44	49	13.5	2.6	9.6
MA	107	112	102	56	60	51	11	13	10	10.5	5.5	26.1
SD	69	73	64	33	35	32	6	6	6	5.8	..	..
SY	124	127	122	74	75	73	15	..	..	10.9	..	..
TN	108	109	106	87	83	91	30	25	35	14.3	7.1	20.5
TR	98	100	95	82	90	74	34	39	30	11.8	4.2**	15.9**
WB&G	80	80	80	92	90	95	41	40	42	13.2	6.5	17.2
YE	85	94	76	46	61	30	9	14	5	8.6	6.4	19.5
MENA-12 avg.	98	101	94	71	74	69	25	26	25	11.3	5.1	16.8
LUMI avg.***	111			70			24				4.5	14.2
HI avg.***	101			101			67				5.1	12.5

Note: A ratio of 95 is considered the saturation point for gross primary and secondary education enrolment.

Sources: UNESCO Institute for Statistics database (2007 or closest three years).
* As reported in MBRF and UNDP (2009).
** Ministry of National Education (2007).
*** World Bank (2009g), p. 82; 2007 data.

match the skills and knowledge requirements of a modern labour market, and improve the standards of technical training to meet the needs of production (UNDP and AFESD 2002). The challenge, as laid out, is to: ensure a high quality of basic education, especially for girls; strengthen tertiary education, particularly in science and engineering; and open more opportunities for lifelong learning. The report also stressed that higher education is in urgent need of upgrading to address shortcomings in research and development (R&D) performance. More recent assessments suggest that flaws in the education system are impeding MENA countries from participating fully in the knowledge economy, creating knowledge capital and closing the gap with the rest of the world (MBRF and UNDP 2009).

Knowledge is a core factor of production and a principal determinant of productivity and human capital as well as being intrinsically linked to growth and poverty; thus increasing the supply of knowledge is one of the main keys to progress in the MENA region (UNDP and AFESD 2002). Apart from the low quality of education, there is an undersupply of knowledgeable people, inadequate ability to exploit existing knowledge and generate new knowledge through R&D, and underdevelopment in the use of information and communication technology (ICT) applications in education, culture and health. Needed are efforts to integrate knowledge better in the education and training system and improve the alignment of education and training and research systems. The 2003 AHDR was dedicated to the issue of 'building a knowledge society' and underlined the importance of knowledge to Arab countries as a powerful driver of higher productivity, highlighting many deficiencies in the existing knowledge system (UNDP and AFESD 2003). These themes were further developed in the 2009 Arab Knowledge Report (MBRF and UNDP 2009).

Education reform in the MENA-12 countries is driven by the need to meet modern labour force needs, to create jobs for cohorts of young people, to supply foreign enterprises with skilled and qualified workers and enhance the performance of domestic SMEs, and to overcome the serious mismatch between the skills needed by the labour market and those provided by the education system. Major donor-assisted reform programmes are under way to expand and improve the quality of primary, secondary and higher education systems and to modernize the vocational education and training systems (for example, Egypt's Quality Education Initiative; the Jordan Education Initiative, Education Reform for Knowledge Economy – ERfKE, and higher education strategy; Morocco's National Education and Training Charter; the Palestinian Education Charter; the Tunisia National Education Strategy; the Modernization of the Vocational Education and Training programme in Syria; and the Yemen National Basic Education Strategy and National General Secondary Education Strategy). Efforts at the vocational education and training level include expansion of education and training centres and student enrolments; improvement of governance systems; curriculum reform; upgrading of instructors; stronger links with the private sector so that labour force requirements are better reflected in training; and, in some cases, introducing entrepreneurship and business management skills modules into technical training programmes. But education reform is not sufficient by itself to produce better economic outcomes; more productive use of investments in human capital is needed (World Bank 2008g). A shift towards private sector export-driven job growth with higher productivity would increase the returns to education (World Bank 2007b).

Most of the MENA-12 countries do not perform very well on the World Bank Knowledge Index (WBI 2008), indicating a relatively low level of preparedness for the knowledge economy and ability to generate, adopt and diffuse knowledge.[17] Turkey and Jordan are the top ranked among the MENA-12, consistently sharing the highest and second-highest scores on each of the knowledge indicators; however all of the MENA countries have a long way to go to close the knowledge gap with upper-middle-income countries.

The challenge for MENA policymakers is to enhance 'knowledge society' educational and skills development programmes both for new entrants and for those who have to retrain and return to the labour market. A huge amount of effort will be required to address this challenge (Blanc and Louis 2007; FEMISE 2008; World Bank 2004d, 2008g; MBRF and UNDP 2009). More information about education reform initiatives in the MENA-12 countries is highlighted in the country profiles in Chapters 8 and 9.

S&T AND INNOVATION CHALLENGE

The next challenge facing the MENA-12 is the S&T and innovation challenge. Increasing productivity is one route to economic growth and use of technology is one of the keys to achieving this. Developing countries are in need of technology to improve their production capacity and competitiveness. In the early stages of development, most of them have to import technology and modern equipment from developed countries and rely on foreign direct investment (FDI) for technology transfer and technical competence. However at some point in the development path countries need to build the infrastructure, institutions and capacity to develop, commercialize, diffuse and export their own technology. This requires investment in science, research and technology development.

The national innovative capacity of a country is its ability to produce and commercialize a flow of new-to-the-world technologies over the long term (Furman et al. 2001). The level of innovative capacity affects a nation's total factor productivity and share of high-technology products in exports. The readiness of an economy to exploit its innovative capacity depends on a number of variables: the level of R&D, the technology infrastructure, its institutional supports and incentives, the supply of scientists and engineers, an educated labour force, openness to international competition, a university system that encourages commercialization of S&T, and the strength of linkages between the research environment and private industry. These factors and others are described by Porter (1990) and Furman et al. (2001) as the building blocks for advancing innovation in a country. The MENA-12 countries do not show significant strength on most of these variables.

Deficiencies in the MENA region's S&T and R&D environment are seen as a major impediment to economic advancement (MBRF and UNDP 2009). The 2009 Arab Knowledge Report indicates that the MENA region suffers from several weaknesses in the institutional S&T and R&D structures; a lack of scientific and research staff; administrative arrangements and legal frameworks that limit the effectiveness of S&T and R&D institutions; low publication and patents output from scientific research; overly modest efforts to transfer innovation knowledge to the production and service sectors; and a lack of private sector R&D investment.[18] According to this report creating policies in support of S&T development is one of the most important steps for MENA countries to respond to the challenges of unemployment among youth, outmigration of talent and growing investment in the consumption of imported technical products. Recommended actions include modernization of innovation structures, increased investment in R&D, creating an innovation-conducive environment, fostering partnerships between governments and private research centres and institutes, and establishing agencies and institutions that can design S&T strategies to bridge the gap between scientific research and economic outcomes through the commercialization of innovations.

Countries in the MENA-12 have varying levels of S&T and innovation performance. One of the indicators for an economy's technology and innovation performance is the share of high-technology exports[19] in total manufactured exports. This is an area where the MENA-12 countries are weak even compared with other LUMI countries. Morocco has the highest share of high-technology exports at 9 per cent of total manufactured exports (less than half the share in LUMI countries), followed by Tunisia at 5 per cent (World Development Indicators – WDI). The share is less than 1 per cent in Egypt, Jordan, Syria, Yemen and Sudan. For the

Table 3.3 R&D expenditures

Country	R&D as % of GDP	Country	R&D as % of GDP
Tunisia	1.02	Egypt	0.23
Morocco	0.64	Algeria	0.07
Turkey	0.71	LUMI countries	0.96
Jordan	0.34	HI countries	2.47
Sudan	0.29		

Source: WDI data for most recent years, 2000–2007 (World Bank 2010).

most part MENA countries are exporting raw materials and low-valued-added products and importing high-value-added and knowledge-content products.

Weak high-technology export performance can be partly explained by another widely used technology and innovation indicator: the low level of R&D expenditures to GDP. Comparable data could not be sourced for all of the MENA-12 countries, but World Development Indicators for seven of the countries indicate that this ratio is less than 1 per cent of GDP, except for Tunisia which invests just over 1 per cent (Table 3.3). The rest of the MENA-12 fall below the average of 0.96 per cent of GDP for LUMI countries and all are far below the average of 2.47 per cent for high-income countries. Unless MENA countries increase their ratio of R&D to GDP to 2 per cent by 2012, the 2002 AHDR predicts that they will fall dangerously behind developed countries in innovation performance (UNDP and AFESD 2002).

The Middle East and Developing Africa (MEDA) countries[20] do not play a significant role in technological innovation on a global or regional scale (AFII-ANIMA 2005). Not only is R&D expenditure very low, but the number of researchers, scientific publications and patents is limited and innovation policies are either modest or symbolic. Although there are numerous science and technology parks, technology and innovation centres and incubators across the MEDA countries, they are weak in management budgets, finance for start-ups, venture capital infrastructure and links to FDI activity. In fact FDI appears to produce a low level of technology transfer in the region.

More efforts are needed to address the insufficient incentives to promote technology development and increase R&D expenditures, particularly in the private sector. Such measures could include favourable tax treatment, risk-sharing schemes, intellectual property laws and developing capital markets, all deficient in the MEDA countries (AFII-ANIMA 2005). Basically a more enabling environment for the development and diffusion of technology and knowledge is required if the MENA region is to become more globally competitive (MBRF and UNDP 2009).

In addition to pursuing strategies to attract FDI through Qualifying Industrial Zones (QIZs), technology zones and so on, most of the MENA-12 countries have started to focus more strategically on S&T and innovation as key elements of their future competitiveness and economic growth. Tunisia and Turkey appear to be furthest along with policy developments as both have taken a more 'innovation systems' approach to the issue. Tunisia has implemented a series of comprehensive measures to promote R&D, S&T skills and innovative enterprises, and has created an S&T Observatoire to track and monitor performance. The government expects to develop 12 technology hubs aimed at encouraging research and innovation by 2015 and has funded several campus-based *pépinières d'entreprise* (incubators) at Tunisian universities and higher-technology institutes. The Turkish government has had a Superior Council on S&T since the 1990s and has adopted a National Science, Technology and Innovation Strategy with a target to increase research intensity to 2 per cent of GDP (OECD 2008c). National technology platforms have been established to increase the R&D and innovation capacity of industry (focusing on industry sectors with the highest share of exports and imports), technology and innovation centres have been set up throughout the country, and other initiatives are under way to support an increase in R&D capacity and to boost the capacity of SMEs to access knowledge from global suppliers.

Many policy and programme initiatives are also under way in the other countries, for example, R&D tax credits, R&D funding to universities, development of intellectual property protection (IPP) and patent rules, and the establishment of technopoles, incubators and technology innovation centres. Ongoing efforts to support R&D and innovation are briefly described in the country profiles in Chapters 8 and 9. However the impact of these efforts is often thwarted by missing elements, such as developed capital markets, a robust venture capital industry and strong entrepreneurial culture and capacity. In Jordan and Algeria, for example, stakeholders are concerned about the lack of appropriate institutions and support for the commercialization of domestic innovations emanating from R&D activity, as well as a weak entrepreneurial and innovation culture. A comprehensive diagnosis of impediments to innovation and an analysis of innovation system deficiencies would make a valuable contribution to policy developments in all of the MENA-12 countries.

The availability of venture capital is very important to the advancement of innovative, technology-driven and high-growth enterprises. Noutary (2008) outlines several deficiencies in the financing of innovation in the MENA region. These include: the very low share of investment funds dedicated to seed and venture capital financing; lack of professional business angels and business angel networks; weak capacity of organizations offering investment services to mentor entrepreneurs on the investor–investee relationship and provide post-investment value-added advice; weak links between incubators and sources of investment capital; information asymmetries between entrepreneurs requiring investment capital and potential sources of equity funds; and few government incentives to stimulate private venture capital activity (such as tax credits and matching funds).

The venture capital industry in the MENA-12 is underdeveloped compared to more developed economies. It is relatively more developed in Morocco, Turkey and Tunisia than in Egypt, Lebanon and Jordan; embryonic in Algeria, Syria and the West Bank & Gaza (AFII-ANIMA 2005); and negligible in Yemen, Sudan and Iraq. The first venture capital company in Morocco appeared in 1993 and by 2007 there were more than a dozen funds in operation. Tunisia has more than 35 Venture Capital Investment Companies (SICARs) for new entrepreneurs, although the culture of private equity is still considered weak. There are few exit options for equity investors because of limitations in most MENA stock markets for listing of emerging growth companies. Only three of the stock exchanges have listings for smaller firms: the NILEX exchange on the Cairo and Alexandria Stock Exchange, the SME Exchange on the Istanbul Stock Exchange and a small cap market in Tunisia.

The issue of patent law and IPP, important in the development of innovative private sector activity, is largely ignored on the policy agenda of MENA governments. Some differences in the treatment of IPP exist depending on national legislative frameworks. Countries with World Trade Organization (WTO) membership, such as Egypt, Jordan, Morocco and Tunisia, are bound by obligations and standards on protecting intellectual property, but others may have fewer or more stringent laws and standards than exist in the multilateral international system. The region suffers from a lack of competent specialists in the legal texts of intellectual property, an area where coordination and sharing of experience among MENA countries would be very helpful (MBRF and UNDP 2009).

In 2004 Algeria, Egypt, Jordan, Lebanon, Morocco, the Palestinian Authority (PA), Syria and Tunisia signed on to the Euro-Mediterranean Charter for Enterprise and accepted to meet the goals and implement actions under the ten principles of good governance for effective actions towards private sector development.[21] One of the policy areas in the Euro-Med Charter for Enterprise is focused on policies to encourage innovative companies. In the Charter performance assessment in 2008 (European Communities and OECD 2008), Egypt and Tunisia scored highest among

Table 3.4 Innovation policy performance

Indicator	AG	EG	JO	LE	MA	SY	TN	WB&G
Enhancing enterprise innovation	2.0	3.5	2.5	3.0	3.0	2.0	3.5	1.0
Establishment of innovation and technology centers	1.5	4.0	3.0	3.0	3.0	2.0	3.5	1.0
Support for innovative enterprises	1.5	4.0	3.5	3.5	2.5	2.0	3.5	1.0
Business incubators	2.0	3.5	2.5	3.0	2.5	2.0	4.0	2.0
MED weighted average = 2.9	*1.8*	*3.8*	*2.9*	*3.1*	*2.8*	*2.0*	*3.6*	*1.3*

Note: Scores are out of a maximum of 5.

Source: Data from European Communities and OECD (2008), p. 62.

the eight MENA-12 countries on implementation of the innovation policy dimension with scores of 3.8 and 3.6 out of 5, followed by Lebanon with a score of 3.1 (Table 3.4). The assessment report noted that the policy framework for innovation varies across countries. A number of countries have innovation-related programmes but have not yet adopted comprehensive innovation strategies. Algeria and the West Bank & Gaza were assessed as having made the least progress on the innovation policy indicators.

A number of European Union-funded projects are working in the MENA region to foster technology development and innovation. Medibtikar, the EuroMed Innovation and Technology Programme, aims to contribute to the development of innovation and to help Mediterranean companies participate in collaborative innovation projects with European partners (Noutary 2008). Nine of the ten MEDA countries involved are among the MENA-12. The ANIMA Investment Network project is devoted to helping Mediterranean partner countries acquire strategies and tools to attract foreign investments through a focus on technology and innovation infrastructure (AFII-ANIMA 2005). In 2008 the European Union launched a project to establish an Innovation Fund to help improve links between universities and industry. Such projects are hoped to stimulate innovation activity in the region as well as more coordinated actions.

WORLD ECONOMY INTEGRATION CHALLENGE

Integration into the global economy for developing countries means trading internationally within a more open system. Their capacity to do so is often constrained by the need for significant upgrading of production to meet international standards and conformity assessments, trade facilitation and a raised level of human capital. Two indicators commonly used to measure the degree of global integration in a country are its FDI and trade performance. Although significant progress has occurred in the MENA countries in recent years to reduce customs duties, dismantle trade barriers and open up to foreign investment, the region continues to lag in world economy integration relative to most regions of the world (World Bank 2006c, 2007b). The FDI and trade openness performance of the MENA-12 countries is elaborated next.

Foreign Direct Investment Performance

Foreign direct investment not only brings capital into a developing country but also can play an essential role in economic growth through the transfer of technology from foreign to domestic firms (Schmidt 2008). The transfer of technology and knowledge creates jobs, boosts overall productivity, enhances competitiveness and helps to reduce poverty. According to Schmidt's analysis, FDI helps poor countries catch up or converge with richer countries, but not equally in all countries; the impact of FDI depends on the context. He concluded that to maximize the economic growth benefits of the transmission of technology (the main factor in the contribution of FDI to economic growth), FDI needs the presence of complementary domestic institutions in sufficient extent and depth, a well-educated labour force, a sophisticated financial system and a threshold level of trade (Schmidt 2008). He also proposed that a minimum level of FDI is required before FDI actually benefits macroeconomic growth.[22]

Consistently from 1989 onwards the MENA region has been less successful in attracting FDI than others, with only a slight increase in the share of global FDI since 1970 (World Bank 2009c). This signals a lack of business opportunities, an unattractive local business environment or higher risk perceptions. Most of the regional FDI has been directed to

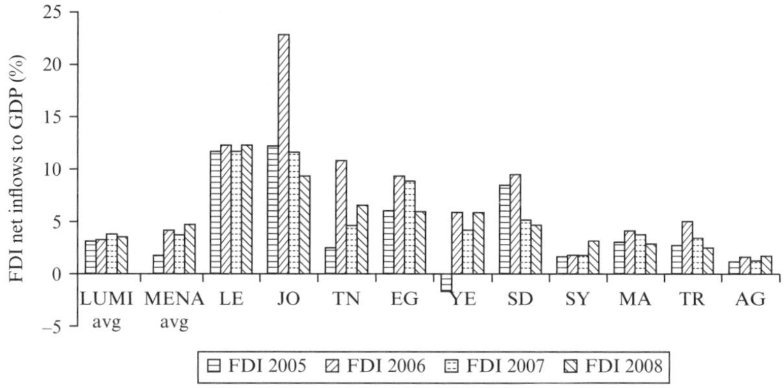

Source: WDI. No data for IQ and the WB&G.

Figure 3.8 Foreign direct investment inflows to GDP, 2005–2008

the non-tradable sectors, such as real estate, housing and tourism, and very little into export-oriented manufacturing. In order to continue rapid development in the MENA region, higher levels of FDI will be required.

Figure 3.8 compares the MENA-12 on FDI inflows for 2005–2008. Top FDI performers have been Jordan and Lebanon with several of the countries attracting FDI in each of the four years at well above the average level for LUMI countries and the greater MENA region. Syria and Algeria were consistent underperformers. The year 2006 was a particularly good one for FDI inflows, especially in Jordan and Lebanon, but since then the situation has deteriorated in a number of the countries.

Attracting foreign investment is a priority for all of the MENA-12 governments because of its potential for bringing in capital, technology and jobs. Consequently all have undertaken many reforms to improve the investment environment. Almost all of these countries have foreign investment laws in place to guide efforts in attracting foreign investors, although they vary with respect to foreign ownership restrictions, investment approval processes and treatment of domestic versus foreign investors. Most of the countries offer generous tax incentives and holidays. They have implemented measures to reduce customs procedures and costs; built QIZs, free trade zones, industrial parks and technology zones; amended investment laws to improve incentive structures and processes; established investment promotion agencies; modernized commercial laws; and set up one-stop investment shops to simplify the business registration and licensing processes and facilitate the dealings of foreign companies with the domestic bureaucracy. Most of the investment promotion agencies are seeking to maximize 'innovative' FDI content. Between 2003 and 2005 the majority of technological FDI in MEDA countries was going to Morocco, Algeria, Turkey and Tunisia in the form of private sector R&D centres, opening of subsidiary locations of large technology-oriented firms, takeovers, acquisition of start-ups, partnerships, joint ventures and call centres (AFII-ANIMA 2005).

However as Schmidt (2008) suggests, other areas of the economy must be strengthened if MENA countries are to compete with other attractive locations for FDI. This will necessitate a skilled labour force (including technicians), a base of developed SMEs to act as partners and/or suppliers to foreign firms, flexible labour laws and good analysis of the investment opportunities in the country. In the meantime a number of country-specific weaknesses persist: a mismatch between the skills of the vocational and technical education system and the skills required by foreign firms (especially those required for a modern and knowledge-based economy); foreign ownership restrictions (in some countries more so than in others); a lack of transparency in the judicial system; outdated financial systems; and a SME sector characterized by very small enterprises, undercapitalization, low-skilled workers, low-value-added production, a low level of diversification and differentiation, and weak competitiveness. Differences in the severity of these weaknesses will have an impact on a government's success with FDI strategies. Political stability, policy certainty, good governance and a country's reputation as a 'good place to invest' are also major contributing factors.

Existing FDI is not likely making its full contribution to the economy in MENA-12 countries. Many foreign companies import management and workers from offshore, while the domestic jobs created are often low-skilled and low-value-added. Also in question is the extent to which FDI has actually facilitated the transfer of knowledge, skills and technology to domestic SMEs, such as through linkages and supply chain arrangements. There is room for further studies on the impact of liberalization and FDI policies on SME development, employment and poverty reduction.

International Trade Performance

There is substantial evidence that greater trade integration and openness (exports and imports relative to GDP), and export diversification are associated with higher rates of economic growth (World Bank 2009c). Exports in the MENA region tend to be heavily concentrated in the extractive sectors, particularly oil and agricultural products, and a few industrial sectors such as clothing and textiles. The level of manufactured exports to GDP has increased only marginally since 1970, reflecting the limited

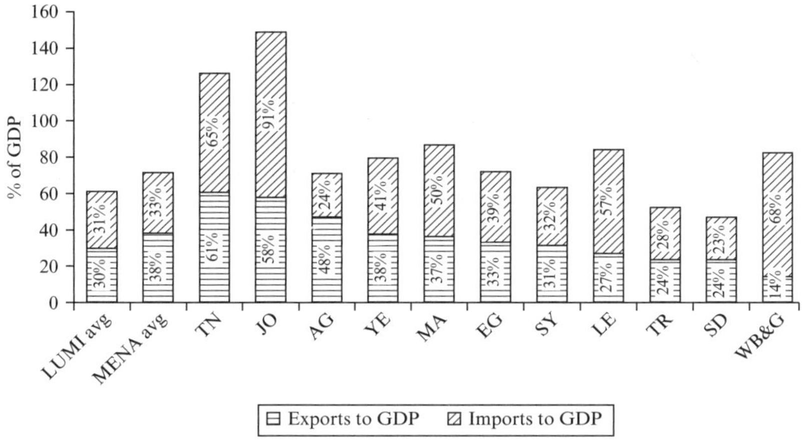

Source: WDI, 2008 data; latest available years for YE and the WB&G. No data for IQ.

Figure 3.9 Trade performance: exports and imports

potential of the MENA private sector to sustain economic growth and diversify the export base, an important strategic goal for the region (World Bank 2009c). High tariff and non-tariff barriers have also acted to hinder access of private enterprises to imported intermediate goods (Noland and Pack 2007).

Figure 3.9 indicates the performance of the MENA-12 countries on trade openness. Jordan, where trade totals almost 150 per cent of GDP, is the most open economy followed by Tunisia at 126 per cent of GDP. The top export performers are Tunisia, Jordan and Algeria, all with export levels exceeding 40 per cent of GDP (and above the average for MENA and LUMI countries). The rest perform below the export average for MENA and LUMI countries. The degree and speed of economic opening varies by country. It appears that the smaller MENA countries tend to have a higher degree of openness if both exports and import levels are considered.

Algeria is the only MENA-12 country with a large trade surplus, mostly due to oil exports, but similar to Egypt and Turkey, the level of export growth has been marginal over the 2006–08 period. On the other hand export performance in Jordan, Lebanon, Tunisia and Sudan has been improving. The West Bank & Gaza, Jordan, Morocco and Lebanon import substantially more than they export, so although more 'trade-open', are running large trade deficits. Trading partners in the West Bank & Gaza are seriously impeded by restrictions on the mobility of goods and services imposed by Israel, so trade activity is not very diversified. Around 90 per cent of Palestinian exports and 70 per cent of imports are accounted for by trade with Israel.

One of the export challenges in the MENA-12 countries, besides the reported lack of production and product quality, and limited ability to meet international specifications and standards, is the lack of industrial diversification. Algeria, Iraq, Syria, Sudan, Yemen and Egypt are largely dependent on oil and gas exports. Petroleum accounts for over 90 per cent of export revenue in Algeria, Iraq, Sudan and Yemen, and over 60 per cent in Egypt. Tunisia, Turkey and Morocco have been highly dependent on clothing and textiles exports. As noted earlier in Chapter 3, the level of high technology in manufactured exports in the MENA-12 countries is extremely low.

Countries in the region have embarked on reforms to liberalize their trade regime and remove impediments to increased trade through regulatory changes, the creation of trade institutions, and a proliferation of regional, bilateral and international Free Trade Agreements (FTAs). Tunisia, Egypt, Morocco and Turkey have been members of the WTO since the 1990s and Jordan was granted accession status in the early 2000s. Algeria, Lebanon, Syria and Yemen are in various stages of preparing for or negotiating accession; Iraq has observer status; the Palestinian Authority is preparing a formal application for observer status; and Sudan has plans to enter. The MENA countries in the Euro-Med region are part of the EU Association Agreement, which will bring full market access to the European Union by 2010–12, and all are part of bilateral trade agreements with a variety of other countries. The trend towards global integration is complemented and reinforced by regional integration efforts through the Greater Arab Free Trade Area (GAFTA), although interregional trade is reported as being low (UNDP and AFESD 2002). The level of regional trade integration, as measured by the number of inter-MED FTAs in place, has improved in recent years, but implementation of the main regional FTAs is at an early stage. Egypt, Jordan, Morocco and Tunisia are the most advanced of the Euro-Med countries and Algeria is the least integrated (European Communities and OECD 2008). The 2002 AHDR recommended moving towards a regional customs union or common market to deepen regional integration and multiply the effects of other association agreements, such as those with the European Union (EU).

To stimulate higher exports and export-oriented industries, several of the governments have established free trade zones, export promotion agencies, trade information centres, trade points and even export development banks. All have carried out some reforms to dismantle tariffs, conform to international quality standards and simplify customs, trade and export procedures, although many obstacles still exist in the customs system (processing delays, excessive red tape, high costs and corruption). Most of the MENA-12 governments have also implemented donor-supported initiatives targeting sectors and SMEs with upgrading and export promotion support.

'Better access to markets' was one of the policy areas assessed in the Euro-Med Charter for Enterprise policy assessment exercise carried out by the OECD in 2007–08. This dimension is concerned with policies to lower trade barriers, including the regulatory framework, reduction of trade transaction costs and adoption of international technical standards. The results of the assessment for eight of the MENA-12 countries are presented in Table 3.5. Egypt and Tunisia are the most advanced in this policy area with overall scores of 3.5 and 3.2 (out of 5) followed by Morocco and Jordan. On the proactive trade policy dimension, having an export promotion agency or government entity responsible for export promotion activities and implementing an export strategy placed Egypt, Tunisia and Morocco in the lead. Jordan also performed reasonably well, but was found to be missing a comprehensive strategy, an issue that the government was seeking to address in 2009. Efforts to develop an export promotion strategy are also under way in Lebanon. Although Syria and Algeria have established export development agencies or commissions to promote non-carbon exports, most of their activities to support export promotion were assessed as 'ad hoc'. On the second policy dimension, 'simplification of procedures', Egypt and Tunisia are again in the lead, but only Egypt and Morocco were reported to have an OSS for export facilitation.

Of the three policy dimensions, the most problematic is related to the Agreement on Conformity Assessment and Acceptance of Industrial Products (ACAA). There is a lot of variation across countries on the six ACAA indicators, but overall the policy progress is not far advanced. Complying with ACAAs (legislative alignment and infrastructure capacity) is critical if countries want to meet technical and other specifications for products exported to European markets. All of the Euro-Med countries have signed on to the ACAA concept as a means of improving their industrial competitiveness and have defined their priority sectors (for example, electrical products, construction, pressure equipment, machinery) and almost all have started the preparatory work for signing of the ACAA. Except for Syria and the West Bank & Gaza, governments have started to adopt harmonized European standards in their priority sectors and to upgrade and restructure their 'quality' infrastructure and conformity assessment bodies.

One of the most significant barriers to trade integration in these

Table 3.5 Implementing policy for 'better market access'

Indicator	AG	EG	JO	LE	MA	SY	TN	WB&G
1. Implementing a proactive trade policy								
Export promotion strategy	1.5	4.0	2.5	2.0	2.5	2.0	3.5	1.5
Intra-MED trade agreements	1.0	4.0	4.0	3.0	4.0	3.0	4.0	3.0
MED weighted average = 2.8	*1.3*	*4.0*	*3.1*	*2.4*	*3.1*	*2.4*	*3.7*	*2.1*
2. Simplification of procedures for international trade								
Level of computerization of procedures for foreign trade	1.5	4.0	3.0	4.0	4.0	3.0	4.0	3.0
Quality of information on foreign trade	1.5	5.0	3.0	3.0	3.0	2.0	3.0	3.0
Virtual one-stop shop	1.5	4.5	2.0	2.0	3.0	1.0	3.5	1.0
MED weighted average = 3.1	*1.5*	*4.5*	*2.7*	*3.0*	*3.3*	*2.0*	*3.5*	*2.3*
3. Agreement on conformity assessment and acceptance of industrial products (ACAA)								
Adoption of EU technical regulations	1.0	2.0	1.0	1.0	2.0	2.0	2.0	1.0
Adoption of EU technical standards	2.0	3.0	3.0	2.0	2.0	2.0	2.5	1.0
Accreditation	2.0	2.0	2.5	2.0	2.0	1.0	3.5	1.0
Conformity assessment	1.0	1.5	2.0	2.0	1.5	1.0	2.0	1.0
Metrology	1.0	1.5	2.0	1.5	2.0	1.0	2.5	1.0
Market surveillance	1.0	1.5	1.0	1.0	1.5	1.0	1.0	1.0
MED weighted average = 1.8	*1.3*	*1.9*	*1.9*	*1.6*	*1.8*	*1.3*	*2.3*	*1.0*
Overall trade policy score	1.4	3.5	2.6	2.3	2.7	2.0	3.2	1.8

Note: Scores are out of 5.

Source: Data from European Communities and OECD (2008), pp. 55–60.

countries is the low capacity and competitiveness of the SME sector. Substantial upgrading will be needed to increase the SME contribution to export performance. The broader issue of the SME sector challenge is the subject of Chapter 4.

GENDER CHALLENGE

Gender-based inequality is also an important issue for PSD. Women in developing economies are subject to significant market, systemic, sociocultural and education failures that restrict their access to property titles, credit, information, employment and other economic opportunities. The presence of sex-segregated labour markets contributes to gender–wage inequality, suppresses investment in human capital and prevents women from entering higher-productivity occupations (OECD 2006). While much more research is needed on the relationships between gender equality, poverty and economic growth (Bibi and Nabli 2010), gender inequality appears to affect economic growth through the quality of human capital inputs (as in access to education), barriers to women's employment in certain sectors or occupations, differential propensities to save and unequal access to secure property rights (Morrison et al. 2007).

The OECD argues that the failure to focus on women's market access reduces the effectiveness of policies to promote pro-poor growth. Consequently, 'enhancing women's market access' was identified as one of the six issues in the donor framework to increase the impact of PSD on poverty reduction (OECD 2006). The gender issue is also in focus in the EuroMed Role of Women in Economic Life (RWEL) programme (RWEL 2008d), the ILO/CAWTAR (Center of Arab Women for Training and Research) joint initiative on Gender Equality and Women's Rights in the Informal Economy of Arab States (ILO and CAWTAR 2008a), and studies by the World Bank (World Bank 2001, 2004b, 2005d, 2009e) and the World Economic Forum (WEF 2008b).

The regional gender gap was highlighted in the 2002 AHDR as one of the three major human development deficits[23] in the region (UNDP and AFESD 2002). The report argued that women in the Arab region suffer from unequal citizenship and legal entitlements, evidenced by a very low share of women in parliaments, cabinets and the workforce generally, and a trend towards the feminization of unemployment. Gender-based occupational segregation and wage structures result in a stifling of women's productive potential and lower family incomes and standards of living. The Economic Commission for Africa (ECA) proposes that gender considerations are the 'missing link' in achieving sustained growth: if gender inequalities in education and formal sector employment were addressed, per capita incomes would rise (ECA 2004). Morrison et al. (2007) present supporting evidence that developing countries with higher gender equality tend to have lower poverty rates.

One of the major issues is the extent to which women in developing countries are benefiting equally from economic growth strategies. The RWEL programme found that liberalization policies have had a negative impact on women in gender-specific ways, resulting in a preponderance of women workers in low-wage manufacturing jobs (RWEL 2007). The ECA (2004) called for gender analysis of all WTO-related trade issues under negotiation to consider the gender-different impacts of trade policies, the way gender inequality affects trade performance and the gender impacts of policies on poverty reduction. The ECA also proposed that gender analysis be incorporated in Poverty Reduction Strategy Papers (PRSPs). RWEL (2008c) concludes that there is a dearth of analysis on the MENA situation with respect to the effect of trade and economic liberalization policies on poor and low-income women and the effects of globalization on households. It further concluded that the issues of women, the economy and gender in the MENA region remain largely unexplored. There is no systematic research investigating the strategies women are using to negotiate economic power or to retain control over their earnings, and limited data on the impact of new job opportunities on empowering women. There is also a need for research on the role of women in private sector and SME development, covering themes such as: the impact of private sector discrimination in hiring practices; the impact of FTAs and FDI on women's employment; how to increase women's role in SME activity; the precise factors resulting in a very low percentage of women as entrepreneurs, especially as employers; and barriers to women's participation in policy dialogue and influence. These issues should be examined in a pan-regional and systematic way.

Chapter 3 has already drawn attention to many of the gender inequities affecting social and economic development in the MENA-12 countries: women's lower literacy rates, lower secondary and higher education enrolment rates, lower labour force participation and employment rates, higher unemployment rates, feminization of certain labour markets and discriminatory hiring practices in the formal private sector. Other indicators reported in the gender-related measures of the Human Development Index (HDI) (UNDP 2009) provide additional evidence of these gender inequities (Table 3.6). Turkey has the highest rank and value of the MENA-12 on the gender-related development index and is in the top half of the 155 assessed countries. It is followed closely by Lebanon.

The gender earned income gap is lowest in Algeria and Sudan, but

Table 3.6 Gender empowerment indicators

Indicator	TR	LE	TN	JO	AG	SY	EG	MA	YE	SD	IQ	WB&G
Rank on gender-related development index (1)	70	71	84	87	88	98	..	111	122	127	..	..
Value	0.788	0.784	0.752	0.743	0.742	0.715	..	0.625	0.538	0.516	..	..
Rank on gender empowerment measure (2)	101	..	..	..	105	..	107	104	109	..	..	..
Value	0.379	..	..	..	0.315	..	0.287	0.318	0.135	..	..	..
Ratio of female to male earned income	.26	.25	.28	.19	.36	.20	.27	.24	.25	.33	..	..
Seats in parliament held by women (% of total)	9	5	20	8	6	12	4	6	1	17	25	..
Female legislators, senior officials and managers (% of total)	8	..	..	..	5	..	11	12	4	..	..	10
Female professional and technical workers (% of total)	33	..	..	..	35	40	32	35	15	..	..	34
Women in ministerial positions (% of total)	4	5	7	15	11	6	6	19	6	6	10	..

Notes:

(1) This index is a composite of four indicators from the Human Development Index: life expectancy at birth, the adult literacy rate, combined enrolment ratio in education and estimated earned income.

(2) Only 109 countries are ranked so Yemen is in last place on this measure.

Source: Data from UNDP (2009).

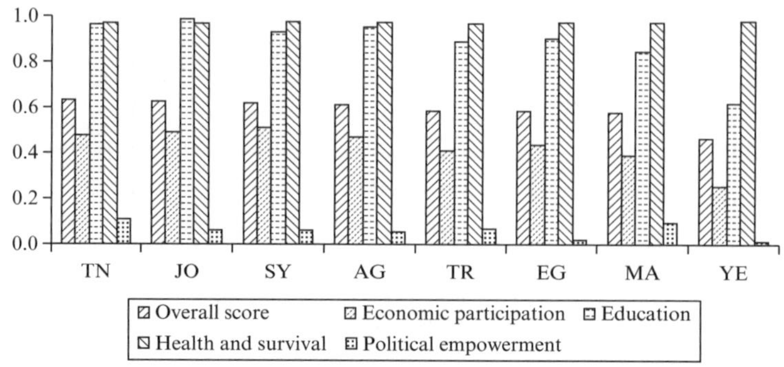

Note: The highest possible score on any one indicator is 1 (equality); the lowest possible score is 0 (inequality).

Source: Data from country profiles in WEF (2008b).

Figure 3.10 Country scores for gender equality

women, at best, earn only 36 per cent of men's income. Iraq has the highest percentage of women in ministerial positions and Syria has the highest percentage of women workers in professional and technical jobs (likely due to the high proportion of women in government employment).

Another tool that can be used to benchmark the gender performance of countries is the World Economic Forum (WEF) Global Gender Gap Index (GGGI).[24] Although only eight of the MENA-12 countries are included among the 130 countries in the 2008 GGGI, the MENA region as a whole was noted as performing less well than any other region of the world, with a gender gap index of 0.58 (WEF 2008b). The interpretation of this is that only 58 per cent of the gender gap has been closed, with the biggest gender gap on the 'economic participation and opportunity' indicators. The scores for the eight MENA-12 countries are compared in Figure 3.10.

These countries are performing reasonably well in terms of gender equality on health and survival and education indicators, with the exception of Yemen, which still has much work to do to close the gender gap in educational attainment. On the other hand they have closed less than 50 per cent of the equality gap on economic participation and opportunity, and 10 per cent or less of the political empowerment gap. In the overall ranking among 130 countries, they are all in the bottom 20 per cent. Yemen is in last place, making it the only country to have closed less than 50 per cent of its overall gender gap.

The 2008 Global Gender Gap report makes the case that in order to maximize its competitiveness and development potential, each country should strive for greater gender equality, reinforcing this position by confirming a positive correlation between gender equality and both the level of development and country competitiveness.[25] The World Bank (2004b, p. 4) makes two propositions: (1) that if rates of female participation in the labour force increased from their actual levels to predicted levels (considering existing levels of female education, fertility and age structure), average household earnings would increase by as much as 25 per cent, making a major contribution to reducing poverty; and (2) that if female participation rates had been at predicted levels during the 1990s, per capita GDP growth rates might have been 0.7 per cent higher per year, a significant loss when compared with an average per capita income growth of 1.9 per cent for the decade. One of the questions raised in the World Bank report was whether the MENA region can afford such a loss in future growth due to gender inequality (World Bank 2004b).

Most of the MENA-12 countries would describe themselves as among the most advanced in the world regarding equality of laws for women, including their legal rights to own land and businesses. However the way these laws are implemented, coupled with patriarchal practices and family pressures, often result in women forfeiting their rights. Improving the environment for the fuller participation of women in society and the economy has been noted as a priority in MENA-12 countries. As examples, the Egyptian government has implemented gender-budgeting and set a target in its Sixth Five-Year Plan to increase women's labour force participation to 25 per cent by 2013; the Iraqi government has a target to increase women's participation in the labour force to 35 per cent and plans to implement inclusive employment policies; Morocco's 2004 labour law included a clause requiring equal pay for equal work; and Jordan's transformation agenda (National Agenda 2006–15) states the government's commitment to remove all forms of discrimination against women. In spite of these official proclamations and actions, it will take time for cultural changes to occur. The rate of change is tempered by the attitudes of this generation of youth. In the 2009 Gallup survey of young Arabs, young men and women held very different views about the role of women in society (Silatech 2009). A much higher percentage of young women than men believe that women should be allowed to hold a job outside the home and to hold leadership positions in parliament.

The 2005 AHDR argues that the rise of women is a prerequisite for an Arab renaissance and that women must be encouraged to develop and use fully their capabilities in all spheres of activity (UNDP and AFESD 2006). Barriers that impede their equal access to education, employment and entrepreneurial opportunities, safe working conditions, representation, personal liberties and equal treatment under the law must be addressed. Donors continue to advocate for gender reforms and to specify targets to be met regarding women as beneficiaries of PSD and SME projects.

Chapter 3 has described six of the major economic challenges facing the MENA-12 countries. The final economic challenge relates to the development of SMEs and entrepreneurship. This issue is discussed separately in Chapter 4 because it has not been as extensively analysed within the MENA region context as the other challenge areas and is central to PSD.

NOTES

1. As a point of comparison less than 16 per cent of the European population is under 15 years of age, 63.5 per cent is 15–59 and 20.6 per cent is over 60; the median age in developed countries is over 40 (UN 2007).
2. Fertility rates range from an average of 3.86 births per woman in Iraq to 5 in Yemen (*World Factbook*, WFB). The lowest fertility rates in the MENA-12 are in Algeria and Tunisia – both below 1.8 births per woman.
3. The size of the under-15 age group is calculated from 2009 estimates in the WFB country profiles.
4. The World Bank job creation projections are for all the MENA countries, which exceed in number the MENA-12.
5. Unofficial rates of unemployment can be considerably higher. For example, the unofficial unemployment rates in Iraq and Jordan are estimated at 30 per cent and in Yemen at up to 35 per cent.
6. By way of comparison the employment rate in Europe is about 64 per cent with a Lisbon Council target to reach 70 per cent by 2010 (World Bank 2007b).
7. Informal enterprises are more likely to be dominated by entrepreneurs of low education and ability (De Paula and Scheinkman 2007; LaPorta and Shleifer 2008).
8. Schneider uses the label 'shadow economy' and includes in his definition of this all market-based legal production of goods and services that are deliberately concealed from public authorities for reasons of avoiding payment of taxes and/or social security contributions, avoiding having to meet certain legal labour market standards, such as minimum wage and safety standards, and avoiding compliance with certain administrative procedures. He devised a sophisticated model to estimate the size of the 'shadow economy' in 145 countries.
9. During the same period the level of informality increased from 30 to 39 per cent in sub-Saharan Africa; from 22 to 28 per cent in South Asia; from 29 to 38 per cent in Latin American countries; and from 18.5 to 20 per cent in East Asia and the Pacific (Zinnes 2009).
10. The average level of informality for 76 developing countries in 2006 was 34.8 per cent of GDP; for 19 Eastern European and Central Asian countries, 36.9 per cent; and for 15 high-income OECD countries, 15.8 per cent (Schneider and Buehn 2009).
11. The formal private sector accounts for only about 10 per cent of total employment in Egypt (Assaad 2007).
12. Hernando de Soto is the author of *The Mystery of Capital* (de Soto 2000) and a strong advocate of the importance of assigning property rights to the poor so that they can participate more fully in the formal economy.
13. PCBS (2008), 'PCBS: Informal Sector and Informal Employment in the West Bank and Gaza Strip', powerpoint slide presentation 15–17 July 2008, available at http://www.pcbs.org.ps (accessed 14 August 2009).

14. Although Barro (1998) did not find that the level of female schooling correlated with economic growth, it was seen to be important for other indicators of economic development, such as fertility, infant mortality and political freedom.
15. The gross enrolment ratio is defined as: 'the ratio of total enrolment, regardless of age, to the population of the age group that officially corresponds to the level of education shown' (World Bank 2009g, p. 87).
16. The new Emergency Education Plan 2009–12 issued by the Morocco government in 2008 seeks to counter high school dropout rates by making education compulsory to the age of 15 and upgrading more than 2500 educational establishments in rural areas.
17. More detail on the Knowledge Economy Index and measures can be obtained from http://www.worldbank.org/kam.
18. Over 95 per cent of funding for scientific research in the MENA region comes from the government, contrary to the considerably lower proportion in developed countries (not more than 40 per cent in Canada, 30 per cent in the US and 20 per cent in Japan) (MBRF and UNDP 2009, p. 192).
19. High-technology exports are defined as products with high R&D intensity, such as in aerospace, computers, pharmaceuticals, scientific instruments and electrical machinery (World Bank 2009g, p. 317).
20. MEDA is a group of 12 partner countries of the European Union: Algeria, Cyprus, Egypt, Israel, Jordan, Lebanon, Malta, Morocco, Palestinian Authority, Syria, Tunisia and Turkey.
21. The Charter for Enterprise requires reporting against ten priority actions: (a) simple procedures for enterprises; (b) education and training for entrepreneurs; (c) improved skills; (d) easier access to financing and investment-friendly taxation; (e) better market access; (f) innovative companies; (g) strong business associations; (h) quality business support schemes and services; (i) strengthened Euro-Med networks and partnerships; and (j) clear and targeted information.
22. The FDI threshold level before growth responds to FDI was estimated by Schmidt (2008, p. 10) as 18 times per capita GDP. He also stated that trade may substitute for FDI in promoting growth in countries where the level of FDI is too small to be effective (p. 11).
23. The other two deficits in the MENA region were noted as a freedom deficit and a deficit of human capability and knowledge relative to income.
24. The Global Gender Gap Index (GGGI) is an initiative of the World Economic Forum to benchmark national gender gaps on economic participation, political empowerment, education and health-based criteria across countries, regions and income groups, and ranks countries on the basis of their gender equality (WEF 2008b).
25. To reach this conclusion the 2008 GGGI index scores were plotted against GDP per capita and the 2008–2009 Global Competitiveness Index (GCI) scores.

4. SME and entrepreneurship challenge

THE ROLE AND IMPORTANCE OF SMEs IN PRIVATE SECTOR DEVELOPMENT

Micro, small and medium enterprises (SMEs) are an integral part of the private sector, contributing significantly to job creation and playing a critical role in increasing competition in selected markets, including markets that matter for the poor (DfID 2004c). The SME sector (particularly formal SMEs) appears to become more important as an economy develops. The Ayyagari et al. (2003) analysis of a 76-country SME database[1] found that the formal SME sector share of the economy increases substantially with the level of development, from an average of 15.6 per cent of gross domestic product (GDP) in low-income countries to an average of 51.5 per cent of GDP in high-income countries. The formal SME share of total employment increases from 17.6 per cent in low-income countries to 57.2 per cent in high-income countries.[2] At the same time the contribution of the informal sector to GDP and total employment declines with the level of economic development. Its share of GDP averages 47.2 per cent in low-income countries but only 13 per cent in high-income countries, and its share of total employment decreases from an average of 29.4 per cent in low-income countries to only 15.2 per cent in high-income countries. The combined contribution of the informal and formal SME sectors remains fairly constant across countries of all levels of development – around 65 to 70 per cent of GDP. What changes is the distribution of the contribution. As national income increases there is a marked shift in the share of GDP and employment from the informal sector to the formal SME sector. The challenge for developing economies is to strengthen and expand the formal SME sector so that it can play a larger role in development of the private sector and make a fuller contribution to economic growth.

Although SMEs are dominant in most economies their smaller size places them at a disadvantage relative to larger enterprises. They have fewer internal resources and less capacity to compete in global markets. Apart from internal factors limiting the survival and growth potential of SMEs, such as lack of management skills, financing and technology, external factors also affect the ability of smaller enterprises to function effectively. These include the markets in which they operate, the policies, laws and regulations affecting business activities, and the organizational and institutional arrangements surrounding the enterprise (White 2008). An unlevel playing field for the growth of SMEs will hinder investment and lead to lower pro-poor growth (OECD 2004a).

SMEs make up of the vast majority of the private sector in the Middle East and North Africa (MENA) countries. Consequently SME policies should be tantamount to private sector development (PSD) strategies, but this is generally not the case. SME policy development is not necessarily accorded the government and policy attention required to improve dramatically the operating conditions, competencies and resource needs of the SME sector so that it can contribute more substantially to economic prosperity. Almost all governments in the MENA-12 countries include statements in their national policy documents about the importance of micro and small enterprises in economic and private sector development; however they differ in the extent to which their policies, strategies and initiatives reflect a view that SMEs really are the engines of private sector economic growth. This has critical implications for a government's policy directions. If SMEs are viewed primarily as a vehicle for absorbing labour at the bottom of the pyramid and reducing poverty, SME development becomes treated more as a social issue. The policy response is often to support income-generating activity of poor households through the use of microfinance schemes. The end result is a high level of subsistence enterprise activity with limited potential for growth. Even when governments target SMEs as a vehicle for economic growth, a paradox often results. Governments will state how important SMEs are to the economy in National Development Plans but in practice SME-related policies will take a back seat to those focused on FDI and large-scale projects of domestic investors. Domestic SMEs present a real opportunity for development of the private sector, but this will require serious reforms to bolster SMEs as part of a central, rather than a marginalized component of strategy for economic development and growth.

A combination of market, systemic, education and government failures prevent SMEs from accessing financing, information, business development services (BDS), land, technology, training and the proper skills to compete in a modern economy; expose them to high transaction costs; and impede their market access. Because market forces are not properly allocating resources and institutional structures are not appropriately meeting SMEs' needs, government actions to remedy the situation are called for.

SME SECTOR OVERVIEW

A wide range of SME definitions are in use in the MENA-12 countries, making it largely impossible to make cross-country comparisons of the SME sector. Governments use different combinations of official definitional criteria including the number of workers, total assets, annual turnover and paid-in capital (Table 4.1). Even when official definitions are in place, the various agencies and SME support entities within a country will use their own variations of the definition. For example, over 30 SME definitions are reported to be in use in Jordan. Furthermore the employment size breakdowns reported in official statistics are not generally comparable across countries.

Across the MENA-12 there are limited statistics on features of the SME sector. Many of the common indicators used to describe, measure and monitor trends in the sector in more developed economies (OECD 2009e) are missing: for example, the size distribution of enterprises (by number of workers), the sectoral and geographical distribution of SMEs (by size), the annual growth rate in the number of SMEs and SME workers, the SME share of employment, the new business entry rate, the business exit rate, the percentage of growing and declining SMEs, the SME share of exporters and export volume, the SME share of value-added and SME productivity.

The comprehensiveness, quality, accuracy and reporting timeliness of SME data in MENA countries are consistently weak. Some governments report details on only industrial SMEs – the case in Syria and to a large extent in Morocco and Tunisia – and do not have metrics on enterprises in all sectors of the economy. None of the MENA-12 countries has accurate estimates on the number of informal enterprises, although these are believed to account for between 40 and 80 per cent of all private enterprises depending on the country. This lack of data renders it difficult to describe the role of SMEs and make cross-country comparisons. The MENA-12 countries share common needs for comprehensive data and statistics on the SME sector, better to grasp its size and economic significance, track developments and performance of the sector over time, and provide essential input for effective policymaking to develop SMEs. This includes information on informal enterprises and enterprises owned by women.

There is also a lack of up-to-date statistics. Most of the countries conduct a census of businesses or establishments every 5–10 years, a household census (usually every ten years) and regular labour force surveys that report on the number of own-account (self-employed) workers and employers (business owners that employ others). Some governments are more advanced than others in both collecting and reporting SME sector

Table 4.1 Diverse official SME definitions

Country	Official SME definitions
Algeria	Microenterprise: 1–9 employees; annual turnover less than DZD20 million; balance sheet assets of less than DZD10 million. Small enterprise: 10–49 employees; annual turnover of less than DZD200 million; balance sheet assets of less than DZD100 million. Medium enterprise: 50–250 employees; turnover of DZD200 million – 2 billion; balance sheet assets of DZD100 million – 500 million. (SME law; RADP 2001)
Egypt	Microenterprise: paid-up capital of less than EGP50 000. Small enterprise: paid-up capital of EGP50 000 – 100 000 and no more than 50 employees. (Small enterprise development law [Law 141/2004]) The law does not include a definition for medium enterprise.
Iraq	No official definition.
Jordan	Microenterprise (handicraft): 1–9 workers or less than JD30 000 in registered capital. Small enterprise: 10–49 workers and more than JD30 000 in registered capital. Medium enterprise: 50–249 workers and more than JD30 000 in registered capital. (Circular issued by the Prime Ministry in 2005 to define industrial SMEs)
Lebanon	No official definition.
Morocco	SME: not exceeding 200 employees and not exceeding annual turnover of MAD75 million or annual balance sheet assets of MAD50 million. New enterprise: in existence for less than two years with an initial investment of up to MAD25 million and a ratio of investment per employee of less than MAD250 000. (SME Charter; Royaume du Maroc 2002)
Sudan	No official definition.
Syria	Microenterprise: less than 10 employees; less than SYP3 million in turnover; up to SYP50 million in capital. Small enterprise: 10–49 employees; SYP50 million – 250 million in turnover; up to SYP250 million in capital. Medium enterprise: 50–249 employees; up to SYP250 million in turnover; more than SYP250 million in capital. (First Syrian SME Strategy; MoET 2009)
Tunisia	No official definition.
Turkey	Microenterprise: less than 10 employees; less than YTL1 million in turnover; up to YTL1 million in balance sheet assets. Small enterprise: 10–49 employees; YTL1 million – 5 million in turnover; up to YTL5 million in balance sheet assets.

Table 4.1 (continued)

Country	Official SME definitions
	Medium enterprise: 50–249 employees; up to YTL25 million in turnover; up to YTL25 million in balance sheet assets.
West Bank & Gaza	No official definition.
Yemen	No official definition.

data, but annual surveys of the SME sector are generally not done. The potential to link data files from business registrations, establishment censuses and the administrative records of the tax and social security offices is not exploited to provide a more holistic picture of the SME sector and developments within it. To address these challenges requires capacity building of government statistical offices and the willingness of relevant ministries and agencies to cooperate in sharing data.

The availability of comparative firm-level micro data is essential to attempts to examine the full and real effects of structural reforms on firm behaviour and performance. Currently it is very difficult to do this in the MENA-12 countries although some efforts are under way to build the statistical capacity of governments in related areas. For example, the Morocco Statistics Directorate has an initiative with MEDSTAT[3] on harmonization of sector statistics, Eurostat has a MEDSTAT project to build capacity in the Syrian Central Bureau of Statistics, and the World Bank has supported the Yemen Central Statistical Office (CSO) on a Household Budget Survey and the 2004 Census. Government bodies in Egypt, Tunisia, Morocco and Syria have proposed the creation of SME observatories or indexes that would report on annually collected SME sector data (see EC 2008a; GAFI 2008; SFD 2009; MoET 2009), efforts that could potentially benefit greatly from a regional collaborative development approach.

Prevalence of SMEs and SME Employment

It is not clear how many SMEs there actually are in most of the MENA-12 countries (for reasons outlined above), although estimates from the data which do exist (for ten countries) suggests almost 7 million, reaching more than 12.5 million if estimates of informal enterprises are included (Table 4.2).

The private sector in MENA-12 countries is comprised of a very large number of microenterprises (with fewer than five workers), a very small

Table 4.2 Number of SMEs in selected MENA-12 countries

Country	Number of SMEs	Total (including estimates of informal enterprises)
Algeria	518 900	1 000 000
Egypt	2 340 000	4 300 000
Iraq	330 000	330 000
Jordan	146 067	146 067*
Lebanon	171 000	171 000*
Morocco	..	1 500 000
Syria	523 000	873 000
Turkey	2 390 000	3 500 000
West Bank & Gaza	109 686	180 000
Yemen	304 131	500 000
Total	6 832 784	12 500 067

Notes:
*No available estimates for number of informal enterprises.
No available data for TN and SD.

Sources: Country statistical reports and other country-level reports for various years 2004–08.

number of small and medium enterprises, and a tiny number of large enterprises (Table 4.3). Enterprises with fewer than 50 workers account for at least 95 per cent of private sector enterprises in the MENA-12 countries and over 99 per cent in Algeria, Egypt, Jordan, Lebanon, Syria, Turkey, the West Bank & Gaza and Yemen. The vast majority of SMEs has fewer than five employees: 89 per cent of those in Jordan, 90 per cent in the West Bank & Gaza, 91 per cent in Syria and Yemen, over 92 per cent in Egypt and over 93 per cent in Lebanon.

MENA-12 economies are particularly deficient in producing medium-sized enterprises, reflecting a 'missing middle' in their enterprise structures. For example, only 0.21 per cent of private enterprises in Egypt have more than 50 employees (about 5000 firms out of 2.34 million); less than 0.60 per cent in Turkey (about 14 000 out of the 2.39 million); and 0.70 per cent in Jordan (1039 out of 146 622). The majority of large enterprises are owned by either foreign companies or prominent families who own groups of companies.

The employment share of SMEs is also difficult to determine and to compare across countries. Some governments report on the SME share of total employment and others on the SME share of non-agricultural private sector employment. In many cases statistical reports are not clear on the

Table 4.3 Distribution of enterprises by size: selected MENA-12 countries

Distribution of enterprises by size (number of workers)	EG	JO	LE	TR	WB&G	YE
Micro (< 5)	92.48%	88.70%	93.53%	96.32%	90.23%	91.50%
Micro (5–9)	5.95%		3.88%		6.79%	4.80%
Subtotal	*98.43%*	10.59%	*97.41%*	*96.32%*	*97.02%*	*96.30%*
Small (10–49)	1.35%		2.28%	3.09%	2.03%	
Subtotal	*99.79%*	*99.29%*	*99.68%*	*99.41%*	*99.77%*	
Medium (50–249)	0.21%	*0.71%*	0.32%	0.48%	0.23%	3.70%
Large (>249)				0.11%		
Total	100%	100%	100%	100%	100%	100%
Employment distribution by enterprise size	EG	JO	LE	TR	WB&G	YE
Micro (< 5)	63.64%	38.19%	..	..	56.80%	83.50%
Micro (5–9)	12.96%		..	..	15.50%	
Subtotal	*76.60%*	25.73%			*72.30%*	
Small (10–49)	8.74%		..	..	17.10%	16.50%
Subtotal	*85.34%*	*63.92%*			*89.40%*	
Medium (50–249)	14.66%	36.08%	..	..	10.60%	
Large (>249)			..	..		
Total	100%	100%			100%	100%
Average enterprise size (number of workers)	2.7	4.2	3.9	3.7	2.6	1.9

Note: Employment distribution by size of enterprise for LE and TR not available.

Sources: EG (SFD 2009; 2006 Census); JO (DOS 2006); LE (MoET 2008; 2004 Census); YE (CSO 2004); WB&G (PCBS 2007); TR (Turkstat 2008b).

base for calculation. Enterprises with fewer than 50 employees account for over 80 per cent of private sector employment in Egypt (Assaad 2007) and 77 per cent of non-agricultural private sector employment in Turkey (Özar 2004). Comparable data are not readily available for other countries.

The firm size and employment distribution in the MENA-12 takes a slightly different shape than in the EU-27. According to Eurostat figures

Table 4.4 Distribution of enterprises and employment by size class in the EU-27, 2007

Size class (number of workers)	Number of enterprises (000s)	Share of enterprises (%)	Number of workers (000s)	Share of workers (%)	Average firm size	Share of value-added (%)
Micro (0–9)	18 778	91.9	38 890	29.7	2.1	21.0
Small (10–49)	1 402	6.8	27 062	20.7	19.3	18.9
Medium (50–249)	220	1.1	21 957	16.8	99.8	17.8
Subtotal	*20 409*	*99.8*	*87 909*	*67.2*	*4.3*	*57.0*
Large (250 +)	43	0.2	42 895	32.8	997.6	42.3
Total	20 452	100.0	130 804	100.0	6.4	100.0
Microenterprise share of SME contribution		92.0		44.2		36.4

Note: Figures for the non-financial business economy.

Source: Audretsch et al. (2009) (Tables 10 and 11).

for 2007, 92 per cent of SMEs in Europe have fewer than ten employees (Table 4.4). This compares to 98 per cent in Egypt, about 97 per cent in Lebanon and the West Bank & Gaza, and 96 per cent in Turkey, as examples. These microenterprises account for over 70 per cent of private sector workers in Egypt, Lebanon, Turkey and the West Bank & Gaza, compared to only 30 per cent in the EU-27, reinforcing the greater dependence of MENA countries on microenterprises for private sector employment and the relative absence of contribution from small and medium enterprises.

The greater dominance of microenterprises in the MENA-12 countries means that the average enterprise size (over all enterprises) tends to be smaller than in European countries. The average firm size in the EU-27 is 6.4 workers (2007), compared to an average of 6.1 in Syria (2004), 4.2 in Jordan (2006), 3.9 in Lebanon (2001), 3.7 in Turkey (2005), 3 in Algeria (2009), 2.7 in Egypt (2006), 2.6 in the West Bank & Gaza (2007) and 1.9 in Yemen (2004).

Longitudinal data allowing calculations of SME growth rates are not readily accessible for the MENA-12 countries, but some evidence suggests that the annual growth rate varies widely across countries. The average annual growth in the number of SMEs over 7–10-year time periods has been 12.3 per cent in Algeria (1999–2007), 7.7 per cent in Turkey (1992–2002), 5.4 per cent in Yemen (1994–2004), 4.2 per cent in Egypt (1996–2006) and 3.4 per cent in the West Bank & Gaza (1997–2007).[4] Missing data on the growth rates of individual enterprises on an annual basis makes it is virtually impossible for policymakers to understand timely developments within the sector and to assess the impact of policy measures.

The literature seeking to explain the greater predominance of micro and very small enterprises in developing countries suggests that the following can all be factors acting to constrain the emergence of medium-sized and larger firms: the low education and skill levels of the MSE owners; a high level of uncertainty or insecurity in the economy (which leads to minimization of investment and risk); weak property rights; the inability to exploit economies of scale due to liquidity constraints and lack of transport infrastructure and services; rigid labour restrictions that make hiring of formal workers difficult and expensive; imperfect information; high transaction costs; and insufficient access to and use of technology. Aterido et al. (2008) find that a weak business environment shifts the size distribution of firms downward. Less access to formal finance and complex business regulations has the effect of reducing the employment growth of all firms, particularly micro and small firms, and corruption and poor access to infrastructure reduce employment growth in medium-sized and large firms. Regulatory constraints and perceptions of stability and risk will also affect the size structure of firms (Naudé 2008). These results indicate that significant reforms are needed in the MENA countries to spur microenterprises to grow into the ranks of SMEs and to alter the size distribution of the stock of enterprises.

Prevalence of Self-Employment

A great deal of SME activity is undertaken in the form of self-employment, either by self-employed persons who do not have any employees (own-account self-employed) or by self-employed persons who create jobs for others (employers). Country-level labour force surveys and census data provide data on the number of own-account self-employed workers and employers and their prevalence in the employed population. The self-employment rate in the MENA-12 countries averages just less than 30 per cent. Between 30 to 34 per cent of all employed workers in Iraq, Lebanon, Morocco and Syria are accounted for by these two categories of worker, between 24 and 29 per cent in Algeria, Egypt, Tunisia, Turkey, Yemen and the West Bank & Gaza, and only 15.2 per cent of employed persons in Jordan (Figure 4.1). Sudan has the highest level of self-employment and employer activity, accounting for almost half of total employment in 1993, the latest year for which official data is available (CBS 2006). Egypt

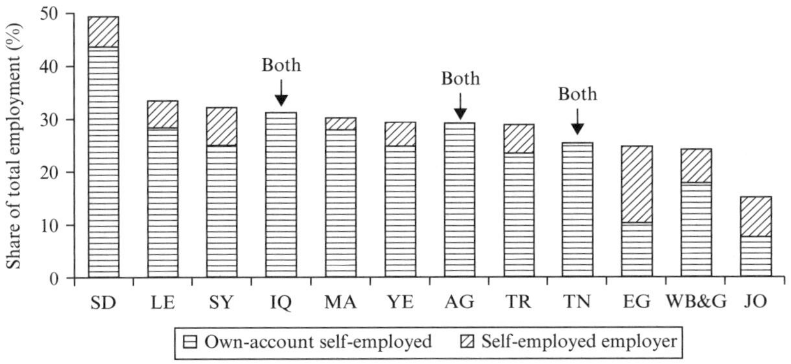

Sources: Various country data sources; years 2004–08. Latest data for SD 1993.

Figure 4.1 Self-employment share of total employment

and Jordan stand out in this comparison because of the high proportion of employers among the self-employed; in the remaining MENA-12 countries the vast majority of the self-employed are own-account with no employees. By comparison, roughly half of the microenterprises in Europe do not have any employees (Audretsch et al. 2009).

A lack of the appropriate education and skills to meet the requirements of employment in the paid private sector and the lack of employment options can be triggers pushing someone into self-employment, so while self-employment is an option for people in the MENA-12 countries to make a living, it does not necessarily contribute substantially to economic growth. In the earlier stages of development, self-employment rates generally decline as the economy grows (Thurik et al. 2008).

Prevalence of Women-Owned SMEs

The rate of SME ownership by women in MENA countries mirrors their low labour force participation and employment rates. According to the World Bank (2007c), women's involvement in entrepreneurship in the MENA region is the lowest in the world. Available labour force survey or census data indicate that women in Sudan have the highest rate of self-employment, accounting for over a third of women's employment,[5] followed by women in Algeria with a self-employment rate of about 30 per cent. In the remaining MENA-12 countries the female self-employment rate ranges from 18 per cent in Egypt to 4.1 per cent in Jordan. The comparison of male and female self-employment rates for own-account self-employment and employers is presented in Figure 4.2.

Source: Country data sources for years 2004–08. Latest data for SD 1993. No data for IQ.

Figure 4.2 Male and female self-employment and employer rates

Employed men in these countries are much more likely than employed women to be self-employed. The male self-employment rate is on average 2.4 times higher than the female rate, but this varies widely from four times higher in Jordan to almost equal in Algeria. The largest gender gaps are in Jordan, Lebanon, Syria and Morocco. In Egypt the percentage of employed men who are own-account self-employed is actually lower than the percentage of employed women who are own-account self-employed. However it should be noted that there are significantly fewer employed women than men, so men still dominate the absolute number of self-employed persons. The female employer rate in the MENA-12 is minimal, ranging from less than 1 per cent in Morocco to 4 per cent in Egypt. Employed men in the MENA-12 are four times more likely than employed women to be employers.

Given these differences in self-employment rates, women's combined share of the self-employed and employers varies from 3 to over 15 per cent depending on the MENA country: 3.1 per cent in Jordan (2007), 4.1 per cent in Syria (2008), 5.1 per cent in Yemen (2004), 7.7 per cent in Lebanon (2004), 10.3 per cent in West Bank & Gaza (2008), and rising to 11.1 per cent in Morocco (2005), 12.9 per cent in Turkey (2006), and over 15 per cent in Algeria (2009), Egypt (2006), Morocco (2004), Tunisia (2004) and Sudan (1993) (Figure 4.3).

Women's share of employer activity ranges from only 3 to 7 per cent (except for Sudan where it was about 15 per cent in 1993). In addition there are miniscule percentages of women with businesses having more than ten employees. Women entrepreneurs in this position are likely to be

Sources: Data from various country labour force survey and census reports, 2006–09. No data for IQ.

Figure 4.3 Women's share of total self-employment activity

highly educated with previous experience in professional or managerial jobs and supportive families (IFC and CAWTAR 2007).

Experience in other countries suggests that research to understand better the barriers to women's participation in entrepreneurial and SME activity can lead to effective policies and measures to reduce the constraints they face in starting and growing businesses (Stevenson and Lundström 2002). There is very little comprehensive research on this issue in MENA countries (see IFC and CAWTAR 2007; FEMISE 2006b). The role of women in entrepreneurial and self-employment activity is of importance because low participation rates represent lost economic and social potential. Not only is entrepreneurial activity a way to integrate more women into the labour market and reduce the dependency ratio, but there are millions of women already engaged in microenterprise activity with low growth potential that could be helped to grow into more substantial enterprises and contribute to job creation.

BARRIERS TO SME DEVELOPMENT

Reports and studies reveal a great deal of similarity in the challenges facing the SME sector across the MENA-12. Common among them are: a low level of education and training; a lack of the management skills and systems required to compete effectively in today's markets; obsolete production systems; a lack of access to external sources of debt and equity finance; inadequate access to information, BDS and training; a lack of the knowledge and experience required for exporting; a lack of broad-based and strategic linkages with larger firms and global supply chains; limited access to markets and distribution channels; poor access to adequately priced inputs due to their size limitations and inability to obtain price discounts through volume purchases; inadequate supply of educated and skilled workers; low utilization of and access to up-to-date technologies; low product quality and competitiveness; and low level of innovation (ECOSC 2003; Özar 2004; UNCTAD 2004; El Mahdi 2006; ERF 2006; El-Meehy 2009; MoET 2009; SFD 2009). In some countries, such as Morocco, access to land and physical premises is noted as a challenge, and in the conflict and post-conflict countries, such as Sudan, Iraq, the West Bank & Gaza and Lebanon, political instability is a major issue.

SMEs are burdened by cumbersome regulatory and administrative procedures, poor infrastructure, underdeveloped financial systems, high loan collateral requirements and largely unattractive tax regimes. Regulatory barriers affecting SMEs are well known. It is complicated, costly and time-consuming to register a business, secure operating licences, register property and comply with complex taxation and other reporting requirements. Access to financing is one of the most significant and persistent barriers. A very small percentage of SMEs in these countries are able to secure financing from commercial banks. The situation is exacerbated in countries where there is limited competition in the banking sector (for example, in Yemen, Syria and Algeria) and banks have little experience in lending to SMEs and offering products that meet their needs for medium- and long-term financing. Although microfinance schemes exist, the demand far exceeds the supply. The venture capital industry in the region is very weak, with Morocco, Tunisia and Turkey standing out as considerably more developed in terms of schemes to fill the equity gap. Leasing is also a nascent concept in the region, although there are several leasing companies in Tunisia and the International Finance Corporation (IFC) is working in other countries, such as in Algeria, Egypt and Yemen, to try to stimulate the industry. Private credit bureaus are rare in the region and public credit bureaus where they exist cover tiny proportions of the population (World Bank 2009b). This means that financial institutions have considerable difficulty in assessing the lending risk of SME borrowers.

The quality of manufactured products has emerged as a critical SME constraint. With the opening of markets through Free Trade Agreements (FTAs), domestic SMEs will have to meet international production and quality standards in order to compete. Euro-Med countries that have signed EU Association Agreements are paying particular attention to preparing their SMEs for the free trade regime; hence the substantial interest in SME upgrading programmes in several of the countries.

The quality of management and entrepreneurial capacity is also a major problem. Entrepreneurship and management education is rarely linked to vocational education and training programmes even if many of the graduates will ultimately end up in micro and small enterprises. Entrepreneurship or small business courses are offered in university education programmes in only a few of the region's universities. Thus SME owners are often unprepared with the skills needed to develop enterprises capable of competing in the global economy.

Another constraint for SMEs in MENA countries is the lack of access to BDS services. Studies in Egypt, for example, suggest that less than 1 per cent of Egyptian SMEs receive any form of BDS (Entrust 2006). The concept of BDS is still nascent in Iraq, Syria and Yemen, with few government or private sector service providers. The provision of BDS services is most developed in Turkey and Tunisia where there are intensive networks of entrepreneurship development centres, SME support offices, technology development centres, and employment bureaus offering advice, counselling and information to new entrepreneurs and existing SMEs. Egypt is expanding its network of Business Resource Centers, SME advice centres and technology and innovation centres, although most efforts have been under way only since about 2006 and services are geared heavily towards industrial and technology-oriented SMEs. The Canadian International Development Agency (CIDA) in Egypt has been supporting a Business Development Services Support Project (BDSSP), the goal of which is to build private sector capacity to deliver good-practice BDS to SMEs. A network of SME facilitation centres has been put into place in Algeria (2003 decree) and the Algerian SME Agency facilitates consulting services to SMEs that want to upgrade their competitiveness. The market for private sector BDS providers and trainers is largely underdeveloped in most of the region. Programmes like the IFC Business Edge business management training and International Labour Organization (ILO) Know About Business training are being offered in various parts of the region, but delivery requires extensive training of private sector companies and individuals due to the lack of related past experience. Besides the reach and capacity issues associated with BDS provision in the MENA countries, there is much discussion of the issue of subsidization of BDS services and the distortion effects this can have on the market. In addition there are questions about whether BDS is best provided by public agencies or the private sector; the strength and capacity of BDS providers; the sustainability of BDS services (that is, the willingness of clients to pay for services); and the impact of BDS on the performance of client enterprises.

To address the barriers faced by SMEs, there is a need for simplified business registration, licensing processes and customs procedures; improved access to external financing and urban and rural BDS; upgrading of technical and management skills, know-how and technology; quality improvements in production systems and products; greater access to information and markets; and stronger linkages with large enterprises.

SME POLICY DEVELOPMENT

Governments in the MENA-12 countries have gradually been designing and implementing policies and programmes to reduce barriers to SME development and growth in hopes of accelerating job creation, reducing poverty and improving domestic productivity, competitiveness and innovation. They differ considerably across countries in the breadth and depth of experience they have in doing this. Governments in Algeria, Tunisia and Turkey have been focusing on policies to develop the SME sector for longer than the other countries. Turkey established the Small and Medium Enterprises Development Organization (KOSGEB) in 1990, the Algerian government has had a Ministry for SMEs and Crafts (and SME Promotion Directorate) since 1992 and the Tunisian government created a special agency for small and medium-sized industries in 1998. The major initial focus was on the delivery of assistance programmes to help industrial SMEs improve their competitiveness. Governments in the remaining countries started taking a serious look at SMEs as drivers of growth in 2000 or later. Some have passed SME laws (Algeria – 2001; Egypt – 2004; and Morocco – passed in 2000, published in 2002); others have prepared White Papers on SMEs (Morocco – 1999; and Algeria – 2004); and most either have SME strategy documents (Algeria, Egypt, Tunisia, Turkey and Yemen) or have been recently engaged in the process of updating existing strategies (Yemen) or preparing new ones (Egypt, Lebanon, Syria and the West Bank & Gaza).

MENA governments have instituted a variety of structures for the development and implementation of SME development policies and programmes. Some have created SME departments or units in line ministries, some have set up dedicated SME agencies, some have SME laws in place, some have interministerial coordinating mechanisms and some have established SME advisory councils to provide advice and input from the private sector. A myriad of arrangements exist for delivering services to SMEs. Table 4.5 identifies some of the SME policy and structural features in the MENA-12.

Multiple ministries and agencies are engaged in SME-related issues in

Table 4.5 Comparison of features of SME policy and delivery structures

Features	AG	EG	IQ	JO	LE	MA	SD	SY	TN	TR	WB&G	YE
Legal features												
SME law or charter	Y 2001	Y 2004	N	N	N	Y 2002	N	N	N	N	N (1)	N (2)
Microfinance law	Y 2004	N (3)	N	N	N	Y 1997	N	Y 2007	0	N (4)	N (5)	Y 2009
Structural features												
SME ministry	Y 1992	N	N	N	N	N	N	N	N	N	N	N
SME department or directorate	Y	N	0	Y 2003	Y 2005	Y	Y 1988	Y 2007	Y	Y	N	1997
Interministerial SME committee	0	Y (6)	0	0	0	0	Y	Y 2008	0	Y	N	N
Dedicated SME agency or institution	Y 2005	Y 2004	N	Y (7)	N	Y 2003	0	Y	Y 1998	Y 1990	N	Y 2006 (8)
SME advisory council/ committee	Y 2004	N	N	N	Y	N	0	Y 2008	0	Y	N	N
Policy features												
SME White Paper	Y 2004	N	N	N	N	Y 1999	N	N	N	N	N	N
SME strategy	Y	Y	0	Y	Y	Y	N	Y 2009	Y	Y	N	Y
Strategy & targets for new enterprises	Y	N	N	N	N	Y	N	N	Y	N	N	N

Table 4.5 (continued)

Features	AG	EG	IQ	JO	LE	MA	SD	SY	TN	TR	WB&G	YE
Infrastructural features												
OSS (business registration)	1	2	0	2	1	2	0	1	3	3	2	0
Network of SME centres	2	2	1	0	2	2	0	1	3	3	1	2
Incubators for start-ups	Y	Y	0	Y	Y	Y	0	Y	Y	Y	Y	0
Microfinance institutions	1	2	1	2	1	3	1	1	3	2	3	2
SME loan guarantee agency	Y	Y	Y	Y	Y	Y	0	Y	Y	Y	N	0
SME Bank	N	N	N	N	N	N	N	N	Y	N	N	N
Venture capital funds	1	2	1	2	1	3	1	1	3	2	1	1
SME stock exchange	N	Y	N	N	N	N	N	N	Y	Y	N	N

Notes:
Y = yes; N = no; 0 = no evidence; 1 = nascent; 2 = established but underdeveloped; 3 = mature and operating well; Year = year of establishment.
(1) An SME law drafted in 2009.
(2) An SME law drafted in 2002 but not yet acted on.
(3) The microfinance law drafted in 2009 for review by Parliament.
(4) A draft law on microfinance institutions presented to the Parliament in the autumn of 2009.
(5) A draft law on microfinance institutions still under review by the Parliament.
(6) The Egyptian Minister of Finance has set up four interministerial committees to examine specific SME policy issues.
(7) Jordan Enterprise has the mandate for SME support, but there are several agencies and funds for different segments of the SME market.
(8) The Small and Micro Enterprise Promotion Service (SMEPS) is a subsidiary of the Social Fund for Development which has key SME responsibilities in Yemen.

most of the countries, creating serious challenges for integrated policy development. For example, the responsibility for SMEs in Tunisia rests with two separate ministries: the Ministry of Industry and Technology[6] deals with industrial SMEs, and the Ministry of Trade and Handicrafts with commercial SMEs, handicrafts and small workshops. In Algeria, Lebanon, Jordan, Morocco, Sudan, Yemen and most recently Syria there is an SME department or unit in a ministry with the lead responsibility for SME issues. Several ministries and agencies are involved in SME issues in Egypt, including the Social Fund for Development (SFD), the Ministry of Trade and Industry (MTI), the Ministry of Investment, the General Authority for Investment (GAFI), the Ministry of Finance and the Ministry of Social Solidarity, a situation which can lead to a lack of policy coherence and coordination. Eighteen entities are reported to be involved in SME issues in Jordan with no systematic coordination of their efforts. The Jordanian government's attempt in the late 2000s to create an overarching SME policy coordination umbrella organization was ultimately abandoned due to the difficulties of performing this role. Dedicated SME agencies have been set up in Algeria, Morocco, Tunisia and Turkey to implement SME programmes and strengthen the environment for SMEs. While an important structural feature for SME support, the potential exists for such agencies to become disconnected from the policymaking process if they are overly involved in the delivery of SME programmes at the expense of policy support. It is not unusual in the MENA-12 countries to see a separation of ministerial and agency responsibility for MSE policies directed towards poverty reduction, and SME policies directed towards competitiveness. This generally results in a less than holistic approach to dealing with SME sector issues, with great potential for creating a schism between the policies for microenterprise development and the policies for SME development. The question of which policy structure works most effectively would be worthy of a comprehensive and comparative analysis.

Although structure matters, what likely matters more is whether a good policy development and implementation process is in place. This requires commitment from the top level of government, an interministerial policy approach, a strong evidence base to inform and underpin policy decisions, an effective process for stakeholder consultation, effective linkages between policy development and implementation, a strong role for private sector advocacy and appropriate mechanisms for delivering and implementing policy measures. Issues such as these are elaborated upon more broadly in the World Bank (2009c) report on unlocking private-led growth in the MENA region, and discussed in more detail in Chapter 6.

SME policies and strategies in the MENA-12 countries are very similar in terms of objectives and measures. These include: financing measures; investments in SME support structures, BDS and information services; business registration and regulatory simplification; technology and skills upgrading; management skills development; SME linkages and cluster initiatives; innovation supports, such as incubators and technology parks; and strengthening of business associations. But governments differ in the weighting balance given to the mix of policy measures, the structures through which these policies and measures are implemented, and the extent to which they are implemented. In some countries more weight is placed on microenterprise support through the use of microfinance, and in others on competitiveness and the upgrading of existing SMEs. The policies of some governments are more interventionist than others in terms of providing direct support to individual enterprises versus reforms to create a business enabling environment for the whole sector. The use of measures targeted to selective SMEs means that the 'enabled environment' for 'all SMEs' is not necessarily addressed as well as that the needs of large segments of the SME sector are not met. Policies focused solely on the enabling environment will not necessarily address a number of other SME constraints. A combination of policies is likely optimal. An analysis of the various policy options and approaches would also make an interesting topic for a comparative regional study.

A summary of the current SME-related policy priorities and actions of each MENA-12 government is included in the country profiles in Chapters 8 and 9. Most governments have been working on reforms to reduce the time and cost of starting a business. One-stop shops for business registration and licensing exist in many of the countries although some are at an earlier stage of implementation than others. There are different models and approaches for this, and limited attempts to share experiences about what approach works best. Egypt, Jordan, Morocco and Tunisia have dramatically reduced the paid-in capital requirements for new limited liability companies, and advocacy groups in Algeria and Yemen are calling for a similar reform. Governments are active to varying degrees in carrying out regulatory reforms to improve the business environment and investment climate, such as modernization of company laws, competition laws, bankruptcy laws and taxation regimes. Egypt is implementing a full-scale 'Guillotine Review' approach to regulatory reform,[7] an approach that is also proposed by the Syrian government.

To help overcome deficiencies in formal lending markets, governments in most of the MENA-12 countries have established SME guarantee funds of various kinds (with different guarantee amounts, ceilings, terms and conditions) that are generally processed through the banks. Limited information exists on the impact of these guarantee funds or the effects of the different sets of terms and conditions on the success of the funds in addressing the SME financing gap, although the reach of these schemes is reportedly limited. Several governments have created small enterprise development funds to finance new start-ups and the upgrading activities of existing SMEs, but again there are no comparative data on the success and impact of these funds. In 2005 the Tunisian government set up a Bank for the Financing of SMEs, the first in the region to do so. Microfinance institutions and programmes are well established in Morocco, Tunisia and the West Bank & Gaza; moderately developed in Egypt; and young or nascent in Algeria, Jordan, Syria, Iraq, Lebanon and Sudan. Governments in Algeria, Egypt, Jordan, Morocco, Syria, Turkey, the West Bank & Gaza and Yemen have already passed or recently drafted a microfinance law to establish a framework for the sustainable operation of microfinance institutions (MFIs) and to regulate the industry. The Sudanese government has issued a regulation requiring Sudanese banks to allocate at least 10 per cent of bank loans in the form of microcredit, and launched a large Microfinance Development Facility with funding from the Bank of Sudan and development partners. Leasing laws to stimulate a private sector SME leasing market are in effect in Egypt, Algeria and Yemen, and the Syrian government is in the process of drafting one. Governments in Egypt, Tunisia and Turkey have launched second-tier stock markets to create an opportunity for small and early-stage growth companies to raise equity capital. There may be useful lessons for countries to learn from each other through a forum for sharing knowledge and experiences of what has worked well and what has not in the whole area of SME access to financing.

Policies and programmes to upgrade the management and production capacity and quality of SMEs is a priority in most of these countries (such as Mise à Niveau programmes in Morocco and Tunisia, the Jordan Upgrading and Modernization Programme (JUMP) and programmes of the Industrial Modernization Centre (IMC) in Egypt), as this is essential if SMEs are to meet the standards required to take advantage of the export market potential offered by FTAs with the European Union (EU) and other countries. The advancement of technology and innovation is also a growing policy area. The development of technology parks and innovation centres is evidence of this (for example, the Smart Village initiative and Technology Transfer and Innovation Centres in Egypt; Technology Parks and technopoles in Morocco and Tunisia; technology incubators and a network of innovation centres in Jordan; Technology Development Centers, Technology Development Zones, and technoparks in universities and research centres in Turkey), as well as the growing emphasis on improving linkages between research and development (R&D)

environments and SMEs. However the level of R&D investment to GDP in these countries is minimal, as noted in Chapter 3.

Nine of the MENA-12 countries benefit from participation in EU-led SME policy exercises. In 2000 Turkey was the first MENA country to sign on to the Bologna Charter for SMEs and to adopt the European Charter for Small Enterprises. Algeria, Egypt, Jordan, Lebanon, Morocco, Palestine, Syria and Tunisia signed on to the Euro-Mediterranean Charter for Enterprise in 2004. These charters are designed as tools to structure policies in support of SMEs and enterprise development at the national level, help foster an entrepreneurial culture and build a framework for private sector reforms. The *raison d'être* of the Euro-Mediterranean Charter for Enterprise is to outline ways to create conditions for businesses to make the most of the Euro-Mediterranean Free Trade Zone, which will mean being prepared for the free trade of goods complying with common standards and technical regulations (EC 2006a). Committing to the charter has led to a series of microeconomic reforms to boost the competitiveness of enterprises, and a shift in policy emphasis to create a favourable environment for business creation and the development of entrepreneurship and innovative enterprises. In 2007 the Organisation for Economic Co-operation and Development (OECD) and the European Commission partnered in an exercise to assess and report on the degree of implementation of enterprise policy as defined in the Charter for Enterprise (European Communities and OECD 2008). Comparisons of the policy assessment for six selected policy areas are presented in Table 4.6. Egypt and Tunisia were the best performers on simple procedures for enterprises; Tunisia on education and training for entrepreneurship; Egypt on improved skills; Egypt and Morocco on access to finance and investment-friendly taxation; Egypt, Tunisia and Morocco on quality business support schemes and services; and Egypt, Morocco and Tunisia on the strength of their business associations.

THE ENTREPRENEURSHIP CHALLENGE

Increasing attention in both developed and developing economies is being given to the role of entrepreneurship in development and growth and the importance of building an 'entrepreneurial society' (Caree and Thurik 2003; Acs et al. 2005; Acs 2006; Stevenson and Lundström 2007; Naudé 2008; Thurik 2009). Most of the research on entrepreneurship has been within the developed-country context. According to Lingelbach and de la Viña (2005): 'entrepreneurship in developing countries is arguably the least studied economic and social phenomenon in the world today'. Naudé

Table 4.6 Policy progress on selected EuroMed Charter for Enterprise priorities

Indicator	AG	EG	JO	LE	MA	SY	TN	WB & G
1. Simple procedures for business								
Institutional framework for enterprise policy								
Delegation of responsibility for enterprise policy	1.5	4.0	3.5	2.0	3.0	2.0	3.5	2.0
Coordination with other ministries, stakeholders and civil society	3.0	3.5	3.0	2.0	4.0	2.0	3.0	2.5
Enterprise development strategies	2.0	4.0	2.5	2.5	3.0	3.0	3.5	1.5
Clear task assignment	2.5	4.0	4.0	2.0	4.0	3.0	4.0	1.5
MED weighted average = 2.3	*2.3*	*3.9*	*3.2*	*2.2*	*3.5*	*2.5*	*3.5*	*1.9*
Better legislation and administrative simplification								
Delegation of responsibility for regulatory reform	2.0	4.0	2.5	2.0	3.0	2.0	3.0	1.0
Strategy for the simplification of legislation	2.0	4.0	2.0	2.5	2.5	3.0	3.0	1.0
Review and simplification of current legislation	2.0	3.5	2.0	2.5	4.0	2.0	2.5	2.0
Elimination of redundant legislation and regulations	2.0	3.5	2.0	2.0	2.0	2.0	3.5	2.0
Cost-benefit analysis of new enterprise legislation	1.0	2.5	1.5	1.0	1.5	1.0	1.0	2.0
MED weighted average = 2.5	*1.9*	*3.7*	*2.1*	*2.1*	*2.7*	*2.2*	*2.8*	*1.5*

Table 4.6 (continued)

Indicator	AG	EG	JO	LE	MA	SY	TN	WB & G
Cheaper and faster start-up and closing								
Number of days to obtain registration certificate	4.0	4.0	4.0	4.0	4.0	1.0	4.0	4.0
Number of steps to obtain registration certificate	4.0	4.0	4.0	5.0	5.0	1.0	5.0	1.5
Official costs to obtain registration certificate	3.0	3.0	2.0	4.0	1.0	1.0	3.0	4.0
Administrative identification numbers	3.0	4.0	4.0	3.0	2.0	1.0	1.0	4.0
Number of days for company identification number(s)	4.0	4.0	5.0	1.0	4.0	1.0	4.0	4.0
Number of days for overall registration process	2.0	3.0	3.0	1.0	3.0	1.0	1.0	1.0
Number of steps for overall registration process	1.0	3.0	2.0	3.0	3.0	1.0	2.0	1.0
Silence is consent	1.0	5.0	1.0	1.0	1.0	1.0	5.0	1.0
Costs of registration for limited liability companies	1.0	1.0	1.0	1.0	1.0	1.0	2.0	1.0
Minimum capital requirements	1.0	3.0	1.0	1.0	1.0	1.0	2.0	4.0
One-stop shops (regional investment centres, etc.)	1.5	4.0	4.0	4.5	4.5	2.0	5.0	2.5
Online registration	1.0	3.0	2.5	1.0	2.5	1.0	4.0	1.0
Time to close a business	4.0	2.0	2.0	2.0	5.0	2.0	5.0	1.0
Cost to close a business	5.0	2.0	4.0	2.0	2.0	4.0	5.0	1.0
MED weighted average = 2.6	*2.2*	*3.3*	*2.6*	*2.5*	*2.6*	*1.4*	*3.5*	*2.3*
Total weighted average	2.1	3.6	2.6	2.3	2.9	2.0	3.3	1.9

Table 4.6 (continued)

Indicator	AG	EG	JO	LE	MA	SY	TN	WB & G
2. Education and training for entrepreneurship								
Policy	1.0	1.5	1.0	1.0	2.0	2.0	3.0	1.0
Lower secondary education	1.0	1.0	1.0	1.0	1.5	1.5	3.0	1.0
Upper secondary education	1.0	1.5	1.5	1.0	1.5	2.0	3.0	1.0
Good practice	1.0	2.5	1.5	1.0	1.0	1.0	3.5	1.0
Non-formal entrepreneurial learning	1.0	4.0	1.0	1.0	1.5	1.5	2.5	1.0
Total MED weighted average = 1.7	1.0	2.0	1.2	1.0	1.5	1.6	3.0	1.0
3. Improved skills								
Availability of training	1.0	4.0	3.0	2.0	3.0	2.5	3.5	2.5
Start-ups	2.0	2.0	1.5	1.5	1.5	1.5	2.0	1.5
Enterprise training	1.0	3.0	1.0	1.0	1.0	1.0	1.0	1.0
Enterprise growth	1.0	4.0	3.0	1.0	3.0	1.0	3.0	1.0
Access to international markets	2.0	4.0	3.0	2.0	2.0	2.0	2.5	2.0
Total MED weighted average = 2.3	1.4	3.5	2.4	1.6	2.2	1.7	2.5	1.7
4. Easier access to finance and investment-friendly taxation								
Credit environment								
Collateral and provisioning requirements	1.0	2.0	2.0	3.0	2.0	1.0	2.0	1.5
Cadastre	3.0	3.0	4.0	3.0	4.0	3.5	4.0	2.0
Laws on distressed companies and bankruptcy	3.0	3.5	4.0	1.5	3.0	3.0	4.0	2.0
Registration systems for movable assets	1.0	3.0	1.0	1.5	1.0	1.0	1.0	2.0

Table 4.6 (continued)

Indicator	AG	EG	JO	LE	MA	SY	TN	WB & G
Credit information services	2.0	3.5	2.5	3.0	2.5	1.0	3.5	2.0
MED weighted average = 2.7	*2.0*	*3.0*	*2.8*	*2.4*	*2.5*	*1.9*	*2.9*	*1.9*
Enterprise financial facilities								
Credit guarantee schemes	3.0	4.0	4.5	4.0	4.0	2.0	3.5	3.5
Availability of risk capital	2.5	4.0	1.5	3.5	4.0	1.0	4.0	1.5
Access to capital markets	1.5	4.0	3.0	3.0	4.0	1.5	3.5	2.0
Microfinance facilities	2.5	4.0	3.0	4.0	5.0	2.0	3.0	3.0
Leasing	3.0	4.0	3.5	4.0	4.5	2.0	5.0	1.5
MED weighted average = 3.2	*2.5*	*4.0*	*3.1*	*3.7*	*4.3*	*1.7*	*2.3*	*2.3*
Investment-friendly taxation								
Analysis of tax impediments to SME equity finance	–	5	1	–	–	–	–	1
Analysis of tax impediments to risky investment in SMEs	–	2	1	–	–	–	–	–
Assessment of compliance costs for SMEs and remedial tax administration	–	5	1	2	–	–	–	1
Assessment of policy measures to lessen tax compliance costs for SMEs	–	5	1	–	–	–	–	2
Assessment of taxpayer assistance to reduce tax compliance burden	–	5	3	4	–	–	–	2
5. Quality business support schemes and services								

Table 4.6 (continued)

Indicator	AG	EG	JO	LE	MA	SY	TN	WB & G
Range of business services	2.0	4.0	3.5	3.0	3.0	2.0	3.0	2.0
Availability of information on business service providers	1.5	4.0	3.5	2.0	3.5	1.5	3.0	1.5
Access to business services	2.0	3.5	3.0	2.0	3.5	2.0	4.0	2.0
Business establishment support services	3.0	4.0	3.5	2.0	4.0	3.0	4.0	2.0
MED weighted average = 3.1	2.2	3.9	3.4	2.3	3.5	2.2	3.6	1.9
6. Strong business associations								
Public–private consultations								
Framework of the consultations	2.5	4.0	3.5	3.0	4.0	3.0	4.0	3.5
Frequency	2.0	4.0	3.0	2.0	3.5	3.5	5.0	4.5
Openness and transparency of the consultation process	2.0	4.0	3.5	2.5	4.0	2.0	3.0	5.0
MED weighted average = 3.5	*2.1*	*4.0*	*3.4*	*2.5*	*3.9*	*2.7*	*3.9*	*4.4*
Enterprise networks and business associations								
Advocacy function and governance rules	2.0	4.0	3.5	4.0	4.5	2.0	4.0	5.0
Provision of services by private sector associations	2.0	4.0	3.0	2.5	3.0	2.5	4.0	3.0
MED weighted average = 3.6	*2.0*	*4.0*	*3.3*	*3.5*	*4.0*	*2.2*	*4.0*	*4.3*
Overall weighted scores	2.1	4.0	3.3	2.9	3.9	2.5	3.9	4.4

Note: The maximum score value is 5.

Source: Data from European Communities and OECD (2008).

(2008) suggests that entrepreneurship performs a different role in developing versus developed economies. While the major entrepreneurship-related concern of advanced economies is obtaining new sources of productivity and growth (which underlie competitiveness), the focus in developing economies is more on the role of entrepreneurship in stimulating and accelerating growth.

Because of its importance and power to 'make business work for the poor', entrepreneurship was promoted by the United Nations Development Programme (UNDP) as one of the key pillars of strategy for developing countries (UNDP 2004). The OECD (2004b) states that countries with high rates of entrepreneurship are more likely to have dynamic private sectors and be better able to deliver and sustain high rates of growth. The World Bank (2006a) concurs that entrepreneurial activity is important for the continued dynamism of a modern economy and for job creation. Barriers to starting a business are significantly and negatively correlated with business density and the new business entry rate, and higher business density and entry rates with a more robust private sector (World Bank 2006a; Klapper et al. 2009).

The World Bank (2006a) concluded from its analysis of entrepreneurship and business environment reforms that if governments reduce barriers to starting a formal business and ease access to credit, rates of entrepreneurship will grow. However this may be too simplistic. Lundström and Stevenson (2005), in their review of the entrepreneurship literature, identified many other factors affecting the level of entrepreneurial activity in a society, such as cultural awareness, education, social security, degree of business support and so on. They also concluded from their review of government practices in developed countries that policies to promote higher levels of entrepreneurship in an economy are broader than those to support SME development. In other words, although related to SME policy, entrepreneurship is a distinctive policy area (Stevenson and Lundström 2002; Lundström and Stevenson 2005). This notion will be elaborated further in Chapter 7.

The focus on entrepreneurship as a policy issue is not well developed in any of the MENA-12 countries. Although governments in Algeria, Morocco and Tunisia have set targets for new enterprise creation in their national development plans and strategies[8] and mandated agencies to achieve those targets, in general the support environment in the MENA-12 countries is not sufficiently in place to facilitate the acceleration of entrepreneurial activity. It is difficult to obtain start-up financing for new enterprises, start-up procedures are often cumbersome, the appropriate level of BDS is not widely available, and the overall culture for entrepreneurship is still weak after decades of government-controlled economies in which there was limited scope for entrepreneurial activity except on the margins.

The issue of fostering entrepreneurship is critical because none of the MENA-12 countries has a substantial enough base of formal domestic SMEs. They will need an increasing supply of private enterprises as well as more growth-oriented and competitive existing ones in order to grow their economies and create employment for large numbers of new labour market entrants. Therefore a higher level of competent entrepreneurship and business start-up activity is required, necessitating a greater supply of motivated and capable entrepreneurs.

Interest in entrepreneurship among MENA countries has been growing. The Jordanian Young Entrepreneurs Association (YEA) produced a White Paper on Entrepreneurship in 2004 (YEA 2004b), which was used to raise the profile of the issue among Jordanian stakeholders. At the same time the YEA initiated Jordan's participation in the Global Entrepreneurship Monitor (YEA 2004a). YEA also carries out public dialogue and advocacy activity to promote a more favourable support environment for entrepreneurship. One of its major positions is that a change in mindset is as important to private sector growth as a change in environment and conditions. The Syrian Young Entrepreneurs Association (SYEA) is also actively involved in promoting entrepreneurship in Syria, and similar efforts by other organizations are under way in Egypt, Tunisia and Turkey.

Entrepreneurial activity levels are an indicator of the level of private sector development. Ten of the MENA-12 countries have some measure of this from their participation in the Global Entrepreneurship Monitor (GEM) Project.[9] The GEM project, led by Babson College and the London Business School, started tracking entrepreneurial activity rates in ten countries in 1999 and now conducts annual studies to measure entrepreneurial activity rates in over 50 developed and developing countries. Formal efforts to join the GEM consortium in Egypt, Syria, Tunisia and Turkey were largely led by private sector and government organizations and/or donors committed to raising awareness about the importance of entrepreneurship and producing the evidence base to inform the government policy agenda better. Funding from Canada's International Development Research Centre (IDRC) enabled collection of GEM data in seven MENA-12 countries in 2009.[10]

The GEM research produces three main measurements of entrepreneurship. The Total Entrepreneurial Activity (TEA) rate measures the percentage of the adult population involved in early-stage entrepreneurial activity. This is comprised of two indicators: the percentage of the adult population actively engaged in trying to start a new business (the nascent entrepreneur rate), and the percentage of the adult population with a young business that has paid salaries and wages for more than three months but less than 42 months ('baby business' owners). The third measurement is of the percentage of the adult population with an established business that is more than 42 months old (established business owners).

The GEM results for ten of the MENA-12 countries reveal that Yemen has the highest TEA rate: 24 per cent of the adult population is either trying to start a business or owns a baby business (Figure 4.4). Next is Algeria with a TEA rate of 16.7 per cent, followed by 15.7 per cent in Morocco, 15 per cent in Lebanon, 13.1 per cent in Egypt, 9.4 and 10.2 per cent in Tunisia and Jordan respectively, and less than 9 per cent in the West Bank & Gaza, Syria and Turkey. These TEA rates suggest that more than 20 million adults in these countries are either actively trying to start a new business or already own a baby business.

Morocco and Lebanon have the highest densities of existing entrepreneurs in the adult population (about 25 per cent) as well as those engaged in all three types of entrepreneurial activity (over 30 per cent). Yemen is interesting in that over 22 per cent of adults are trying to start a business but only 4 per cent own an existing business. This situation may reflect the difficulties of finding paid employment in the country, coupled with an unfriendly regulatory and financial environment. Thus people explore the option of starting their own business but few are actually able to get one started. In contrast, a small proportion of adults in Tunisia, the West Bank & Gaza and Turkey are trying to start businesses.

The TEA rate by itself is interesting, but more insight is gained by

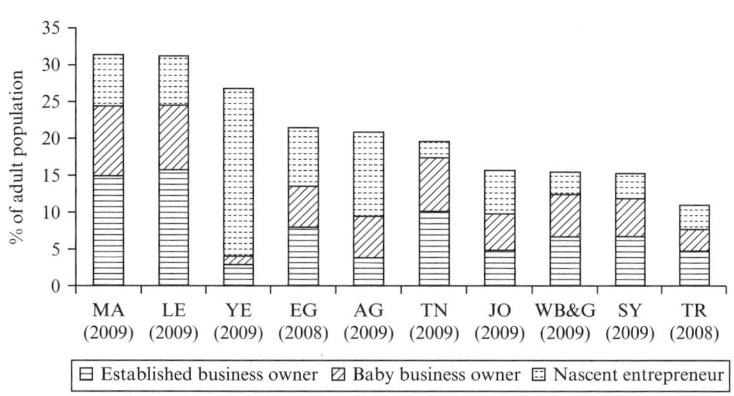

Source: GEM Adult Population Survey (APS) data

Figure 4.4 Adult population involved in entrepreneurial activity

considering the relationship between TEA and the level of country development. The GEM results indicate that TEA rates generally decline across countries as their level of economic development increases until per capita GDP reaches between US$27 000 and US$30 000, at which point there is a tendency for TEA and per capita GDP to rise together (Bosma and Levie 2010).[11] Countries fall on one side or the other of a line approximating a U-shaped curve. Except for Lebanon, Algeria and Yemen, which have TEA rates above the curve (meaning that they have more than the expected level of entrepreneurial activity for their level of economic development), the remaining seven of the MENA-12 countries fall below the U-shaped curve (meaning that they have less than the expected level of entrepreneurial activity for their level of economic development) (Figure 4.5).

It would be very useful if more MENA countries were involved in the GEM research on a longitudinal basis, as it would produce important monitoring data on entrepreneurial activity rates to guide policy directions. Apart from the valuable data gleaned from participating in the GEM project (IDRC 2010), additional research to examine the social, cultural and environmental constraints to the decision to become an entrepreneur would be very valuable. Studies are needed on the changing profile of entrepreneurs in each country (and the different types of entrepreneurs); the impact of regulations, economic reforms and support programmes on business-start-up, survival and growth rates; the impact of cultural aspects on entrepreneurial activity levels; the influence of entrepreneurship education on the motivation to become an entrepreneur; and the different approaches and mechanisms for developing the entrepreneurial potential of young people and women.

Evidence suggests that the Tunisian government may have the most comprehensive approach to policies stimulating entrepreneurship. Not only has the government set a target to achieve the creation of 70 000 new enterprises between 2005 and 2009, but the Agency for Promotion of Industry within the Ministry of Industry and Technology has the Centre de Soutien de la Création d'Entreprise with many measures to promote new enterprise activity and entrepreneurship development. Such measures include entrepreneurship training, start-up financing schemes, university incubators (*pépinières*), advice and support at both national and regional levels, and the introduction of entrepreneurship courses in university curriculum. The MIEPME (renamed the Ministry of Industry and Technology in 2010) and the Ministry of Higher Education (MHE) have even signed an accord whereby the MHE agreed to launch *pépinières* on university campuses and to promote entrepreneurship among university students and graduates. In April 2005 the MIEPME launched a national campaign for the creation and development of SMEs that included programme

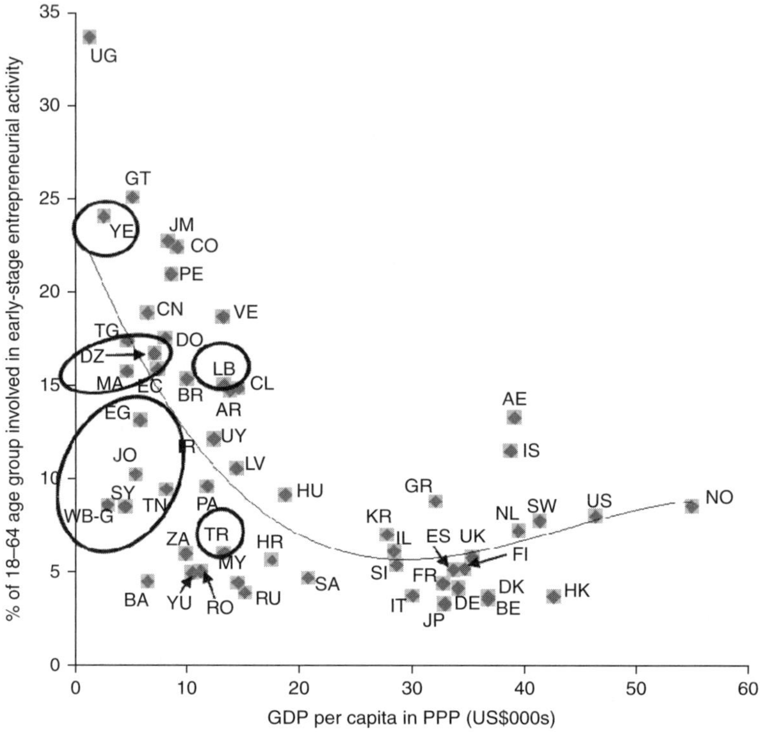

Note: DZ is Algeria.

Sources: GEM data, 2008, 2009.

Figure 4.5 Early-stage entrepreneurial activity and per capita GDP

measures for creation, quality and coaching with a particular emphasis on creating an entrepreneurial culture among young Tunisians. Governments in Algeria and Morocco also set 2005–09 targets for the new number of new enterprises and have agencies and programmes in place to stimulate enterprise creation activity among university graduates; however Tunisia's approach appears the most integrated. It is interesting to note that in Iraq and Morocco television programmes are used to create more awareness of entrepreneurial opportunities by profiling stories on SME owners.

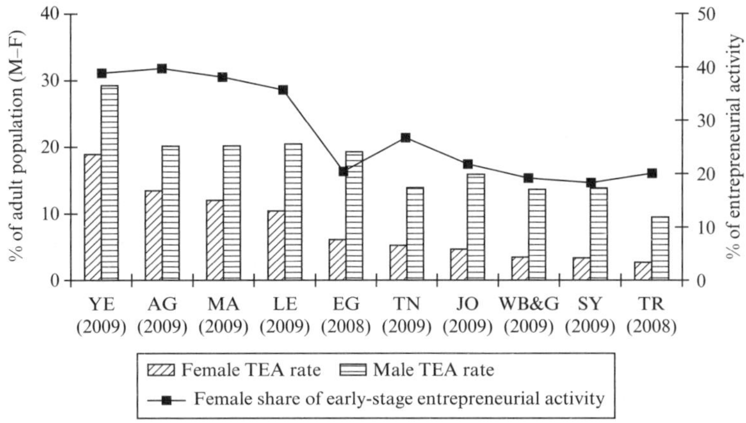

Sources: GEM APS data, 2008, 2009

Figure 4.6 Female entrepreneurial activity levels

Women's Entrepreneurship

As pointed out in Chapters 2 and 3, cultural, social, economic and familial barriers affect women's level of participation in economic activity in MENA-12 countries. Their low rate of participation in the labour force naturally spills over to their entrepreneurship and business ownership activity levels, as discussed earlier in Chapter 4. Many barriers have been identified as being critical to women's greater involvement in entrepreneurship, such as culture, collateral, credit, capability, mobility, discriminatory gender practices, gender segregation in labour markets and so on (FEMISE 2006b; IFC and CAWTAR 2007).

Until recently there has been very little data on the level of female entrepreneurial activity. GEM results for 2008 and 2009 reveal that women's early-stage entrepreneurial activity rates vary considerably across the ten MENA-12 countries (Figure 4.6). The male entrepreneurial activity rate is more than four times the female rate in the West Bank & Gaza and Syria, and more than three times higher in Turkey, Jordan and Egypt. The female share of early-stage entrepreneurial activity in these five countries is around 20 per cent, in contrast to above 35 per cent in Algeria, Yemen, Morocco and Lebanon, where male TEA rates are around one and a half times those of females.

The interest in women's entrepreneurship in MENA countries is relatively recent. Women-owned enterprise only became a policy issue in Jordan when it was raised in the UN *Country Assessment Report* presented to the Jordanian government in 2006. Subsequently the Royal Court asked the Jordan Forum for Business and Professional Women (JFBPW) for a strategic action plan on women's entrepreneurship to be added as a component in the government's five-year National Agenda Plan. In 2000, the Egyptian Prime Minister created a National Council for Women (NCW) to advise the government on strategies to increase the role of women in SMEs. Some policy attention is being paid to women's entreprencurship in Morocco, but mostly at the programme level. There is no evidence that any of the countries has a strategic policy framework for the development of women's entrepreneurship.

Given that the formal private sector in many MENA countries discriminates against women in its hiring practices, entrepreneurship is a strong option for women who want to become economically active. In addition to the need for policies and actions to remove gender biases in formal private sector hiring practices, policies to enhance the opportunities for women to be more successfully involved in entrepreneurship activity are also needed. Small-scale programme initiatives have been implemented in some of the countries. Egypt's NCW has established a Women Business Development Center to provide training, counselling and assistance to existing SMEs owned by women and to women trying to start new enterprises; the Moroccan Agence Nationale pour la Promotion de la Petite et Moyenne Enterprise (ANPME) delivers a Promotion of Women Entrepreneurship programme funded by German Technical Cooperation (GTZ), offers training to women entrepreneurs through the Taahil Almokawalat scheme and cooperates with the Association des Femmes Chefs d'Entreprises du Maroc (AFEM) on the Women's Financing Programme. In Syria the Modernizing and Activating Women's Role in Economic Development (MAWRED) non-governmental organization (NGO) operates a network of business incubators to encourage women's inclusion in business, and the Syria Trust for Development coordinates the Women Village Incubators project. The Jordan MicroLoan Fund for Women is one of the largest in that country. In Yemen the Women Economic Empowerment Association (WEEA) has formed over 60 lending groups of women in microenterprises, where the women manage their own savings and lending projects.

Donors and NGOs are providing various forms of support for women's entrepreneurship development in some MENA countries. This includes targeting women clients in donor-funded microfinance programmes, building the capacity of businesswomen associations and advocacy NGOs, and conducting research. Businesswomen associations exist in most of the MENA-12 countries but they differ substantially in their capacities, services and advocacy strengths. One of the most developed is the Jordan Forum for Business and Professional Women, which has been conducting comprehensive research on women entrepreneurs and their enterprises to influence government policy. Other organizations such as the Egyptian Business Women Association (EBWA), the Association des Femmes Chefs d'Entreprises du Maroc (AFEM), the Women Entrepreneurs Association of Turkey (KAGDIR), and the Lebanese Business Women Association have done much to raise the profile of women entrepreneurs through conferences, promotion and advocacy activity.

There is little evidence of substantial efforts at the policy and programme level to increase the participation of women in enterprise activity and to accelerate the growth of their firms. Only a few studies have been done on the state of women's entrepreneurship in MENA countries. The International Finance Corporation report on women entrepreneurs[12] recommended that further research be done to compare the characteristics, contributions and challenges of women and men business owners (IFC and CAWTAR 2007). The report also recommended that policymakers consult more extensively with women entrepreneurs on policy formulation, and stressed the importance of building capacity in businesswomen associations.

There are no regional networks for policymakers to exchange knowledge and experience on the issue of women's enterprise development and there may be merit in encouraging such an exchange. The Women Business Leaders Forum, launched at the November 2007 OECD-MENA Investment Programme ministerial meeting in Cairo, is intended to create a platform for regular dialogue between the OECD-MENA Investment Programme and regional bodies working on improving the economic status of women in the MENA region (OECD 2007c). One of the anticipated outcomes of the forum will be actions to improve the framework for women's entrepreneurship, including the adoption of policies and initiatives which could improve the current challenges facing women business leaders and encourage a higher participation of women in economic activities. An Action Plan will guide the forum's activities through Forum Chapters to be established in each of the participating MENA countries, but progress on operationalizing these chapters has been very slow.

This concludes the description of the major economic challenges in the MENA-12 countries and sets the stage for exploring in more detail the context for private sector and enterprise development. Chapter 5 examines the capacity and conditions for unleashing of the market economy, and brings together a number of indicators to compare countries on the extent of their private sector dynamism.

NOTES

1. Turkey was the only country in the MENA-12 included in the SME database. The time period covered by the analysis was 1990–99. The authors differentiate between SMEs, which in their database refers to 'formal' enterprises, and the informal sector, which includes non-registered enterprises.
2. In low- and middle-income countries the informal sector accounts for 29.14 per cent of total employment and formal SMEs for only 17.56 per cent; the respective shares in high-income countries are 15.16 per cent and 57.24 per cent (Ayyagari et al. 2003, p. 10).
3. MEDSTAT is a regional statistical programme of cooperation between the European Union and various Mediterranean countries – specifically Algeria, Egypt, Israel, Jordan, Lebanon, Morocco, Palestine, Syria, Tunisia and Turkey.
4. The SME growth rate in the West Bank & Gaza accelerated to 4.5 per cent in the 2004–07 period.
5. Sudan data are from 1993 and were the latest available.
6. Prior to this renaming in 2010, the Ministry was called the Ministére de l'Industrie, de l'Energie et des Petites et Moyennes Enterprises (MIEPME).
7. The Guillotine Review method to regulatory reform involves a rapid three-step review of existing legislation and regulations with the intent of eliminating regulations that are not needed and simplifying ones that are too complex.
8. Algeria had a target to create 100 000 new enterprises from 2004 to 2009, Morocco had a target for 30 000 new enterprises and Tunisia had a target for 70 000 new enterprises.
9. See www.gemconsortium.org for more information on the GEM project.
10. The IDRC pilot project supported GEM research in Algeria, Jordan, Lebanon, Morocco, Syria, the West Bank & Gaza and Yemen.
11. The country with the highest TEA rate in the 2009 GEM study is Uganda – 33.6 per cent; the lowest TEA rate is in Japan – 3.3 per cent (Bosma and Levie 2010).
12. The IFC project produced a comparative study of women's entrepreneurship in Bahrain, Jordan, Lebanon, Tunisia and the United Arab Emirates in cooperation with the Center for Arab Women Training and Research (CAWTAR).

5. MENA countries, the market economy and the environment for private sector development

A market-led economy is one largely driven by the private sector with a minimal role for government in economic activity, except as regulator and facilitator, and intervening only where there are clear market failures (World Bank 2005f). The key elements in transition to a market economy include privatization of state-owned enterprises (SOEs); creating a market-friendly business environment by reducing rules, administrative burden and costs, promoting competition and limiting monopolistic behaviour; fostering a viable financial sector that channels resources to productive investments (liberalization); stimulating a willing and able cadre of entrepreneurs to take up the supply response with confidence that investment climate improvements are permanent; and openness to trade that will allow global integration. Actions in these areas are believed to contribute to a stronger, more vibrant private sector.

Although the Middle East and North Africa (MENA) region has made progress in implementing market economy reforms, the World Bank (2007b) describes it as among the least business-friendly in the world, with burdensome and costly procedures that thwart business development and a broad range of practices hindering the full emergence of the private sector. Key sectors in many of the countries remain closed to competition due to high levels of industry concentration (Sekkat 2010) and regulatory restrictions. Overall progress on service sector reform, including liberalization of financial services, transport, telecommunications,[1] power and water falls below that of other economies in transition (World Bank 2007b). In spite of evidence that direct engagement of the state in the productive sector has serious negative effects on private initiative and dynamic, competitive markets (OECD 2004a), privatization of SOEs in the MENA region has been slow and barriers to entry often discourage investors. Corruption and deficiencies in governance and administrative reform in the public sector persist, calling for further efforts to increase public sector accountability in the areas of transparency and contestability of government policies (World Bank 2009c).

AT DIFFERENT STAGES OF MARKET ECONOMY TRANSITION

Following long periods of a development approach based on heavy state intervention and a very limited private sector role, the MENA-12 countries are at different stages of transition to being market-led economies. Some of the governments started to move towards the market economy model in the mid-1980s and by the 1990s most had done the same. Early initiatives focused on macroeconomic stabilization programmes, privatization and reforms to encourage investment and exports. Turkey, Jordan and Morocco began the liberalization reform process in the 1980s; Tunisia, Algeria, Egypt, Sudan, Syria and Yemen in the 1990s; and Iraq and the West Bank & Gaza in the early part of the 2000s. Due to political instability, interruptions caused by war and conflict or changes in government, even countries that started earlier with liberalization and opening-up reforms entered a 'new phase' of national reforms in the post-2000 era. A major impetus for this new phase of reforms in individual countries is associated with meeting requirements for accession to the World Trade Organization (WTO), European Union (EU) Association Agreements or entry to the Gulf Cooperation Council (GCC), but can also be related to changes in regime and political leadership, where 2000 appears to have been a pivotal time point in many of the countries.

The MENA-12 are also in different phases of their privatization efforts, an important policy action in the transition to a private sector-led market economy.[2] The first recorded privatization transactions took place in Turkey in 1988 (OECD 2007a), although the government first established a Privatization Administration in 1985 (EC 2005c). Its initial emphasis was on divesting the smaller SOEs operating in competitive sectors, mainly industry and tourism, later turning to network utilities and infrastructure. Tunisia, Egypt, Morocco and Sudan were next to embark on privatization activity. Since then most of the MENA-12 governments have adopted privatization plans to divest or restructure state-owned and controlled enterprises, although some have been more forceful than others in implementing their plans. These governments also have different policies with respect to privatization[3] and adopt different mechanisms – sale of shares and assets, restructuring SOEs into 100 per cent owned independent corporations, management buyouts, joint ventures and 'corporatization'.[4]

Many divestments have been made in Turkey, Tunisia and Morocco,[5] while governments in Algeria, Iraq, Yemen and Syria still own a large number of SOEs in key industry sectors. The Moroccan government approved its first privatization programme in 1989 and with most of its privatization completed is considered one of the most advanced in the region (World Bank 2006c). The Algerian government launched its privatization programme in 1995, but according to the World Bank, 'a comprehensive scheme for large-scale privatization is far from being set up' (World Bank 2006c) even though many small-scale SOEs have been sold. The Sudanese government also started early (Privatization Plan in 1992) and has gone through two phases of privatization activities that peaked in 1993. Suliman (2007) describes Sudan's efforts as largely unsuccessful due to corruption and a lack of democratic accountability, and because privatizations led to substantial increases in unemployment with no social protection for retrenched workers. Jordan and Iraq[6] embarked on privatization plans in 2000 or later, and although the Syrian government passed a law in 2001 to end state monopolies it is still considering alternative options to full-scale privatization. Governments that are holding on to their SOEs often fear the potential negative impact of privatization on employment, given already high unemployment rates and a limited private sector to absorb possible labour surpluses. On the other hand some governments that have privatized report employment gains from divestment as well as increased foreign direct investment (FDI) inflows.

Governments in some of the MENA-12 countries have also acknowledged later than others the importance of enabling a private sector-led market economy. According to the assessments and conclusions of international organizations and donor agencies about the market economy status of the 12 countries: Turkey is considered a functioning market economy; Tunisia as a 'newly industrialized country' and the most competitive economy in the African and Arabian region (being one of the first countries in the region to open its economy and introduce measures to improve the business climate); Morocco as a country that has embraced the principle of a market-based economy but lacks a truly competitive environment for the private sector (Bertelsmann Stiftung 2008c); the West Bank & Gaza as one of the most open economies in the Middle East (MNE 2005), although conflict issues prevent it from realizing the benefits of that openness; Lebanon as one of the Middle East's most advanced economies, with a history of liberalism and private sector dominance (Holmes et al. 2008); Jordan as a country that has made impressive gains in full implementation of a market economy (Bertelsmann Stiftung 2008b); Egypt as a top reforming country on the ease of doing business (World Bank 2008i), but one where the institutional framework of the market economy suffers from structural weaknesses; Syria as a 'largely state-controlled economy that only recently embarked on a reform path' (WEF 2008a, p. 33) or as a self-proclaimed 'social market economy' on the way to reform (SEBC 2007, p. 20); Algeria as a country where economic

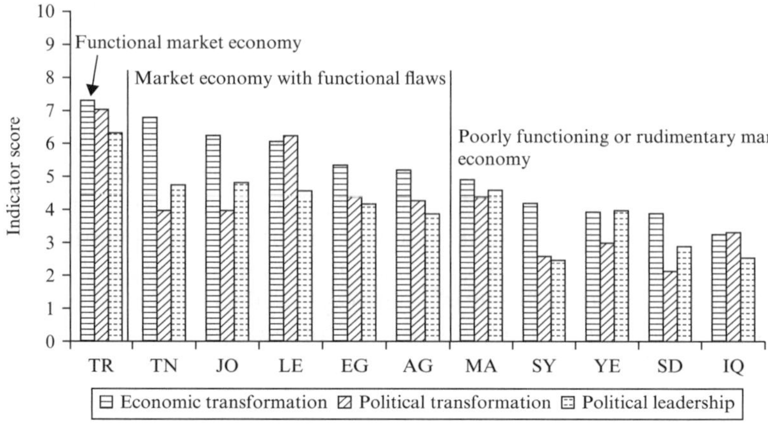

Note: Scores are based on a scale of 1–10, with 10 being the best.

Source: Data from BTI, Bertelsmann Stiftung (2008a).

Figure 5.1 Market economy transition status, MENA countries

reform is stifled by easy access to oil and gas revenues and where many of the market economy framework structures are still to be developed (Bertelsmann Stiftung 2008a); Iraq as a nascent market economy (World Bank 2004a), which until 2005 had virtually no private sector; and Yemen as one of the least competitive economies in the world (UNDP 2006a) that, along with Sudan, has made little progress toward being a market economy and shows limited evidence of the emergence of a dynamic private sector (Bertelsmann Stiftung 2008a).

The Bertelsmann Transformation Index (BTI) examines the market economy development and transformation processes of 125 countries using 52 indicators on 17 criteria to measure the level of political transformation, the level of market economy transformation and the degree of political leadership in implementing market economy reforms (Bertelsmann Stiftung 2008a).[7] The BTI 2008 results for 11 of the MENA-12 countries are presented in Figure 5.1. Only Turkey meets the BTI criteria of a functional market economy. Five of the MENA-12 countries are categorized as market economies with functional flaws, and five are categorized as poorly functioning or rudimentary market economies. Turkey ranks in the top quarter of the 125 countries (32nd place) and Syria, Iraq and Sudan are in the bottom 10 per cent. Turkey, Algeria and Egypt recorded the most improvement in their economic transformation scores since the 2006 BTI, while Syria and Sudan did not progress at all.

PRIVATE SECTOR SCOPE AND CAPACITY

It would be ideal to have a clear set of indicators and data to measure where a country is in terms of its private sector development (PSD). Unfortunately that does not appear to be the case, as highlighted in Chapter 1. Indicators such as the private sector share of gross domestic product (GDP), employment and investment would give an indication of the relative size of the public and private sectors. Measuring the inflow of FDI would provide an indication of the openness of the economy for private sector activities. Domestic credit to the private sector to GDP could be used as an indicator for the capital available for private sector growth. Indicators such as the density of private sector SMEs would provide a measure of the prevalence of independent enterprise; business entry and exit rates[8] would measure of the level of economic dynamism in the economy, and so on. Because of the lack of comparable data on some of these indicators, it is difficult to monitor changes within countries over time and to make cross-country comparisons. Attempts to analyse the capacity of a country for PSD and pro-poor, inclusive growth outcomes must also include human development indicators, such as literacy and education, poverty levels, inequality and gender equity – all issues of growing concern in MENA-12 countries.

The following presents comparative data on key available indicators (not already covered in Chapters 3 and 4) to assist in a better understanding of the scale and scope of the private sector and the environment for private sector expansion in the MENA-12. Indicators to measure the relative size of the public and private sectors and their role in employment and capital formation, the scale of private credit availability, the friendliness of the business-enabling environment and the level of economic freedom are used in the analysis. These are combined with other indicators discussed in previous chapters, such as GDP growth rates, employment-related rates, entrepreneurship density rates and human development indicators, to categorize the MENA-12 countries on the relative status of their PSD performance.

The Relative Size of the Public Sector: Spending, Employment and Capital Investment

The first set of PSD indicators has to do with the size of government. Three measures are used for this: the level of government spending, the public–private sector share of total employment and the public–private share of gross capital formation. Another key useable indicator would be the private sector share of GDP, but recent comparable data for all

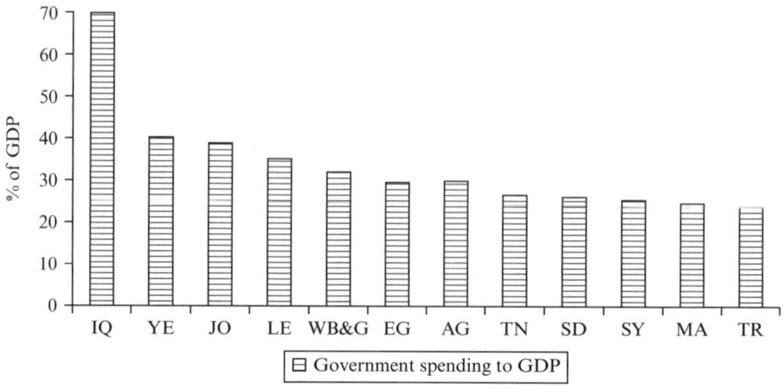

Sources: Data from country profiles in Heritage Foundation (2010). Data for the WB&G from the WDI database.

Figure 5.2 Government spending to GDP

MENA-12 countries are not available. However the World Bank (2009c, p. 26) indicates that the private sector share of non-hydrocarbon GDP is in the 70–75 per cent range for Egypt, Morocco and Tunisia; 80 per cent or higher for Algeria, Syria, Jordan and Lebanon; and more than 90 per cent for Yemen. (It should be noted that if hydrocarbons were included, the share of private sector GDP in Algeria and Yemen would fall to between 40 and 50 per cent.) Growth in the private sector share of GDP in MENA countries has been relatively static since at least 2000.

The level of public expenditure is one way in which the state exerts its influence on the economy and society.[9] The comparison of MENA-12 countries on the level of their government spending to GDP is illustrated in Figure 5.2. This ranges from a high of 70 per cent of GDP in Iraq, to less than 25 per cent in Turkey and Morocco. Five of the countries – Iraq, Yemen, Jordan, Lebanon and the West Bank & Gaza – have government spending exceeding 30 per cent of GDP, which is treated as a key threshold by the Heritage Foundation in their calculations for the Index of Economic Freedom, beyond which they start to penalize countries in their rating on this indicator (Heritage Foundation 2009). Some level of government expenditure is warranted for the provision of public goods and services that are more efficiently provided by the state than the market, or to correct market failures, but if excessively high this can crowd out the private sector, lead to market distortions and create long-term damage to a country's growth potential.

Another indicator to measure the size of the public versus the private

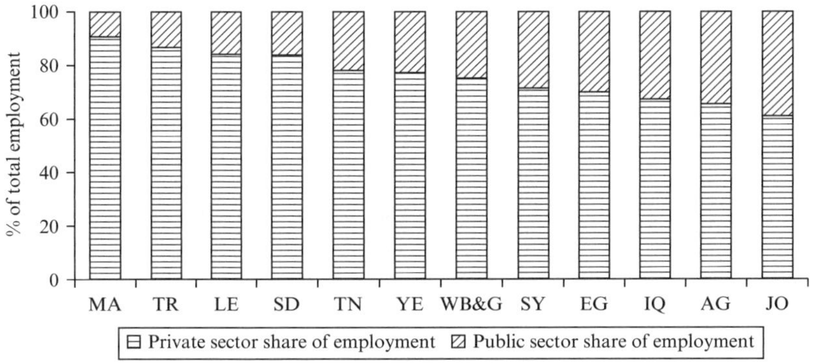

Sources: Various country-level data sources for latest year 2004–2008.

Figure 5.3 Private and public share of employment

sector is the share of total employment. Iraq, Algeria and Jordan have the largest public sector shares of total employment, exceeding 32 per cent. On the other hand, the share of private sector employment in Morocco, Turkey, Lebanon and Sudan exceeds 80 per cent of total employment[10] (Figure 5.3).

The level of gross investment in fixed capital is one of the key indicators of growth in economies. Total investment in developing countries tends to fall in the range of 15–30 per cent of GDP, with the public sector share between 20 and 40 per cent and the private share between 60 and 80 per cent (Harberger 2005). Gross investment in high-growth countries typically exceeds 25 per cent of GDP, and it falls below 20 per cent in low-growth countries (OECD 2004a). Blanc and Louis (2007) suggest that an investment to GDP ratio of 30 per cent or more is needed to foster strong economic growth performance. When investment is low, the productive capacity of the economy fails to increase, leading to lower rates of job creation and fewer opportunities for the poor to improve their standard of living (OECD 2004a). However it is not only the level of investment that matters, but the share of investment in productive sectors, modern technology and innovation that leads to increases in labour productivity.

The proportion of private capital formation in gross investment provides some indication of the role and strength of the private sector in the economy. A higher share of private investment in gross investment could indicate a more favourable investment climate – one that reduces costs, risks and barriers to competition (World Bank 2005c). A lower share of private investment in a country may indicate crowding out by public investment.

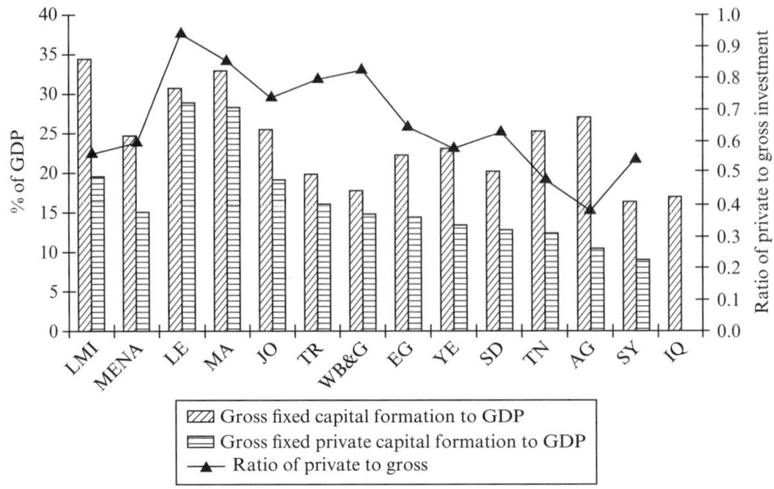

Sources: World Bank 'Private Sector at a Glance' country data, 26 April 2010 (2008 data); UN database, 2007, for the WB&G and IQ. No available private capital formation data for IQ.

Figure 5.4 Private share of gross capital formation

Gross capital formation in the MENA-12 amounted to an average of 23.2 per cent of GDP in 2008, lower than the average for lower-middle-income (LMI) countries (34.5 per cent) and for the MENA region as a whole (24.8 per cent), which includes the oil-rich Gulf countries. However it ranged from a high of 33 per cent in Morocco to a low of 16.4 per cent in Syria (Figure 5.4). Only Lebanon, Morocco, Jordan and Tunisia exceeded 25 per cent, and Turkey, the West Bank & Gaza, Syria and Iraq fell below 20 per cent. Private capital formation to GDP averaged 16.3 per cent, above the average for LMI countries and just below the MENA region average; it ranged from almost 30 per cent in Lebanon and Morocco to 9 per cent in Syria. The ratio of private to gross investment was highest in Lebanon, Morocco, Turkey and the West Bank & Gaza (80 per cent or more of gross investment) and lowest in Algeria and Tunisia (less than 55 per cent). Eight of the MENA-12 countries outperformed the LMI country average on this indicator, and seven outperformed the MENA region.

During the 2000–2008 period only Jordan, Sudan and Turkey achieved annual growth in gross capital formation of more than the lower- and upper-middle-income (LUMI) country average of 9.8 per cent. Growth in the private investment share of GDP was uneven across the MENA countries between 1995 and 2006, increasing moderately in Egypt, Morocco,

Yemen and Tunisia and declining in Jordan, Lebanon, Algeria and Syria (World Bank 2009c, p. 53).

The Relative Level of Private Sector Credit

Access to private credit is a key factor in economic and private sector growth. The critical determinants of growth in private credit are: (1) the extent of public sector crowding out; (2) the effectiveness of regulatory institutions, legal systems and contract enforcement; (3) the presence of informational and transactional infrastructure (such as credit bureaus); and (4) the structure of the banking system in terms of ownership and concentration (OECD 2004a). Common causes of low private sector credit growth are poor regulatory supervision of the banking system, crowding out by the public sector, government-imposed policies directing bank lending, and lack of competition in the banking system.

The level of domestic credit to the private sector to GDP[11] and the level of domestic credit provided by the banking sector[12] as a percentage of GDP are used as important PSD indicators. The private sector credit to GDP indicator points to the proportion of capital in the country being utilized by the private sector and is evidence of the extent of financial deepening. Rapidly growing economies have significantly higher levels of private sector credit to GDP than low-growth economies (OECD 2004a). The level of domestic credit provided by the banking sector is an indicator of the level of banking sector liberalization as well as the level of competition from private banks.

On the first indicator Jordan, Morocco, Lebanon and Tunisia were the top MENA-12 performers in 2008, each outperforming the average for LUMI and MENA-wide countries (Figure 5.5). Domestic credit to the private sector would appear to be relatively more constrained in Syria, Algeria, Sudan, Yemen and the West Bank & Gaza. Lebanon is by far the best performer of the MENA-12 on the level of domestic credit provided by the banking sector as a percentage of GDP (173 per cent) and, together with Jordan, Morocco and Egypt, is above the average for both LUMI and MENA-wide countries. The performance of Yemen, the West Bank & Gaza, Sudan and Algeria is well below the average for both LUMI and MENA region countries. Algeria, Iraq, Syria and Yemen have very recent experience with liberalization of the banking sector, while the five top-performing countries have been encouraging the entry of foreign and private banks for much longer. However there is evidence of public sector crowding out of private sector access to financing, and banks would still prefer lending to public entities, SOEs and large firms than to SMEs. The low level of domestic credit in the case of Sudan is affected by large domestic arrears and

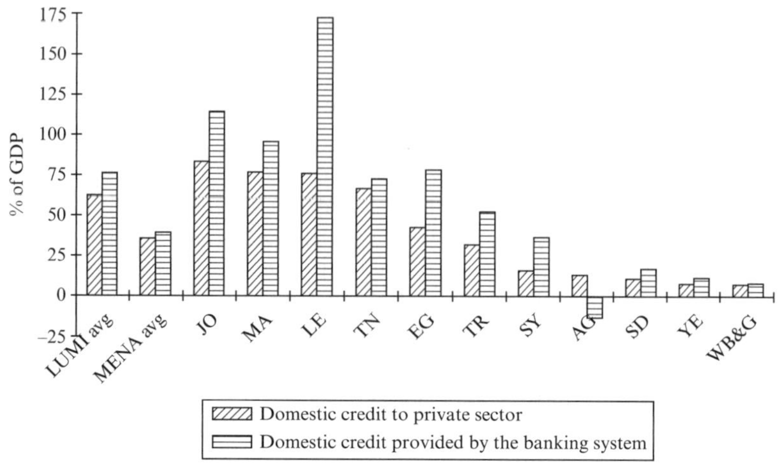

Source: WDI, World Bank (2010), data for 2008 or latest year. No data for IQ.

Figure 5.5 Private sector credit and credit provided by the banking sector to GDP

non-performing loans (IMF 2008a). The lack of credit information sources in the MENA countries and limited sharing of what does exist creates high information asymmetries.

Financial services in MENA countries are in great need of further liberalization, development and expansion. The World Bank (2007b) reports that only 12 per cent of the financing of MENA firms comes from the banking sector, lower than in any other region of the world. The high level of public ownership of banks, the lack of competition and restrictive lending practices are among the major problems. State-owned banks hold over 90 per cent of bank assets in Algeria (FSAP 2004) and Iraq, and at the end of 2007 still owned 94 per cent of all bank assets in Syria (OBG 2009). The government's share of bank assets in Morocco, Turkey and Yemen is around a third. This compares to an average of less than 7 per cent in East Asia and Pacific countries, and 12 per cent in Europe and Central Asia (World Bank 2006c, p. 77).

The Enabling Business Environment

Two global indexes are used in this chapter to compare MENA-12 countries on the enabling business environment, a critical dimension for PSD: the World Bank Doing Business Index and the Heritage Foundation Index of Economic Freedom (IEF).

Sources: *Doing Business* reports (World Bank 2007a, 2008b, 2008c, 2009b).

Figure 5.6 Country rankings on Doing Business

Rankings in the World Bank Doing Business survey are becoming routinely used as an indicator of the business-friendliness of country environments and their capacity for increased private sector activity. The Doing Business indicators measure the extent to which regulations affecting business and the protection of property rights act as enhancements or constraints in ten areas of activity: (1) starting a business; (2) dealing with construction permits; (3) employing workers; (4) registering property; (5) getting credit; (6) protecting investors; (7) paying taxes; (8) trading across borders; (9) enforcing contracts; and (10) closing a business. Values and rankings for 183 countries on these indicators reflect the comparative ease of doing business.

Tunisia and Turkey have the highest rankings among the MENA-12 in the *Doing Business 2010* report (World Bank 2009b) and most favourable environments for business, and Iraq and Sudan have the lowest rankings (Figure 5.6). Over the four years from 2007 only Egypt has consistently improved its rankings on a year-to-year basis, moving from 165th place in the 2007 report to 106th place in the 2010 report, and recognized by the World Bank as one of the top reformers among all countries during this period. On the other hand the relative performance of Lebanon, Algeria, the West Bank & Gaza and Iraq has consistently deteriorated. In the 2010 report, only Tunisia, Yemen, Jordan, Egypt and Morocco recorded improvements in their ranking performance over 2009. Turkey lost the most ranking positions in 2010, moving from 63rd place in 2009 to 73rd place in 2010. The scores for each of the *Doing Business 2010* indicators for the MENA-12 countries are presented in Table 5.1.

The Level of Economic Freedom

The Index of Economic Freedom (IEF), published annually by the Heritage Foundation, is based on the principle that free exchange, openness and competition are the foundation for economic growth and well-being. As part of its definition of economic freedom, the Heritage Foundation states: 'individuals in an economically free society would be free and entitled to work, produce, consume, and invest in any way they please under a rule of law, with their freedom at once both protected and respected by the state' (Heritage Foundation 2009, p. 11). The IEF is built on analysis of the ten freedom components listed in Table 5.2, which taken together provide a portrait of a country's free market economic policies and assess the strengths and weaknesses of its institutional quality relative to cross-country comparisons and benchmarks.

The Heritage Foundation analysis of cross-country performance over the 15 years from 1995 to 2009 indicates that countries which have opened up to the 'productivity-boosting competition of the global marketplace' have experienced higher levels of prosperity than countries where economic freedoms are constrained (Heritage Foundation 2009, p. xii). It has demonstrated that economic freedom is key to creating an environment where entrepreneurship and innovation can flourish, resulting in rapid economic growth, sustainable development, higher per capita income and improvements in overall human development. The Heritage Foundation also asserts that higher economic freedom environments empower the poor and build the middle class.

Nine of the MENA-12 countries were included among the 179 countries in the *2010 Index of Economic Freedom*[13] (Heritage Foundation 2010). Jordan has the highest level of economic freedom for this set of nine countries with a global ranking of 52 (Table 5.3). Both Jordan and Turkey are assessed as being 'moderately free' (keeping company with the top 40 per cent of all countries); while the remaining countries, with the exception of Syria, are considered 'moderately unfree' (keeping company with the bottom half). Syria has the lowest level of economic freedom of the nine MENA-12 countries, down almost two points from 2009 and slipping into the 'repressed' economy category.

The nine MENA countries performed best in the category of fiscal freedom (average score of 82) and relatively well against the other 179 countries on business freedom, fiscal freedom and government size. They

Table 5.1 *Scores on* Doing Business 2010 *indicators*

Doing Business ranking/ scores (2009) (*Doing Business 2010* report)	TN	TR	YE	JO	EG	LE	MA	AG	WB&G	SY	SD	IQ
Overall rank	69	73	99	100	106	108	128	136	139	143	154	150
Starting a business												
Number of procedures	10	6	6	8	6	5	6	14	11	7	10	11
Time in days	11	6	12	13	7	9	12	24	49	17	36	77
Cost (% of income per capita)	5.9	14.2	83.0	49.5	16.1	78.2	16.1	12.1	55.0	27.8	36.0	75.9
Minimum paid-in capital requirement (% of income per capita)	0.0	9.5	0.0	19.9	0	51.0	11.8	31.0	220.4	1012.5	0.0	30.3
Dealing with construction permits												
Number of procedures	20	25	15	19	25	20	19	22	21	26	19	14
Time to deal with permits	84	188	107	87	218	211	163	240	199	128	271	215
Cost to deal with permits (% of income per capita)	998.3	218.8	144.1	697.1	331.6	194.8	263.7	39.6	1110.6	540.3	206.4	915.0
Employing workers												
Rigidity of employment index	40	35	24	24	27	25	60	41	31	20	36	24

Table 5.1 (continued)

Doing Business ranking/ scores (2009) (*Doing Business 2010* report)	TN	TR	YE	JO	EG	LE	MA	AG	WB&G	SY	SD	IQ
Firing cost (weeks of salary)	17	95	17	4	132	17	85	17	91	80	118	0
Registering property												
Number of procedures	4	6	6	7	7	8	8	11	7	4	6	5
Number of days	39	6	19	21	72	25	47	47	47	19	9	8
Cost (% of income per capita)	6.1	3.0	3.8	7.5	0.9	5.8	4.9	7.1	0.7	28.0	3.0	7.7
Getting credit												
Public registry coverage (% of adults)	19.9	15.9	0.2	1.0	2.5	8.3	0.0	0.2	6.5	0.0	0.0	0.0
Private registry coverage (% of adults)	0.0	42.9	0.0	0.0	8.2	0.0	14.0	0.0	0.0	0.0	0.0	0.0
Depth of credit information (out of 10)	5	5	0	2	6	5	5	2	3	0	0	0
Strength of legal rights index (out of 10)	3	4	2	4	3	3	3	3	0	1	5	3
Protecting investors												
Investor protection index (out of 10)	5.3	5.7	4.0	4.3	5.3	5.0	3.0	5.3	6.0	4.3	3.3	4.3

Paying taxes												
Number of payments per year	22	15	44	26	29	19	28	34	27	20	42	13
Hours spent dealing with tax payments	228	223	248	101	480	180	358	451	154	336	180	312
Labour tax and contributions (%)	24.6	24.5	11.3	12.4	28.9	24.1	21.5	30.2	0.0	19.3	19.2	13.5
Total tax rate (% of profit)	62.8	44.5	47.8	31.1	43.0	30.2	41.7	72.0	16.8	42.9	36.1	28.4
Trading across borders												
Number of documents for export	5	7	6	7	6	5	7	8	6	8	6	10
Number of days to export	15	14	27	17	14	26	14	17	25	15	32	102
Cost to export (US$ per container)	$783	$990	$1129	$730	$737	$1002	$700	$1248	$835	$1190	$2050	$3900
Number of documents to import	7	8	9	7	6	7	10	9	6	9	6	10
Number of days to import	21	15	25	19	15	35	17	23	40	21	46	101
Cost to import (US$ per container)	$858	$1063	$1475	$1290	$823	$1203	$1000	$1428	$1225	$1625	$2900	$3900
Enforcing contracts												
Number of procedures to enforce a contract	39	35	36	38	41	37	40	46	44	55	53	51
Number of days to enforce a contract	565	420	520	689	1010	721	615	630	600	872	810	520
Cost to enforce a contract (% of claim)	21.8	18.8	16.5	31.2	26.2	30.8	25.2	21.9	21.2	29.3	19.8	27.3

Table 5.1 (continued)

Doing Business ranking/ scores (2009) (*Doing Business 2010* report)	TN	TR	YE	JO	EG	LE	MA	AG	WB&G	SY	SD	IQ
Closing a business												
Number of years to go through insolvency	1.3	3.3	3.0	4.3	4.2	4.0	1.8	2.5	..	4.1	..	..
Cost of insolvency (% of estate)	7.0	15.0	8.0	9.0	22.0	22.0	18.0	7.0	..	9.0	..	..
Recovery rate (cents on the dollar)	$0.523	$0.202	$0.286	$0.273	$0.168	$0.190	$0.351	$0.417	..	$0.295	..	..

Source: World Bank (2009b).

Table 5.2 Components of the Index of Economic Freedom

Component	Measurement
Freedom # 1: Business Freedom	Measure of the ability to start, operate and close a business without interference from the state. It assesses the level of overall burden of regulation and efficiency of government in the regulatory process (uses indicators from the World Bank *Doing Business* assessment).
Freedom # 2: Trade Freedom	Measure of the openness of an economy to imports and the ability of citizens to interact freely as buyers and sellers in the international marketplace (absence of tariff and non-tariff barriers).
Freedom # 3: Fiscal Freedom	Measure of the burden of government, particularly from taxation, and the freedom individuals and businesses have to keep and control their income and wealth.
Freedom # 4: Government Size	Measure of the size of government spending.
Freedom # 5: Monetary Freedom	Measure of price stability and assessment of market-determined prices (as opposed to price controls).
Freedom # 6: Investment Freedom	Measure of overall investment climate (policies towards the free flow of foreign and domestic investment capital).
Freedom # 7: Financial Freedom	Measure of banking security and independence from government control.
Freedom # 8: Property Rights	Measure of the degree to which a country's laws protect private property rights and are enforced.
Freedom # 9: Freedom from Corruption	Measure of the level of corruption in the country.
Freedom # 10: Labour Freedom	Measure of aspects of the legal and regulatory framework that restrict a country's labour market (regulations on minimum wage working hours and severance requirements, laws inhibiting lay-offs, regulatory burden on hiring and so on).

Source: Heritage Foundation (2009).

Table 5.3 Index of Economic Freedom scores, 2010

Country	2010 rank	2010 score	Business freedom	Trade freedom	Fiscal freedom	Govern-ment size	Monetary freedom	Invest-ment freedom	Financial freedom	Property rights	Freedom from corruption	Labour freedom
Jordan	52	66.1	65.6	78.8	83.0	55.1	73.2	**65.0**	**60.0**	**55.0**	**51.0**	**74.2**
Turkey	67	63.8	68.9	**86.4**	78.1	**82.9**	70.0	**65.0**	50.0	50.0	46.0	41.1
Lebanon	89	59.5	56.6	80.5	**91.0**	62.8	71.4	55.0	**60.0**	30.0	30.0	57.0
Morocco	91	59.2	76.1	71.2	68.5	81.5	**78.4**	60.0	**60.0**	40.0	35.0	21.7
Egypt	94	59.0	65.0	74.0	**89.7**	73.4	64.2	50.0	50.0	40.0	28.0	55.6
Tunisia	95	58.9	**80.2**	53.5	74.4	78.5	76.5	35.0	30.0	50.0	44.0	67.4
Algeria	105	56.9	71.2	70.7	83.5	73.4	**77.2**	45.0	30.0	30.0	32.0	56.4
Yemen	121	54.4	74.4	76.1	83.2	51.3	65.1	45.0	30.0	30.0	23.0	65.4
Syria	145	49.4	59.2	54.0	87.0	80.2	63.3	20.0	20.0	25.0	21.0	64.7
Avg for the nine MENA countries		*58.6*	*68.6*	*71.7*	*82.0*	*71.0*	*71.0*	*48.9*	*43.3*	*38.9*	*34.4*	*55.9*
Avg for 17 MENA countries		*60.4*	*67.1*	*75.2*	*87.0*	*68.9*	*68.9*	*45.3*	*45.9*	*41.5*	*40.2*	*64.1*
Avg for 179 countries		*59.8*	*64.6*	*74.2*	*75.4*	*65.0*	*70.6*	*49.0*	*48.5*	*43.8*	*40.5*	*62.1*

Note: Scores are out of 100. A score of 80–100 indicates a high degree of freedom economy; 70–79.9 a 'mostly free' economy; 60–69.9 a 'moderately free' economy; 50–59.9 a 'mostly unfree' economy; and below 50 a 'repressed economy'. 179 countries were ranked.

Source: Heritage Foundation (2010).

did not perform very well relative to the global average on financial freedom, property rights, freedom from corruption and labour market freedom, all freedoms that play a large role in promoting business and competitiveness. Particular note is made of the scores for property rights because the ability to accumulate personal property is the main motivating force in a market economy and vital to a fully functioning free market economy (Heritage Foundation 2009). If individuals and businesses do not have secure property rights, their ability to undertake commercial activities and borrow money for investment will be thwarted as well as their confidence in making long-term plans. This will act as a serious constraint on PSD, including the ability of the poor to improve their livelihood, a critical argument made by de Soto (2000). Only Jordan, Tunisia and Turkey have scores above the average for all countries on the property rights dimension and then only at the lower level for a 'mostly unfree' economy. The other six countries are among the 'repressed' economies on this dimension. This is obviously a policy area where MENA governments need to exercise more proactive efforts.

There is a great deal of variability in the performance on the different freedom dimensions within and across the nine MENA-12 countries. Tunisia has the highest level of business freedom; Turkey has the highest level of trade freedom and freedom from government; Lebanon and Egypt have the highest levels of fiscal freedom; Morocco and Algeria have the highest levels of monetary freedom; Jordan and Turkey have the highest levels of investment freedom (only 'moderately free'); Jordan, Lebanon and Morocco have the highest levels of financial freedom (only 'moderately free'); and Jordan has the highest level of property rights freedom, freedom of corruption (although at the 'mostly unfree' level) and labour freedom.

The most significant gains in economic freedom between 2005 and 2010 were achieved by Egypt, Morocco and Turkey, with slight improvements recorded by Lebanon, Tunisia and Yemen, and no measurable change by Jordan. Syria's performance on the IEF had improved considerably up until 2009 but deteriorated in 2010 (Heritage Foundation 2010).

The Level of Entrepreneurial Activity

The level of entrepreneurial and SME activity can also be used as an indicator of the level of PSD. Finding comparable measures for this indicator is somewhat difficult, as discussed in Chapter 4. The commonly used measure of SME density (SMEs per 1000 population) would be useful if MENA country data were complete and comparable, but this is not the case. However entrepreneurial activity rates from the Global

Entrepreneurship Monitor (owners of 'baby' and established businesses from Figure 4.4 in Chapter 4) and country-level self-employment rates (and share of employers) (also presented in Chapter 4) can be used as proxy measures. Including a measure for the proportion of the adult population that is actively trying to start a business (nascent entrepreneurs) can be used as another indicator of a country's entrepreneurial propensity. The level of informality might also be used to provide an indicator of the level of PSD in a country, but the direction of the relationship could be seen as either positive or negative. A high level of informality could be seen as positive because it indicates a high level of participation of independent enterprise in the economy, or as negative because it reflects a poor environment for the establishment of formal enterprises.

MAKING SENSE OF THE PSD INDICATORS

Key indicators suggestive of the level of PSD in a country have been described in Chapter 5 and preceding chapters. Using a selection of these indicators, an attempt is made to categorize the relative PSD positions of the MENA-12 countries. This categorization is the result of analysis based on their relative rankings[14] on a number of indicators associated with both private sector dynamism and economic outcomes. Private sector dynamism was also considered in relation to certain structural features of the economy that are believed to have an influence on PSD, such as government size, human capital and gender dimensions. The indicator variables used in the analysis are listed in Table 5.4.

The results for the positioning of countries on private sector dynamism and economic outcome indicators are illustrated in Figure 5.7. This analysis suggests that Lebanon, Morocco, Jordan, Egypt and Tunisia are doing comparatively well on both (Quadrant I), while Turkey is doing comparatively well on private sector dynamism but not as well on economic outcomes (Quadrant II). On the other hand Algeria is doing comparatively well on economic outcomes but not as well on private sector dynamism indicators (Quadrant III). Yemen, Sudan, the West Bank & Gaza, Syria and Iraq have comparatively weak performance on both economic outcomes and private sector dynamism indicators (Quadrant IV).

The positioning of each country on the three sets of indicators is illustrated in Figure 5.8. Lebanon, Jordan and Tunisia are the only three that have above-average private sector dynamism, economic outcomes and structural features. Yemen, Sudan and Iraq are below average on all three sets. Morocco and Egypt have above-average private sector dynamism and economic outcomes, in spite of below-average structural features.

Table 5.4 Variables for private sector dynamism, economic outcomes and structural features

Criteria	Variable	Sign for inclusive PSD
Private sector dynamism		
Private share of investment, credit and employment	• Net private FDI to GDP	+
	• Gross private fixed capital formation to GDP	+
	• Private share of gross fixed capital formation	+
	• Private sector share of employment	+
	• Domestic credit to private sector to GDP	+
	• Domestic private credit provided by the banking system to GDP	+
Dynamics of entrepreneurship	• Informal sector to GDP	+ *
	• Self-employment rate (own-account and employers) (as percentage of total employed workers)	+
	• Employer share of total self-employment	+
	• Nascent entrepreneur rate	+
	• Density of entrepreneurs per 100 population (owners of young and established enterprises)	+
Environment for business	• 2010 Doing Business ranking	+
	• Index of Economic Freedom score	+
Economic outcomes		
	• Real GDP growth rate (2008)	+
	• Rate of growth of GDP per capita	+
	• Labour force participation rate	+
	• Unemployment rate	-
	• Exports to GDP	+
	• Gross fixed capital formation (investment)	+
Structural features		
Quality of human capital and labour inputs	• Population age index (proportion of under age 15 population to the 65 and older population)	+
	• Life expectancy index (from HDI)	+
	• Education Index (from HDI)	+
	• Literacy rate	+
	• Female literacy gap	+
	• Share of women in employment	+
	• Population below the national poverty line	-

Table 5.4 (continued)

Criteria	Variable	Sign for inclusive PSD
Sector structure	• Service sector share of GDP relative to agricultural sector share	+
Size of government	• Government expenditure to GDP	-
	• Public sector share of employment	-
	• Public debt to GDP	-

Notes:
Plus and minus signs relate to whether high levels of each indicator would produce a positive or negative effect.
* A large informal economy may have negative effects on PSD because of the unfair competition to formal firms and generally reflects a poor business environment. On the other hand it also indicates a high level of private sector activity in the economy, even if not reflected in formal GDP statistics. For the purposes of this assessment the informal economy is treated as a positive measure for private sector dynamism.

Turkey is above average on private sector dynamism and structural features but below average on economic outcomes. The West Bank & Gaza is an interesting case. It has relatively weak private sector dynamism and economic outcomes, but with the exception of a high level of poverty, has relatively strong human capital dimensions. If the West Bank & Gaza was to achieve a higher level of freedom and action, it might well expect to improve its private sector performance. Algeria is above average on economic outcomes and below average on the other two, while Syria is above average on structural features and below average on private sector dynamism and economic outcomes.

Although there is a tendency for countries with higher private sector dynamism to have favourable structural features and better overall economic outcomes, and for countries with lower private sector dynamism to have weaker structural dimensions and overall economic outcomes, there is a high degree of intercountry variance on specific indicators of country context (Table 5.5). The scale and character of PSD therefore also differs. The possibilities for growth of the private sector in the West Bank & Gaza are much less than in Jordan and Tunisia, for example. Table 5.6 summarizes the results of the PSD context description for each country. Since these countries are at different points of transition and achieving at different levels of performance, they can potentially learn a lot from each other about how to improve their relative performance.

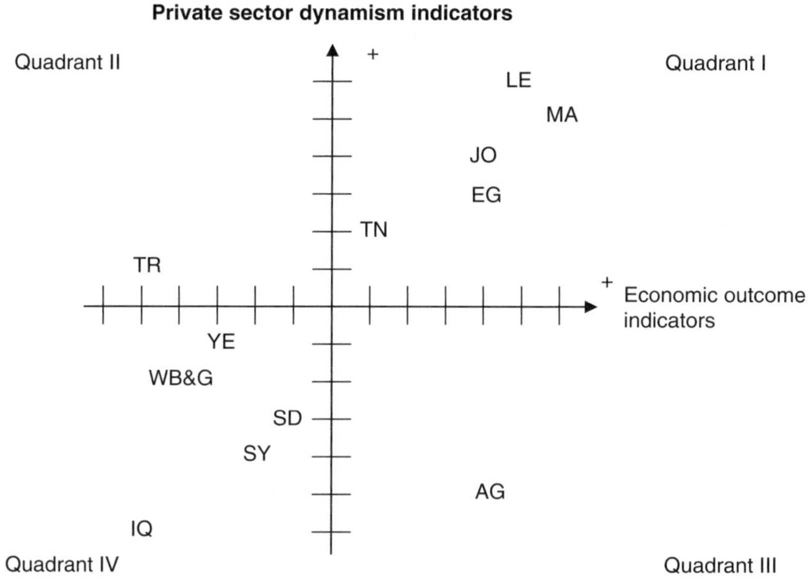

Figure 5.7 *Relative country performance on private sector dynamism and economic outcomes*

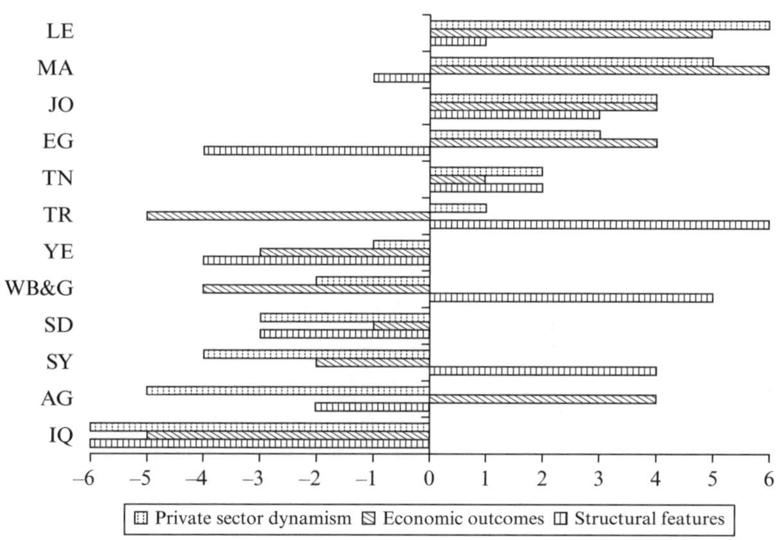

Figure 5.8 *Relative country positions on private sector dynamism, economic outcomes and structural features*

Table 5.5 Relative positions of MENA-12 countries on private sector performance indicators

Private sector dynamism	LE	MA	JO	EG	TN	TR	YE	WB&G	SD	SY	AG	IQ
A. Private share of investment, credit and employment												
Net private FDI	1	8	2	4	3	9	5	..	6	7	10	..
Gross fixed private capital formation	1	2	3	6	9	4	7	5	8	11	10	..
Private to gross fixed capital formation	1	2	5	6	10	4	8	3	7	9	11	..
Domestic credit to the private sector (% of GDP)	3	2	1	5	4	6	10	11	9	7	8	..
Domestic credit provided by the banking system (% of GDP)	1	3	2	4	5	6	9	10	8	7	11	..
Private sector share of employment	3	1	12	9	5	2	6	7	4	8	11	10
B. Dynamics of entrepreneurship												
Informal sector (% of GDP)	3	2	8	5	1	6	7	..	..	9	4	..
Self-employment rate (% of total employed workers)	2	5	12	11	9	8	6	10	1	3	7	4
Employer share of self-employment	9	11	2	1	5	6	8	3	10	4	7	..
Density of nascent entrepreneurs (% of adult population)	5	4	6	3	10	8	1	9	..	7	2	..
Density of entrepreneurship (% of adult population)	1	2	7	4	3	9	10	5	..	6	8	..
C. Business environment												
Doing Business 2010 rank	6	7	4	5	1	2	3	9	12	10	8	11
Index of Economic Freedom score	3	4	1	5	6	2	8	..		9	7	..
Overall rank	*1*	*2*	*3*	*4*	*5*	*6*	*7*	*8*	*9*	*10*	*11*	*12*

Structural features												
A. Quality of human capital and labour inputs												
Age index (youngest/oldest)	11	8	6	7	12	10	1	4	2	5	9	3
Life expectancy index (HDI)	6	8	4	9	2	7	11	3	12	1	5	10
Literacy rate	3	11	2	9	6	3	12	1	10	5	8	7
Education index (HDI)	3	10	2	8	6	4	10	1	12	5	7	9
Female literacy gap	3	10	1	11	5	5	12	2	7	4	6	9
Share of women in employment	7	2	10	6	4	3	5	8	1	12	11	9
Population below the poverty line	8	4	3	6	1	6	10	11	9	2	7	..
B. Size of government												
Government expenditure (% of GDP)	9	2	10	6	5	1	11	..	4	3	6	12
Public sector share of employment	3	1	12	9	5	2	6	7	4	8	11	10
Public debt (% of GDP)	10	6	7	8	5	4	3	..	9	2	1	..
C. Sector structure												
Service sector to agriculture sector	3	11	1	7	6	4	5	2	12	9	8	10
Overall rank	*6*	*7*	*4*	*10*	*5*	*1*	*10*	*2*	*9*	*3*	*8*	*12*
Economic outcomes												
Real GDP growth	1	3	8	4	11	12	6	1	6	10	9	5
GDP per capita growth	1	5	4	3	6	11	10	7	2	7	9	..
Labour force participation rate	10	2	5	6	6	6	9	11	2	4	1	12
Unemployment rate	1	5	6	3	9	7	10	12	11	1	4	8
Exports/GDP	8	5	2	6	1	9	4	11	10	7	3	..
Gross capital formation	2	1	4	7	5	9	6	10	8	12	3	11
Overall rank	*2*	*1*	*3*	*4*	*6*	*11*	*9*	*10*	*7*	*8*	*3*	*11*

Note: A rank of 1 indicates the best-performing country.

Table 5.6 PSD context description, MENA-12

Quadrant I: Above-average private sector dynamism and economic outcomes (Lebanon, Morocco, Jordan, Egypt and Tunisia)

Country	Private sector dynamism	Economic outcomes	Structural features	Summary implications for private sector growth
Lebanon	• Strong FDI performance. • Highest level of private capital formation. • Highest level of domestic credit provided by the banking system in the MENA-12; third-highest level of domestic credit to the private sector. • High self-employment rate, but lower share of employers. High level of informality. High density of entrepreneurs in the adult population, but percentage of people trying to start a business is lower than average. • Higher-than-average ranking on the ease of doing business and about average on the IEF.	• High recent GDP growth and GDP per capita growth. • Lower-than-average level of exports. • Second-highest gross capital formation performance. • Below-average labour force participation rate; lowest level of unemployment.	• High education index; high literacy rate; one of the lowest female literacy gaps. • Slightly-below-average share of women in employment. • Above-average poverty level. • Low public sector share of employment. • One of the highest levels of public debt; relatively high level of government spending. • Highly service-driven economy.	*Strong on private sector dynamism, above average on structural features and above average on economic outcomes.* • Relatively favourable business environment and level of economic freedom and high level of human capital indicate good conditions for private sector development. • Strong entrepreneurial culture, level of entrepreneurial activity and open credit system, but conditions or opportunities for new entrepreneurs and private investors may be constrained by political instability and high business transaction costs. • FDI likely driving growth (plus high level of remittances).

Morocco	• Below-average performance on FDI to GDP. • High share of private capital investment to GDP; high ratio of private to total capital formation. • Relatively strong availability of credit to the private sector and domestic credit provided by the banking system. • Highest share of private sector employment. • Above-average level of informality, one of the highest. • Average self-employment rate, but lowest employers rate and proportion of employers among the self-employed. • High density of entrepreneurs and proportion of the adult population trying to start a new business. • Below-average rank on Doing Business and slightly-above-average on economic freedoms.	• Above-average GDP growth; average GDP per capita growth. • Highest level of gross capital formation. • Just-above-average level of exports to GDP. • Second-highest labour force participation rate. • Lowest unemployment rate.	• Among the lowest literacy rates, highest female literacy gaps and lowest education indexes. • Below-average poverty level. • One of the highest shares of women in employment. • Lowest share of public sector employment. • Below-average government spending to GDP; moderate level of public debt. • Low ratio of service sector to agricultural sector. Agriculture still plays a key role in the economy.	*Strong on private sector dynamism, above-average on economic outcomes and below average on structural features.* • GDP growth is not resulting in per capita income growth, which implies it is not pro-poor. • High capital formation and private share of investment, but may not be in productive sectors. • Although the density of entrepreneurs and level of entrepreneurial activity is relatively high, the business environment is not that favourable. May explain high informality and low rate of employers in self-employment (low level of human capital could also be an explanation). • Not fully utilizing the labour force, but low level of human capital will constrain productive growth. The high share of women in employment may be in low-skill jobs.

Table 5.6 (continued)

Quadrant I: Above-average private sector dynamism and economic outcomes (Lebanon, Morocco, Jordan, Egypt and Tunisia)				
Country	Private sector dynamism	Economic outcomes	Structural features	Summary implications for private sector growth
Jordan	• Strong relative performance on FDI, private capital investment, share of private investment in total, domestic credit to the private sector, private credit provided by banking system. • Relatively small share of private sector employment. • Much smaller informal sector. • Lowest level of self-employment, but second highest share of employers in the total self-employment rate. • Below-average density of entrepreneurs in the adult population and proportion of adults actively trying to start a business. • Above-average rank on Doing Business and highest rank on the IEF.	• About average GDP growth. • High performance on exports and gross capital formation to GDP. • Slightly-above-average labour force participation rate; average unemployment rate (but still over 13 per cent).	• High level of literacy and education, including low female literacy gap; and relatively low level of poverty. • Low share of women in employment. • Much-higher-than-average share of public sector employment and one of the highest levels of government spending. • Relatively strong service sector.	*Strong on private sector dynamism, economic outcomes and structural features.* • Growth is primarily driven by FDI and exports. • High level of human capital and participation in the labour force. • Signs of a lower level of entrepreneurial activity, even though private investment level and availability of private credit are relatively high and the business environment relatively favourable. Low levels in certain areas of economic freedom and the strong role played by government in employment may indicate some crowding out of the private sector. • Not taking advantage of the educated supply of women for growth in employment.

Egypt	• Higher-than-average level of FDI to GDP. • Lower-than-average private capital formation to GDP and share of private in total. • Above-average level of private credit to the private sector and share of credit from the banking system. • Below-average private sector share of employment. • Among the lowest self-employment rates, but highest share of employers among the self-employed. Above-average level of informality. Relatively high density of entrepreneurs; just-below-average proportion of adults trying to start a new business. • Above-average ranking on ease of doing business and average on economic freedoms.	• Relatively high GDP and GDP per capita growth. • Below-average exports to GDP. • Average labour force participation rate; third-lowest official unemployment rate.	• Below-average level of literacy, one of the highest female literacy gaps, and lower than average education index. • Close-to-average poverty level (but 20 per cent). • Relatively high level of government employment. • Above-average level of public debt to GDP. • Below-average and relatively low role of the service sector in the economy.	*Above average on private sector dynamism and economic outcomes and below average on structural features.* • Relatively high level of entrepreneurial activity, but low level of human capital and high share of government employment. • Private sector growth will require higher education levels and competitive space for productive private sector activity, especially in the service sector. • Business environment is improving, but informality remains high.

Table 5.6 (continued)

Quadrant I: Above-average private sector dynamism and economic outcomes (Lebanon, Morocco, Jordan, Egypt and Tunisia)				
Country	Private sector dynamism	Economic outcomes	Structural features	Summary implications for private sector growth
Tunisia	• Third-highest FDI performance. • Lower-than-average private capital formation to GDP, and share of private capital in the total. • Well-above-average availability of private credit and the share of domestic credit provided by the banking system. • Higher-than-average share of private sector employment. • Largest informal sector. • High density of entrepreneurs in the adult population, but lower-than-average self-employment rate and very low incidence of people trying to start a new business. • Top ranking on Doing Business and average score on IEF.	• Second-lowest GDP growth, but average GDP per capita growth. • Strongest level of exports to GDP. • Above-average gross capital formation rate. • Average labour force participation rate, but higher-than-average unemployment rate (above 14 per cent).	• High life expectancy, with average literacy rate and education index performance. • Literacy gap for women slightly higher than average, but women's share in employment is above average. • One of the lowest levels of poverty. • Below-average public sector share of employment and public debt.	*Above average on private sector dynamism, economic outcomes and structural features.* • Human capital performance is relatively good but declining trend in economic growth. • Favourable business environment and availability of private credit is above average, but realizing low share of private capital formation in gross investment. Signs that entrepreneurship culture may be weak; may be barriers to formalization.

Quadrant II: Above-average private sector dynamism and below-average economic outcomes (Turkey)

Country	PSD performance	Economic outcomes	Structural features	Summary and implications for private sector growth
Turkey	• Higher-than-average private capital investment and private share of total investment. • High share of private sector employment. • Low relative level of FDI performance. • Low density of entrepreneurs and people trying to start a business. • Lower-than-average self-employment rate, although higher-than-average level of informality. • High rank on ease of doing business and on economic freedoms (second-highest after Jordan).	• Lowest GDP growth and growth in GDP per capita. Low relative export performance. • Slightly-below-average labour force participation rate. • Unemployment rate above 14 per cent.	• High literacy rate; lower-than-average female literacy gap; high education index. • Lower-than-average poverty level (but still 20 per cent). • Relatively high share of women in employment. • Low public share of employment; lowest level of government spending; relatively low level of public debt.	*Above average on private sector dynamism and structural features and below average on economic outcomes.* • Economic performance indicators have been declining. • In spite of relatively favourable assessments of business environment and economic freedoms, the level of entrepreneurship is low. • Could be a matter of low entrepreneurial culture or other barriers to the choice of having a business. • Barriers to formalization likely exist. • High level of human capital but not being fully utilized.

Table 5.6 (continued)

Quadrant III: Below-average private sector dynamism and above-average economic outcomes (Algeria)

Country	PSD performance	Economic outcomes	Structural features	Summary and implications for private sector growth
Algeria	• Second-lowest level of FDI to GDP. • Second-lowest level of gross private capital formation to GDP and lowest share of private in gross capital formation. • Among the lowest levels of domestic credit to the private sector (as percentage of GDP) and virtually no domestic credit being supplied by the banking system. • Second-lowest share of private sector in total employment. • Relatively high self-employment rate, low employer rate, and below-average share of employers in self-employment rate. • Higher-than-average level of informality.	• Below-average GDP growth; one of the lowest levels of GDP per capita growth. • Third-highest level of exports to GDP and level of gross capital formation. • Highest labour force participation rate. • Lower-than-average unemployment rate (but still above 10 per cent).	• Average literacy rate, female literacy gap (although still over 19 per cent) and education index. • Above-average poverty level. • Second-lowest share of women in employment. • Second-highest share of public sector in employment. Lowest level of public debt to GDP. • Second-smallest service sector share of GDP.	*Very weak on private sector dynamism, above average on economic outcomes and below average on structural features.* • Relatively unfavourable business environment and investment climate. • Average level of human capital but not fully utilized in the labour market, especially women. • High public sector employment share may be crowding out the private sector. • Strong export and gross capital investment performance, but FDI and private investment are low. • Signs that the culture of entrepreneurship may be weak, although the nascent entrepreneur rate is relatively

Country	PSD performance	Economic outcomes	Structural features	Summary and implications for private sector growth
	• Above-average proportion of adults trying to start a business, but low density of existing entrepreneurs. • Well-below-average ranking on ease of doing business; just below average on economic freedoms score.			high. The low availability of private credit is likely to be a constraint to entrepreneurial activity.

Quadrant IV: Below-average private sector dynamism and below-average economic outcomes (Yemen, the West Bank & Gaza, Sudan, Syria and Iraq)

Country	PSD performance	Economic outcomes	Structural features	Summary and implications for private sector growth
Yemen	• Above-average level of FDI to GDP. • Below-average private capital formation and share of private in gross capital formation. • Very low share of domestic credit to the private sector (second lowest) and credit provided by the banking system. • Just above average in private sector share of employment. • Below-average size of the informal sector, the rate of self-employment and the share of employers among the self-employed.	• Above-average GDP growth; second-lowest performance on GDP per capita growth. • Above-average level of exports to GDP; average gross capital formation to GDP. • Below-average labour force participation rate, among the highest unemployment rates.	• Youngest age population. • Lowest literacy rate; largest female literacy gap; third-lowest education index. • Second-highest poverty level. • Above-average share of women in employment. • Just-below-average public sector share of employment; high level of government spending; relatively low level of public debt.	*Below average on private sector dynamism and economic outcomes with weak structural features.* • Although the business environment is assessed as being relatively favourable (for the MENA-12), there are signs of constraints to starting and operating a business (high nascent entrepreneur rate yet low entrepreneur density). • Low human capital and low utilization of the labour force. • The young population will create employment creation pressures, but the low level of human capital is likely a

Table 5.6 (continued)

Country	PSD performance	Economic outcomes	Structural features	Summary and implications for private sector growth
Quadrant IV: Below-average private sector dynamism and below-average economic outcomes (Yemen, the West Bank & Gaza, Sudan, Syria and Iraq)				
	• Very high proportion of nascent entrepreneurs, but very low density of existing entrepreneurs. • Above-average ranking on the ease of doing business; second-lowest score for economic freedoms.		• Weak service sector; well below average in relation to agricultural sector.	deterrent to private sector and enterprise growth, as is the low level of private credit and the weak economic freedoms.
West Bank & Gaza	• Below-average private capital formation to GDP, but third-highest share of private investment in gross capital formation. • Lowest on credit to the private sector and the second-lowest on credit provided by the banking system. • Average share of private sector in employment. • Below-average self-employment rate, but above-average share of employers among the self-employed.	• Highest GDP growth; lower than average GDP per capita growth. Very low level of exports and gross capital formation to GDP. • Second-lowest labour force participation rate; highest reported unemployment rate.	• High life expectancy; highest literacy rate and education index. Lowest female literacy gap, but below-average share of women in employment. • Highest level of poverty. • Average share of public sector employment. • Highly service-driven economy.	*Low on private sector dynamism and economic outcomes, but high on structural features.* • Very high level of human capital, but underutilized. • Opportunities for export growth and private investment are limited. • Low nascent entrepreneur rate may be related to limited opportunities for starting a new business, low availability of credit and relatively unfavourable business environment.

	• One of the lowest in percentage of the adult population trying to start a business, but density of existing entrepreneurs is above average. • Below-average ranking on the ease of doing business (fourth lowest).			The same conditions may make it difficult for existing entrepreneurs to grow their enterprise. • If more opportunities were available, high human capital would bode well for successful entrepreneurship. • Being a conflict country poses additional severe challenges to PSD.
Sudan	• Average level of FDI to GDP (although low). • Below-average private capital formation and private share of gross investment. • Low level of credit to the private sector and domestic credit being provided by the banking system although levels improving. • Above-average private sector share of employment. • High self-employment rate; below average incidence of employers among the self-employed. • Poorest ranking on the ease of doing business. (No data on level of informality or density of entrepreneurs.)	• Above-average GDP growth; second-highest growth in GDP per capita. • One of the lowest exports to GDP ratios; below average on gross capital formation. • Above-average labour force participation rate, but one of the highest unemployment rates.	• Lowest life expectancy and education index; third-lowest literacy rate. Female literacy gap is large, but just below average for MENA-12 countries. • Highest share of women in employment. • Below-average share of public sector employment and government spending; high level of public debt. • Low service sector economy; dominated by agricultural sector.	*Below average on private sector dynamism and low on economic outcomes and structural features.* • Unfavourable business environment, low level of human capital, low exports and gross capital formation, low private credit, and high public debt do not bode well for PSD and growth. • Being a conflict country poses additional severe challenges to PSD. • Entrepreneurial activity most likely of a subsistence nature and not poised for growth.

Table 5.6 (continued)

Country	PSD performance	Economic outcomes	Structural features	Summary and implications for private sector growth
Quadrant IV: Below-average private sector dynamism and below-average economic outcomes (Yemen, the West Bank & Gaza, Sudan, Syria and Iraq)				
Syria	• Below-average level of FDI to GDP. Second-lowest level of private capital formation; below-average share of private in gross capital formation. • Below-average level of domestic credit to the private sector to GDP and share provided by the banking system. • Below-average share of private sector employment. • Lowest informal sector (as share of GDP), but third-highest self-employment rate and one of the highest shares of employers among the self-employed. • Close-to-average density of entrepreneurs in the adult population, but relatively	• Below-average GDP and GDP per capita growth. • Below-average ratio of exports to GDP. • Lowest gross capital formation to GDP. • Above-average labour force participation rate; lowest unemployment rate (less than 10 per cent).	• Highest life expectancy. • Above-average literacy rate (82 per cent) and education index, and below-average female literacy gap. • Lowest share of women in employment. • Relatively low poverty level. • Above-average share of public sector employment. • Second-lowest level of public debt to GDP. • Smaller than average service sector, especially in relation to the agricultural sector share of GDP.	*Very weak on private sector dynamism, below average on economic outcomes and above average on structural features.* • Relatively unfavourable business environment and investment climate. Various forms of economic freedom in question. Several constraints on private sector dynamism. • Relatively high level of human capital and utilization of the labour force in employment. • Public sector employment benefits may be crowding out the private sector. • Signs that the entrepreneurship culture may be weak.

	low proportion of nascent entrepreneurs. • Third-lowest ranking on the ease of doing business and lowest score on the IEF ('repressed' economy).			
Iraq	• Low private sector share of employment. • Above-average self-employment rate. • Low rank on ease of doing business (second-lowest among the MENA-12). (Many missing variables for Iraq.)	• Higher-than-average GDP growth. • Second-lowest level of gross capital formation to GDP. • Lowest labour force participation rate. • Relatively high reported unemployment rate (above 15 per cent).	• One of the youngest populations. • Below-average literacy rate and education index; slightly higher than average female literacy gap. • Low share of women in employment. • Highest level of government spending to GDP; high public debt; third-highest public sector share of employment. • Smallest service sector share of the economy; low ratio of service sector to agricultural sector.	*Below average on private sector dynamism and low on economic outcomes and structural features.* • Unfavourable business environment and investment climate will deter private sector development. • Below-average level of human capital and underutilization of the labour force, particularly women. • Will need job creation to absorb new entrants. • Being a conflict country poses additional severe challenges to PSD.

A key issue in monitoring the PSD performance of a country is being able to link policy measures directly to PSD indicators. Some of this was inherent in the preceding analysis with the inclusion of values on the ease of doing business and IEF indicators in the list of private sector dynamism variables. However Doing Business and the IEF deal almost exclusively with policies to improve the business environment and investment climate. They do not focus on many of the micro-level policies that are needed to 'facilitate enterprise development', the third pillar in the PSD framework in Figure 1.1 of Chapter 1.

Policies such as those to reduce the time and cost of doing business, open trade possibilities and promote more competition in the financial sector will certainly contribute to a more favourable environment for the operation of private enterprises, but will not be sufficient to stimulate the surge in domestic entrepreneurship that is required in MENA countries to accelerate employment, innovation and growth. Absolutely essential are micro-level policies and measures to promote a stronger culture of entrepreneurship, build the know-how and capacity of entrepreneurs and the competitiveness of their enterprises, and address the barriers that entrepreneurs face in accessing financing, business development services (BDS), guidance, training, information, markets, technology and technical assistance – issues elaborated in Chapter 4.

Focus on the importance of these micro-level policies has tended in recent years to take a back seat to the business enabling environment (BEE) policy agenda. One initiative that keeps the spotlight on the enterprise policy agenda is the Euro-Mediterranean Charter for Enterprise that eight of the MENA-12 countries have adopted (also, Turkey is a partner in the European Charter for SMEs). The Organisation for Economic Co-operation and Development (OECD)–European Commission effort to assess the progress of Euro-Med countries in implementing the charter's ten policy areas (see Chapter 4) is one of the few examples of policy assessment initiatives. At the same time the lack of data has thwarted efforts to link enterprise policy improvements with improvements in the scale and scope of entrepreneurial and SME activity. It is interesting to note that Tunisia, Egypt, Morocco, Lebanon and Jordan, countries that performed well in the PSD categorization above, were assessed by the OECD–European Commission as making more progress in implementing enterprise policies than Syria, Algeria and the Palestinian Authority, with overall assessment scores of close to or above 3 (out of 5) versus less than 2 in the other countries. (See the comparative assessment scores for each of the policy areas in the relevant discussions in Chapters 3 and 4.)

More effort is clearly needed to refine a comprehensive and manageable set of indicators to measure and monitor performance in the level of private sector dynamism. The framework outlined in this chapter is intended as a step in that process.

NOTES

1. The World Bank (2007b) did note that Algeria, Egypt, Jordan, Morocco and Tunisia have undertaken telecommunications reforms.
2. In advanced industrial economies the benchmark used for private ownership of enterprise assets of large-scale enterprises is more than 75 per cent and for small enterprise is 100 per cent (European Bank for Reconstruction and Development, EBRD Index of Privatization).
3. For example, Tunisia is strongly opposed to the privatization of basic services and Algeria to that of its energy companies.
4. Corporatization is an approach whereby the government maintains ownership of the enterprise but enters into agreements with private sector companies to manage the SOE in a 'corporate' manner.
5. By 2005 the Turkish government owned only 5 per cent of Turkish enterprises (EC 2005c) and the Tunisian government had divested of over two-thirds of its assets (MIEPME 2005).
6. The Iraqi government set up a special Privatization Commission in 2004 but abolished it in 2005. In 2005 the government still owned 192 SOEs that employed a half a million workers. Options for a mixed sector where the private sector can participate with the public sector are being considered (MPDC 2005b; World Bank 2006c).
7. The BTI includes indicators to assess political participation, rule of law, stability of democracy institutions and political and social integration (political transformation); market organization, private property, welfare regime, economic performance, education and environment and structural constraints (economic transformation); and efficiency in political leadership in the prioritization, coordination and implementation of policies (management performance and political leadership).
8. Business entry and exit rates are an important indicator of the dynamism of the SME sector. This type of data is virtually non-existent in the MENA countries. The Turkish Statistical Office reports monthly figures for new business registrations and business closures and the Algerian statistical office reports annually on SME entries and closures – the closest examples in the MENA-12 countries. It is possible to obtain data on the number of new registered limited liability companies from country sources, but more difficult to obtain an accurate measure of the existing stock of enterprises. This leads to imprecision in calculating new business entry rates and especially in making comparisons across countries. Another problem in using registrations of limited liability companies as a proxy for business entry rates is that the vast majority of new and existing enterprises are sole proprietorships and this is not captured.
9. Equally if not more important than the level of government spending is how the spending is allocated across sectors, such as health, education, social welfare, defence and infrastructure, and the resulting impacts on both economic growth and social equity. The management of government resources is critical to growth, human capital formation and the welfare of the poor, and public expenditure adjustments are very important in the development of a market economy. An analysis of government expenditure patterns in MENA-12 countries is beyond the scope of this book, but is a large consideration in determining the extent to which spending is supporting priorities of market-led and inclusive growth.
10. Public sector employment in the Gulf countries is an average of 13 per cent of total employment ('Weaker Outlook for Private Sector Employment in 09' by National Bank of Kuwait, 17 February 2009), available at http://www.arabtimesonline.com/

NewsDetails/tabid/96/smid/414/ArticleID/144257/reftab/73/Default.aspx (accessed 12 February 2010).

11. The World Bank defines domestic credit to the private sector as: 'financial resources provided to the private sector – such as loans, purchases of non-equity securities, and trade credits and other accounts receivables – that establish a claim for repayment' (World Bank 2010, p. 295).
12. Domestic credit provided by the banking sector is defined as: 'all credit to various sectors on a gross basis, except to the central government, which is net. The banking sector includes monetary authorities, deposit money banks, and other banking institutions for which data are available' (World Bank 2010, p. 311).
13. Iraq and Sudan were also reviewed but due to lack of data were not scored or ranked in the 2010 IEF.
14. The relative positions of the MENA-12 countries were calculated using a Borda ranking procedure (see Moulin 1988) used by Lundström and Stevenson (2005) in their context categorization of 13 developed countries. In this procedure the MENA-12 countries were first ranked from 1 to 12 on the quantitative results for each indicator (1 was used for the highest-performing country and 12 for the lowest-performing country). Based on the average ordinal ranking for each of the three sets of variables (private sector dynamism, economic outcomes and structural features), Borda ranking values of +6 to −6 were then assigned: +6 to the ordinal rank of 1, and −6 to the ordinal rank of 12.

6. Policy, research and capacity issues

The previous chapters of this book have laid out the major socio-economic challenges faced by the MENA-12 countries, indicating that the slow development and growth of the private sector is one of the key strategic deficiencies. The critical policy question is how to foster the conditions for a more substantial and vibrant private sector. MENA governments have undertaken many structural reforms to improve their macro-economic frameworks since the end of the 1990s, but these have not evidently been sufficient to foster strong private sector-led investment and meet employment demands (World Bank 2006d). Efforts to engage in structural reforms of the micro-economic environment affecting enterprises have proven to be much slower and more difficult to implement (Noland and Pack 2007) although governments in each of the MENA-12 countries have expressed commitment to such reforms and made some progress.

The private sector response to policy reforms has been more robust in resource-poor countries, such as Jordan, Morocco, Tunisia, Egypt and Turkey, than in the resource-rich countries of Algeria and Syria, although less responsive in MENA countries than in higher-growth countries where similar reforms have been pursued (World Bank 2009c). This led to the World Bank's conclusion that the relatively low level of private investment and dynamism in MENA countries is more due to greater policy uncertainty and the unequal, discretionary and preferential implementation of policies than to insufficient reforms (World Bank 2009c). In other words the lack of impact has had less to do with the reforms than with how they are applied and the credibility of the government in its commitment to reform. Muasher (2008) suggests as other reasons for the lack of progress on reforms: the Arab–Israeli conflict, oil wealth (which reduces the need), the lack of democracy, the lack of employment and quality education, and the lack of a system of checks and balances. He stresses the importance of a widened base for public participation in decision-making processes and more political and economic freedom.

As MENA governments continue their efforts to improve the business environment and investment climate, they will have to overcome a variety of policy, research and institutional deficiencies. Not only are there many remaining policy gaps, but also serious constraints and fundamental weaknesses in the statistical systems; a lack of data, research and public information; and a lack of private sector input in the process of identifying, designing, monitoring and evaluating reforms. Private sector development is a multisectoral agenda that requires a broad-based reform process involving interministerial coordination and alliances with external stakeholders (World Bank 2009c). Structures for achieving this are rare in MENA countries.

Micro, small and medium enterprises (SMEs) are a major part of the private sector and so their growth is essential for its advancement, yet the existence of coherent and cohesive policies and strategies for strengthening the SME sector and creating a favourable environment for the creation of new entrepreneurial ventures is sporadic. Policy frameworks virtually ignore the issue of entrepreneurship development as a priority. SME policy units, where they exist, are weakly resourced and do not generally have strongly institutionalized structures. The dedicated SME agencies that exist in some countries are largely focused on delivering donor-funded support programmes and do not necessarily have strong linkages to the policymaking machinery. Gaps exist in programmes, services and support for key target groups, and there are weak ties between the SME agenda and liberalization and investment policies.

There is limited evidence of FDI benefits spilling over to the domestic SME sector or improving the livelihoods of the poor (Bibi and Nabli 2010), with little attention being paid to this as an important policy issue. The informality issue is becoming more prominent on the government agenda in some of the countries, especially in Sudan, Turkey, Morocco and Syria, where the approach is to draw the informal sector into the modern economy. However most governments tolerate or tacitly encourage informal sector activity as a social safety net. The role of women in the private sector poses a major policy dilemma, but not one that has gained much traction in economic policy circles. World Bank research has generated heightened awareness of the economic benefits to be gained by increasing women's participation in the economic sphere, particularly as entrepreneurs, but policy support for improving the current situation is underdeveloped.

The region suffers from a limited evidence base to support policy development. Comprehensive statistical data on SMEs is generally not available and its quality, comparability and timeliness are poor. Information on the level of entrepreneurial activity and analysis of the behaviour of nascent and early-stage entrepreneurs is very limited. There are few efforts to examine the impact of legislation and regulations on SMEs and private sector development (PSD) more generally. Few researchers in the MENA region are studying SME sector issues and the role of civil society organizations (CSOs) in the policymaking and reform process is limited. Private sector and SME advocacy groups have weak capacity to produce solid, evidence-based studies so do not have sufficient grounds for knowing what policies will be effective in improving the operating environment and conditions for private enterprise, particularly the activities of SMEs, and for monitoring policy outcomes. This leads to a situation of low accountability within the government in responding to the priorities and needs of smaller private sector entities.

The remainder of Chapter 6 presents the perspectives of regional stakeholders on the state of PSD in their countries, and the weaknesses and priorities that need to be addressed.[1]

STAKEHOLDER VIEWS ON PSD WEAKNESSES AND PRIORITIES

During International Development Research Centre (IDRC)-led consultations, stakeholders in the MENA-12 countries enumerated a long list of PSD challenges. In Algeria these include the following: slow privatization efforts, with the government still owning many large enterprises that compete with the private sector or shut it out of certain sectors completely; a low level of FDI with too many foreign ownership restrictions; lack of diversification in the economy with overdependence on the oil sector; deindustrialization; over-regulation; corruption; complexity in commercial laws; customs barriers; low liquidity in the banking system; lack of risk capital and innovation infrastructure (such as incubators); hurdles to starting a business; lack of SME competitiveness, management skills and capital; and high taxes. Although the private sector has been developing since the early part of the 2000s, there are strongly held views that not much progress is being made on improvements in the investment climate or on PSD generally. Algerian stakeholders emphasized the need to diversify the economy beyond oil and to establish a structure for SMEs to emerge, one of the main purposes behind the SME law and the framework for SME development.

Jordanian stakeholders emphasized: weaknesses in the SME sector, such as limited marketing, low capacity for quality and limited access to financing; structural weaknesses, specifically the concentration of large firms in many sectors, the small manufacturing sector and the small size of the majority of enterprises; weaknesses in the research and development (R&D) and innovation system (low level of R&D investments, universities do not promote R&D activity or provide incentives to professors to do applied research, and poor linkages exist between R&D facilities and the private sector); a mismatch between the education system and the labour market; the relatively high cost of Jordanian labour; and coordination weaknesses within the government which leads to problems in implementing the country's vision. Decades of government employment and control over the economy have created a generation of Jordanians who lack entrepreneurial capacity, and of enterprises accustomed to working in a protected market. Both are finding it difficult to make the shift to a private sector-led and competitive market economy. Thus cultural change was an underlying dimension of stakeholders' concerns.

In terms of what to do next, stakeholders focused on improvements to the vocational training system so Jordanians could acquire more skills; upgrading SMEs; stimulating bank lending to SMEs; shifting to more higher-value-added activity in promising sectors and knowledge-based areas; implementing an innovation policy with an 'innovation systems' approach and all of the institutional elements and linkages that would entail; and mobilizing the private sector to create an umbrella 'voice' to the government on PSD needs. They also advocated streamlined and better-coordinated government structures for the implementation of PSD and SME policies and actions.

Moroccan stakeholders stressed weaknesses in the investment environment (such as the lack of transparency in the judicial system, red tape, the high cost of doing business and high taxes on income and salaries); insufficient attention to the quality of education in the expanding vocational and technical training system and lack of coordination among the 14 ministries offering sector-specific vocational training; the lack of innovation, including weak links between universities and the business community; weaknesses in the SME sector (low product quality, limited product differentiation, lack of production organization and poor access to financing); and reticence on the part of some factions of society regarding privatization and the implementation of reforms. As priorities, stakeholders stressed pushing innovation as a key concept of business development, improving the quality of skills development and training to prepare new graduates for the skills demanded in the labour market, and continuing efforts to reduce the costs of doing business.

Syrian stakeholders commented on a variety of PSD challenges. Although the government's latest five-year development plan stresses the importance of private sector GDP growth, the strategy for achieving this was stated as 'missing'. No one government ministry 'is in charge of' PSD, and the vision for it is not necessarily shared by all Cabinet members, some of whom view it as 'threat to socialism'.[2] Several key informants focused on the need to deal with the privatization issue. Public monopolies exist in many areas of the economy (for example, oil and gas, electricity, parts of the textile production chain, procurement monopolies in cotton, sugar cane and other commodities) and public sector companies are competing with the private sector in several sectors. Although, as informants stated, over half of the public industrial companies are losing money and the rest are producing low value-added, the government is reluctant to privatize and is deliberating on other options, such as corporatizing or joint venturing, where it would still maintain a high level of ownership and control. Other stated weaknesses were capacity gaps in private sector enterprises (human resources, industrial standards in all sectors, production control, sector linkages, education–industry linkages and information); the low-value-added, labour intensive nature of SMEs that are used to working in protected markets and cannot compete on price and quality with products coming in under the Greater Arab Free Trade Area (GAFTA); restrictive labour laws that discourage the private sector from formal hiring; weak university and vocational education systems; low R&D expenditures; low entrepreneurial capacity (many graduates prefer to work in the public sector or move to the Gulf); and lack of integration of environmental issues at the sector level.

> 'The private sector is still a small part of the overall economy.' 'Everything needs to be done . . . the field is empty for new interventions.' (Key informant, Syria)

Syrian stakeholders had a long list of PSD priorities. This included the need for: work on cultural reform; changes in the regulatory environment; consensus on harmonization of Syrian laws and regulations in order to enter European Union (EU) markets; huge investments in infrastructure (roads, ports, rail, transport, water); changes in the labour law to encourage formal hiring; creation of a social safety net programme; changes in the non-governmental organization (NGO) law to allow more involvement of civil society and NGOs in development discussions and activities; a policy framework and private sector institutional support infrastructure; and capacity building to enable the private sector to become more efficient, better financially managed, with better human resource development, better marketing and more access to foreign market opportunities.

In general, stakeholders felt that Syria needed a government policy on PSD that sets its benchmark at the international level. They recommended that the government establish a Private Sector Development Council to initiate policies and activities related to: financial services; consulting services; overhaul of the regulatory framework (including the Company

Law, labour laws, customs laws and the foreign exchange and tax regime); professional management of family enterprises; development of sector associations; harmonizing standards with the EU; and upgrading of businesses. A major challenge for the work of the government, donors and international organizations in Syria is the general lack of data and information. The lack of data is related to weaknesses in institutional capacity, insufficient expertise, a lack of capability to link data effectively to the policy process with political neutrality, and a culture that is reluctant to share information (UN 2005). There is insufficient collection and reporting of timely data on private enterprises, particularly micro and small enterprises (MSEs), and no efforts to monitor business entry and exit activity and other indicators of entrepreneurial dynamism and performance. The need to improve data sources, develop baseline data, implement a single business number registration system and deploy methods for evaluating the impact of policy changes have been advocated (SEBC 2007).

The main PSD challenge in Yemen was described as a weak investment climate that is deterring investment from non-Arab countries. Private sector investment in Yemen since 1991 has been very small, and several major problems were cited: corruption; lack of a land registry; foreign property ownership restrictions; monopolies in several sectors; lack of liquidity in the banking system; absence of a stock exchange; and a weak industrial base. Weaknesses in the banking system are illustrated by the ownership of large non-public banks by big industrial companies that have preferential lending practices; restrictions in the Bank Act that constrain the entry of foreign banks; and the low flow of savings into investment (less than 5 per cent of Yemenis have bank accounts). Other stated deficiencies include an inadequate infrastructure; poor quality of university and vocational education and training and a lack of competent management training institutes; an uncompetitive SME sector (characterized by very small firms, family business structures not poised for growth, low capacity and industrial SMEs used to working in protected markets); and weak involvement of the private sector in the government's investment discussions and decisions. The government system and structure was seen as one of the main problems. There is no central planning ministry, no system to advance private sector views up to Cabinet, no clear definition of which ministries are involved in which sectors, and several ministries are heavily engaged in running state-owned enterprises (SOEs). Reform progress was reported as being slow because of implementation weaknesses in the government. The lack of solid studies and indicators on private sector growth was also stated as a problem, resulting in a lack of capacity to measure growth in private sector areas and determine its future directions.

Yemen stakeholders stressed the need to: simplify investment procedures;

invest in vocational training to upgrade labour force skills; restructure the Central Bank of Yemen (so that it is not operating as a commercial bank for the government); promote the role of entrepreneurship in the culture; strengthen SME management skills and capacity; and target growth opportunities in agriculture, fisheries, tourism and manufacturing.

Stakeholders in Egypt, Jordan, Morocco and Syria raised concerns about the growing income disparities between the rich and the poor and the urban and rural populations, which they believe are related to the outcome of economic reforms. They stressed the need for research on the impact of World Trade Organization (WTO) accession, Free Trade Agreements (FTAs), and foreign investments laws on equality and poverty, and recommended that these themes, as well as women's empowerment, should be integrated in economic reform strategies.

The major challenge in the West Bank & Gaza is seen as one of creating more market competition and linking this to the private sector. However it is important to consider the country's context. Palestine is a conflict territory and this affects the environment for SME and private sector growth. Because the borders are closed, for example, special problems are created for SMEs in reaching markets. SMEs do not have a collective 'voice' and thus do not play an active advocacy role in policy processes. Most of the research in Palestine is focused on foreign direct investment (FDI) and sectors where large firms can do business, which means insufficient policy attention to the development of SMEs.[3] Brain-drain has resulted in a lack of competent and trained researchers and limited capacity to build research skills.

Iraqi stakeholders held the view that excessive regulation is the major deterrent to PSD, but that more laws and regulations will not solve the problem. One of the critical issues is that the pattern of privatization and investment in Iraq is not sufficiently geared to the production sectors. Performing competitiveness analysis at the sector level and identifying sector opportunities, underlying skill sets and market demand are seen as the keys to the creation of jobs and markets. For SME development, Iraqi stakeholders recommended moving towards sectoral approaches in the offering of business development services (BDS) and Small Business Development Centers' services, linking BDS with financing and offering Islamic financing products.

One of the critical issues in Sudan was stated as the relationship between the public and private sectors, and the capability of government employees, who come mostly from a planned economy experience, to understand the behaviour of the private sector and design policy measures that appropriately serve its needs.

A major issue for Lebanese stakeholders is the lack of statistical databases and indicators to confirm whether private sector and SME performance is actually improving. Baseline research is needed to identify performance indicators for the level of competitiveness of Lebanese enterprises and to examine how a National Accounts System for SMEs might be formulated. Efforts to set out the parameters for this would result in better-informed and redirected policies. Other regional stakeholders also confirmed the need for an agreed-to set of appropriate indicators to measure PSD performance (for example, job creation, the share of SMEs in gross domestic product, the entry and exit of firms, or others).

Because incentives and structures in each country are quite different, it is clear that 'cookie-cutter' approaches to policy reform are unlikely to meet the specific needs of individual countries. Stakeholders differed in their prioritization of the gaps to be addressed. Specific research gaps (research issues, capacity building and exchange platforms) were noted by stakeholders in Jordan, Morocco and Yemen. NGOs, donors and business associations in Jordan felt that one of the biggest needs is capacity building for government officials – knowledge, capability to do policy development and capacity to implement it better. They also stressed that private sector and SME advocacy efforts are not very well developed and that NGO associations, mostly young, need capacity building and training in advocacy approaches. Syrians expressed the need for a forum for generating independent policy advice to government and donors, suggesting that a public policy institute would fill the gap. Yemeni officials also stressed the need for a public policy institute and for technical expertise and experiences from other countries. Lack of coordination between stakeholders and government departments was seen as another major problem in Yemen. Morocco stakeholders indicated that there are weaknesses in networking the different providers of SME services and pointed to facilitation of networks as a gap.

The next four sections present a discussion of four categories of relevant needs and gaps identified in the IDRC assessment: (1) policy capacity; (2) capacity of business associations and development NGOs; (3) research capacity; and (4) country-and regional-level fora for policy dialogue and exchange.

POLICY CAPACITY

Regional stakeholders acknowledge the existence of a number of progressive ministers who are trying to advance policy reforms, but low capacity within the bureaucracy, weak policy development processes, inadequate consultation and low use of research evidence to underpin policy decisions are limiting factors. In countries where the government tasks itself with running many SOEs, policy capacity is even more seriously affected because ministries are busy managing these enterprises – agricultural supply chains, railways, mining operations, hotels and energy and industrial companies – and have little time to devote to policy development work. Comprehensive frameworks and processes to guide policy development are largely missing. Although there are clearly differences in the capacity of governments across the MENA countries to design and deliver PSD policies, authors of the Bertelsmann Transformation Index suggest that the real issue is lack of political will for far-reaching reforms that may upset the status quo of power relations (Bertelsmann Stiftung 2008a). The World Bank asserts that policymakers in some MENA countries are not wholly committed to reform, coupled with the fact that private sector institutions do not have a 'loud and unified voice' to demand reforms and government accountability (World Bank 2009c, p. 13).

In line with the World Bank (2009c) view that policy implementation is a key problem, regional stakeholders point to a number of weaknesses. Vision documents, five-year plans, strategies and laws may be in place – most countries are credited with being good at delivering these – but follow-through is more problematic. Lack of implementation plans, dedicated resources, know-how and cooperation between ministries and agencies are among the major reasons given for poor implementation performance. Others include the lingering presence of government officials who resist political reform, which makes reaching consensus difficult; the high turnover of high-ranking officials, which often delays progress on policy dialogue; and changes of government and ministerial restructurings, which lead to a lack of continuity and consistency in the policy course.

Stakeholders in several of the MENA-12 countries emphasized problems with SME policy development and implementation processes. Governments are seen as better at preparing policy and strategy documents than at carrying out their implementation. There is considerable overlap among both national and international bodies on SME issues within countries, and confusion about who leads on SME policy in some. SME policies are not well integrated with other relevant policies areas, such as industrial policy, trade and investment policy, labour market policy and taxation policy; policy areas that are all in one way or another linked to policies to foster private sector development. In other words an integrated policy development approach is missing.

To overcome weaknesses in policy capacity, representatives from MENA governments suggested the need for external expertise on new ideas and ways of doing things, capacity building agreements with donors to enable the hiring of qualified experts at more competitive salaries, training of staff and implementation of medium-term strategies for institutional development. It is also important to bridge the gap between policy and research by providing funding to policy research institutes, producing good-practice studies on policy coordination mechanisms, and working on the set of indicators that can be applied to measure the role and performance of the private sector and of SMEs in the economy and monitor the extent to which their contribution is growing. Countries would benefit from studies and exchanges to review and discuss good-practice experiences in policy structures and the application of lessons learned within their own contexts. There would also be value in exchanging experience and intelligence about how to link SME development into the broader PSD policies and initiatives. Some MENA governments have been working in the SME policy area since the 1990s but most have only started focusing on this since the early 2000s. Useful lessons could be learned from examining the strengths and weaknesses of the various approaches and mechanisms in place. There would also be merit in examining PSD coordinating and consultation structures and their impact on policy implementation.

'There is no really meaningful public–private dialogue . . . Business associations have meetings with government, but nothing ever comes from it.' (key informant, Algeria).

'The private sector, SMEs and SME service providers are not well consulted. Even if the government consults with the Chambers of Commerce and Industry as a matter of routine, it is always with the same people, largely people who already sit on government boards.' (key informant, Jordan).

'The government is not working well with the private sector and not involving them in investment discussions and decisions.' (key informant, Yemen).

Stakeholders from the business and NGO communities in many of the MENA-12 countries perceive that governments do not consult stakeholders on policies and legislative changes either sufficiently or adequately, describing consultation processes as passive and ineffective. Even government ministries and agencies cite the lack of consultation processes, with particular reference to SMEs, although they are more likely than donors and the private sector to report that governments are trying to involve the private sector in decision-making, having come to the realization that top-down policymaking is not effective. It is also clear that some government agencies within countries are more committed to conducting consultations than others, a situation that appears to be linked to the openness of the relevant minister or agency head to private sector input. Although the private sector in MENA countries would like to see more consultation being done and on a more inclusive basis, it is not always easy for governments to do this efficiently because private sector bodies are highly fragmented and not organized into effective consultative mechanisms.

CAPACITY OF BUSINESS ASSOCIATIONS AND DEVELOPMENT NGOs

The prevalence of business and sector associations and development NGOs varies across the MENA countries. This depends on the legal framework for establishment of independent business associations and NGOs and the rights of association and assembly. These laws appear to be more mature and flexible in Algeria, Egypt and Morocco, where a large number of such organizations exist. NGO laws in Iraq, Syria and Yemen are more recent and have many restrictions, thus one finds considerably fewer and weaker NGOs in these countries. Many of the development NGOs in Jordan have been in existence only since the mid-2000s; there are only about ten development NGOs in the whole of Syria; and association formation in Yemen is described by stakeholders as 'a very new concept'. Even in countries where there are more numerous NGOs, the lack of human resource capacity is one of the main problems, particularly in the skill areas of project management, financial budgeting and advocacy. Civil society organizations in the MENA region remain underdeveloped and in some cases subjected to extreme repression (Bertelsmann Stiftung 2008a). NGOs are not considered as advocacy groups that can contribute to the system of checks and balances, but according to Muasher (2008) such groups are necessary to help counteract corruption, nepotism and stagnation in Arab societies.

Business and sector associations are generally aware of the importance of advocacy efforts and the need to build capacity to carry out this function, particularly on behalf of SMEs. Chambers of commerce and industry exist in all of the MENA-12 countries but are not seen as able to play an adequate role in representing the views of SMEs to government. Other types of membership-based business associations exist in parts of the region, for example: associations of young entrepreneurs in Syria, the West Bank & Gaza, Turkey and Jordan; business women associations in Algeria, Egypt, Iraq, Jordan, Lebanon, Morocco and Turkey; and entrepreneurs' confederations, clubs or forums in Algeria, Egypt, Jordan,

Morocco and Tunisia. These associations take on the role of representing the views of independent enterprises, but for the most part have limited capacity. Notable exceptions are the Young Entrepreneurs Association (YEA) in Jordan and the General Confederation of Moroccan Enterprises (CGEM). The YEA is in the process of establishing a Public Policy Advocacy Project to advocate for legislative and structural reform to improve the business environment for SMEs and start-ups (YEA 2009). The priority issues for the new advocacy initiative are: introducing temporary business licences, enabling electronic registration, imposing the 'silence is consent' rule and removing the requirement for SME owners to personally hold vocational licences in the technical skill areas of the businesses they want to start. The CGEM, which represents the broader interests of private sector entrepreneurs in Morocco, is particularly active in representing the interests of SMEs at the national policy level and in 2007 established a Commission on SMEs to raise the level of attention to SME issues in its dialogue with the government.

The weak capacity of private sector business and SME associations is considered to be an important issue, particularly the need to improve their ability to carry out dialogue with government and the public on the operating environment for SMEs, and to build their capacity to assess the impact of policies, legislation and regulations on SMEs and perform the advocacy function. Efforts to strengthen business and sector associations are undertaken by the government and donor organizations in some countries. The EU has a project in Morocco to help sector associations improve their governance so that they can become more effective partners with government, SMEs and donors, and to improve their ability to participate in discussions with government on policy issues. It also fosters links between sector associations so that they can benefit from sharing information and knowledge and discussing the problems of SMEs and how to solve them. Jordan Enterprise works directly with sector associations in Jordan on policy development and supports capacity building plans for each association.

Private sector organizations are better organized to engage with the public sector on policy dialogue in some countries than in others. In a few of the MENA-12 countries, private sector associations have come together in federations or councils to present a collective voice to governments on private sector issues, sometimes assisted by the government. In 2004 the Algerian Ministry of SMEs and Crafts encouraged the formation of more than 90 local business associations, employer federations and professional syndicates into a National Consultative Council for the Promotion of SMEs. This council, which has a General Assembly chaired by the Minister of SMEs and Crafts, acts as a forum for continuous dialogue between government, SMEs and CSOs on SME issues, policy reforms and development programmes. Chambers of commerce, federations of industry and sector and business associations in Palestine have formed a Private Sector Coordination Council to represent their views to government. However, even with better organization and strengthened capacity, the ability of business associations and development NGOs to influence policy reforms is dependent on the effectiveness of public–private sector consultation processes within a country.

RESEARCH CAPACITY

According to the perceptions of consulted stakeholders, the overall research capacity in MENA-12 countries is weak, although variable across countries. It is considered to be very low in Jordan in terms of the numbers of researchers working on SME research issues. On broader economic and reform policy issues capacity exists in the Centre for Strategic Studies at the University of Jordan and the Jordan Centre for Public Policy Research and Dialogue (JCPPR) formed by the Higher Council for Science and Technology in 2003, but the use of evidence-based research to underpin policy was stated as a big challenge.

Research capacity is also weak in Syria and Yemen. The absence of an economic research institute in these countries is considered a barrier to informed policy development. In Syria members of the Syrian Economic Society perform quality research and the society itself provides a platform for creating policy debates by holding presentation sessions on a regular basis. The Syria Trust for Development is gaining research strength and the Syrian Enterprise and Business Centre (SEBC) conducts studies on aspects of SME development. The University of Kalamoon and the SEBC have both called for the formation of a public policy research centre dedicated to performing independent studies and research to inform public policy (Husrieh 2005; SEBC 2008). This is seen as a necessary initiative to strengthen local capacity for critical policy analysis and maximizing policy impact.

> 'We need to establish Centers of Excellence and build them to train people from here and attract them from the outside.' (key informant, Yemen).

Several stakeholders in Yemen highlighted the need for research and the lack of research capacity in Yemeni universities. There are no solid studies on the current state of the private sector and limited knowledge on how to measure growth in private sector areas. There is no network of researchers, no roster of researchers or consultants, and a big need to upgrade research skills and capacity in the country. Donors indicated a need for people trained to do quick assessment and baseline studies to underpin donor programme interventions. An initiative to build research capacity of graduate students was recommended as a partial solution to the demand for quality research.

Research capacity is perceived as being ‘adequate’ in Algeria, Egypt and Morocco. The Centre de Recherche en Economie Appliquée pour le Développement (CREAD) is the most dynamic research institute in Algeria, with a unit dedicated to research on SMEs. Egypt has several research centres, the foremost of which are the Egyptian Center for Economic Studies (ECES) and the Economic Research Forum (ERF). The ERF, which operates through a regional network, has a number of research programmes, offers research methodology training workshops, hosts an annual economic research conference, publishes a working paper series, and launched the *Middle East Development Journal* in 2009. The Centre Marocain de Conjoncture is a key research institute in Morocco with a number of economists on its staff who were educated and trained in North America and Europe. The 14 universities in Morocco use networks such as the Forum Euroméditerranéen des Instituts Economiques (FEMISE) and the Economic Research Forum (ERF) to access expertise, and have developed effective links with researchers in European countries: however not much of the research deals directly with SME issues. There are also identifiable credible economic and policy research institutes in the West Bank & Gaza, Lebanon, Turkey and Tunisia. Iraq is a mostly weak economic policy research-oriented environment. A regional network of researchers interested in entrepreneurship issues is evolving through the IDRC-supported pilot initiative to build research capacity and support the Global Entrepreneurship Monitor research in MENA countries.

Regional stakeholders identified three research-related priorities to meet the current gaps: impact and SME-related studies; expanded research infrastructure and training; and quality PSD and SME statistics and data.

Impact Studies

Numerous research topics were raised, about which more knowledge is critical. The first set of studies concerns assessments of the impact of economic policies on private sector and SME performance and social development outcomes. The list of suggested studies in this area is long. It includes topics such as: the impact of WTO accession on SMEs; the impact of FDI strategies on the transfer of technology; the impact of liberalization and FDI policies on poverty reduction; the impact on PSD of the outmigration of talent; the impact of the economic growth agenda on social issues (for example, the consequences of growth for employment and social dimensions); the social impact of privatization; the impact of economic reform on SMEs; the impact of past SME interventions and analysis of future policy options; the impact of business services and programmes on entrepreneurs; the impact of leasing and guarantee schemes on SME access to financing; the impact of government and donor policies and programmes on private sector and SME performance; the socio-economic impact of current policies and analysis of the costs of alternative policy options for achieving economic growth; the effectiveness of mechanisms for transferring science and technology (S&T) knowledge to the mainstream economy; the social cost of transition to a market economy; and the impact of donors' priorities and funding on government's actions and allocation of resources (are donors doing the right things in terms of problems and solutions or is donor-funding causing market distortions?).

SME-Related Studies

There is significant demand for SME-related research. Stakeholders expressed a need for: studies on how to foster more regional integration of SMEs; updated baseline studies on SMEs; research on women entrepreneurs and their role in SMEs; research on the entrepreneurial landscape; research on promising and high-opportunity sectors for SMEs and new businesses; research on the role of Islamic financing in improving the financing environment; research on the demand for microfinance; research on the financing gap in segments of the financial market and what types of financing are needed; knowledge of how credit guarantee programmes work in other countries; studies on the potential for setting up guarantee funds to encourage venture capital investments in emerging firms; research on growth SMEs; research on skilled labour and the needs of SMEs; and analysis of policy options for SME development. They also indicated the need for research on the 'real' role of the SME sector in private sector growth, evidenced by employment trends, value-added, entry and exit dynamism, level of formalization and growth trends (both sector-wide and within individual enterprises). There is virtually no research on the make-up of the entrepreneurial class to help guide policy decisions and targets, such as their demographics, motivations, objectives, backgrounds, behaviours and strategies. This knowledge gap also needs to be addressed.

More research on the youth challenge and longitudinal employment and labour market trends and outcomes; capacity studies of the NGO environment (mapping of what they do and what their capacity is); research on the exact nature of barriers to the commercialization of innovations in the region; and detailed analysis of the innovation system to underpin policy proposals were also noted.

Research Infrastructure and Training

Stakeholders pointed to weaknesses in research capacity, emphasizing the need to build a larger cadre of competent researchers through training and knowledge transfer, and efforts to encourage and support young regional researchers. There is also a need for an expanded research network and knowledge in performing microeconomic analysis, SME-related research and policy impact assessments. With funding support, existing research centres and networks could form the nucleus for a regional network of policy research institutes to build more research capacity in these areas.

Statistical and Data Needs

There are weaknesses in the statistical systems in most of the MENA-12 countries, which not only presents a challenge for policymaking, but also results in a lack of information about sectors, markets, growth opportunities and performance of the microeconomy. Stakeholders across the region consistently emphasized the lack of statistics and data on the SME sector. Data incompleteness, inaccuracy and lack of access were cited as

'Lack of statistics and information on the SME sector is a big gap.' (key informant, Jordan)

'We don't have good data on the SME sector . . . so it's hard to see where the policy gaps are.' (key informant, Morocco)

'SME data is a mess. There's a problem with data accuracy and reliability. The quality of data is poor and what does exist always has to be validated.' (key informant, Yemen)

'It is very difficult to get business start-up data. Every new enterprise must register with the Chamber of Commerce but data is not published.' (key informant, Jordan)

'Statistics are a problem in Syria.' (key informant, Syria)

key informant, major problems in being able to gain a better understanding of the sector and its developments over time. Data and information on the informal sector are lacking in all countries. Information on informal enterprise activity is often picked up in population censuses, but in most of the MENA-12 countries these take place only every ten years. This lack of information is problematic for governments attempting to reduce the level of informality.

Regional stakeholders suggested that the need for better statistics and data on the SME sector could be addressed by establishing a MENA Observatory on SMEs. Member countries in such an Observatory could work on harmonized SME definitions, reach consensus on the use of key indicators to describe the sector, and implement the appropriate statistical systems and sampling surveys to monitor needs and track longitudinal developments in the sector, including business entry and exit rates. There have been other regional efforts around the world to implement SME Observatory projects (for example, the European Observatory for SMEs[4] funded by the European Commission and the Latin American SME Observatory funded by the Inter-American Development Bank).[5] These efforts have resulted in building the capacity of individual governments and researchers to produce country-level SME Observatories and improving country-level statistical systems to produce quality data on the SME population on a timely basis as input to the policymaking process. These SME Observatories have become the key source of knowledge and information on the SME sector in countries and regions where they exist.

There are currently no SME Observatories in the MENA-12, although serious interest and demand has been generated at the country level. The Ministère de la Petite et Moyenne Entreprise et de l' Artisanat (MPMEA) in Algeria has proposed the establishment of a Center for the Study and Development of SMEs and Crafts (an Observatory) to produce a system of economic information on the functioning of the SME sector. The Ministry of Industry and Trade (MIT) SME Support Unit in Lebanon is planning to develop an SME Observatory to report more fully on the contribution of SMEs to the economy. The Tunisian government has also identified the need for a SME Observatory, in line with the Employment Observatory and the S&T Observatory, to add value to the base of evidence to support SME policy development. A twinning project is under way between the Tunisia Institute of National Statistics (INS) and the EU for the establishment of a reliable system to trace data on enterprises, improve data quality and make better usage of administrative resources (EC 2008a). The National SME Agency in Morocco has expressed the need for more regular research and surveys on the needs of SMEs to measure the impact of SME support programmes. It has proposed the creation of an Enterprise Observatory to meet this need (ANPME 2007). The CGEM has further reinforced the need for an SME Observatory in order to produce an annual report on the situation of SMEs in Morocco. Recent SME strategy documents in Egypt have noted the need for more comprehensive and timely data on the SME sector and its performance trends (GAFI 2008; SFD 2009). The General Authority for Investment (GAFI) strategy proposed development of an SMI Index as a numerical tool to measure changes in the different aspects of small and medium investors (SMIs) and monitor the evolution of entrepreneurship performance, including the entry, growth, survival and exit of enterprises. The Turkish Statistical Office has streamlined its activities with other ministries for data collection and has better capacity than most other MENA countries to report on new business registrations and exits. Under the EU harmonization process Turkstat will be seeking to upgrade the Business Register and reporting of enterprise statistical data to EU standards. In light of the early stage of all of this work, a collaborative effort to create a regional SME Observatory would be very beneficial to participating MENA countries.

Regional stakeholders also support the execution of annual Global Entrepreneurship Monitor (GEM) studies in MENA countries (IDRC 2008b). The objectives of the GEM project are to measure differences in entrepreneurial activity between countries, uncover factors determining national levels of entrepreneurial activity and identify policies that may enhance the national level (and quality) of entrepreneurial activity. Over 50 countries were involved in this global research in 2009. Over the years GEM research findings have played a key role in influencing policy developments, with numerous concrete examples of country-level reforms to contribute to a more favourable policy environment for new venture activity (a building block of private sector growth) that were initiated in response to GEM report recommendations. In addition the GEM project has further stimulated more intensive research on the entrepreneurial process and the determinants that give rise to higher new business start-up rates and early-stage growth enterprises in different country contexts, and created an expanding international network of knowledgeable entrepreneurship researchers. The MENA region is not well represented in the GEM research project, thus there are large gaps in understanding the dynamics of entrepreneurship in the region and in the capacity to benchmark regional performance.

POLICY DIALOGUE AND EXCHANGE

During IDRC regional workshops in 2007 and 2008, there were several expressions of interest in a regional platform for the sharing of experience,

> 'There are not many opportunities for researchers, government officials, financiers, and BDS providers to get together to exchange good practices.' (key informant, IDRC regional workshop)

policy debate and creation and dissemination of knowledge (IDRC 2008a, 2008b). Exchange and dialogue between policymakers, researchers and the private sector is happening in some countries but is recent and not very systematic. Key research organizations, government officials and donors in a number of the countries stressed the need for good-practice sharing and regional exchange forums that would facilitate policy dialogue and mutual learning, perhaps leading to governments identifying studies or projects that they could work on together.

CONCLUSIONS

The MENA-12 countries are at different stages of transition to a market economy but their governments are all undertaking reforms to modernize their economies and to become more competitive in the global economy. In this process they are facing many of the same contextual challenges. They share many of the knowledge needs and questions about the optimal policy choices to expand private sector growth effectively, and some of the same weaknesses in policy, research and institutional capacity. There is scope for adding value to PSD and SME development efforts in the region through cooperative efforts to build research and policy capacity, develop and carry out a research agenda to fill knowledge gaps, create opportunities for regional exchanges of knowledge, experience and information, and build the advocacy capacity of NGOs and business associations.

NOTES

1. The views in Chapter 6 are largely those expressed by key informants during study visits to six of the MENA-12 countries, and complemented by input from government officials, researchers and business association stakeholders in the other six countries who participated in two regional workshops hosted by IDRC in 2007 and 2008 (IDRC 2008a, 2008b). Other reflections on the issue of PSD-oriented policy, research and institutional capacity are supported by various published works on the topic.
2. Comments from a key informant during interviews in Syria in 2007.
3. IDRC has been providing funding to the Palestine Economic Policy Research Institute (MAS) to carry out a programme of micro, small and medium enterprise

(MSME)-related research and to build the capacity of Palestinian researchers in this field. Publications produced by this project can be accessed at http://www.pal-econ.org.

4. The major benefits of the European Observatory for SMEs were seen as: (a) providing systematic examination of the situation of SMEs by improving their statistical coverage and analysing the reaction of SMEs to a wide range of economic policy initiatives; (b) contributing to regional debates on SMEs and the economic and policy issues they face; and (c) providing a unique reference document for researchers, economists, policymakers, SME support organizations and SMEs.
5. The 1992 European Observatory for SMEs started with 12 countries; the 2007 Observatory work included 30 countries. It has been a role model for SME Observatories in Latin America, South Africa and Russia. The Latin America SME Observatory includes 25 countries.

7. Entrepreneurship: a platform for future private sector growth

Numerous private sector development (PSD) challenges facing the MENA-12 countries have been described in the preceding chapters. The scope of these challenges and types of policy response depend on the specific context in each country. The situation in poor and conflict countries will demand a broader PSD policy reform effort than in countries with greater political stability and more supportive PSD environments. However there is room in each of the countries for improvements in private sector performance as the mechanism for addressing their socio-economic and growth challenges.

Policy advice to MENA-12 countries by international organizations emphasizes macro- and meso-level reforms to improve the business environment and investment climate with the expectation that benefits will trickle down to the level of domestic micro, small and medium enterprises (SMEs). However this policy advice may not be sufficiently focused on micro-level reforms to strengthen the capacity of existing SMEs to take advantage of the opportunities offered by a better investment climate and to foster a larger supply of competent entrepreneurs motivated to invest in and start new enterprises. Stronger SMEs and more competent entrepreneurs do not just automatically spill out from regulatory and structural reforms. Their capacity has to be built within the context of a supportive culture. Potential and existing entrepreneurs need guidance in how to recognize and assess business ideas and opportunities, and support in converting these opportunities into successful businesses that can meet the needs of local and foreign markets. The premise of this chapter is that SME and entrepreneurship policy needs to be elevated on the government and donor policy agendas in order to achieve a more inclusive approach to development and growth in MENA-12 countries. It is now time to integrate entrepreneurship as a strategic component of economic development policy and commit to forming the interministerial alliances and public–private partnerships necessary to carry out a plan of action to unleash its potential as a platform for future private sector growth.

Future growth in gross domestic product (GDP), GDP per capita and employment will come predominantly from expanded market opportunities, the expansion of existing SMEs and new venture creation and growth. Easing the entry requirements for new firms will be important, but without efforts to stimulate a stronger entrepreneurship culture and provide the right balance of institutions, incentives and supports to enable the successful emergence of a larger supply of motivated and capable entrepreneurs from within society, the take-up of macro- and micro-level policy reforms to grow the private sector will likely continue to make slow progress.

Depending on the assumptions held about how development happens and what matters most for growth in a particular country context, governments will place priority on different targets and policy options. Given that growth happens at the level of the productive enterprise, the PSD framework presented in Figure 1.1 of Chapter 1 identifies five potential sources of private sector growth generation: foreign investors, large enterprises, SMEs, existing informal enterprises and new entrepreneurs. Different policy options exist for exploiting the growth potential of each of these target groups, depending on the decisions made about how these groups might contribute to growth. The framework of possible PSD policy targets and decisions is presented in Figure 7.1.

Firstly, private sector growth can be stimulated through macro- and meso-level reforms that will increase the amount of foreign direct investment (FDI), international trade and privatization activity. The primary policy objectives in this case will be to attract multinationals and foreign enterprises and to create 'national champions' among larger domestic firms. The extent to which domestic SMEs will benefit from this approach depends on how well they are able to take advantage of supply chain linkages and the transfer of technology and know-how.

The second policy target for private sector growth is strengthening the existing base of domestic SMEs. In this case governments have to make

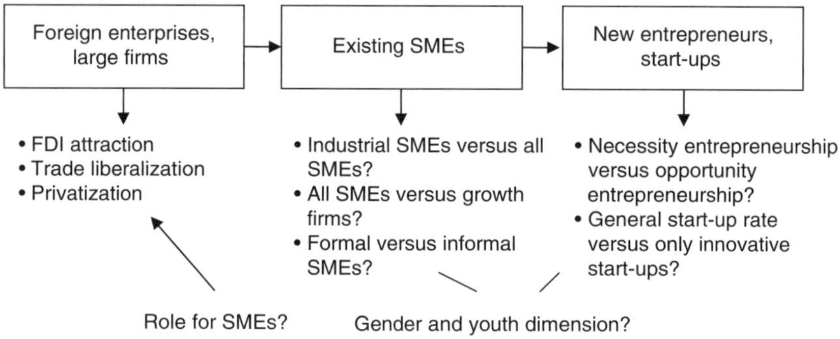

Figure 7.1 Framework of possible PSD targets and policy decisions

decisions about whether to create conditions that will improve the operating conditions for the SME sector as a whole or only industrial SMEs, whether to support the strengthening of all SMEs or only the ones with growth potential,[1] and whether and how to address the needs of informal enterprises.

The third policy target is to encourage new entrepreneurs and start-ups. In this case possible decisions are about whether to encourage higher overall business start-ups rates or only innovative quality start-ups, whether to encourage all forms of entrepreneurial activity or only opportunity-driven entrepreneurs, and whether to target specific groups of the population with growth potential, such as women and young people. If the goal is to increase the overall level of entrepreneurial activity, then attention must be paid to the cultural and societal values supportive of entrepreneurship.

The key to making the right policy choices will be understanding of the nature of the policy problem to be solved and the existing state of SME and entrepreneurship development. The ultimate objective should be to develop a balanced set of strategies directed at the three policy targets and to maximize the interconnectedness of these strategies. Based on an assessment of the situation in MENA-12 countries it appears that policies to target foreign enterprises and large firms are more sophisticated and higher on the governments' agendas than policies to target the development of SMEs, and that comprehensive policies to stimulate higher levels of entrepreneurial activity are lacking (see country profiles in Part II of this volume). In the next phase of robust private sector growth MENA governments should turn to entrepreneurship as a major policy orientation – building the capacity of the population to engage in and generate entrepreneurial activity and creating the conditions to facilitate this. Not only existing SMEs, but new entrepreneurs, are a critical part of long-term private sector growth.

THE IMPORTANCE OF ENTREPRENEURSHIP IN DEVELOPMENT AND GROWTH

Kirzner (1980) referred to entrepreneurship as the prime mover of progress, stating that to disregard the role of entrepreneurship in development would neglect an important mechanism in the growth process. Over twenty years later the topic of entrepreneurship in developing economies is described by Lingelbach and de la Viña (2005) as one of most under-studied and under-researched phenomenon; yet studies of the developed economies confirm the importance of entrepreneurial activity and new business entries to job creation, increasing competition and productivity, new product market combinations, innovation and inclusive growth (Sobel et al. 2007). Ovaska and Sobel (2005) conclude from their extensive analysis of the literature that entrepreneurship is important for a healthy, well-functioning market economy. Evidence suggests that the entry of new firms is at least as important for employment creation and productivity gains as improving the capacity of existing SMEs, if not more important (Djankov 2008). New entries, for example, introduce competition to existing firms that are then forced to improve, or decline and exit. The exiting firms are replaced by new and more productive and competitive enterprises. This higher level of dynamism in the economy is a known contributor to economic growth, illustrating the Schumpeterian 'creative destruction' concept.

Lingelbach and de la Viňa (2005) argue that entrepreneurship in the developing-economy context is distinct from that practised in advanced economies and that understanding these distinctions is critical to PSD in developing countries. Although there are pervasive opportunities for new businesses in developing economies, potential and existing entrepreneurs are operating in environments with much more economic, political and regulatory uncertainty. To reduce their risks, entrepreneurs often spread their resources over a number of related businesses; so if one does not succeed, they have others to fall back on. Entrepreneurs in developing economies depend much more heavily on informal financing through family and social networks to start their enterprises, with limited access to alternatives, such as bank financing and leasing. The lack of external financing and risk capital poses a severe limit on the growth potential of entrepreneurial enterprises. In the absence of access to external sources of financing, the cash flow from one business is used to finance the others. Because of underdeveloped and fragmented retail and distribution channels, the entrepreneurs are more likely to start businesses that have direct access to the end customer, which also reduces their initial capital requirements, and then gradually to develop businesses in vertically integrated parts of the production chain. There are fewer opportunities for entrepreneurs to gain the requisite skills and experience to grow significant businesses because of deficiencies in the education system and the lack of formal private sector jobs where they might learn about marketing, sales and organizational strategies. Furthermore many of the developing-economy environments do not have a private sector tradition, developed entrepreneurship culture and supportive institutional structures. All of these situational and environmental factors outlined by Lingelbach and de la Viňa (2005) have an impact on how entrepreneurship evolves in developing countries.

In addition larger numbers of people in developing economies are pushed into informal and subsistence forms of entrepreneurial activity due to a lack of employment opportunities and social safety nets. While these microenterprises, largely of a self-employment nature, play a role in curbing household poverty, they do little to contribute to economic growth. This leads to the critical question in entrepreneurship development of whether the type of entrepreneurship matters to growth. Naudé (2008) concludes that different contexts will produce different types and kinds of opportunities for entrepreneurs, not all of which are tied to growth. Baumol (1990) outlines three types of entrepreneurship: productive (innovative, growth-enhancing); unproductive (subsistence); and destructive (rent-seeking or illegal activities), indicating that only productive entrepreneurship produces economic growth. Acs (2006) observes from his analysis of opportunity-motivated versus necessity-motivated entrepreneurship[2] that only opportunity-entrepreneurship correlates positively with economic development. Opportunity-entrepreneurship is associated with higher growth aspirations and employment creation potential. This is an important concern for developing economies since their new enterprises are often started by people motivated by necessity. A large proportion of these necessity-entrepreneurs would prefer to be employed in paid jobs if employment opportunities were available, and many of their enterprises have limited potential for moving beyond a subsistence level. On the other hand even necessity-driven enterprises are a seedbed for experimentation and could lead to the development of higher-opportunity ventures in the future, especially for the better educated entrepreneurs.

The implication of Acs's analysis is that developing economies should focus on stimulating opportunity-entrepreneurship. However the 'opportunity environment' is influenced by the size and role of the private sector relative to the public sector in the economy; the transportation infrastructure (getting products to market); the urban–rural distribution of the population (access to services and markets); the openness of the economy to competition and trade; the sector distribution in the economy (the size of the agriculture sector versus industrial and service sectors); the level of access to technology and financial markets, and so on, which suggests that a range of policies are necessary to pave the way for productive and opportunity-motivated entrepreneurship.

In addition to the question of what kind of entrepreneurship contributes to economic growth is the question of how much entrepreneurship is good for economic growth. Carree et al. (2002) found a U-shaped curve relationship between the business ownership rate (business owners and self-employed individuals as a percentage of the labour force) and per capita

GDP in Organisation for Economic Co-operation and Development (OECD) countries. Countries with lower GDP per capita in any given time period had higher business ownership rates than those in more economically developed countries. A country's business ownership rate was found to decline with increases in GDP per capita until GDP per capita reached about US$18 000 at which point business ownership rates started to increase with rises in GDP per capita.[3] These researchers propose that there may be an equilibrium rate of business ownership and that countries falling above or below the U-shaped curve may have either too few or too many business owners. Countries with too many business owners (and possibly too many marginal enterprises led by low-ability entrepreneurs), usually developing economies, may not be benefiting sufficiently from economies of scale and scope. Countries with business ownership rates falling below the curve may not have enough entrepreneurial activity, leading to the underdevelopment of opportunities for innovation and competitive undertakings. In both cases there is a penalty – either too few or too many business owners will lead to lower economic growth rates. Government intervention may be called for to adjust the level of entrepreneurship, but the implications for appropriate policy actions will differ depending on the country's level of economic development (Wennekers et al. 2008). The policy prescription must also take into consideration the net effect of annual business entry and exit rates and an estimation of how many new enterprises are needed each year to maintain a certain level of business ownership and employment. This issue is rather moot in the context of MENA countries since there are virtually no data on business entry, survival and exit rates, and limited reliable data on the business ownership rate.

There have been few successful attempts to relate the level of entrepreneurship to economic growth and development variables. One of the major constraints to do doing this has been the lack of comparable international data on entrepreneurial activity levels. The Global Entrepreneurship Index (GEINDEX) project is one such attempt (Acs and Szerb 2009). It compares the entrepreneurial performance of different countries at different stages of development by taking into consideration measures of the quality of entrepreneurial activity, such as the capacity of the entrepreneur and growth aspirations, and relating it to the quality of the institutional and business environment. Analysis from the preliminary work on the GEINDEX reveals that although raw entrepreneurial activity levels are higher in most developing countries than in developed countries (as noted in Chapter 4), the quality of entrepreneurial activity and its contribution to growth is higher in developed countries.

However high rates of business ownership are important in developing countries because both their private sectors and economies are underdeveloped. Self-employment provides an important vehicle for employment creation and experimentation. So even if the business ownership rate is high compared to developed countries, it does not necessarily mean that the primary challenge is to move people out of self-employment and microenterprise activity. In fact increasing the rate of business formation may be necessary to continue to build the base of productive SMEs. Gries and Naudé (2008) argue that new entrepreneurs and firms are critical in transition economies since they are less encumbered with the historical influence of protectionism and a low market orientation. The challenge is more in improving the quality of start-ups, shifting the size structure of the stock of enterprises and the balance of formal versus informal enterprises, and helping MSEs overcome the limitations and disadvantages of their 'smallness'. The growth of individual SMEs in developing economies is hampered by a lack of markets, finance, infrastructure, technology and management skills. In some respects they are destined to function under some kind of maximum size threshold arbitrarily set by microfinance ceilings or the excessive cost of business registration. Removing these growth barriers is also essential.

DETERMINANTS OF ENTREPRENEURSHIP

Many factors influence the motivation of people to start businesses and become entrepreneurs. People decide to start businesses for a variety of reasons that are shaped by their family backgrounds, social environments, work experiences and personal aspirations. The desire for autonomy and economic independence, the drive to 'prove it can be done' and the expectation of a higher income are among the established motivations for starting a business. Situational forces are known to play a key role in the individual decision process (Wennekers and Thurik 1999; Verheul et al. 2001; Gabr and Hoffman 2006; Wennekers 2006), which can be triggered by necessity, the presence of compelling opportunities or some sort of inspiration.

Entrepreneurial ability, comprised of human capital (education and skills), social capital and cognition, is certainly one of the key determinants of the level and quality of entrepreneurial activity and increasingly seen in economics as a vital form of human capital (Gries and Naudé 2008). Entrepreneurial ability, when matched to profitable market opportunities and low opportunity costs of bringing a new firm to market, stands out as the central determinant of business start-up rates and ultimate business success (Naudé 2008).

People are not born with entrepreneurial ability, they acquire it over time. Entrepreneurship skills are learned and nurtured through exposure, education, experience and acquisition of knowledge and know-how. If a society wants more competent entrepreneurs, it has to invest in their know-how. The education system and training system is only one vehicle for doing this. People also learn entrepreneurial skills by growing up in a family business environment, working in small enterprises or through self-employment experiences.

Socio-economic and cultural factors, labour market characteristics, financial wealth and the quality of institutions play a strong role in the emergence of entrepreneurship in a society. Entrenched cultural perceptions and attitudes regarding risk, economic security and socially valued occupations, education systems, the nature of employment options and the incentive structure can be major hindering or supporting influences (UNECE 2008a). The determinants of entrepreneurship can be influenced through a variety of interventions geared to create awareness of entrepreneurship as an option; profile entrepreneurs as role models; open doors to opportunity; reduce fear, uncertainty and disincentives; and provide access to the necessary resources for establishing an enterprise, such as counselling, advice, financing, training, information and technical support.

On the other hand certain government policies and actions can, inadvertently or otherwise, deter entrepreneurial activity. Disincentives to entrepreneurship can be found in the taxation and regulatory environment, labour laws, social security regimes, bankruptcy laws, the system of property rights, financial markets and the intellectual property regime. Thus one of the critical factors in determining differences in entrepreneurial activity levels among countries is the presence and quality of institutions that favour the emergence of entrepreneurship. Variances in the rate of entrepreneurship can be explained by differences in economic policies and the design of formal institutions (laws and regulations) that set the rules of the game for conducting business (Hall and Sobel 2008). The incentives in this system can result in producing either higher or lower levels of productive entrepreneurship versus unproductive or destructive entrepreneurship (Baumol 1990) and, through the way that regulation affects social networks, working status, business skills and attitudes towards risk, influence an individual's decision about whether to engage in opportunity-entrepreneurship (Ardagna and Lusardi 2008).

Several links have been found between economic freedom and entrepreneurship levels, indicating that the quality of institutions matters for entrepreneurial growth. If the institutional framework does not safeguard economic freedom, people who want to start new businesses will face more risk and uncertainty and may become discouraged or channelled into informal activity (Amoros 2009). If incentive structures, such as property rights, savings policies, taxation, the regulation of labour markets and the costs of enforcing contracts and obtaining information work to encourage unproductive entrepreneurial activities (subsistence enterprises) or destructive entrepreneurial activities (rent-seeking), then even higher measured levels of entrepreneurship will lead to less economic prosperity. Weak property rights, for example, will encourage unproductive entrepreneurship. Institutions, such as high tax rates, determine the distribution of business activity between the formal and informal sectors of the economy (van Stel et al. 2007) and rigid labour and social security regulations discourage the employment growth of SMEs and possibly the levels of self-employment (Henrekson 2007). Overall, higher economic freedom leads to higher levels of productive entrepreneurial activity (Sobel et al. 2007), particularly a smaller government sector, better legal structure, secure property rights and less regulation of credit, labour and business (Nyström 2008). The economic freedom indicator with the highest relationship to entrepreneurial activity levels is the size of government (Sobel et al. 2007; Bjørnskov and Foss 2008; Nyström 2008). A large government sector (high tax rates and levels of public investment and consumption) has the effect of decreasing entrepreneurial activity levels.

Naudé (2009) argues that good governance[4] and lower start-up costs are insufficient to promote entrepreneurship in developing countries, especially opportunity-entrepreneurship. Proactive policy measures to improve entrepreneurial ability through education and training support are justified, as are policies to create a supportive environment that allows entrepreneurial learning and experimentation to take place; policies to reduce obstacles to start-ups, especially finance; and in the case of innovation, policies to support R&D activities and venture capital (Gries and Naudé 2008; Naudé 2009).

The Global Entrepreneurship Monitor (GEM) research further identifies a grouping of nine Entrepreneurial Framework Conditions (EFCs) that set the context for the emergence of entrepreneurial activity (Bosma et al. 2009): financial support; government policies and regulations; government programmes; education and training systems; research and development (R&D) transfer; the commercial, legal and professional services infrastructure; internal market openness; ease of access to physical infrastructure; and social and cultural norms. More or less of the appropriate levels and types of the EFC inputs will influence the allocation of effort into entrepreneurship by acting as an incentive or an inhibitor (Levie and Autio 2008).

THE FRAMEWORK FOR SME AND ENTREPRENEURSHIP POLICIES

The above discussion supports the case for more dedicated policy attention to the emergence of entrepreneurship. As reported in Chapter 4 most MENA-12 countries are pursuing the development and implementation of SME policy, but according to the analysis of Stevenson and Lundström (2002) and Lundström and Stevenson (2005) entrepreneurship policy encompasses a broader domain. Although they are related, SME policy and entrepreneurship policy are distinctive. They differ in their overall goals, strategic objectives, targets, policy rationale, measures and time periods for realizing results. The primary aims of SME policy are to level the playing field for smaller firms by introducing measures to help overcome their disadvantages in the marketplace due to their smallness and resource poverty, and to improve their competitiveness. The primary target is established firms. The specific aims of entrepreneurship policy are to increase entrepreneurial activity levels, enhance entrepreneurial capacity and foster a favourable environment for the emergence of new and early-stage growth firms. Because firms do not start themselves, the unit of policy analysis and focus must shift away from the firm to the individual entrepreneur or potential entrepreneur. This emphasis on individuals versus entities is one of the most distinguishing features of entrepreneurship policy vis-à-vis SME policy.

The interacting scope of these two policy domains by stages of the entrepreneurial and SME development processes is illustrated in Figure 7.2. Entrepreneurial activity starts before a firm is created, so entrepreneurship policy applies during the awareness creation and pre-start phases as well as during the early-stage start-up, survival and growth phases. SME policy assumes that assisted firms already exist and have built sufficient capacity to absorb the benefits of any assistance.

The role and appropriate type of policy intervention will depend on which market, systemic or cultural failures the government is aiming to address, and at what phase of the entrepreneurial or SME development process. However the foundation for an efficient SME policy will be limited without efforts to foster the development of positive attitudes and a supply of motivated individuals, nascent entrepreneurs, start-ups and young emerging firms; thus specific policies to encourage entrepreneurship are essential. Policies to improve the environment for entrepreneurship will also improve the operating conditions for existing SMEs, so in some respects, entrepreneurship policies can be seen as the base.

The framework for entrepreneurship policies is illustrated in Figure 7.3.[5] It includes policies in six major areas: reduction of entry and exit

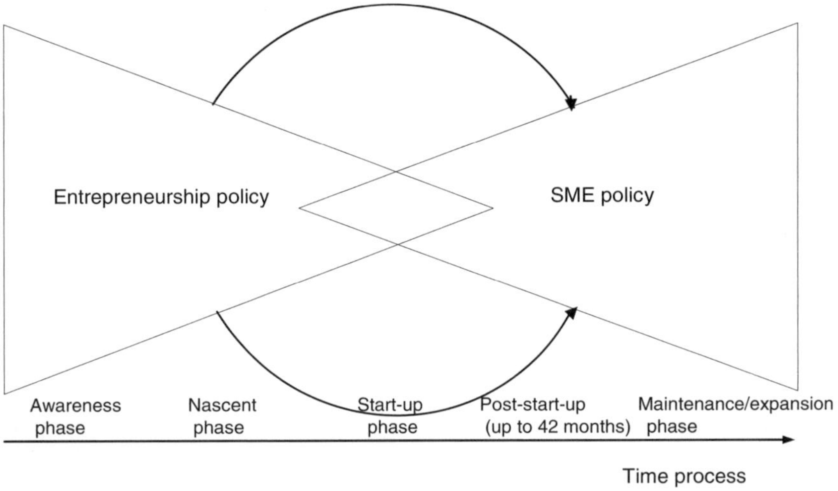

Source: Stevenson and Lundström (2002), p. 27.

Figure 7.2 The interface between entrepreneurship policy and SME policy

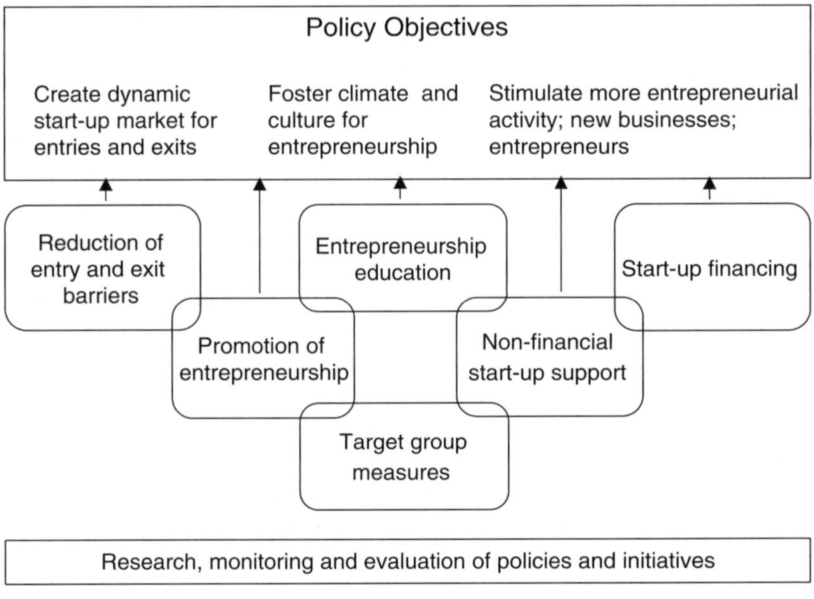

Figure 7.3 Framework for entrepreneurship policies

barriers; promotion of entrepreneurship; entrepreneurship education; start-up financing; non-financial start-up support; and target group measures. The framework also includes research and the monitoring and evaluation of policies and initiatives as one of its components. The mix of policies selected as priorities by individual governments will very much depend on the context for entrepreneurship and the strength of the existing SME and entrepreneurial sector.

ENTREPRENEURSHIP POLICY CONFIGURATIONS

Stevenson and Lundström (2002) described four dominant entrepreneurship policy typologies, each one specific to a set of contextual factors in a country. Firstly, in countries with already high levels of self-employment and entrepreneurial activity for their level of economic development – for example, Canada, the United States (US) and Australia – governments tend not to have a specifically identifiable 'entrepreneurship policy'. These are countries that have long-standing SME policies in place with few barriers to starting a business, and well-developed cultures of entrepreneurship. The approach of these governments to entrepreneurship development is to improve the level of service and programming in their existing SME support structures to accommodate the needs of start-ups and new entrepreneurs. Often special initiatives will be targeted to particular groups of the population that are underrepresented in the entrepreneurial population, such as women, or to groups where starting a business could be an option to unemployment, such as the unemployed and people with disabilities. The area of entrepreneurship policy where these countries do tend to exert dedicated effort is to increase the level of innovative entrepreneurship. The policy agenda here involves simplifying the patenting process, ensuring the appropriate level of intellectual proportion rights and protection, funding R&D and early-stage commercialization processes, stimulating a supply of early-stage risk and venture capital, and promoting an innovation culture. It is important to note that innovation-oriented entrepreneurship policy will be most effective when it builds on an already strong base of SMEs and entrepreneurial activity.

The second typology highlights a policy orientation geared to specifically foster new venture creation. This approach tends to be dominant in countries with administrative, regulatory and structural barriers to starting a business and disincentives to entrepreneurship and new firm entry in labour, competition, taxation and bankruptcy regimes. Even though the level of self-employment in these countries may be high, typical of countries at a lower level of economic development, so is the level of unemployment and informality. A typical case might also be one where the culture of entrepreneurship is weak due to recent transformation to a market economy. The SME sector is likely large but underdeveloped in terms of its capacity. Having an SME policy is critical to strengthening the whole sector, but new venture creation is an important pillar within the framework of this SME policy. The policy challenges are to reduce the administrative and regulatory time and cost of starting a business, facilitate the formalization process for existing SMEs, and improve access to microfinancing, entrepreneurial skills and business development services (BDS). The overall objective is to create employment. For example, in the early 2000s the Spanish government launched a number of initiatives to facilitate the new company creation process and, through interministerial cooperation and coordination, to reduce incentives to entrepreneurship in labour laws, taxation rules and the financing system. It launched one-stop information shops, single business windows for business registration, mutual guarantee funds, entrepreneurship education initiatives in the secondary and vocational education systems, and entrepreneurship training programmes for the unemployed, youth and women. The government also created a new form of legal business, that of an 'autonomous society', to encourage micro and informal economy enterprises to shift to the formal economy. The autonomous society was a form of business somewhere between a sole proprietorship and a limited liability company that could be created with a minimum of cost and legal complexity and would apply for the first two years of a firm's existence.

The third typology is characterized by policies tailored to increase entrepreneurial activity and start-up rates among specific groups of the population. These might include groups that are under-represented among entrepreneurs, such as women and youth, or groups with higher potential to start innovative, technology-oriented ventures, such as university graduates, researchers and scientists. The US and Canada stand out as countries where target group policies for women, youth and the unemployed are well developed. This form of 'niche entrepreneurship policy' is most appropriate in contexts where the base of entrepreneurs and SMEs is relatively strong and where 'niche' approaches will increase overall growth activity as well as greater social inclusion.

The final typology is characterized by a holistic approach to entrepreneurship policy. Countries with this approach have entrepreneurship policy documents and frameworks that lay out objectives, targets and measures to increase the level of entrepreneurial activity and dynamism in the economy. They tend to be economies with low business ownership, self-employment and new firm entry rates and weak entrepreneurship cultures. The policy framework generally includes measures to promote an entrepreneurship culture; reduce barriers to entry, growth and exit; embed entrepreneurship in the education system; improve access to start-up financing, business information, technical assistance and networks; and address the needs of specific target groups, including innovative entrepreneurs. The governments taking this approach are attempting to address the range of failures to entrepreneurship development: systemic failures, social failures, education failures, information asymmetries, externalities and market failures. In the mid-2000s Denmark, Finland and the United Kingdom (UK) provided good examples of the holistic entrepreneurship policy approach.

Obvious from this discussion of entrepreneurship policy typologies is that context matters in the choice of approach. The MENA-12 countries tend to have relatively high self-employment rates, high levels of informality, weak SME sectors and, perhaps with the exception of Lebanon and Morocco, relatively weak entrepreneurship cultures. Their experience with SME policy is relatively recent, in some cases only emerging. According to the European Communities and OECD (2008) only Morocco and Tunisia (among the eight MENA-12 countries included in their policy assessment exercise) have gone so far as to set policy guidelines for enterprise development. The idea of entrepreneurship policy is a new concept in these environments, with only a few isolated and fragmented initiatives. The most appropriate approach to entrepreneurship policy is likely integration as a strategic pillar within existing SME policy frameworks, but at the same time encompassing the scope of policy objectives and measures characteristic of holistic entrepreneurship policy. The alternative is a companion policy framework to complement the existing SME policy. Since so many issues of institutional quality need to be addressed, implementation of entrepreneurship policies will require an interministerial approach.

The following presents an elaboration of the policy objectives and measures within the framework for entrepreneurship policies presented in Figure 7.3 with brief reference to current practices in MENA-12 countries.

Entrepreneurship Promotion

The major objectives of policies to promote entrepreneurship are to reduce the cultural and psychological barriers to entrepreneurship and raise the status of entrepreneurship as a valued activity in society. Positive exposure to entrepreneurship is an important factor in creating awareness of the possibilities of starting a business and motivating more of the population to consider entrepreneurship as a feasible career and employment option, as well as in reinforcing the social legitimacy of entrepreneurial activity and enhancing its level of desirability. This is particularly important in economies where the culture of entrepreneurship is weak. Examples of initiatives might include campaigns to stress the value of entrepreneurship to job creation and economic prosperity, media stories profiling entrepreneurship and credible role models, award programmes to recognize and reward successful entrepreneurs, and public events to call attention to entrepreneurial activity and the support that is available to it.

In the MENA context, promotion efforts are very important because the social legitimacy of entrepreneurship is not well engrained. This is particularly evident in countries like Algeria where much lower shares of the adult population consider entrepreneurship as a desirable career choice, perceive that entrepreneurs have high status within society and agree that they often see stories about successful new businesses in the public media (Table 7.1). Although relatively high percentages of the adult population in the MENA countries perceive that entrepreneurship is a desirable career choice, a large share would actually prefer to work in the public sector. The exceptions to this are in Lebanon and Morocco. Yemeni adults indicate favourable attitudes to entrepreneurship, however few would prefer to be self-employed if they could choose their work environment, or expect to start a business in the next three years.

A survey poll of almost 9000 young people in MENA countries, conducted by Gallup in 2009, found that a high proportion of 15–29-year-olds would prefer to work in government jobs than to be self-employed, assuming similar pay and working conditions (Silatech 2009). Only in Algeria, Lebanon and Morocco is self-employment the preferred employment choice of young people (Figure 7.4). The self-employment preference rates in these three countries are close to the EU-25 average of 44.6 per cent (Gallup Organization 2007). The lowest preference levels for self-employment are among young people in Egypt, Yemen, Iraq and Syria. The legacy of public sector employment continues to affect the culture with respect to desired forms of work, although it is interesting to note that, in spite of high preferences for government jobs in Sudan, Iraq and Tunisia, young people in these countries are the most likely to indicate that they plan to start their own business within the next 12 months.

Very few of the MENA-12 governments include the promotion of entrepreneurship (as defined above) in official policy initiatives. Syria is one of the few where the government has integrated 'promoting SMEs and entrepreneurs' as a priority in its SME strategy (MoET 2009). Its objectives for doing this are to generate a more positive image of entrepreneurship and to ensure that entrepreneurship and a career in the private sector are viewed positively. Consultations conducted by the Syrian government revealed that: 'entrepreneurship is not promoted positively or effectively

Table 7.1 Entrepreneurship perceptions and attitudes, MENA countries

	AG	EG	JO	LE	MA	SY	TN	TR	WB&G	YE
Indicators of entrepreneurship culture (% of 'yes' responses, adult population)										
Entrepreneurship is a desirable career choice	57	73	82	85	83	90	87	72	87	94
Entrepreneurs have high status within society	55	..	84	79	87	91	94	..	79	97
Often see stories about new businesses in the media	39	57	68	66	73	58	70	63	53	95
Perceptions and attitudes towards entrepreneurship (% of 'yes' responses, adult population)										
See good opportunities for starting a business	50	40	46	56	51	59	15	47	52	16
Have the skills and knowledge to start a business	56	53	63	82	75	66	40	44	63	62
Fear of failure would prevent them from starting a business	31	25	36	18	25	16	34	39	33	61
Expect to start a business in the next 3 years	22	35	25	22	27	54	54	21	24	9
Current and preferred work environment (% of adult population)										
Would prefer to be self-employed	46	..	48	63	70	53	..	..	46	15
Would prefer to work for the public sector	44	..	43	19	18	39	..	..	40	56

Source: GEM APS data, 2008, 2009.

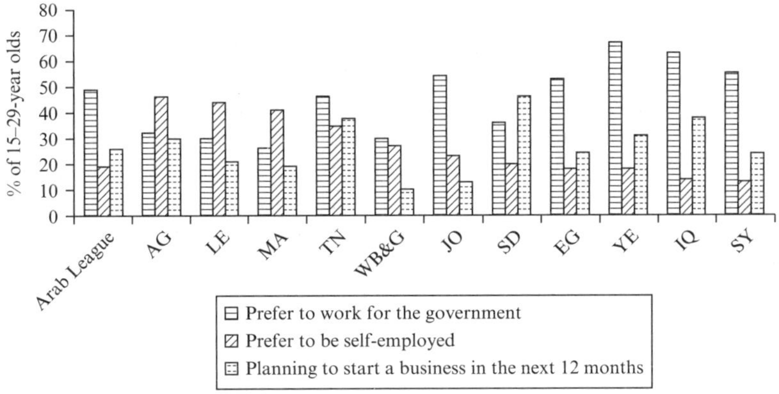

Source: Silatech (2009).

Figure 7.4 Work preferences of young people, 15–29

in Syrian media, there are few inspirational role models who could be used to promote the entrepreneurial positives; and . . . there are few examples . . . of signposting in the Syrian media as to where would be entrepreneurs could go to for encouragement, support and advice' (MoET 2009, p. 61). This yet to be implemented strategy will include a communications and promotional campaign with development of media and print material packages. Governments in Egypt, Jordan, Lebanon and Morocco joined with private sector and non-governmental organization (NGO) partners to support Global Entrepreneurship Week activities in 2009 and there are isolated examples of entrepreneur competitions and entrepreneurship conferences and events in the various countries. It is also likely to be important in the MENA context to target government officials in any promotional efforts as they too need to be educated about the value of entrepreneurs in a modern society. Increasing awareness among policymakers will have an influence on the allocation of effort and resources into supporting entrepreneurship.

Entrepreneurship Education

Entrepreneurship education is considered one of the determinants of the level of entrepreneurship, an indicator of a country's entrepreneurship performance (Levie and Autio 2008; OECD 2009e) and essential for developing the human capital necessary for the society of the future (WEF 2009a). However it is an issue that has only gained policy traction since the late 1990s (Stevenson and Lundström 2002). The goals of entrepreneurship education policy are to promote an entrepreneurial mindset from an early age, adopt entrepreneurship as a key competency in curriculum outcomes of the primary and secondary education system, and expose students to the principles and practices of entrepreneurship and starting a business at all levels of the education system. The rationale behind entrepreneurship education efforts is that entrepreneurship is a learned way of thinking, behaviour and set of skills. Education for entrepreneurship is expected to enhance the supply of entrepreneurs through three mechanisms: a cultural effect on students' attitudes and behavioural dispositions (mindset aspects); enhanced cognitive ability to recognize and assess opportunities; and provision of the skills required to start and grow a business (Levie and Autio 2008). By introducing entrepreneurship in the curriculum, countries can build their entrepreneurial capacity and ability. Although there is evidence that students who take entrepreneurship courses are more likely to become future entrepreneurs, the skills and knowledge learned in these courses can provide better preparation for all forms of work.

Component parts of entrepreneurship education strategies include: liberalizing the education system to teach creative thinking and problem-solving and independent learning; developing age-appropriate entrepreneurship-related curriculum and resource materials; training teachers in their use; providing classes in how to start and manage a business as part of vocational education and training programmes and university courses; and supporting extracurricular activities to expose students to the practice of entrepreneurship. Good practices in entrepreneurship education initiatives in developed economies are described in Stevenson and Lundström (2002), OECD (2009b) and EC (2009).

Education and training for entrepreneurship is an enterprise policy area where MENA countries did not fare very well in the OECD assessment of progress towards implementing the Euro-Mediterranean Charter for Enterprise (European Communities and OECD 2008). Tunisia, with an assessment score of three out of five, fared better than the other countries (see Chapter 4). Promoting the entrepreneurial spirit and key entrepreneurial competencies are embedded in the Tunisian National Education Strategy and related competencies and skills are taught at the secondary school level. The Moroccan National Charter on Education and Training emphasizes promotion of an entrepreneurial mindset in general and vocational education programmes, and is achieving progress at the secondary school level through the 'one school, one enterprise' initiative. Progress is less advanced in the other MENA-12 countries. In 2009 the Egyptian Minister of Education approved expansion of the International Labour Organization (ILO) Know About Business curriculum in secondary schools, following a successful pilot in 2007–08, and the Minister of

Higher Education is supporting the integration of entrepreneurship learning in faculties of engineering and other cross-campus disciplines. The European Training Foundation is working with the Syrian Ministry of Education and Minister of Higher Education to promote entrepreneurship education in schools and universities; this initiative will be supported within Syria's new SME strategy framework (MoET 2009). In Lebanon the Ministry of Education has given INJAZ-Lebanon access to all public schools to deliver entrepreneurship-related courses.

These efforts are recent and have not had much time to impact on the knowledge base of the population. A very low proportion of the adult population in MENA-12 countries has taken any courses in starting a business as part of their formal in-school learning experience; generally fewer than 5 per cent (IDRC 2010). This rises to an average of over 11 per cent in more developed economies, with rates higher than 20 per cent in Columbia, Ecuador, Chile, Belgium and Slovenia (Bosma et al. 2009).

Efforts to introduce students to the world of entrepreneurship in the MENA-12 countries are more prevalent as an extracurricular activity. NGOs, such as INJAZ, the Syrian Young Entrepreneurs Association, the Syria Trust for Development, the Queen Rania Centre for Entrepreneurship in Jordan and the Egyptian Junior Business Association are among those playing a key role in promoting entrepreneurship as a career option for young people. INJAZ, which is affiliated with Junior Achievement Worldwide, offers its curriculum and experiential programmes in over 100 schools in Jordan as well as several in Egypt, Lebanon and Syria. Country-specific programmes are offered through such initiatives as the Bader Young Entrepreneurs Program in Lebanon and the BIDAYA youth business programme and SHEBAB entrepreneurship training and entrepreneurship promotion projects in Syria. University business plan competitions take place in several countries to encourage students to develop business ideas. Entrepreneur societies have been formed by students at universities such as the Princess Sumaya University for Technology (PSUT) in Jordan and the American University in Cairo; interest is rapidly growing on a number of other campuses but this will be best supported by faculty advisors and community entrepreneurs.

Reduction of Entry and Exit Barriers

This area of entrepreneurship policy has as its objectives to remove the regulatory barriers to the entry and exit of businesses, simplify the administrative procedures for starting and operating a business, and remove the disincentives to self-employment and entrepreneurship that are often found in the labour laws and taxation regimes. Restrictions on entry and exit inhibit the market process with a negative impact on growth by protecting incumbent firms and reducing the level of competition in the marketplace, discouraging the registration of new firms and creating opportunities for corruption and rent-seeking. Government policies attempting to limit competition have the effect of reducing the level of entrepreneurship, new product market combinations and innovation (Sobel et al. 2007). On the other hand, without regulatory restrictions market concentration can emerge. If competition laws and policies are inadequate to curb anti-competitive practices of incumbent firms, then collusion practices and abuse of market power by dominant firms will also serve to prevent and deter market entry (Joekes and Evans 2008; Sekkat 2008; Sekkat 2010).

Simplified business entry regulations and less costly procedures lead to more new firms being established and reduced levels of informality (Djankov 2008). High start-up costs result in both fewer entrepreneurs and higher unemployment (Naudé 2008). The link between entrepreneurship and institutional quality has already been established. The quality of rules in the formal legal and regulatory system (strongly associated with the economic freedoms) can impact on the level, type and distribution of entrepreneurial activity.

The whole area of regulatory policy related to improving the environment for smaller enterprises has a long history dating back to the late 1970s. As an entrepreneurship policy issue, it has been gaining considerable momentum in OECD countries and EU member states since the late 1990s (Stevenson and Lundström 2002). Since that time governments in these economies have been scrutinizing, amending and reforming existing legislation, regulations and procedures, and subjecting proposed new legislation and regulations to assessments of their potential impact on new businesses and existing SMEs. In particular, market entry barriers, regulated markets, government regulation and complicated administrative procedures and tax systems present obstacles to nascent and new enterprises. Flexible labour markets, streamlined administrative requirements (that reduce time and cost), simplified tax policies and reporting systems, and reformed bankruptcy laws are among those most conducive to enhancing entrepreneurial activity levels. The process of adjusting the regulatory environment is ongoing. Countries all over the world, including advanced economies, are in a race to the top of the rankings on the World Bank's ease of doing business reports, losing and gaining places on an annual basis.

Governments in MENA-12 countries have a long road ahead to improve the regulatory and administrative environment for SMEs and entrepreneurs. Many of the existing laws and regulations affecting business were developed under planned-economy regimes and are inappropriate in a market economy context. The cost to the economy is a high level of informality, in terms of both enterprises and employment. The process of entry and exit of firms in MENA countries is less dynamic than in the transition countries of Eastern Europe, except in Turkey (Sekkat 2010). The issue of intensifying the 'creative destruction' process by encouraging new entries and easing the process of exit of unproductive enterprises warrants further policy attention.

Governments in most of the MENA-12 have undertaken massive reform programmes since 2000 to adjust their regulatory environments. One-stop shops have been created to facilitate the business registration process, company laws and commercial codes have been amended, tax regimes simplified and land registration systems implemented or improved. Most of the MENA-12 governments have launched extensive regulatory reform initiatives to improve the business climate, including preparation for the Guillotine approach in Egypt and Syria. Not as much progress has been made on competition policy,[6] bankruptcy laws, labour market flexibility and the protection and enforcement of property rights, as evidenced by results in the World Bank Doing Business and Index of Economic Freedom assessments.

An area of regulation that advanced economies have already dealt with is the regulation of banks and non-banking financial institutions to improve access to financing for SMEs and start-ups. Undertaking this work is critical in MENA-12 countries. Microfinance frameworks are in place in Jordan and Syria; the Egyptian and Turkish governments have drafted microfinance laws; and Yemen adopted a bank microfinance law in 2009 that opened the door for microsavings. With minor exceptions, stock exchanges, where they exist, are small and inflexible with respect to the listing of new firms. Regulatory frameworks for venture capital and microfinance are rare (Morocco and Jordan being exceptions), although there are efforts in certain countries to change this.

It is paramount for these countries to complete their review of all existing laws and procedures to remove disincentives to entrepreneurial activity (in the areas affecting economic freedoms) and to apply the 'think small first' principle to all new legislation and regulations. It is also essential for them to make clear and accessible information available to the public on regulations and procedures for starting and closing a business.

Start-Up Financing

It is a well-known fact that entrepreneurs have difficulty securing financing for the start-up of a new enterprise, particularly if they lack collateral and a track record in business. To address market failures in the allocation of financing to new and small enterprises, governments in many countries develop policy measures to fill the gap. These measures can take the form of microloan funds, seed capital funds, government-backed credit guarantee schemes to encourage bank lending or incentive programmes to stimulate private venture capital investments in early-stage growth-potential enterprises. There are many more types and sources of financing available to start-ups and SMEs in developed than in developing countries. Financial and capital markets are deeper and more fully developed and there is a longer history of bank financing of SMEs and entrepreneurial ventures.

This diversity and depth of financing types and sources for SMEs and new start-ups does not exist in MENA-12 countries. The overwhelming majority of new firms are started without the benefit of any formal external financing. The major financing instrument is microcredit and the penetration of the potential market is low. Results from the 2009 Global Entrepreneurship Monitor research studies in seven MENA countries reveal that less than half of nascent entrepreneurs expect to fund their start-up from their own money (IDRC 2010). Those who expect financing from others are much more likely to seek it from their immediate family members and relatives than from banks, microfinance providers or government programmes. The pattern differs somewhat across countries. For example, Algerian start-ups are much more likely than in other countries to expect financing from banks, and Yemeni start-ups from microfinance providers.

As described in Chapter 4, microfinance is well established in Morocco, Tunisia and the West Bank & Gaza; moderately developed in Egypt and Turkey; and young or nascent in Algeria, Jordan, Syria, Iraq, Lebanon, Yemen and Sudan. Although a certain level of microfinance is delivered through government agencies, the majority is funded by donors and delivered through NGOs. There is also evidence to suggest that microcredit is more accessible to existing MSEs than to start-ups (PlaNet Finance 2008). Government guarantee programmes exist in most of the countries but the reach and impact of these programmes are unknown. Special initiatives to finance the start-ups of unemployed graduates and young people are supported by governments in Algeria, Morocco, Tunisia and Turkey. The venture capital industry is weak in all countries except in Morocco, Tunisia and Turkey, although technology development funds exist in some countries to provide start-up funding for technology-intensive and information and communication technology (ICT) start-ups. The lack of credit information bureaus is a hindrance to enabling banks to assess the risk of new entrepreneurs as clients, even if they were predisposed to lending in this market. The OECD assessed more progress on enterprise policy in the area of access to financing in Egypt and Morocco, with the lowest level of performance in Syria (European Communities and OECD 2008). (See Table 4.6 in Chapter 4.)

To improve the availability of start-up financing in the MENA countries, there is a need to expand microfinance programmes; explore the potential for increasing Islamic financing schemes; provide incentives for the establishment of seed capital and venture capital funds; be more aggressive in encouraging banks to offer credit to start-ups and early-stage enterprises (more flexible credit guarantee terms, training of bank officers in SME lending practices); develop systems for the provision of credit information; provide information to entrepreneurs on sources and types of financing; and offer programmes in economic and financial literacy to improve the ability of SMEs and new entrepreneurs to attract external financing.

Start-Up Support: Services and Infrastructure

The goal of business support services (defined as the provision of information, advice, counselling, entrepreneurial and management training, mentoring and technical assistance) is to assist new entrepreneurs and SMEs in acquiring knowledge, skills and know-how. The rationale for policy measures in this area is linked to evidence that the use of professional advisory and training services has an impact on enterprise survival and growth rates. In ideal markets these services would be provided to new entrepreneurs and SMEs at affordable prices by the private sector. However the reality is that until the business has reached a certain scale the entrepreneurs cannot afford the services of professional consulting and training firms, or are unaware of its value. This indicates some form of market failure or information asymmetry. The situation is more extreme in developing countries because the capacity of the private sector in providing services to start-ups and SMEs is underdeveloped. Thus a role for public provision of services and the eventual creation of a private market can be justified.

The types of information and guidance needed by entrepreneurs will depend on the stage of the entrepreneurial or business development process they are in. Nascent entrepreneurs trying to obtain assistance with refining their business idea or assessing the potential of an opportunity will have substantially different needs than an existing entrepreneur who is trying to access international markets. Governments in developed economies tend to have mature, well-established and coordinated business support systems in place that serve the needs of groups of entrepreneurs at different stages of development. These might include entry points that help new entrepreneurs access relevant information on starting a business; online portals for start-ups; entrepreneurship or enterprise centres to help potential entrepreneurs explore their aspirations and capabilities in developing business ideas and opportunities; 'just-in-time' and flexible entrepreneurship training approaches; business advisory centres that perform diagnostic and counselling services; networks of business incubators providing space, networking and advisory services; and technology and innovation centres assisting with technology transfer and commercialization activities.

Effective provision of these various services requires a network of institutional providers and a base of capable professionals with the requisite set of knowledge, skills and competencies. Governments in a number of countries develop professional standards for the delivery of business support services and invest in professional development programmes to improve the standards of performance. The United Kingdom is a good-practice example of this, although there are institutes for business advisors and certified small business counsellor initiatives in many European countries and throughout the Asia-Pacific Economic Cooperation (APEC) countries, including Indonesia and Malaysia.[7]

The system of formal support in the offering of guidance, advice, counselling and information to new entrepreneurs and existing SMEs is not well developed in any of the MENA-12 countries, an issue highlighted in Chapter 4. In addition to varying levels of access to government-managed business support systems at the national level, NGOs and business associations play a role in providing business advisory and training services. Most of these services are heavily reliant on donor funding, and while donor support is beneficial to building capacity in the region, vacuums in services to entrepreneurs and SMEs are created when programme funding comes to an end. Issues of capacity, coordination, the range and quality of services offered, the number of clients assisted, resourcing and rural access are prevalent throughout the business support system. Fewer than 10 per cent of early-stage entrepreneurs in seven of the MENA-12 countries make use of advisory services from public agencies, NGOs and business associations; the vast majority of start-up entrepreneurs use their informal networks of family and friends for business advice (IDRC 2010), much more so than in the case of developed countries. What would be useful is a country-level analysis of the institutional capacity of the national system of business support to identify areas for enhancement.

Various types of entrepreneurship and business management training programmes are available and being delivered, primarily supported by donors. Countries make use of the ILO and International Finance

Corporation (IFC) training materials and in-house approaches developed by NGOs to raise the competence of entrepreneurs and SME owners. Again there are coordination, reach, cost and capacity issues. A base of knowledgeable private sector trainers and advisors is gradually being developed, but the task remains large.

Consideration should be given to creating networks of entrepreneurship or enterprise centres; opening one-stop shops (OSSs) as sources of information on markets, business opportunities, suppliers, steps to take in starting a business and referral services; developing partnerships with private sector organizations and business associations and building their capacity to deliver quality and appropriate BDS to new and early-stage entrepreneurs; encouraging successful entrepreneurs to act as mentors and coaches to start-ups and early-stage growth firms; and expanding the number of incubators to provide premises and advisory services for new start-ups. The provision of these services should be consistently available to entrepreneurs in rural as well as urban centres.

Target Group Policies

The majority of governments in developed countries adopt policy measures to increase the participation of groups of the population that are under-represented in entrepreneurial and SME ownership activity. An analysis of which demographic groups have lower than average business start-up and business ownership rates will often reveal that they do not have equitable access to the necessary resources, opportunities, knowledge and support. The particular groups for targeting will differ across countries depending on the context. In the US, for example, lower rates of business ownership among Hispanics and African-Americans led to implementation by the US Small Business Administration of policies and measures to address the barriers they faced in accessing skills, financing and markets. The US government also has entrepreneurship programmes targeted specifically to war veterans.

Governments in many countries have special policies targeting the entrepreneurial development of women, some dating as far back as the early 1980s. Self-employment became a way for the influx of Western women entering the labour force to create meaningful employment for themselves during a time when there were widespread discriminatory hiring practices in private firms. However many of these women lacked work histories, management experience and access to the male-dominated business networks, had difficulty accessing bank financing for their businesses and faced a range of social and cultural barriers, not dissimilar to the current situation facing women in MENA countries.

Legislative actions to give women the right to access credit in their own name without the requirement for a male co-signer, efforts to change attitudes about women's role in economic activity, and the establishment of women's business development centres, training and mentoring networks and dedicated loan guarantee funds were among the policy measures adopted to level the playing field for women entrepreneurs (Stevenson and Lundström 2002).

Other common groups for targeted entrepreneurship policies are the unemployed and young people. Entrepreneurship is seen as a viable employment alternative for a certain percentage of unemployed people and supported by government programmes in Canada, the US, the UK, Sweden and many other countries that have unemployment insurance schemes. By offering incentives for unemployed persons to participate in entrepreneurship training programmes that will help them develop business ideas and entry strategies, they can be assisted back into the labour market. Policies to assist young people to become entrepreneurs are grounded in evidence that they lack awareness of entrepreneurship as a career option, as well as experience and entrepreneurial know-how, and have difficulty accessing external financing. The response in developed countries has been to promote youth entrepreneurship, establish youth enterprise centres, create special financing schemes for young entrepreneurs and support the formation of young entrepreneur networks.

The lessons learned from the target group policy experiences of other countries suggest two types of appropriate actions: (1) actions to reduce barriers and obstacles endemic to the particular group; and (2) tailored financial and non-financial support services to improve their access to information, role models, markets, advice, entrepreneurial skills, financing and networks.

The nature of the youth employment and gender challenges for the MENA-12 countries were articulated in Chapters 3 and 4. To achieve expansion of the private sector and ensure future employment for youth and women, more inclusive entrepreneurship strategies will be necessary. Governments in Algeria, Morocco, Tunisia and Turkey, in particular, have national programmes to support young entrepreneurs, for example, the Moukalatawi programme in Morocco and the Agence Nationale de Soutien à l'Emploi des Jeunes (ANSEJ) young entrepreneurs programme in Algeria, both mentioned in Chapter 3. The extent of national level policy emphasis on the promotion of women's entrepreneurship is much lower in MENA-12 countries with few examples of good-practice policy initiatives. With the increasing supply of educated young men and women entering the labour market in MENA countries and the lack of available public and private sector jobs, governments would do well to step up their efforts to design and implement targeted entrepreneurship development strategies.

This completes a brief description of the six entrepreneurship policy areas. Given the nature of private sector, SME and entrepreneurship development in the MENA-12 countries, it appears that a higher emphasis should be placed on fostering an entrepreneurial society, accelerating the take-up of entrepreneurship as a viable career option, and providing the necessary support for the start-up and growth of viable ventures. The high-level entrepreneurship policy challenges are to: increase the number of entrepreneurs and formal SMEs to accelerate growth in the stock of private enterprises; improve the capacity and quality of new entrepreneurs to influence stronger and more opportunity-focused start-ups with higher survival rates and growth potential; and improve the level of access to the required resources and support to start and grow successful businesses. This suggests that a holistic and integrated entrepreneurship policy approach is the most appropriate for MENA-12 countries, but one closely linked to a comprehensive SME strategy that aims to: inject innovative attitudes and practices into existing enterprises, especially microenterprises; upgrade the management competencies and competitiveness of existing SMEs; and increase the percentage of high-growth and innovation-related firms.

CONCLUDING REMARKS

Private sector development is very important as a driver of employment and economic growth in the MENA-12 countries. Yet the private sector in these countries remains relatively small, as well as concentrated in a small number of large firms that have benefited from protective policies and a large number of very small firms that have limited access to formal finance, markets and support programmes. The private sector is largely uncompetitive in global markets and its growth is hindered by a high level of informality. The World Bank (2006d) outlines the main structural issues constraining investment and the growth of private enterprises in the MENA region as:

- the regulatory and administrative environment for business, which limits entry, exit, growth and competition;
- the lack of access to finance and other business supports;
- inadequate trade facilitation infrastructure and logistics;
- the lack of access to land and the cost and complexity of titling and registration of property; and
- the still heavy role and intervention of the state in the economy.

These and other issues affecting PSD, such as increasing the supply of entrepreneurs and strengthening the entrepreneurial capacity of the population, are among the top policy priorities to be addressed. However there is considerable diversity among the MENA countries, as demonstrated throughout this book. While there are some common PSD-related deficiencies, such as the low representation of women in entrepreneurial activity, the relatively low quality of education systems, bureaucratic regulatory environments and the absence of external formal financing, countries differ dramatically in their contexts and capacities. Thus tailored policy responses will be needed.

Part I has described the framework for PSD; analysed the economic and social challenges facing the MENA-12 countries; examined their comparative PSD performance; and emphasized the critical importance of strengthening their entrepreneurial capacity for future growth. The concluding message is that entrepreneurship development has been an overlooked area of PSD. Needed is a comprehensive set of policies and strategies to unleash the entrepreneurial potential of each country in companion with an elevated status for policies to develop existing SMEs and improve their competitiveness. It is time to bring the development of SMEs and entrepreneurship into the mainstream of economic policymaking.

Given the different contexts in each country with respect to levels of human capital, political stability, current policy orientations and initiatives, institutional quality, financial and non-financial support structures, levels of entrepreneurial activity and capacity for private sector development, the platform for moving forward is very much country-level specific. However from a generic perspective, several priorities emerge.

Invest in Raising the Average Education Level of the Population

This will pay off in human capital development, and matters to private sector development and growth. The type of education is a critical issue for improving the knowledge and skills, quality and capacity of SME owners and new entrepreneurs, in addition to ensuring that they have access to appropriately skilled labour to meet the demands of a modern economy. Apart from investments to raise the overall education level of the MENA-12 population, efforts to integrate entrepreneurship in the school curriculum should be accelerated. The quality of the output of entrepreneurship education initiatives has a direct bearing on the future level and quality of entrepreneurial activity. This implies that there should be strong ties between the economic and education ministries. Only a small minority of the population in MENA countries has ever taken any entrepreneurship courses in the education system or had training in how to start a business. So even when they embark on entrepreneurial activity, they are doing so with limited formal knowledge. Investing in the development of entrepreneurial skills and capacity of young people and women is an imperative.

Greatly Facilitate Access to Financing

Entrepreneurs in the MENA countries generally start with small amounts of capital and little opportunity for leveraging the scale of their start-ups or the growth of their enterprises through the use of external financing. Problems of collateral constraints, property rights, property registration and credit information exacerbate the situation. The banking systems in MENA countries are not predisposed to targeting the small business sector and there are often few financial alternatives, especially for medium- and longer-term financing required by growth firms. Guarantee systems are not having much impact on changing the lending behaviour of banks, and seed and venture capital markets are underdeveloped.

Reduce Barriers to Entry for New Businesses

This crosses a number of regulatory and procedural areas. More open competition is needed through sector deregulation, continued privatization of state-owned enterprises (SOEs) and more effective implementation of competition policy to reduce the control of markets by monopolistic and other anti-competitive activity. There needs to be further reduction of the complexity in laws, regulations and procedures governing business registration and licensing, and streamlined processes for facilitating business start-ups and closures. Incentives are also needed to encourage the formalization of a large number of informal enterprises. Reduction of the statutory non-wage labour costs and other labour market rigidities is necessary to foster hiring opportunities and the creation of more jobs in the formal private sector.

Significantly Expand Support Systems and Institutional Infrastructure to Provide Non-financial Services and Assistance

This should be tailored to new entrepreneurs, SMEs and growth-oriented enterprises. In most of the MENA-12 countries the reach of existing support structures and services is limited, especially in non-urban areas. There is a general absence of entrepreneurship or enterprise centres to provide guidance to new entrepreneurs who are trying to develop their business ideas, get businesses started and pursue early-stage growth.

Reinforce the Social Legitimacy of Entrepreneurship and Encourage a Stronger Entrepreneurship Culture

Initiatives are needed to promote the importance of entrepreneurship and entrepreneurs in society, as well as to create more opportunities for exposure to knowledge about entrepreneurship and to entrepreneurial skills and know-how. Integrating entrepreneurship as part of the core curriculum in the education system would be an important step towards preparing a more capable supply of future entrepreneurs.

Build the Capacity of all Institutions and Professionals Connected with Supporting Entrepreneurship Development

This includes government regulators, policymakers and administrators, competition authorities, business support providers, development NGOs, trainers, microfinance lenders, bankers, venture capitalists, business associations, teachers, researchers and even the media.

Develop Improved Systems for Coordination and Implementation of Policies and Initiatives

This also entails more inclusive consultation mechanisms to advise the government on policy actions.

Design Systems for Evaluating the Effectiveness and Impact of Policies, Measures and Programmes on SME and Entrepreneurship Development

This includes mechanisms for measuring the impact of major laws, regulations and policies on SMEs and entrepreneurial activity levels. To accomplish this will require more sophisticated and comprehensive national statistical systems with the capacity to collect data on SMEs (number, size, employment effects, export activity and investment patterns) and business entry, growth and exit rates on a regularized basis, and to track development trends and performance over time. The development of an SME and Entrepreneurship Observatory, one of the suggestions coming out of Chapter 6, should be seriously considered. The work of such an Observatory could also advance the work on measurements of PSD, SMEs and entrepreneurial activity and carry out studies to monitor the impact of business environment reforms and support programmes on SMEs and entrepreneurship development.

Support and Carry Out a Research Programme

This research should be directed to producing answers to some of the questions raised by stakeholders and outlined in Chapter 6 – studies on the impact of macro- and meso-level policies on private sector, SME and entrepreneurship development and on gender, inclusive growth and poverty; and studies relevant to the whole range of issues dealing with the role of the SME sector in the economy and its behaviour. The knowledge generated from this research is absolutely essential to the underpinning of effective policy development. In countries where research capacity is weak or policy research institutes do not exist, efforts should be made to support their development. The ultimate aim should be to create a Regional Centre of Excellence in SME and Entrepreneurship Research that will produce studies, build research capacity and develop a cadre of SME and entrepreneurship research experts.

Facilitate Intercountry Exchanges

Given that the MENA-12 countries each have a somewhat different context, are at different stages of transition to the market economy, have made varying degrees of progress on building PSD capacity and have a variety of experiences in designing and implementing SME and entrepreneurship-related policies, measures and initiatives, there is great potential for intercountry exchanges of practice and policy learning. There is also great potential for collaborating on developing solutions to some of the key policy challenges.

Part II presents individual country profiles. Chapter 8 includes a synopsis of the six countries with comparatively stronger private sector dynamics based on the categorizations produced in Chapter 5 – Morocco, Lebanon, Jordan, Turkey, Egypt and Tunisia. Chapter 9 profiles the six countries with less dynamic PSD environments – Yemen, Sudan, the West Bank & Gaza, Syria, Algeria and Iraq. These profiles briefly summarize the context for PSD, recent policy developments, aspects of the institutional set-up in support of SMEs and entrepreneurship, and initiatives in support of enhancing growth in private sector activity.

NOTES

1. This policy question is raised by several researchers (see Storey 1994; Lazonick 2008; Naudé 2008, among others) who suggest that economic growth is driven more by the small percentage of new or young firms that grow rapidly. Thus the issue of the quality of entrepreneurial activity comes into play.
2. The opportunity-entrepreneurship and necessity-entrepreneurship categorizations were

derived from the Global Entrepreneurship Monitor research based on responses of the adult population to a question about why they started a business or were trying to start a business (Reynolds et al. 2003). Although it is an interesting and somewhat useful concept, researchers may make too much of the distinction between necessity and opportunity entrepreneurship. First of all, entrepreneurs' motivations often change once they are in business and become more aware of opportunities and, secondly, there are a range of intervening variables or factors that trigger the decision to start a business and these do not necessarily dictate the future of the enterprise and its ultimate contribution to growth.

3. As an economy develops and wages increase, entrepreneurs with less ability will exit and become wage labourers; entrepreneurs with more ability will face better incentives to grow their enterprises (Naudé 2008).
4. However Naudé (2009) concedes that good governance may reduce the role of destructive entrepreneurship with the result of impacting positively on economic growth.
5. The Stevenson and Lundström (2002) entrepreneurship policy framework was derived from their analysis of policy measures to stimulate entrepreneurship in ten developed countries.
6. Competition authorities are beginning to be active in Morocco, Tunisia and Egypt, so the situation may be changing.
7. See http://apec-ibiz.org for more detail on the APEC International Network of Institutes for Small Business Counsellors (APEC-IBIZ).

PART II

Profiles of the 12 MENA countries

8. Profiles of more dynamic PSD environments

This chapter includes brief profiles of the six MENA-12 countries with above-average levels of private sector dynamism based on the categorization in Chapter 5. These are presented in the following order: Lebanon, Morocco, Jordan, Egypt, Tunisia and Turkey.

THE CASE OF LEBANON

Context for Private Sector Development

The Lebanese Republic is a small, upper-middle-income country with an estimated population of 4 million, growing at a rate of 1.1 per cent a year, and 2009 gross domestic product (GDP) per capita (purchasing power parity – PPP) of US$14 266 (IMF 2010 database). Lebanon is a major service, transport and financial hub in the MENA region with a tradition of liberalism and a history of private sector domination. It is described as one of the Middle East's most advanced economies (Holmes et al. 2008).

Some indicators suggest that state involvement in the economy is rather significant. Government expenditures as a share of GDP averaged 36 per cent from 2002 to 2005, above the average for other upper-middle-income countries by a wide margin (EC 2005a). Progress on privatization has been slow and the process complicated by investor hesitation due to the unstable political situation (EC 2005a). Lebanon has the second-highest gross capital formation in the MENA-12 (about 31 per cent of GDP in 2008) and highest level of private capital formation (29 per cent of GDP), a dramatic increase over 2007. Private investment accounts for almost 95 per cent of the gross. The private sector share of employment is almost 85 per cent (CAS 2007).

Lebanon's GDP growth, hampered by its political and fiscal situation, has fluctuated in recent years from a high of 7.5 per cent in 2004 to a low of 1 per cent in 2006, averaging 4 per cent annual growth during the 2000–2008 period (World Development Indicators – WDI), the fourth-lowest among the MENA-12. GDP rebounded in 2008 to 8 per cent, the MENA-12 highest growth rate, but dropped slightly to 7 per cent in 2009 (World Factbook – WFB). Recent improvements in economic performance have been driven mainly by private consumption (rather than by private investment), net exports to growing markets in neighbouring Middle East countries and tourism spending of Lebanese expatriates (Bank Audi 2008).

The government is engaged in a number of multilateral agreements with obligations and reforms to further liberalize the economy. Exports in 2008 amounted to 27 per cent of GDP, below average for the MENA-12, however the level has increased from 21 per cent in 2006 (WDI). Access to European markets will increase as a result of Lebanon's partnership agreement with the European Union (EU) and its companies are expected to benefit from technology transfer and know-how resulting from foreign direct investment (FDI). Despite the unstable political condition, Lebanon was able to attract FDI amounting to 12.3 per cent of GDP in 2008, the highest relative FDI inflow of the MENA-12 countries and well above the MENA average. It has managed to maintain consistent levels of FDI to GDP over the 2005–08 period. The economy has been further assisted by capital inflows from the EU and other donors to support restoration and rebuilding efforts, and from remittances (which amount to almost a quarter of GDP). The Lebanese economy is largely service-oriented; the service sector is responsible for over 75 per cent of GDP and 70 per cent of the labour force (WFB). The manufacturing output contributes to about 10 per cent of GDP.

Lebanon has a well-developed, competitive and regulated banking sector and performs much better than other MENA countries with regard to the level of domestic credit provided by the banking system – 173 per cent of GDP in 2008, compared to the MENA average of almost 40 per cent (WDI). However some public sector crowding-out in terms of access to loans (MoET 2005) and a high concentration of lending to a few clients are noted. Only 3 per cent of beneficiaries account for 75 per cent of total private sector credit (OECD 2007b).

On global indicators of economic freedom, knowledge economy and doing business, Lebanon fares in the upper half of the MENA-12 countries. It ranked 108 out of 183 countries in *Doing Business 2010* (World Bank 2009b) and is assessed as a 'mostly unfree' economy in the Index of Economic Freedom (Heritage Foundation 2010). It has a 'high degree' of fiscal and trade freedom; is 'moderately free' on monetary and financial freedoms; and 'mostly unfree' on business, investment and labour freedoms. It falls into the category of a 'repressed' economy on property rights and freedom from corruption.

The major macro-level constraints impeding private sector development (PSD) are the unstable political condition, the country's high level of indebtedness (among the highest in the world), the lack of supportive infrastructure, the slow pace of productive sector modernization and delays in public service reforms (EC 2004, 2005a). The competitiveness of the business sector is hampered by the high cost of doing business, which acts as a disincentive for expansion of production and exports, particularly in manufacturing and services (Bank Audi 2008); high customs duties; high labour costs, especially for social security; high land rental prices and electricity costs; a lack of marketing capability and market information; cumbersome administrative procedures; and government-controlled barriers to competition (Nasnas 2007).

In addition to economic development and growth issues, the country has a number of social problems to address, such as high unemployment, poverty and poor and unequal assess to basic services and infrastructure. Before the 2006 crisis almost 7 per cent of the Lebanese population was living under the poverty line; following hostilities, a third of Lebanese could not meet their basic needs with their post-war income, resulting in widening social gaps (UN-ESCWA 2006). The literacy rate in Lebanon is among the highest in the MENA-12 (87.4 per cent), with a relatively low female literacy gap (10.9 points), and comparatively strong performance on education indicators.

Lebanon has a labour force participation rate of 45 per cent, an employment rate of 46 per cent and an official unemployment rate of just over 9 per cent (much higher among young people). The share of women in employment is only 20.5 per cent. About one-third of the workforce is self-employed (the second-highest in the MENA-12), with a low share of women in self-employment – less than 8 per cent. There appears to be a high level of informal sector activity in Lebanon, amounting to over 36 per cent of GDP (Schneider 2005). Up to half of MSEs and 40 per cent of their workers are informal (FEMISE 2006a).

SMEs in Lebanon face a number of environment-related, market and institutional disadvantages. SME performance is affected by a lack of access to new technologies, finance, and information and advisory services; inadequate basic infrastructure; distortion in the structure of costs and prices; a shortage of skilled labour in some professions; and low investments in R&D and training that could lead to innovation and potentially rapid growth (FEMISE 2006a; MoET 2006a, 2006b). The most severe obstacle is security and political instability, which contributes to investment aversion and low competitiveness (MoET 2006b). Access to formal credit is exacerbated by the lack of transparency of mostly family-owned Lebanese SMEs. High taxes, cumbersome licensing procedures and high custom duties discourage the formalization of SME activity and inhibit growth. Poor-quality and insufficient services by business associations do not support the growth of SMEs in Lebanon, and the limited access of SME owners to international quality standards and requirements means that local products cannot compete in international markets, even with Lebanon's open economy policy (ECOSC 2003).

The entrepreneurial culture in Lebanon appears stronger than in most MENA-12 countries. Preliminary data from the 2009 GEM-MENA study indicates a high density of existing entrepreneurs. Almost a quarter of the adult population owns a business. It has the highest density of entrepreneurs per 100 adults in the ten GEM-MENA countries (24.6 per cent) (IDRC 2010). About 7 per cent of the adult population was actively trying to start a business in 2009. In the Silatech (2009) survey of young Arabs, 44 per cent of Lebanon's 15–29-year-olds stated that they would prefer to be self-employed, assuming similar pay and working conditions, than to work for the government (30 per cent) or as an employee in a private business (15 per cent). Over 60 per cent of adults in the GEM-MENA study stated their preference for self-employment, much higher than in Syria, Jordan, Algeria, the West Bank & Gaza and Yemen (see Table 7.1 in Chapter 7).

Government Priorities and Recent Policy Developments

The government has a number of urgent social and economic priorities, among which are macroeconomic and financial stability, post-conflict restoration of infrastructure, restoring credibility in the education system, improving the economic conditions and social protection of low-income groups, job creation, civil service reform, and improving the trade and investment environment.

Regulatory and administrative reform

Starting in 2005, and with the 2007 formation of a high-level administration simplification programme, Lebanon has been working on a number of reforms to improve the regulatory environment for businesses. This follows a complete review of the business and commercial legislation affecting the private sector (Mallat 2006). The Ministry of Economy and Trade (MoET) is working on legislative amendments to facilitate company establishment, new laws on mergers and acquisitions, a revised bankruptcy law that will meet international standards,[1] and preparation of the new Capital Market Law and the organizational structure of the Capital Market Authority. The Office of the Minister of State for Administrative Reform is implementing a strategy for simplification of administrative procedures (European Communities and OECD 2008). The MoET has established OSSs in national post offices (LibanPost) throughout the country to simplify company registration, saving entrepreneurs €1300 in registration costs, and the Ministry of Finance is undertaking tax system reforms to achieve a better distribution of the tax burden. Electronic registration of taxpayers and declaration of income tax by post and payment through commercial banks is now possible. A new draft Competition Law has been submitted to the Parliament to regulate anti-competitive practices and preparation has begun for the establishment of an independent national competition council (EC 2008c). This is considered critically important as half of Lebanon's domestic markets are assessed as being oligopolistic to monopolistic, with a high concentration of market share in the hands of a few enterprises (Berthélemy et al. 2007). Some of these monopolistic practices are natural, given economies of scale or fixed costs, but others are artificial, rent-seeking and restrict entry of new businesses (CRI 2003; Berthélemy et al. 2007).

To improve the performance of Lebanese exports in the international market, the government is working on simplification of trade and export procedures, establishing the basis for leading laboratories and companies to comply with international standards, creating awareness of quality-related matters and drafting a law on standardization. To attract foreign investors, the government has opened an OSS to facilitate bureaucratic and regulatory processes. The government has also prepared a public administration reform agenda geared to creating a transparent public administration with increased control and oversight so as to combat corruption.

The Government of Lebanon's Reform Programme and its Association Agreement with the EU serve as tools for monitoring the implementation of the economic, social and institutional reforms to which the Lebanese authorities committed themselves at the Paris III International Donor Conference in January 2007.

SME and entrepreneurship policies and programmes

The government of Lebanon adopted the Euro-Mediterranean Charter for Enterprise in 2004 and subsequently launched the Integrated SME Support Programme. This was the country's first policy effort to focus specifically on SMEs. The objectives of the programme were to implement an integrated approach for SME development, facilitate access to finance and business services, and create a conducive environment for doing business. It is heavily involved in the formulation of business enabling environment policy and SME support initiatives, has successfully established four business development centres focusing on incubation of innovative business ideas, and has undertaken efforts to develop the financial sector and create SME financing schemes (OECD 2007b).

The MoET created an SME Support Unit in 2005 that, in cooperation with the Ministry of Finance, is the main coordinating body for SME development. The MoET established an SME Advisory Committee of government and private sector bodies to identify concrete actions to eliminate regulatory barriers and to lobby for policies to level the playing field for SMEs. Progress is being made towards setting a formal SME strategy[2] for the country as part of Lebanon's commitment under the Euro-Med Charter for Enterprise (MoET 2008). The strategy's major policy objectives are to: (1) improve the macroeconomic environment to overcome the low propensity to invest; (2) improve the cost structure of firms and encourage diversity in products and export markets; (3) reduce regulatory and compliance costs, burdens and entry and exit barriers; (4) ensure fair competition; and (5) improve roads, industrial areas, access to electricity and telecommunications, and business development services (BDS). The SME Support Unit is planning to develop an SME Observatory to report more fully on the contribution of SMEs to the economy.

In 2000 the government, in partnership with the private sector, established Kafalat, a limited credit guarantee society to provide loan guarantees to undercollateralized but innovative SMEs[3] and start-ups. Under a protocol with the European Bank for Investment, Kafalat also offers subsidized interest rate loans for SME clients in sectors associated with traditional crafts, high technology, agriculture, tourism and industry. Development of a microfinance industry is relatively new to Lebanon, but a number of public sector institutions and NGOs are facilitating access to sources of microfinance. Leasing is not a common practice, although leasing companies are covered under a fully implemented Leasing Law. The private equity and venture capital market is in its nascent stages with very few funds directed at SMEs and high-potential start-ups. There have been additional initiatives to help finance improvements to the facilities of private sector enterprises that incurred direct or indirect damage from physical disaster, and to respond to the short-term financing needs of enterprises reopening in the post-conflict period (OECD 2007b).

Modest efforts are under way to support the development of entrepreneurship. In 2006 the Ministry of Education entered into an agreement with INJAZ-Lebanon giving it access to all public schools to deliver entrepreneurship courses. INJAZ is at the same time working to strengthen the capacity of the Ministry's Career Counselling Unit to include entrepreneurship and self-employment as career options. The Bader Young Entrepreneurs Program[4] aims to promote private initiative by inspiring the young generation to start businesses, and providing support to these entrepreneurs through education, finance and networking. Initiatives include participation in the Arab Business Plan Competition and the creation of a US$17 million Building Block Equity Fund to invest in new enterprises with innovation potential. The Olayan School of Business at the American University of Beirut (AUB) has recently launched an Entrepreneurship Initiative to expose its students to the world of entrepreneurship. The long-term goal of the school's initiative is to be a regional nucleus for supporting and developing entrepreneurship-related research, training material and knowledge dissemination in the Arab world.

Innovation policies

Research and innovation activities in Lebanon are modest. It has a small but diverse and multicultural science and technology community, and limited private sector investment in R&D (EC 2005a). A Science and Technology and Innovation Policy Plan was launched in 2006 (CNRS 2006); however its implementation was thwarted by the civil war. The new Parliament endorsed a plan to reform science and technology in the summer of 2008, but it needs an action plan to strengthen existing research institutes and organizations as well as to invest in new laboratories and upgraded technological capabilities of educational institutions. Technopoles and incubators are part of the required infrastructure as well as improvements to intellectual property protection (IPP).

Conclusions

Future development and economic growth are heavily dependent on restoring financial and political stability. The disruption in policy developments and reforms due to political upheaval, civil strife and conflict has had a negative effect on private sector investment and as well as on the acceleration of reform activity. However the basic conditions for private sector growth are positive and the trade and entrepreneurial orientation of the population is strong. Concerted efforts are needed to mobilize this potential.

THE CASE OF MOROCCO

Context for Private Sector Development

The Kingdom of Morocco is a lower-middle-income country with an estimated population of 31.3 million, growing at a moderate rate of 1.1 per cent, and GDP per capita (PPP) of US$4600 in 2009 (IMF 2010). Morocco has embraced the principle of a market-based economy and has been implementing economic liberalization policies since the 1980s.

Most of the state-owned enterprises (SOEs) have been privatized, an area in which Morocco is considered the most advanced in the MENA region (World Bank 2006c). The promotion of foreign direct investment (FDI) started in the early 1980s, much of it initially privatization-driven. Improvements to the investment climate for foreign and domestic investors are made through specific programmes designed to expand and upgrade public infrastructure, form public–private partnerships (PPPs) for infrastructure development and promote the development of tourism. New technology parks and offshoring zones have been built to accommodate new factories coming in through FDI activity. FDI reached 2.8 per cent of GDP in 2008,[5] which is below average for MENA countries, and at a low level compared to Jordan, Lebanon, Tunisia and Egypt. It has been declining since 2006. Privatizations have accounted for a large share of FDI with relatively limited spillover effects. Remittances to Morocco made up about 8 per cent of GDP in 2008, a substantially greater level than from FDI.

Trade liberalization has been on the government's agenda since the late 1980s. It is one of the four MENA-12 countries to be a member of the World Trade Organisation (WTO), signed its first Euro-Mediterranean Association Agreement in 1996 and has entered into a number of multilateral and bilateral Free Trade Agreements (FTAs) with Arab countries and the US. Morocco's total trade in 2008 amounted to 87 per cent of GDP – exports totalling 37 per cent of GDP and imports totalling 50 per cent (WDI). In accordance with provisions in the FTAs executed with both the EU and the US, Morocco must upgrade its quality standards. As a result, ISO 9000 certification has become a priority for enterprises and factories.

Growth has been sporadic. From 2000 to 2008 the annual average GDP growth was 4.8 per cent (WDI), but this has fluctuated from a low of 1.8 per cent in 2000 to a high of 7.8 per cent in 2006. GDP grew at 5.1 per cent in 2009, down from 6.2 per cent in 2008 (WFB). These swings are largely the result of variable performance of the agricultural sector, which is highly susceptible to the amount of annual rainfall. Morocco's growth has been underpinned by superior investment levels. Gross capital formation reached 33 per cent of GDP in 2008, the highest level among the MENA-12, and averaged annual growth of 9.1 per cent over the 2000–2008 period, higher than the MENA average rate of 7.5 per cent (WDI). Over 85 per cent of the gross capital formation is derived from the private sector, the second-highest share in the MENA-12, trailing only Lebanon.

The banking system is becoming more competitive through mergers and linkages with regional and international banking systems. All of the Moroccan banks have private shareholders, although the government still holds controlling shares in a few banks and financing companies. Domestic credit to the private sector in 2008 was reported at 77.4 per cent of GDP, higher than the MENA average of 35.8 per cent of GDP (WDI), and up from 52 per cent of GDP in 2003. The amount of domestic credit provided by the banking system was 95.5 per cent of GDP, again much higher than the MENA average of 39.7 per cent, and third-highest in the MENA-12. The opening of a privately managed credit bureau in 2008 should improve financial intermediation.

Morocco has one of the most robust venture capital markets in the MENA region, with 18–20 privately owned venture capital companies and venture capital arms in most banks. Risk capital is growing in part due to investments by the European Investment Bank, but legislation in 2006 also improved the regulatory framework for venture capital and provided incentives to venture capital funds investing in small and medium enterprises (SMEs).

Morocco ranked 73 out of 134 countries in the 2009–10 Global Competitiveness Index, down from 64th place in 2007–08, owing largely to a weakening security environment and deterioration of the education system (WEF 2009b). The regulatory and business environment is seen as becoming more conducive to business activity and creation, and a rigid labour market as the major deterrent to the country's competitiveness. Morocco is assessed as being a 'mostly unfree' economy on the Index of Economic Freedom (Heritage Foundation 2010). Its best-performing scores are on government size ('high degree' of freedom); monetary freedom, business freedom and trade freedom ('mostly free'); and fiscal freedom ('moderately free'). Its lowest score is on labour freedom, followed by property rights and freedom from corruption – each falling in the 'repressed economy' category. The *Doing Business 2010* report ranks Morocco 128 out of 183 countries (World Bank 2009b), down from 115th place in the first *Doing Business* report. Morocco's performance has deteriorated on a number of indicators and improved in others, with the overall result that Morocco is losing competitive position against other countries that have made more progress on doing business reforms. Among the MENA-12 countries, Morocco was placed in seventh position in the 2010 rankings. The implication of these global rankings is that a number of barriers must be addressed to improve Morocco's productivity and global competitiveness.

Agriculture contributed almost 19 per cent to GDP in 2009, but accounts for 45 per cent of labour force activity (WFB) and up to 75 per cent in rural areas. The government is committed to improving the productivity of the sector, while at the same time diversifying into other areas of economic activity. The industrial sector contributes about a third of GDP, but represents only about 20 per cent of the labour force. The manufacturing share of GDP in 2008 was 14 per cent (WDI). The service sector accounts for almost 49 per cent of GDP (and growing), and over a third of the labour force.

The labour force participation rate in Morocco is 50.6 per cent: 75.9 per cent for men and 26.6 per cent for women (HCP 2009). Women's share of employment is about 27 per cent, higher than in many of the MENA-12 countries, but there are serious gender biases in the paid labour market. The majority of all employed women are classified as unpaid family workers (World Bank 2009e). The unemployment rate in 2009 was over 10 per cent, but is disproportionately high in urban areas and among youth. Just over one-fifth of working-age youth were unemployed in 2008, accounting for almost 42 per cent of total unemployment (HCP 2009). The unemployment rate for women is close to the national average, unlike the case for many of the MENA-12 countries.

Morocco has a low level of human capital. The adult literacy rate has increased from 52.3 per cent to 58.8 per cent between 2004 and 2007 (KOM 2008), but is still the second-lowest among the MENA-12, and there is a sizeable gap of almost 25 points between the literacy rates for women and men. This reflects weak performance on most of Morocco's education indicators. Compared to the average for MENA countries, Morocco has low gross school enrolment rates, especially at secondary and tertiary levels and particularly for girls (USAID 2008b). Less than one in ten Moroccan workers has completed secondary education and returns to education are low (USAID 2007). The poverty level has declined significantly since 2001, from over 20 per cent of the population living on less than US$2 (PPP) a day to less than 9 per cent in 2007 (KOM 2008). Despite reduced poverty levels, Moroccans still experience high inequality in income distribution, a situation that has not changed at all since 1985.

Although the public sector still competes with the private sector in some areas of economic activity, the public sector share of employment is only 9.2 per cent (HCP 2009), the lowest in the MENA-12. The private sector is responsible for the majority of capital formation (gross investment). The private sector accounted for almost 90 per cent of gross capital formation in 2007, reaching 27.2 per cent of GDP. This is among the highest levels of private investment for the MENA-12, suggesting that there are many opportunities for private sector involvement in the economy. However monopolies exist in certain industries and the Competition Council formed under the 2001 antitrust law rarely meets, making Morocco weak in terms of fighting cartels and monopolistic practices (Bertelsmann Stiftung 2008c).

Private sector enterprises face many challenges: inadequate

transportation infrastructure; a high cost of doing business; bureaucratic, time-consuming and corrupt administrative procedures; restrictive labour regulations; low quality standards; and lengthy and corrupt commercial arbitration processes. They view tax rates as the major constraint to doing business, followed by access to financing and corruption.[6] There is a lack of qualified staff, especially at middle management levels, as well as a gap between the skills produced by the education system and the needs of the private sector labour market. Scarcity of real estate is another severe constraint, but property rights are well defined and the acquisition of property is regulated.

The level of informality is high, a situation encouraged by the government in the 1980s and 1990s to ease poverty. Schneider and Buehn (2009) calculated the informal economy at close to 37 per cent of GDP in 2006. Some experts estimate that 50 to 60 per cent of private sector enterprises are informal. The annual fiscal loss attributable to the informal sector is equal to MAD7.5 billion (UNCTAD 2007). The primary disincentive to formalize in Morocco appears to be the prohibitive cost of insurance and taxes[7] (ERF 2006).

SMEs are very important in the Moroccan economy. They account for 95 per cent of all enterprises, 50 per cent of employment, 30 per cent of exports and 40 per cent of private investment (European Communities and OECD 2008). However there is very poor availability of data on the SME sector, such as the distribution of SMEs by sector, size and employment. Most Moroccan SMEs are family-run and poorly diversified. They tend to be concentrated in low-value-added sectors and suffer from undercapitalization, poor productivity, limited management skills and weak linkages with FDI investors and activities (World Bank 2006b; European Communities and OECD 2008). SMEs encounter low access to financing and information, high tax rates, a complex tax regime and complex registration requirements (ERF 2006).

NGOs and business associations are active in supporting SMEs and advocating their concerns, including the Federation of SMEs, the National Union of SMEs (UNPME), the Association des Femmes Chefs d'Entreprises du Maroc (AFEM) and the General Confederation of Moroccan Enterprises (CGEM). The CGEM established a Commission on SMEs in 2007 to raise the level of attention to SME issues in its dialogue with the government.

In 2008 there were about 2.8 million self-employed Moroccans, accounting for 30.4 per cent of total employment (HCP 2009). The self-employment rate for men is more than three times the rate for women, and self-employed men are even more likely to employ others. The 2009 Global Entrepreneurship Monitor reports that 24.5 per cent of adults own a business, giving Morocco the second-highest density of existing entrepreneurs in the GEM-MENA countries (IDRC 2010). The proportion of adults trying to start a business is almost 7 per cent, close to the level one might expect for a country at Morocco's level of development. These data suggest that the culture of entrepreneurship is relatively strong. Morocco is one of the few Arab countries where the majority of 15–29-year-olds state that they would prefer to be self-employed than to work for the government (41 per cent versus 26 per cent) (Silatech 2009). The number of new business entries doubled between 2000 and 2007, perhaps one of the outcomes of reforms to reduce entry barriers and increase business opportunities (European Communities and OECD 2008).

Government Priorities and Recent Policy Developments

The Moroccan government is committed to stimulating economic growth through a stronger investment climate, increased private sector activity and improved competitiveness. Job creation, particularly for youth, is at the centre of the government's economic and social development strategy. The private sector is not growing fast enough to absorb labour force growth, so incentives are offered to motivate private sector hiring as well as to encourage young people to start their own enterprises. SME upgrading and stimulation of new economy sectors are a key part of the government's recent policy efforts. Gender equality and poverty reduction are also priorities, as the government is keen to meet the Millennium Development Goal (MDG) targets.

Industrial and sector strategies

There are a number of national sector strategies to increase the performance of industries and enterprises. The 2005 Emergence Plan, that set out the strategic objectives for industrial policy to 2015, proposed a private sector, export-led, investment-attraction strategy that would focus on a number of promising sectors as the drivers of economic growth: offshoring (software development, call centres, data processing and information and communication technology – ICT); auto parts; aeronautics; specialized electronics parts; agrifoods with regional competitive advantages; sea products; and textiles and handicrafts.

With the initial Emergence Plan falling short of expectations, the government released a new Emergence Plan (2009–15) in 2009 to be implemented in partnership with business and sector associations. The National Pact for Industrial Emergence plan contains over 100 measures to promote industrial sector activity, many dealing with the competitiveness of Moroccan SMEs. Priority sectors are to be supported to meet quality standards through company training funds and specialized training institutes. The targets are to create 220 000 new jobs, reduce urban unemployment levels, boost private sector investment by MAD50 billion and increase exports by MAD95 billion.

Other sector strategies exist for the trade sector (the Rawaj Plan), the crafts industry (Vision 2015) and tourism sector (Plan Azur de Tourism). Each of these plans has aggressive targets for job creation and includes massive investments to build capacity and sophistication of the sector. The government's goal is to establish Morocco as an international trade and production platform and, as such, it is focusing on modernization of the transportation infrastructure and developing 'small cities' with industrial zones that will encourage new enterprise creation and clusters.

Education and training policies

Skills development and training are among the top priorities of the government. Reinforcing their importance, the government declared 2000–2010 'the decade of education and training'. The goals are to provide more appropriate training and knowledge to prepare young people coming out of the education system with the skills demanded by the labour market, and to enhance the competitive modernization of enterprises and access to markets by offering training to upgrade standards and certification competencies within industry sectors.

The Office de la Formation Professionnelle et de la Promotion du Travail (OFPPT) is the central government training entity responsible for developing the government's training strategy to mitigate the youth employment gap. The OFPPT plan for 2008–12 is to train 650 000 young people in the skills required by new economy sectors identified in the Emergence Plan (AfDB and OECD 2008c). Consequently it faces pressure to increase the number of centres and students and to develop training capacity. The national jobs and skills promotion agency, l'Agence Nationale de Promotion de l'Emploi et des Competences (ANAPEC), facilitates employment by providing tax and social security incentives to employers and skills training to job seekers in new sectors of the economy. The government's budget for training is funded through a 1.6 per cent training tax on the wage bill of companies that pay into the social security fund. Although there is intergovernmental agency tension regarding vocational training responsibilities and policy formulation, the Moroccan vocational training system is regarded as the best in the region in terms of systems and approaches.

Education reform laid out in the 2008–10 National Education and Training Charter aims to have at least 90 per cent of children completing primary education and 80 per cent completing junior secondary school.

The charter specifies measures to make more effective use of educational resources and infrastructure, improve curriculum design, expand course offerings, utilize forms of apprenticeship and other workplace-based training, and adopt a competency-based education approach. The charter also emphasizes the promotion of an entrepreneurial mindset and provides for the development of entrepreneurial skills in general and vocational education, but the framework for entrepreneurial learning is not well integrated and nor is the integration of entrepreneurship as a key competence in the curriculum guidelines (European Communities and OECD 2008). The new Emergency Education Plan 2009–12, issued in 2008, seeks to counter high school dropout rates by making education compulsory to the age of 15 and upgrading more than 2500 educational establishments in rural areas. More broadly the government's aim is to reduce illiteracy to less than 20 per cent by 2010 and to eradicate it by 2015 through an extensive literacy campaign and adult basic education programme.

Regulatory reform policies

The government is committed to boosting the growth of the private sector by modernizing business laws and resolving tax problems. Licensing and permits procedures have been streamlined through the creation of Regional Investment Centres (RICs) that serve as one-stop shops (OSSs) for commercial registration and investment. The minimum paid-in capital for a new limited liability has been reduced from MAD100 000 to MAD10 000, customs procedures have been modernized, and a law passed on normalization and certification related to standards accreditation. The Improving the Business Climate in Morocco (IBCM) programme aims to develop tools for assessing the business climate and competitiveness factors and to improve the 'quality' infrastructure (USAID 2007). Morocco is undertaking a major effort to align itself with EU legislation, rules and standards to access the internal EU market (EC 2007a).

SME and entrepreneurship policies and programmes

Developing and upgrading SMEs is one of the pillars of government policy. The Ministry of Industry, Commerce and New Technologies (MICNT) is the lead institution for the coordination of enterprise policy, although it does not have a separate SME unit. The government's heightened policy emphasis on SMEs began in the late 1990s. A White Paper on SMEs was released in 2000 (MAGG 1999), followed by the SME Charter in 2002, which specified the establishment of l'Agence Nationale pour la Promotion de la Petite et Moyenne Enterprise (ANPME). Morocco adopted the Euro-Mediterranean Charter for Enterprise in 2004, and in 2005 the government formed a National Committee on Support for

Enterprise Creation to promote measures to encourage new enterprises (MICMANE 2005).

The role of ANPME is to coordinate the delivery of SME programmes and services and to elaborate a programme of technical assistance for the creation, promotion and competitive modernization of SMEs. Its main programme effort is delivery of the *Mise à Niveau* scheme, a programme focused on upgrading the technological and managerial capacity of SMEs. ANPME's primary targets are enterprises with high growth potential and enterprises with limited competitiveness in a restructuring or modernization phase. Tailored programmes have been designed to meet the needs of the two groups of enterprises.

The government has been promoting self-employment as an employment option since the late 1980s through such policy initiatives as the Young Entrepreneurs Loan that offered preferential interest rates or tax exemptions to vocational education and training and post-secondary graduates who wished to start a business. One of the most prominent recent policy initiatives is the Moukawalati programme, a national entrepreneurship programme targeting unemployed young graduates. Launched in 2006 and implemented by ANAPEC, the Moukawalati programme provides start-up training and a year's worth of follow-up coaching support to young people who will establish a microenterprise that creates jobs for others. ANAPEC established a network of 100 'windows' through partner banks for dealing with Moukawalati clients and the government agreed to provide guarantees for 85 per cent of the loan values. However the programme had very disappointing results during the first two years. The launch of Moukawalati enterprises was impeded by difficulty in finding suitable business premises, and many of the potential young entrepreneurs could not secure bank financing even with the special government guarantees.[8] The government introduced a revised programme in 2009. The target was lowered to the creation of 10 000 new enterprises (a third of the original target), and the programme eligibility criteria extended to young people without graduation qualifications from professional training institutions. The number of Moukawalati offices and trained advisors has been expanded and stronger financing commitments agreed to by banks.

To help SMEs access financing, the government funds credit guarantees. Eleven credit guarantee schemes are operated by the Caisse Centrale de Garantie (CCG), a 100 per cent government-owned loan guarantee company that provides 60–85 per cent guarantees for bank loans extended to qualifying SMEs. Morocco has been building microfinance facilities since the 1990s and has proven itself as a leader in the greater Middle East region. Regulation and governance of the microfinance industry has been in place since the promulgation of the Microfinance Law in 1999 and the largest of the 12 microfinance institutions (MFIs) in Morocco follow international best practices in microlending. Microcredit enjoys strong backing from the government.

The government also has an informal sector policy to encourage formalization. The Rawaj strategy to reduce the informal sector proposed public awareness campaigns, tax incentives, a franchise initiative with various incentives, and provision of medical and social insurance. The principle is that by offering these benefits to formal enterprises, informal enterprises will be encouraged to formalize.

Innovation policies

The government places a high priority on innovation, ICT and research and development (R&D), but R&D investments are low. This is in spite of the presence of a number of bodies for the promotion of R&D (for example, the National S&T Research Centre, the National Fund for Scientific Research and a national fund to help technological investors). Efforts are being made to strengthen universities and R&D centres, provide fiscal incentives, foster knowledge and technology transfer networks, build industrial technology centres and innovation parks, and offer innovation awards. At least 12 incubators are networked throughout the country to support start-ups, including with financial support for incubator-hosted projects. A number of these incubators are associated with higher education institutions and funded by the Ministry of Higher Education and the MICNT.

Much of the innovation system is still in a pilot phase and needs further adoption of good policy practices (European Communities and OECD 2008). In the meantime the government continues with implementation of the Plan of Action 2006–10 to modernize and strengthen the national research system. ICT is a major emphasis of the government's actions to develop an information and knowledge economy to foster jobs and growth (MICNT and DPTIT 2007). The E-Morocco 2010 strategy, launched in 2005, is linked to the modernization of the education system, promotion of innovation, e-government and adoption of ICT by enterprises.

Conclusions

Although Morocco has a stronger private sector than most of the MENA-12 countries, it has a long way to go in establishing a truly business-friendly environment and ameliorating structural imbalances and human capital weaknesses in the economy. Economic stabilization and other reforms have not resulted in meeting job creation expectations or decreasing income inequality. The lack of sustained high growth and job creation are the country's major challenges, and Morocco needs an expanding, more diversified and competitive private sector that will create higher value-added jobs, exports and innovations. Building on the strong entrepreneurial inclination of its population will be key.

THE CASE OF JORDAN

Context for Private Sector Development

The Kingdom of Jordan is a middle-income country with an estimated population of 6.3 million, growing at 2.2 per cent, and 2009 GDP per capita (PPP) of US$5620. Jordan is the most urbanized society of the MENA-12; 78 per cent of the population lives in urban areas (WFB). Located in the centre of an area of political instability, its economic and political progress is heavily influenced by developments in neighbouring Iraq and the West Bank & Gaza.

In the late 1990s Jordan privatized a number of SOEs, initiated liberalization processes and started to reduce barriers to trade and FDI. There are more than 13 Qualifying Industrial Zones (QIZs) in Jordan, which have put Jordan on the foreign investment map since 2000. The volume of foreign capital flow into Jordan increased rapidly from less than 2.5 per cent of GDP in 2001 to 23 per cent in 2006. The level of FDI has declined since 2005, but still plays a much larger role in Jordan (9.3 per cent of GDP) than in most of the other countries in the MENA region (WDI). Although very successful at attracting foreign investment, the QIZs have been less successful in creating employment for Jordanians.[9] Jordan is the most trade open of the MENA-12 countries with WTO membership since 2000 and FTAs with the US, the European Union (EU) and several Arab countries. Exports reached 58 per cent of GDP in 2008, and imports amounted to 91 per cent of GDP (WDI), resulting in a persistent trade deficit.

Jordan achieved solid economic performance during the 2000–2008 period with annual GDP growth averaging 7.2 per cent (WDI). This was the second-highest level of growth in the MENA-12. However GDP dropped to 5.6 per cent in 2008 and to 3.1 per cent in 2009. Growth has been fuelled by a boom in construction and real estate projects, tourism and remittances. Remittances amounted to 18 per cent of GDP in 2008, far higher than the average for MENA (4.8 per cent) or other middle-income countries (1.9 per cent) (WDI). Over the past few years Jordan has consistently benefited from one of the highest levels of official development assistance in the Arab world. This amounted to US$126 per capita[10] and over 3 per cent of gross national income (GNI) in 2008 (WDI).

The Jordanian economy is heavily driven by the services sector (two-thirds of GDP) with a relatively minor contribution from the agricultural sector (3.7 per cent of GDP). The manufacturing sector, at over 20 per cent of GDP and two thirds of industrial output, is dominated by resource-based, labour-intensive and low-tech industries. Jordan's industrial dynamism has been largely a product of foreign capital and foreign labour seeking to benefit from its preferential trade agreements with the US.

The level of gross capital formation is high compared to most of the other MENA-12 countries (25.6 per cent of GDP) with almost three-quarters accounted for by the private sector. However much of the private investment is diverted into real estate and construction projects rather than value-added production activity due to the higher investment returns.

The Jordan banking system is well developed, internationally competitive and in compliance with basic international banking standards (Bank Audi 2009b). There are no state-owned banks in the country (Lyman and Lauer 2005), unlike most of the other MENA-12 countries, but there are some government-controlled credit institutions that are all involved in subsidized microlending. Domestic credit to the private sector reached 84 per cent of GDP in 2008, considerably higher than the MENA average of almost 36 per cent and first among the MENA-12. The level of domestic credit provided by the banking system climbed to 115 per cent of GDP, considerably higher than the MENA average of about 40 per cent. Capital markets are well developed and the boom in the stock market has pushed changes in the rules to allow listings for start-ups. The Amman Stock Exchange is beyond reach for most Jordanian SMEs and a junior stock market is needed.

Jordan has a relatively favourable business environment for private sector growth. It has the highest score among the MENA-12 countries on the Index of Economic Freedom and is categorized as a 'moderately free' country (Heritage Foundation 2010). It has a high degree of fiscal freedom; is 'mostly free' on monetary and trade freedoms; 'moderately free' on investment and financial freedoms; but assessed as a 'repressed' economy on freedom from corruption and property rights. Jordan has lost position in the World Bank *Doing Business* rankings, dropping from 80th place in 2007 to 100th place in *Doing Business 2010* (World Bank 2009b).

Past extensive reform initiatives to promote private sector-led growth and a knowledge-based economy have included investments in human capital. Jordan has one of the highest literacy rates in the region (90 per cent for adults and rising to 99 per cent for the 15–24 age group) (WDI). It has rapidly narrowed gender differentials in education levels and access, and boasts one of the highest female literacy rates in the MENA region (WFB). Public and private institutions for education and training and

R&D are strong and education levels are high (Bertelsmann Stiftung 2008b). However the Jordanian economy has derived little benefit from its human capital investment given the low utilization of labour and high unemployment rates among better-educated Jordanians.

The labour force participation rate in 2008 was 50 per cent (WDI). The employment to population ratio is less than 40 per cent, one of the lowest in the MENA-12 countries. One of the reasons for this is the low participation of women in economic activity. Women's share of employment is less than 16 per cent. High fertility rates, gender-based wage and non-wage discrimination, underemployment, occupational segregation and untapped potential of the private sector to utilize the capabilities of women workers are the major impediments to women's role in the labour force (World Bank 2005b).

The official unemployment rate of 13.5 per cent[11] has remained persistently high. The rate of unemployment for women is more than twice the rate for men (10.2 per cent versus 24.7 per cent) (HKJ 2008) and over three-quarters of the unemployed are between the ages of 15 and 29 (DOS 2008). The highest unemployment rates are, by far, for young highly educated women – about 58 per cent for women holding a bachelor degree or higher (DOS 2008). One of the major challenges for Jordan is being able to generate sufficient new quality jobs to absorb an estimated 50 000 new labour force entrants each year[12] and to ensure social protection for workers who cannot adjust to changing circumstances and skill requirements (ILO 2006).

The percentage of the population living below the national poverty line has decreased from 21.3 per cent in 1997 to 14.2 per cent in 2007 (UNDP 2009), but poverty rates are much higher in rural areas and efforts to reduce poverty have not led to a reduction in income inequality (Saif and Tabbaa 2008). It appears that much of Jordan's recent growth performance has not been pro-poor, reducing neither unemployment nor poverty levels.

The government plays a strong role in the economy, accounting for over 30 per cent of GDP (MPIC 2006) and almost 40 per cent of employment, and is heavily involved in key economic sectors. Public sector employment is seen as an attractive employment option because of its job security and social benefits. Young, educated Jordanians are willing to wait for long periods of time for the few available pubic sector jobs or will opt for employment outside Jordan rather than accept the available low-skilled and low-paid private sector jobs. Almost two-thirds of newly created jobs since 2001 have been filled by non-Jordanians (Razazz and Iqbal 2008).

Indigenous private sector activity is concentrated in low-value-added wholesale and retail trade, motor vehicle repair, and personal and household goods (61 per cent of establishments and almost one-third of employment). Various surveys confirm weaknesses in the manufacturing sector, demonstrated by its low contribution to GDP and economic growth. Jordan enterprises view tax rates, corruption and obtaining business and licensing permits as among their top constraints.[13]

The SME contribution to GDP is reported as 27 per cent, much lower than in many other countries (MPIC 2006). The employment share of under-50-employee establishments (64 per cent) is lower than in most of the other MENA-12 countries. In Egypt and the West Bank & Gaza, for example, enterprises with fewer than 50 employees account for more than 85 per cent of private enterprise employment. Jordan's SMEs encounter many of the same challenges faced by SMEs in other MENA-12 countries. They have weak management capabilities and internal management systems; inadequate financial and accounting systems; poor marketing skills; unsophisticated production processes and technology; and inadequate access to information on markets, distribution channels, product specifications required for export markets and good-practice production and management techniques. Most SMEs will not be able to respond competitively to the opportunities offered under the FTAs without upgrading. One of the major external barriers is access to finance (Al-Anagreh et al. 2005). What SMEs need most is financial access, marketing know-how, development of export capability and linkages, SME-friendly government regulations and devoted advocacy efforts.

The self-employment rate in 2007 was only 15.2 per cent (DOS 2008), less than half the rate in most of the MENA-12. Employed men are four times more likely to be self-employed than employed women. The female self-employment rate is 4.1 per cent compared to 17.3 per cent for men. This female self-employment rate is the lowest in the MENA-12. Jordan stands out with Egypt as one of the countries where the self-employed are more likely to create jobs for others (almost half of the total self-employed are employers).

Jordan's informal sector was estimated at 21.6 per cent of GDP in 2006 (Schneider and Buehn 2009), actually low for a country at Jordan's level of economic development. This could indicate a more favourable environment for the formalization of enterprises or it could indicate a lower level of subsistence economic activity generally.

About 6 per cent of Jordanian adults in the 2009 GEM survey of entrepreneurial activity were in the process of trying to start a business (nascent entrepreneurs) and 10 per cent already owned an operating business (IDRC 2010). The density of existing entrepreneurs in the adult population is among the lowest in the ten GEM-MENA countries. The comparatively low self-employment rate and density of nascent and existing entrepreneurs in Jordan seems to suggest that many fewer people are involved in entrepreneurial activity, although some of the other conditions favourable to this are in place. Until the late 1980s Jordanians were mostly reliant on government employment, so the culture of entrepreneurship may not be well entrenched. Over half of 15–29-year-olds reported in a 2009 Gallup survey that they would prefer to work for the government, assuming similar pay and working conditions, than to work in the private sector (16 per cent) or be self-employed (23 per cent) (Silatech 2009). Promoting entrepreneurship as an option among young people and ensuring the proper supports are in place to unleash entrepreneurship is likely very important to Jordan's future private sector growth.

Government Priorities and Recent Policy Developments

Since 1999 and the coming to the throne of King Abdullah, developing the country's domestic economic potential and improving its living standards have become the main policy priorities. The aim of the government is full implementation of a market economy and full integration in the world market (Bertelsmann Stiftung 2008b). Acknowledgement of the role of the private sector as a main partner in economic activity was confirmed in the government's National Social and Economic Development Plan 2004–2006 (MPIC 2004).

The National Agenda 2006–15 lays out the renewed vision for Jordan's transformation and the main topics of reform over the coming ten years (MPIC 2006). Targets are set to achieve annual real GDP growth of 7.2 per cent, double per capita income, reduce unemployment to 6.8 per cent by creating 600 000 new jobs, increase women's share of employment to 20 per cent, reduce public debt to 36 per cent (from 91 per cent), increase FDI inflow to 40 per cent of GDP and reduce the poverty rate to 10 per cent. The agenda was developed in consultation with stakeholders from different sectors, civil society associations and the public. The new agenda was divided into three phases of implementation to transition Jordan from a factor-driven to an efficiency-driven economy and finally to an innovation-driven economy. The three phases include reforms to promote export-oriented, labour-intensive industries and traded services; expand vocational training and employment support; invest in key infrastructure to support private sector growth; improve public sector governance; eliminate all forms of discrimination against women; liberalize state-controlled markets; upgrade and strengthen the industrial base to create value-added jobs; and support selected sectors to make the transition to the knowledge economy. The agenda also emphasizes greater inclusion of civil society organisations (CSOs) and public participation in decision-making and development processes. This entails new legislation to guarantee freedom in establishing NGOs and reducing barriers to their creation.

Regulatory and administrative reform

Implementation progress on regulatory and administrative reforms has been made on several fronts (EC 2008b). These include a new investment law, drafting of a new labour law, an anti-corruption law, revision of competition and company laws, modernization of the bankruptcy law, changes to the tax law to provide incentives for smaller firms and significantly lower their tax payments, and changes to the Social Security Code to help eliminate discriminatory practices in the hiring of female workers.[14] The cost of registering a limited liability has been reduced from JD30 000 to JD1000, business registration processes have been simplified, and OSSs established by the Jordan Investment Board (JIB) and the Ministry of Industry and Trade (MIT). Online company registration is now possible. Major steps have been taken to increase private sector awareness about quality standards to facilitate access to global value chains. A Ministry of Public Sector Reform has been created to simplify systems and procedures and promote performance measurement and accountability (UN 2008).

The Ministry of Industry and Trade (MIT) created a Jordan National Competitiveness Team (JNCT) to monitor and assess the status of Jordan's competitiveness and to establish a Competitiveness Observatory. The first national report of the team recommended that Jordan target investments towards the fastest-producing sectors, resolve the brain-drain issue, develop education and vocational outputs in line with market needs, increase cooperation between the public and private sector, and focus coordinated efforts on strengthening the capacity of manufacturing firms through support for marketing, business linkages, BDS, clustering and information provision (JNCT 2007).

Education and training policies

Developing a high-quality labour force is a priority of the National Agenda. Education reform started in 2003 with the launch of the Jordan Education Initiative, the Education Reform for Knowledge Economy (ERfKE) and the Jordan higher education programme. These initiatives include reforms to update the curriculum, develop comprehensive training programmes for teachers of all grades, adopt online learning systems, build new schools and reform early childhood education.

A major challenge for Jordan is the mismatch between the education system, especially the technical and vocational education and training (TVET) system, and the needs of the job market (UNESCO 2008).

Although a number of key donor-assisted reforms have been initiated, the lack of a formal coordination process for the harmonization of education and training, the lack of capacity of social partners and stakeholders to handle human capital development reforms, and the lack of multi-donor coordination pose risks to achievement of the National Agenda goals (ETF 2009).

SME and entrepreneurship policies and programmes

Jordan lacks a coherent policy or strategy on enterprise and SME development, although the United States Agency for International Development (USAID) is supporting the MIT to prepare such a document (European Communities and OECD 2008) and the United Nations (UN) has identified development of a gender-sensitive SME policy as an area for support (UN 2008). The SME Department in the MIT, established in 2003, has responsibility for SME policies. This is shared with Jordan Enterprise, which is the implementing body for all enterprise support programmes, including the Jordan Upgrading and Modernisation Programme (JUMP), the Services Modernisation Programme to upgrade service sector SMEs, the SME Equity Financing Programme and other programmes of direct support to start-ups and existing SMEs. However many government and quasi-government entities are involved in SME development issues. The National Fund for Enterprise Support (NAFES) was established in 2001 to help create a BDS market in Jordan and subsidizes up to 80 per cent of consulting and training fees paid by SMEs to approved service providers. The Jordanian Business Development Center (BDC) provides support to SMEs with 5–250 employees in the areas of export development, financial management and operations and competitiveness upgrading, including a programme for women-owned and managed businesses. The Development and Employment Fund (DEF) is a non-bank financial institution established in 1992 to provide services to poor, low-income and unemployed individuals so that they can start MSEs. The Arab Academy for Banking and Financial Services established an SME Center in 2006 to develop the skills of entrepreneurs through high-standard training courses and consulting services to improve their businesses.

To improve access to financing, the Central Bank has been encouraging the professionalization of bankers in SME lending. A few banks have slowly started to enter the SME market, setting up separate SME loan departments and experimenting with credit-scoring models. The government established the Jordan Loan Guarantee Corporation (JLGC)[15] in 1994 to provide commercial banks with loan guarantees (up to 85 per cent) to encourage them to lend to low-collateralized SMEs. The government also established specialized institutions to extend long-term loan facilities to SMEs in the agriculture and industrial sectors at subsidized interest rates.

The microfinance industry in Jordan is emerging. There are five large MFIs with a strong commercial orientation and commitment to industry norms, a dozen or so other MFIs that provide microfinance as one of their activities, and around 200 local microcredit schemes (PlaNet Finance 2007). The five-year National Strategy for Microfinance Development launched in 2008 provides a supervisory and regulatory framework for expansion of MFI activity (MPIC 2008).

To address the private venture capital gap, especially for early-stage start-ups and SMEs, the government mandated Jordan Enterprise to create two government-backed programmes – a €5 million Early Stage Fund and a €20 million Capital-for-Growth Fund. A request for proposals to select private fund managers for the two funds closed in June 2009 (JEDCO 2009). In addition to government budget resources, the European Investment Bank (EIB) and other donors are investing in these funds.

A number of NGO activities promote entrepreneurship, although are somewhat fragmented and uncoordinated. The IFC launched its Business Edge entrepreneurial and business management training programme in Jordan with the goal to train 5000 SME owners by 2009. Business Edge training is complementary to Start Your Own Business (SYOB) and Expand Your Business training programmes offered by the ILO. The Jordan Forum for Business and Professional Women (JFBPW) offers advice and counselling to women entrepreneurs, hosts an incubator for women who own an enterprise or want to start one, and acts as a voice for women-owned SMEs with the government and the public by conducting research and advocating for more favourable laws and regulations. The Young Entrepreneurs Association (YEA) is active in entrepreneurship promotion and advocacy and has produced key policy and research reports to influence policy attention on the issue (YEA 2004b). The AlRiyadi ('entrepreneur') website (www.alriyadi.net) is part of YEA's larger initiative to spur economic growth by encouraging entrepreneurship and providing easy access to information and learning. The YEA organizes promotional campaigns for university students and entrepreneurship forums in communities and is in the process of establishing a Public Policy Advocacy Project to advocate for legislative and structural reform to improve the business environment for SMEs and start-ups (YEA 2009). INJAZ, established in Jordan in 1999, offers entrepreneurship-related courses to university and secondary school students as part of classroom and extracurricular activity. Over 100 schools and universities are involved. Other official efforts by the government ministries to integrate entrepreneurship in the education system are not very advanced.

The Princess Sumaya University for Technology (PSUT) established the Queen Rania Center for Entrepreneurship (QRCE) in 2006 to promote knowledge-based entrepreneurship and foster the commercialization of technology. One of its key initiatives is the National Entrepreneurship Competition – a tech-based business plan competition intended to turn innovation into commercialization.

Innovation policies

R&D is currently high on the national agenda. The Higher Council for Science and Technology (HCST), established in 1987, serves as an umbrella to coordinate the science, technology and innovation activities of ministries, institutions and private sector organizations. The latest HCST strategy identifies a number of performance targets to realize achievements in the areas of information, human resources, transfer of technology and R&D (HCST 2004). The Jordan Industrial Estates Corporation has established a network of innovation centres to promote cooperation between universities and industry and to commercialize R&D, and existing incubators have formed the National Consortium for Technology and Incubation of Business. A scientific research fund was established within the Ministry of Higher Education to support research and strengthen dialogue between the private sector and academia. Funds for R&D and start-up companies are provided by the HCST through the EU project, Support to Research and Technological Development and Innovation Initiatives and Strategies in Jordan. Efforts are needed to integrate initiatives into a broader policy encouraging the promotion of entrepreneurship and the availability of seed and risk capital for start-ups and high-growth companies (European Communities and OECD 2008).

Conclusions

Jordan is one of the top PSD performers among the MENA-12 countries. However its relatively strong growth is driven by FDI and capital investments in non-productive sectors. Jordan is not as strong as it could be in terms of entrepreneurial activity for employment creation and growth, and is not taking advantage of its supply of educated women to contribute to economic development.

Growth of the private sector, and specifically SMEs, is necessary, not only for economic growth but for employment creation, one of the biggest challenges facing Jordan. Although recent developments have contributed to a more conducive framework for private sector and SME development, concerns remain about the institutionalization of these efforts. The lack of a clear consensus on the direction of free market economy reform, frequent changes of Jordanian cabinets during reform periods,[16] the lack of full participation of civil society in the reform process (Bertelsmann Stiftung 2008b) and the lack of capacity to implement bureaucratic reforms, especially if they might impact on public sector jobs or interests of privileged groups (Alissa 2007a) have been issues in the past. Improved coordination and capacity building are needed in most areas of policy affecting private sector, entrepreneurship and SME development.

THE CASE OF EGYPT

Context for Private Sector Development

The Arab Republic of Egypt is a lower-middle-income country with an estimated population of 79 million, growing at just over 2 per cent, and 2009 GDP per capita (PPP) of US$6123 (IMF 2010). It is the most populous country in the Arab world. Egypt's 'open door' policy was initiated in 1976. In 2004 the government of Egypt began a new reform movement, following a stalled economic reform programme started in 1991 that had been waning since the mid-1990s. The strategic commitment is to further Egypt's integration in the global economy.

Privatization efforts have accelerated since the creation of the Ministry of Investment in 2004. State-owned enterprises in all sectors are subject to privatization, including public utilities and petroleum, but the Egyptian economy relies heavily on tourism, oil and gas exports, and Suez Canal revenues, much of which are state controlled. Better-coordinated FDI efforts have resulted in a steady pace of growth in the level of FDI inflows from 3.4 per cent of GDP in 2002 to 8.9 per cent in 2007, although declined to 5.9 per cent in 2008 (WDI). Tourism and real estate are attracting the largest share. Egypt has foreign trade and investment agreements with over 40 countries, including several in the Arab League. The Association Agreement with the EU entered into force in 2004. Exports to GDP amounted to 33 per cent in 2008 and imports to 39 per cent of GDP (WDI), both slightly higher than in 2007. Hydrocarbons and agricultural products account for up to 80 per cent of exports (USAID 2008a). In order to take advantage of trade agreements and increase the share of exported manufactured products, Egyptian enterprises will have to upgrade their product quality and competitiveness and be encouraged to diversify their product base.

Annual GDP growth averaged 4.7 per cent from 2000 to 2008 (WDI). It reached about 4.7 per cent in 2009, down from 7.2 per cent in 2008 (WFB), but in both years Egypt achieved the third-highest growth in the MENA-12. Egypt's growth performance is largely attributable to increases in revenues from the Suez Canal, tourism, oil and remittances of Egyptians working in the Gulf,[17] however it has not been particularly pro-poor. During the 1991–2006 period GDP growth did not translate into lower poverty levels, improved income distribution or higher per capita expenditure, despite broadly improved market conditions for wage workers and those seeking employment (Assaad and Roushdy 2006; Kheir-El-Din and El-Laithy 2006). Almost 20 per cent of the population lives on less than US$2 a day (UNDP 2009).

The service sector accounts for almost half of GDP and half of the labour force (WFB). About 12 per cent of GDP is attributable to the oil and gas sector. A third of Egyptian labour is engaged in the industry sector, which makes up 38 per cent of GDP, and about a third in low-productivity agricultural activities.

Gross capital formation totalled 22.4 per cent of GDP in 2008 (WDI), placing Egypt in the bottom half of the MENA-12 countries. Private capital formation reached 14.5 per cent of GDP, about two thirds of the gross investment, up from 47 per cent in 2003–04. Private investments remain crowded in oil and gas, real estate and construction, transportation, communications and storage.

More than half of the banking system is in private hands (Enders 2007) although the public sector still dominates the sector and absorbs a significant portion of the available credit. Domestic credit to the private sector was 43 per cent of GDP in 2008 (WDI), above the average for the MENA region. The level of domestic credit provided by the banking system reached 78 per cent of GDP in 2008, also higher than the MENA region average (WDI). The distribution of bank financing is uneven, with most loans going to a few large and well-established enterprises. Half of the total loans in Egyptian banks are held by 0.20 per cent of the clients (World Bank 2008a). Egypt launched an SME Exchange (NILEX) on the Cairo and Alexandria Stock Exchange in 2007[18] but the formal venture capital industry is very nascent. Equity finance and leasing mechanisms are underdeveloped and lack sufficient depth to serve the SME market.

Egypt moved slightly up in the rankings on the 2009–10 Global Competitiveness Index over the previous year, largely due to upgrading of infrastructure and positive developments related to labour market efficiency and financial markets sophistication (WEF 2009b). However the labour market continues to be overregulated and employment opportunities for youth and women are underdeveloped. Labour market rigidities, along with macroeconomic instability caused by high government debt (85 per cent of GDP in 2007), budget deficits and inflation, and low confidence in the banking system, are seen as Egypt's major competitiveness challenges. Egypt ranks between Morocco and Tunisia on the 2010

Index of Economic Freedom, in 94th place out of 179 countries (Heritage Foundation 2010). It is categorized as being a 'mostly unfree' economy; although has a high degree of fiscal freedom and is 'moderately free' on trade freedom and government size. Its lowest scores are on property rights and freedom from corruption. Egypt has performed very well on the World Bank's Doing Business assessments over recent years. It has moved up from 165th spot in the first report to 106th spot in the *Doing Business 2010* report (World Bank 2009b), placed fifth among the MENA-12 countries. In comparison Egypt performs very favourably on the time and cost of starting a business, and trading across borders, but has the highest employee dismissal costs, number of days required to register property,[19] cost to enforce a contract and cost of insolvency.

The literacy rate is 71.4 per cent (WFB), with a significant gender gap of almost 24 points. Education indicators place Egypt in eighth place among the MENA-12. This suggests that the quality of the labour force is relatively low. The labour force participation rate is 48 per cent: 71 per cent for men and 23 per cent for women (WDI). The employment rate is only 43 per cent, one of the lowest in the MENA-12. Women's share of employment is 23 per cent, just above average for the MENA-12. The unemployment rate in 2009 was 9.7 per cent (WFB), although the unemployment rate for women in Egypt is four times higher than that for men. There are over 1 million women in the labour force who would like to work but cannot find employment. The highest rate of unemployment is among educated youth (Assaad 2006) and there is mounting pressure to absorb an annual estimate of 800 000 new entrants into the labour force. Economic growth alone is unlikely to generate sufficient employment to deal with this inflow and offset unemployment.

The private sector share of GDP has declined from its peak of just over 70 per cent in 2002 to less than 65 per cent in 2008. The public sector share of total employment is about 30 per cent,[20] the fourth-highest of the MENA-12 countries. Only about 10 per cent of total employment in Egypt is in the formal private sector. The rest of employment is distributed among the informal sector (over a third) and the agricultural sector (over a quarter). The formal private sector has lacked capacity and scale to absorb the country's growing labour force. Informal business practices and corruption, an inadequately educated workforce, tax rates and access to finance and land are the top constraints for private enterprises.[21]

The SME sector contributes an estimated 25 per cent of GDP (GAFI 2008). Micro and small enterprises, defined as those with fewer than 50 workers and paid-in capital of less than EGP1 million, make up the vast majority of the non-agricultural private sector. Microenterprises (with fewer than five workers) alone account for 92.5 per cent of private establishments and almost two-thirds of private sector employment (SFD 2009). Only 1.6 per cent of establishments have more than ten employees, pointing to a serious structural imbalance in the distribution of enterprises by size. The share of MSE employment in the private sector increased from 75 per cent in 1996 to 85 per cent in 2006, but the contribution of SMEs to manufacturing value-added and exports is low (SFD 2009).

SMEs in Egypt suffer from several constraints: a lack of the management skills and systems required to compete effectively in global markets; obsolete production systems; lack of access to finance, information, BDS and training; limited access to markets, distribution channels and supply linkages with larger firms; and low utilization of and access to modern technology (SFD 2009). Fewer than 1 per cent of SMEs access BDS (Entrust 2006), only a small percentage receive any technical education prior to starting their enterprises (El Mahdi 2006) and fewer than 10 per cent report that their workers received any form of training (Entrust 2006). The legal and regulatory burden imposes high transaction cost on SMEs (ENCC 2007). Bank financing is not readily accessible to SMEs and financial leasing is a relatively new phenomenon in Egypt. Microfinance is the major external source of financing for MSEs, although demand exceeds supply.

Owing largely to the difficult business environment for MSEs, informality is a dominant characteristic of the Egyptian SME landscape. The informal economy is estimated at 35 per cent of GDP (Schneider and Buehn 2009). Over 83 per cent of enterprises are informal (El Mahdi and Rashed 2007) and over 70 per cent of all private sector wage workers are employed as informal workers. While the degree of informality declines with firm size, even the largest firms (with over 50 employees) hire nearly a quarter of their workers informally (without a secure contract or social insurance coverage). This particular feature of private sector development is one of those most seriously in need of attention.

Almost a quarter of employed Egyptians are self-employed – 5.3 million people. Egypt stands out among the MENA-12 countries on the high share of employers among the self-employed: 58.5 per cent of the self-employed are employers of others. Self-employed men outnumber women by a little more than four to one. Impediments to women's participation in self-employment and SME activity include social and cultural resistance; low education and literacy levels; limited access to financing, training, BDS and markets; and low property ownership and exercise of property rights (El Mahdi 2006). With efforts to increase women's labour force participation, there will be greater opportunities to present business ownership as an option if the appropriate support is offered.

Entrepreneurship in Egypt is not a deeply engrained cultural value. Over half of 15–29-year-olds in a 2009 Gallup survey stated that they would prefer to work for the government, assuming similar pay and working conditions, than to work in the private sector (10 per cent) or be self-employed (18 per cent) (Silatech 2009). Although a growing number of young Egyptians are becoming interested in entrepreneurship, entrepreneurship training is virtually absent from the educational system. Promoting entrepreneurship as an option among young people and providing the technical assistance to unleash their entrepreneurial potential is likely very important to Egypt's future private sector growth. About 8 per cent of Egyptian adults in the 2008 GEM survey of entrepreneurial activity were in the process of trying to start a business (nascent entrepreneurs) and 13.5 per cent were already owners of an established business (Hattab 2009). The density of entrepreneurs in the adult population is among the highest in the ten GEM-MENA countries. However the entrepreneurial framework conditions in Egypt are less favourable than in most GEM countries, particularly in the areas of entrepreneurship education, R&D support, access to financing for new and growth firms and provision of government support programmes for new and growth firms (Hattab 2009).

Government Priorities and Recent Policy Developments

The government announced very aggressive economic and social development targets in the Sixth Five-Year Plan 2007/08–2011/12: annual GDP growth of 8 per cent, annual per capita income growth of 6 per cent, creation of 3.8 million job opportunities, reduction of the official unemployment rate to 5.5 per cent, an increase in the investment rate to 24 per cent of GDP, a doubling of FDI inflows, a 12 per cent annual increase in exports, reduction in the level of poverty to 15 per cent (and to 6 per cent by 2022), reduction in the illiteracy rate to 20 per cent and an increase in the female labour force participation rate to 25 per cent (Arab Republic of Egypt 2007). The plan includes a massive public expenditure programme to establish 1000 new factories, build 415 000 housing units for low-income groups and 3000 new schools, expand tourism infrastructure and establish 30 villages. Explicit in achieving these targets is a policy orientation to accelerate economic reforms that will foster an enhanced level of private sector participation in economic activity, investments and employment creation. Financing for the plan is to come from the government, donors, FDI and private sector contributions.

Regulatory and administrative reforms

Egypt has made considerable progress in the area of regulatory and administrative reform since establishment of the new government in 2004 and been consistently rated as one of the top ten reformers in the World Bank ease of doing business exercise. Since 2004 the Companies Law has been simplified; customs tariffs dramatically cut; customs procedures streamlined; costs of registering property and the time and cost of starting an enterprise reduced; and a new law passed to establish the system of Economic Courts that will improve the predictability and speediness of justice in areas related to intellectual property rights, anti-monopolies and competition, capital markets and banking (CEC 2009). Tax reforms resulted in a 50 per cent reduction in tax rates and an increase in government revenues. The government is working on badly needed modernized bankruptcy legislation.

Through the Egyptian Regulatory Reform and Development Activity (ERRADA) initiative that started in 2008, the government is using the Guillotine Review methodology to review, simplify and eliminate tens of thousands of existing regulations across several ministries. This process will ultimately lead to adoption of a Regulatory Impact Assessment regime that will improve the quality of new legislation and regulations.

One of the major initiatives to reduce the time and cost of registering an enterprise in Egypt is the establishment of OSSs. The Social Fund for Development (SFD) has opened OSSs for micro and small enterprises (MSEs) in each governorate and the General Authority for Investment (GAFI) has implemented OSSs in major cities to streamline business registration and licensing processes for investors. GAFI has also reduced the costs of incorporating a limited liability company from EGP50 000 to EGP1000, which has resulted in an increase in the number of incorporations of joint-stock companies. The Ministry of Finance has undertaken tax reforms to simplify the method of determining taxes from micro and small enterprises and is adopting international standards in simplified accounting and reporting systems for small firms.

In spite of these diligent efforts by the government to improve the institutional set-up that affects the start-up and operations of enterprises, little progress has been made in reducing informality levels.

Education and training policies and initiatives

Upgrading the skills of the labour force is one of the government's top priorities. The 2002 national training and employment strategy included a reform agenda to upgrade training centres and instructors' qualifications in the technical and vocational education and training (TVET) system. The Ministry of Higher Education (MHE) has been implementing the Egyptian Technical Colleges Program to establish eight super regional colleges and upgrade 45 local technical colleges with improved curriculum and equipment as well as the Technical Education Cluster Project to provide advanced technological education and training.

The National Skills Standards Project (NSSP) provides demand-driven vocational training for SMEs in the construction, manufacturing and tourism sectors, working closely with employers' organizations to assess the skills needs of private sector firms. The NSSP developed a National Vocational Skills Standards and Certification System that has produced qualifications for hundreds of trades and a system for accrediting training providers. The SFD and the MHE are working with Vocational Training Centers to establish sections dealing with the management and operation of small enterprises.

In 2006 the Ministry of Trade and Industry (MTI) formed the Industrial Training Center (ITC), with EGP4 billion of funding over five years, to provide subsidized skills training to industrial sectors and firms and to upgrade the technical skills offered by some training centers to meet local job needs. The goal is to train 250 000 workers annually.

SME and entrepreneurship policies and programmes

Egypt's first national SME policy framework was drafted in 1998 (MoE 1998). With funding and technical assistance from CIDA and IDRC during 2000–2008, the Government of Egypt implemented the Small, Medium and Micro Enterprise Policy (SMEPol) Development Project that was geared to producing research and formulating policies to remove barriers to the development of SMEs in the regulatory environment and to enhance their access to financial and non-financial support and services. In 2004 the government passed the Small Enterprises Development Law (SME Law 141/2004) laying out the provisions for enhancing the role of MSEs (with less than 50 employees) in the economy and giving the sole mandate for implementing and coordinating MSE policies and programmes to the SFD. Since the passing of the SME law, three SME strategies have been drafted, one by the Ministry of Finance focused on improving the competitiveness of small and medium enterprises (MoF 2004), one by the Ministry of Investment targeting small and medium investors (SMIs) (GAFI 2008) and the third by the SFD targeting micro and small enterprises (SFD 2009). The lack of a clear government-wide mechanism for coordinating policies for the whole sector has led to overlap and some confusion.

Egypt has a relatively large number of government bodies, NGOs and business associations working in the field of SME development. Most of the support initiatives are donor-funded and largely uncoordinated. Regional SFD offices provide micro and small loans and advisory services to MSEs. The Industrial Modernisation Centre (IMC), affiliated with the MTI, offers a range of defined programmes to improve the local and national competitiveness of industrial SMEs, including technology transfer, quality improvements and cluster development initiatives. The IMC focuses primarily on enterprises with more than ten workers. The provision of BDS in Egypt is in the early stages of development and availability and outreach of services are limited. The Canadian International Development Agency (CIDA)-funded Business Development Services Support Project (BDSSP) has been building the capacity of existing business associations and NGOs to deliver non-financial business services to SMEs and training BDS providers.

NGOs, the SFD, government ministries and agencies, donors, banks and private sector companies all play a role in trying to address SME financing issues. The major instrument at present is microcredit. Almost 300 NGOs and banks dealt with over 1 million microfinance clients in 2007, quadruple the estimates from five years earlier (USAID and EMFN 2008). A National Microfinance Strategy was developed in 2005 (EBI and CBE 2005) and a microfinance law drafted in 2009 to provide regulations for the microfinance sector. A growing number of banks are establishing SME units or departments, but they tend to target SME clients with well-established track records. The SME Unit within the Egyptian Banking Institute is training financial institutions on SME lending and helping to build the capacity of SMEs to develop bankable proposals. Some donors have been issuing soft loans to banks to encourage downscaling of bank lending practices or funding guarantee facilities. The Cooperative Insurance Society (CIS) for SMEs, the Credit Guarantee Company for Small Scale Enterprises and the Microenterprise Guarantee Facility programme for small and emerging businesses provide credit guarantee services for small enterprise bank borrowers in the different governorates. In 2009 the Ministry of Investment announced an EGP500 million SME Fund to finance the development plans of small and medium investors. Egypt passed a leasing law in 2001 and the IFC is working to promote the emergence of new leasing companies. In 2007 the government supported the launch of I-score, a credit information bureau that is expected to make a significant impact on the SME lending market.

A focus on entrepreneurship education and training is becoming increasingly popular in Egypt. In 2008 the Ministry of Education, in cooperation with the ILO, piloted the introduction of the Know About Business (KAB) curriculum in a small number of selected secondary schools, and trained teachers in its delivery. The Minister of Education has approved the expansion of this curriculum throughout the system and the Minister of Higher Education has agreed to adopt the initiative in higher education facilities.

There are few concrete initiatives at the university level, but growing interest in offering small business management and entrepreneurship courses. The SFD has supported 17 public universities and seven private universities and academies to offer a 40-hour course on entrepreneurship that has the potential to reach 40 000 college and university students and graduates annually when fully implemented. Establishment of a network of university entrepreneurship centres and incubators is proposed within the strategic framework of GAFI's new SMI strategy.

INJAZ-Egypt, started in 2006, aims to create a new generation of empowered youth who will become entrepreneurs by delivering a range of age-appropriate educational products to encourage students to think about starting a business as a career option, identify their entrepreneurial skills and gain experience in starting and running their own businesses for a school year with coaching and mentoring by corporate executives. These programmes are offered in cooperation with schools and universities. There are also other isolated entrepreneurship training initiatives, largely offered by business associations and NGOs. For example, Intilaaqah-Egypt offers the Shell LiveWIRE Youth Enterprise Programme on how to start and develop a business to young people and the Future Generation Foundation offers the Basic Business Skills Acquisition Program to new university graduates through various training centres. The Entrepreneurs Business Forum (EBF) organizes a Business Idea Award competition for commerce and engineering students, Nahdet El Mahroussa sponsors a Young Innovator's Award and the Egyptian Junior Business Association (EJB) sponsors the National Business Plan Competition with the MTI.

Innovation policies

Egypt's R&D intensity is very low, less than 0.5 per cent of GDP, and large-scale R&D projects are relatively modest. Private R&D investment is very low. One of the most aggressive R&D policy efforts is in the ICT sector (MCIT 2007), but the government is also establishing a more elaborate R&D and commercialization support infrastructure. This includes the Smart Village initiative, R&D Centers of Excellence, business and technology incubators, a network of Technology Transfer and Innovation Centers (TTICs) and a Technology Development Fund that provides risk capital to technology and ICT start-ups, specifically technology and higher-value-added start-ups. This infrastructure does not exist in all parts of the country at the present time.

Conclusions

Egypt has made significant progress in its market economy transition in recent years, improving its performance on macroeconomic and business environment indicators. However, unattended, the high level of informality in the enterprise sector, the preponderance of microenterprises in its structural base and the low level of competitiveness of its SMEs will counteract efforts to attract FDI and expand export activity. Promoting quality entrepreneurship and the growth of SMEs will be key to creating jobs and reducing poverty. At present there is insufficient consultation with SMEs and the broader civil society on the reform agenda, and a lack of accountability mechanisms to ensure inclusiveness in policy design and implementation (Alissa 2007b). This deficiency needs to be addressed.

THE CASE OF TUNISIA

Context for Private Sector Development

The Tunisian Republic is a relatively small, middle-income country, with an estimated population of 10.5 million, growing at less than 1 per cent a year, and 2009 GDP per capita (PPP) of US$8254 (IMF 2010). This makes it the third-richest economy of the MENA-12 and the one with the slowest population growth rate. Until the 1970s Tunisia was ruled by a socialist regime and managed as a centrally planned economy with state control of the main productive sectors.

It was one of the first countries in the region to open its economy and is now one of the most trade-liberalized of the MENA-12 economies. One of the pillars of its liberalization policy was the establishment of free trade zones, which became operational in 1995. It has been a member of the WTO since 1995 and was the first MENA country to enter into an Association Agreement with the EU. To deal with the initial pressure on the capacity of Tunisian industries to compete on the European level, the government launched a global upgrading programme (Mise à Niveau) in 1996, as well as technoparks to encourage innovative industrial activities in the high-tech and IT sectors. Exports to the EU quadrupled from 1995 to 2007 as a result of these initiatives. Tunisia also has FTAs with several MENA region and other countries. In 2008 exports and imports amounted to 126 per cent of GDP (WDI), second only to Jordan. Although the level of exports to GDP has grown from 50 per cent in 2006 to 61 per cent in 2008, imports have been growing at a faster rate than exports,[22] resulting in a small international trade deficit.

Tunisia has achieved significant progress in attracting foreign investment. FDI reached 6.5 per cent of GDP in 2008 (compared to the MENA average of 4.6 per cent) (WDI), up from 3.2 per cent in 2000, but down from 10.8 per cent in 2006. The transfer of production knowledge to local private enterprises has not occurred to a great extent, thus hindering the upgrading of local private enterprises (WEF 2008c).

The country has experienced steady economic growth in recent years, averaging annual GDP growth of 4.9 per cent over the 2000–2008 period (WDI). However GDP growth declined in 2009 to 0.3 per cent (WFB), the second-lowest in the MENA-12. Past growth was led by strong domestic and European demand, largely attributed to the recovery of Tunisia's agricultural sector and increases in investment and exports. Tunisia's growth has relied largely on public investment, with a private investment share of gross capital formation of 50–55 per cent (12–13 per cent of GDP), one of the lowest in the MENA-12.[23] The government's target is to increase the private sector share to 65 per cent by 2011 (AfDB 2007).

The Tunisian economy is diversified with a growing services sector. Services account for 54 per cent of GDP (of which tourism is a large share) and about half of the working population.[24] Manufacturing accounts for about 60 per cent of the industry sector and 18 per cent of GDP.

The banking sector has been privatized, but the government maintains firm control over the three largest public banks and was reported to own 47.2 per cent of total bank assets in 2004 (World Bank 2006c). The banking and financial sectors are not well integrated into the international market and the small size of banks does not enable economies of scale in transactions (IMF 2008b). Domestic credit to the private sector is relatively high (66.7 per cent of GDP in 2008 compared to the MENA region average of 35.8. per cent), as is the level of domestic credit provided by the banking system (73 per cent versus 39.7 per cent).

Tunisia performs relatively well on global index assessments. It was placed in the top 27 per cent of all countries on the Global Competitiveness Index in 2009–10 and ranked 69 among 183 countries in the *Doing Business 2010* report, both number one spots for MENA-12 countries. On the other hand Tunisia was assessed as being a 'mostly unfree' economy in the *2010 Index of Economic Freedom* (ranking of 98 among 179 countries and 6th among the nine MENA-12 countries); even though it was rated as having a high degree of business freedom and being 'mostly free' on fiscal and monetary freedoms and government size (Heritage Foundation 2010). Low scores on trade and investment freedoms and freedom from corruption were among those pulling down its comparative performance.

Tunisia has a medium level of human capital compared to the MENA-12 with a population literary rate of 76 per cent and a relatively high level of education. The labour force participation rate in 2008 was 48 per cent: 70 per cent among men and 26 per cent among women (WDI). The employment rate is 41 per cent (WDI), one of the lowest in the MENA-12 countries. The female share of the labour force and employment (about 26 per cent) is among the highest in the MENA-12. Early decisions of the government, dating to the 1960s, to ban polygamy, promote birth control and family planning, and make education compulsory for both girls and boys are largely responsible for the increased level of women's participation in economic activities (Ayadi et al. 2005). Tunisia has the highest ranking of the eight MENA-12 countries assessed in the 2008 WEF Global Gender Gap Index with a placement of 103 among 130 countries (WEF 2008b). The institutional set-up is highly favourable to the emancipation of women and places Tunisia ahead of other Arab countries on gender dynamics (AfDB and OECD 2008d).

The unemployment rate is high at over 15 per cent (WFB). Even though GDP growth has been strong since the late 1990s, much of the growth has been capital-intensive and insufficient to absorb the rise in job seekers and reduce high unemployment levels (AfDB 2007). Tunisia has a relatively low poverty level, leading analysts to conclude that Tunisia's economic growth has been consistently pro-poor (Ayadi et al. 2005; Bibi 2006). The slowdown in population growth, active female participation in the labour force and pro-poor social policies, such as social assistance, microcredit programmes and free public education, have accounted for much of the success in pro-poor growth (Ayadi et al. 2005). The poverty headcount index (population living on less than US$2 a day) decreased from 20 per cent in 1980 to 3.8 per cent in 2005. The 2005 estimate of people living below the poverty line was 7.4 per cent (WFB); lower than in the other MENA-12 countries.

The lack of robustness of the private sector is one of the country's main weaknesses (AfDB and OECD 2008). Private sector growth and competitiveness continues to be hampered by state control over major sectors, suggesting that further reforms to competition policy and practices are needed (World Bank 2008j). Private sector enterprises continue to face a number of constraints: access to financing (high collateral requirements) and technology (low technological capacity); rigidities in the Labour Code; high social charges on employee wages; high customs tariffs; and low infrastructure quality.

Data on SMEs, except for industrial enterprises, are limited. Some estimates indicate that more than 75 per cent of the private sector in Tunisia is composed of SMEs with 100 or fewer employees (Di Tommaso et al. 2001), a lower proportion that would generally be found in a developing economy. SMEs in Tunisia suffer from inadequate capacity and competence, particularly in marketing, management and R&D. Financing of technology acquisition is rather limited and consequently SMEs rely on obsolete technology with little prospects for development and innovation. SMEs need improved access to financial resources for initial start-ups and financial restructuring and to short, medium and long term credit.

The self-employment rate in Tunisia in 2007 was 25.4 per cent (ONEQ

2008), up from 20.2 per cent in 2004. The share of employers among the self-employed is average for MENA-12 countries. Women's share of overall self-employment is 15.8 per cent: 17.5 per cent of own-account self-employment and 11.6 per cent of employer self-employment. This is one of the largest shares of women in total self-employment in the MENA-12. Informality in Tunisia is estimated at 39.3 per cent of GDP (Schneider and Buehn 2009) – the highest level among the MENA-12 countries for which comparable data is available. About 38 per cent of Tunisian businesses operate in the informal economy (World Bank 2004c).

In 2009, supported by the German Technical Cooperation (GTZ), the University of Sousse became a partner in the Global Entrepreneurship Monitor project and collected survey and interview data to enable a baseline assessment of the level of entrepreneurial activity in Tunisia and its entrepreneurial framework conditions. Preliminary data indicate that Tunisia has a relatively high density of entrepreneurs. Over 17 per cent of the adult population owns their own business. Only Lebanon and Morocco have more entrepreneurs per 100 adults in the ten GEM-MENA countries (IDRC 2010). However a very low percentage of the adult population is actively trying to start a business – only 2.2 per cent. This is the lowest nascent entrepreneur rate among the ten GEM-MENA countries, implying that the pipeline for new entrepreneurial ventures is small. A very low proportion of Tunisian adults in the GEM 2009 research (only 15 per cent) 'sees good opportunities to start a business in the next 6 months', substantially lower than the average for all GEM countries and the GEM-MENA group (Bosma and Levie 2010). This may be a contributing factor in the low rate of nascent activity. The GEM-Tunisia project will contribute to the information base on the level of entrepreneurial activity in Tunisia and provide important benchmark data to monitor enterprise creation policies and initiatives.

Government Priorities and Recent Policy Developments

The government sees two major challenges going forward: increasing FDI and cutting unemployment. In Tunisia's 11th Five-Year Economic and Social Development Plan 2007–11, the government set targets to accelerate economic growth to about 6.5 per cent a year; lift per capita income to TND5700; create jobs, especially for young graduates; and reduce the unemployment rate to less than 11 per cent (MDIC 2007). The plan provides for measures to promote greater liberalization, including reform of restrictive labour regulations; promote exports; upgrade and modernize industry and service sectors; establish business creation structures and support funds, including seed capital and risk capital guarantee funds;

reform the educational and training system; develop technological centres, technopoles and business incubators to encourage research and innovation; and offer tax and financial incentives to achieve more balanced regional development (AfDB 2007).

Business environment reforms

Tunisia has made significant progress in improving the business climate since passing of the new Law on Economic Initiative in 2007 (République Tunisienne 2007). The establishment of OSSs[25] has substantially reduced and simplified the process of registering a business; online registration services are available; the minimum paid-in capital requirement for new limited liability companies has been abolished; and dramatic revisions have been made to simplify the time and cost of closing a business, especially in cases where insolvency or bankruptcy is involved (European Communities and OECD 2008). The law also included chapters reducing the tax burden; facilitating the financing of professional training and development of business incubators, *pépinères d'entreprise* and cyber-parks;[26] and encouraging regional development zones.

Education and training policies

One of the major challenges in boosting the ability of the labour market to create more jobs is building the capacity of the educational system to prepare students better for integration into the labour market and to train young people who wish to engage in self-employment (AfDB 2007). To achieve this requires efforts to increase standards of the educational system, address geographic disparities in education access and improve the quality and relevance of teaching to facilitate transition from the classroom to the workforce. A vast reform programme to ameliorate deficiencies in the education system was laid out in the government's strategy, Schools of the Future 2002–2007. The Secondary and Primary Education Law of July 2002 reaffirmed education quality as an absolute national priority to prepare youth for the knowledge economy. Reforms of the higher education system began in earnest in 2005 when the President of Tunisia announced his decision to develop the university system and bring it into line with the standards and systems of advanced countries. The aim is to make university training an important factor in promoting the development process and employability of graduates. There has been a major expansion of both public and private vocational training centres since 2006. In January 2008 the Chamber of Deputies adopted a government bill on vocational training to increase the intake capacity of training centres, reinforce option-based and sandwich training schemes in partnership with enterprises, and set up bridging between general education and technical learning so students can transfer from one to the other (AfDB and OECD 2008d).

SME and entrepreneurship policies and programmes

The Tunisian government has been focusing on the SME industrial sector since the late 1990s. The Support Center for Small and Medium Size Industry was established within the Ministère de l'Industrie, de l'Energie et des Petites et Moyennes Entreprises (MIEPME) in 1998. Responsibility for the SME sector is shared with the Ministry of Trade and Handicrafts, which is responsible for handicrafts, small workshops and commercial SMEs in commercial services. The Company Creation Support Center was set up in 1993 and has established networks in all governorates to encourage new enterprise activity. It also manages the national business incubator network consisting of 19 business incubators located at the Higher Institutes of Technological Studies, engineering schools, universities and technopoles. A Higher Council for the Creation of Enterprises and Development of Innovative Projects, and regional committees for development of creative projects, were created in 2002. Although there is no evidence of a comprehensive SME policy document in Tunisia, the creation and development of SMEs is a part of the new national priorities. A Directorate-General for SME Promotion was established in the MIEPME (the Ministry of Industry and Technology since 2010) for the purpose of setting policy guidelines and coordinating implementation through a number of executive agencies.

The two major SME policy directions are geared towards: (1) improving SME competitiveness by upgrading their skills, technology, product quality and management competencies to ensure they can compete globally; and (2) increasing the level of entrepreneurial activity, especially among young people for whom the unemployment level is highest. The strategy for doing this is built around four key pillars: (1) an attractive and favourable business environment; (2) a diversified financing system; (3) a generous incentive system for regional development; and (4) a system of guidance and technical assistance throughout the process of enterprise creation. The government commits one-fifth of its annual budget for a professional training programme focusing on enhancing the entrepreneurship spirit among youth, creating and supporting business incubators to develop links between universities and businesses, and other initiatives, such as the Salon de la Création d'Entreprises campaign.[27] The Ministry of Industry and Technology partners with the national and regional network of support structures to deliver the strategy, including business centres, incubators,[28] 'single windows', technology centres, technopoles, regional coaches, universities, banks, guarantee funds, Salon de la Création and SME forums.[29]

Tunisia appears to be more advanced than most of the MENA-12 countries in the areas of promoting entrepreneurial spirit among young people, integrating entrepreneurship in the education system and providing non-formal entrepreneurial learning. Entrepreneurship is being addressed as a key competency in secondary schooling (as part of the National Education Strategy since 2002), coaching is provided to micro-enterprises through the employment and self-employment agency, the Agence Nationale pour l'Emploi et le Travail Independant (ANETI), and many other self-employment and business start-up training schemes are offered. The presidential programme of 2005–09 set a target to create 70 000 new enterprises during the plan period, particularly based on innovative ideas. This strategy for entrepreneurship development includes promotion, financing, training, assistance with business plans, mentoring and post start-up support. A National Campaign for the Creation and Development of SMEs was launched by the MIEPME in 2005 with three national programmes to support business creation, quality production and management, and coaching by Tunisian and international experts. Regional business centres and business establishment support centres are available throughout the country to provide technical assistance, counselling and coaching to new entrepreneurs and SMEs.

The government has implemented a number of policy measures and structures to provide microfinance, SME loan guarantees and risk capital. The Banque de Financement des PME (BFPME) was launched in 2005, the first MENA-12 country to have a bank for the financing of SMEs. Tunisia has a leasing law and over a dozen leasing companies, making Tunisia the most progressive of the MENA countries in access to this form of SME financing. There are more than 38 venture capital companies in the country, again rendering Tunisia one of the most developed of the MENA countries.

Innovation policies

Developing innovative enterprises through modernization of the R&D system, improving the level of transfer of knowledge between public research institutes and industry, and financing industry R&D are also priorities for the government. The promotion of innovative enterprises, encouragement of inventors and setting of targets for innovation outcomes (for example, R&D intensity and number of science and technology graduates) were part of the 2005 innovation policy. The government expects to develop 12 technology hubs aimed at encouraging research and innovation by 2015 and is in the process of establishing Competitiveness Centers (AfDB and OECD 2008d).

Conclusions

The policy and institutional framework in Tunisia suggests a strong national commitment to PSD, particularly concerning FDI and trade policies. Development of the SME sector is also seen as important and major efforts are under way to promote entrepreneurship. However growth in trade and investment activity has not resulted in increased employment and the private sector share of investment has fallen short of expectations. The country is far from reaching its full economic potential and much more needs to be done to improve the competitiveness, flexibility and entrepreneurial dynamism of the country. Easing entry and competition in regulated sectors of the economy, diversifying economic activity into more innovative areas, reducing rigidities in employment policies and costly social security for workers, and enhancing business environment reforms are areas still in need of attention.

THE CASE OF TURKEY

Context for Private Sector Development

The Republic of Turkey is a large, upper-middle-income country with an estimated population of 76.8 million, a population growth rate of 1.3 per cent, and GDP per capita (PPP) of US$12 746 in 2009. Until 1980 Turkey was largely an isolated state-driven economy with an industrial structure dominated by large-scale, state-owned and private enterprises. During the 1980s the Turkish government undertook ambitious reforms to make the transition to a free market economy. The Turkish economy is now a mix of modern industry and commerce with a traditional agricultural sector. The industry sector contributes about a quarter of GDP, the service sector about two-thirds and the agricultural sector about 10 per cent (WFB). Manufacturing makes up a large share of the industry sector, amounting to 18 per cent of GDP, the second-highest level among the MENA-12 countries.

Inward FDI, at 2.5 per cent of GDP in 2008, weaker than in previous years, was lower than the MENA region average of 4.6 per cent of GDP (WDI). Reforms associated with the EU accession are expected to boost FDI levels. The Foreign Direct Investment Law has been in force since 2003 and, in 2006, the government established the Investment Support and Promotion Agency – the absence of such an entity believed to be a major factor in the low level of FDI for an economy of Turkey's size. Turkey is just below average for all MENA countries in terms of the level of trade openness. The 1996 Customs Union with the EU resulted in an increase in the volume of trade with EU member states; however, Turkey continues to have a trade deficit. In 2008 exports to GDP totalled 24 per cent and imports reached over 28 per cent (WDI).

Average growth in GDP between 2000 and 2008 was 5.7 per cent (WDI), peaking in 2004 at 9 per cent. Much of Turkey's growth during this period was jobless, and economic prosperity did not lead to lower unemployment. GDP growth slowed down to 0.9 per cent in 2008 and dropped to negative 5.6 per cent in 2009 (WFB). Gross capital formation in 2008 amounted to about 20 per cent of GDP (in the bottom half of the MENA-12 countries), with the private sector share accounting for 80 per cent (16 per cent of GDP).

There is a well-developed banking sector with many private banks and openness to foreign stakes. In 2007 the seven public banks owned 28.6 per cent of total bank assets (SPO 2008), a much lower level than in many of the MENA-12 countries. Domestic credit to the private sector was 32.6 per cent of GDP in 2008, and the domestic credit provided by the banking system was 52.6 per cent of GDP (WDI), below the average for other lower- and upper-middle-income (LUMI) countries, suggesting some constraints on private sector financing. The Capital Markets Authority provided the legal basis for opening an SME Exchange on the Istanbul Stock Exchange in 2003.

Turkey compares reasonably well to the MENA-12 countries on global indicators of competitiveness, freedom, knowledge economy and doing business. It ranked 61 out of 134 countries on the 2009–10 Global Competitiveness Index (WEF 2009b), but behind Tunisia and Jordan. Placed behind Jordan on the 2010 Index of Economic Freedom, with an overall rank of 67 out of 179 countries (Heritage Foundation 2010), Turkey is considered a 'moderately free' economy. It performed particularly well on trade freedom and government size. Its weakest performance was on labour freedom and freedom from corruption indicators, both assessed as 'repressed'. It is the second-best MENA-12 performer on ease of doing business (World Bank 2009b) with particularly competitive scores on the time and cost of starting a business, the ease of registering property, the availability of credit information and enforcing contracts. Turkey is the top performer among the ten MENA-12 countries on the Knowledge Economy Index (WBI 2008).

A labour force participation rate of 46.9 per cent, an employment rate of 41.7 per cent and an unemployment rate of 14.2 per cent[30] (Turkstat 2009) indicate a low utilization of labour in the country, a situation that has been deteriorating since 2000 (World Bank 2006f). The share of women in all forms of employment is about 26 per cent, high compared to other MENA-12 countries, but low given Turkey's level of economic development. About 40 per cent of women's labour market involvement is as an unpaid family worker (Turkstat 2008a). Although adult literacy rates are approaching 90 per cent, 70 per cent of working-age persons in Turkey have below upper-secondary education. This is the third-highest in 27 Organisation for Economic Co-operation and Development (OECD) countries, a factor seen as impeding employment rates and labour productivity (OECD 2009b). With an average education of the adult population of 8.8 years, the Turkish private sector does not have a highly skilled workforce from which to draw (UNDP 2008). Poverty levels are rather high; an estimated 20 per cent of the population is below the national poverty line (WFB). Turkey has a wide gender gap, ranking 123 out of 130 countries on the WEF Global Gender Gap Index with particularly low scores on women's economic participation and political empowerment (WEF 2008b).

Turkey has a rapidly growing private sector that employs 87 per cent of workers and is responsible for 85 per cent of gross capital formation. Yet in spite of many efforts to end government monopolies and privatize SOEs, the state still plays a role in infrastructure, basic industry, banking, transport, communication and energy sectors. The Competition Authority, set up in 1997, plays an important role in ensuring open, competition-oriented markets, but government control over strategic sectors still hampers private sector competition. Major reforms have taken place since 2001 to open the Turkish market to global competition and to meet the requirements for accession to the EU. These changes have altered the fundamentals of the market economy and created a different environment for private entrepreneurs, one that requires improvements in productivity and competitiveness and technological upgrading (Turan and Kara 2007).

Private sector growth in Turkey is hampered by a lack of certainty regarding public governance conditions; a lack of transparency and legal certainty of the judicial system; high energy costs; a complex and unstable taxation system; and low human capital (World Bank 2007e; OECD 2008b). A number of regulatory barriers also exist. In the OECD stocktaking of structural reforms in 27 OECD countries, Turkey was assessed as having the second most restrictive product market regulation, the most restrictive state controls[31] and regulations affecting barriers to entrepreneurship,[32] and the sixth most restrictive barriers to trade and investment[33] (OECD 2009a). The OECD recommended continuing strong reform efforts to simplify product market regulation, in particular sectoral licensing rules which hinder market entry in many parts of the service sector; to advance privatizations; encourage greater competition in network industries; reduce the cost of labour; improve educational attainment; and reduce rigidities in the employment protection legislation that are encouraging the informalization of labour (OECD 2009a).

One of the major structural imbalances in the Turkish private sector is the high level of informality. Schneider and Savaşan (2005) estimated the size of the informal sector for the 1999–2005 period to be 31–35 per cent of GDP. The OECD (2004c) suggested that up to 50 per cent of SME activity could be informal. Less than half of the employed labour force during 2002–05 was in the formal sector and registered in the social security system (Papps 2008). Davutyan (2008) concludes that a large pool of unemployed persons combined with high employment costs (among the highest in the OECD), weak legal enforcement and competitive pressures from low-wage countries create a set of conditions leading many Turkish firms to turn to unofficial production.

SMEs dominate the private sector in number but have low labour productivity and insufficient access to finance, face barriers to the entry of foreign markets and lack competitiveness (EC 2008d). Turkish SMEs are characterized by low awareness of quality and environmental standards; insufficient use of technology; inefficient production; low value-added; a lack of knowledge and experience with exporting; deficiencies in management and human capital; low labour competitiveness; weak linkages with other SMEs; and insufficiency in R&D and innovation activities and investments (Özar 2004; World Bank 2008k). The OECD attributes much of the poor competitiveness performance of SMEs to the lack of institutional support for technological development and the lack of cooperation between academia and the private sector (OECD 2004c). Çetindamar and Çetinkaya (2008) add the lack of capacity and know-how of SMEs and entrepreneurs to commercialize research results through the start-up of innovative businesses to the list of factors. Addressing these obstacles requires an improvement in SME support systems and a more comprehensive and better-integrated service network (Çetindamar and Çetinkaya 2008; SPO 2008).

Self-employment rates are relatively high at 27 per cent of the working population (Turkstat 2008a), but there has been virtually no growth in the self-employment rate during the first nine years of the 2000s. Working men are twice as likely as working women to be own-account workers and over four times as likely to be employers. Factors such as a patriarchal society, traditional gender roles, lack of education, lack of experience in the labour force, low access to credit and resources, and few role models to act as mentors are among those affecting women's low participation in entrepreneurial activity in Turkey (OECD 2004c). The lack of a cohesive policy framework for developing women's entrepreneurship is not helpful in terms of improving the situation (Ecevit 2007).

Turkey has a low level of entrepreneurial dynamism (only about 6 per cent of the adult population is either actively trying to start a business or already owns a young business that is less than 42 months old) and density of existing entrepreneurs (7.8 per cent of the adult population), although almost three-quarters of the adult population consider entrepreneurship a desirable career choice and about a fifth expect to start a business within the next three years (Bosma et al. 2009). These positive attitudes towards entrepreneurship, coupled with a dynamic and changing market for goods and services, indicate favourable conditions for entrepreneurship if they can be exploited. However the framework conditions for entrepreneurial activity appear to need improvement in areas such as the availability of financial support for new and growing firms; government programmes supporting technology development and incentives for R&D investments; stronger intellectual property rights; government regulation policies to reduce taxes and the time it takes to obtain permits and licences; and support for new and growing firms as a top-level policy priority (Karadeniz and Ozdemir 2009).

Government Priorities and Recent Policy Developments

Job creation remains a major challenge for the Turkish government. Up to 700000 new jobs per year are necessary to absorb the growing influx of new labour market entrants while maintaining unemployment at its present level. An annual job deficit has been in play for the past several years (EC 2007c; UNDP 2008). Measures to improve the labour market and the level of labour force participation include youth employment schemes; labour force training for women; a review of the social security system; modernization and capacity building of vocational education and training systems to meet the needs of the labour market better; employment-guaranteed training programmes; and encouragement of entrepreneurship (SPO 2008).

The overall objective of the Ninth Development Plan 2007–13 is to increase the economy's competitiveness by ensuring effective infrastructure equipped with high-technological and adaptable human resources capacity (SPO 2006). A number of policy measures have implications for PSD: a tax law review to simplify the taxation regime and reduce informality; further improvements to the business environment; credit guarantee systems and venture capital to improve SMEs' access to finance; new industrial centres; and enhanced technological infrastructure, particularly in ICT. The Prime Ministry established a Permanent Special Ad Hoc Committee on Competitiveness of Industry in 2007 to evaluate general and sectoral problems and design policy proposals. The 2008 Annual

Programme presented a number of actions to alleviate regional disparities, diversify economic activity and reinforce local governments, to improve the quality of life and business opportunities in the regions (SPO 2008). Developing regional growth centres (through expansion of Organized Industrial Estates, free zones and clustering initiatives), the establishment of regional development agencies and promotion of entrepreneurship are among the key measures.

Complying with the requirements for accession to the European Union is driving the Turkish government's economic and social policy priorities.

Regulatory and administrative reforms

Turkey initiated its Reform Programme for Improving the Investment Environment as a priority of the Eighth Development Plan 2001–05. A Coordination Council for the Improvement of the Investment Environment was formed as the key structure to solicit policy input from the private sector (an international model of success for a public–private platform). This council conducts an agenda with the help of 12 Technical Committees[34] and the participation of both public and private sector institutions. The major aims of the council are to rationalize investment regulations, develop policies to enhance the competitiveness of the investment environment and generate solutions to the administrative barriers encountered by domestic and foreign investors (OECD 2009f). Several measures have been introduced. Amendments to the Turkish Commercial Code in 2003 enabled registration of a company in one day by granting authority to Trade Registries. A new law came into force in 2005 allowing craftsmen and tradesmen to register their businesses online with the Confederation of Tradesmen and Artisans of Turkey. New regulations on opening business premises and obtaining a work licence dramatically reduced the number of required documents. Public service OSSs were established in districts in an effort to decentralize many government functions. In 2007 the government adopted a Regulatory Impact Assessment regime that will assess existing regulations and provide better insight on their possible improvement, the first of the MENA-12 countries to do so. Many reforms have been carried out to adjust legislation to be in conformity with that of the EU.

Reducing the level of informality is another of the government's priorities to improve the competitiveness of the economy. Plans are under way to implement a comprehensive strategy to combat informality through efforts to inform society of the negative aspects of an informal economy, decrease the financial and social burdens on formal employment, and provide more effective coordination among public institutions to address and monitor the informality issue (SPO 2008). Part of this process is to carry out a systematic analysis of the reasons behind, and consequences and dimensions of the informal economy, and to formulate proposals to eliminate its causes. Turkey stands out among the MENA-12 countries as one of the few where the government has made informality reduction a high government priority.

SME and entrepreneurship policies and programmes

Turkey started developing SME-related policies in the late 1980s, early for the MENA-12 group of countries. These were specifically oriented to strengthening small-scale industrial enterprises through technology upgrading and improved product quality. The Small and Medium Enterprises Development Organization (KOSGEB), an associate body of the Ministry of Industry and Trade (MIT), was established by law in 1990 to execute industrial policies for SMEs. Its current role is to implement support mechanisms for increasing the competitiveness of SMEs in all sectors and to encourage entrepreneurship and start-ups.

As an OECD member country Turkey signed on to the Bologna Charter on policies for SMEs in 2000, agreeing to enhance the availability of financial and non-financial instruments to promote SME development. The European Charter for Small Enterprises was adopted in 2002 and the government began concrete steps towards SME development in the ten policies areas[35] outlined in the charter, and in accordance with the SME-related sections of the Accession Partnership Agreements.

The first SME Strategy and Action Plan was launched in 2004 (SPO 2004). The objectives of the revised SME Strategy and Action Plan for 2007–09 are to improve the efficiency and international competitiveness of SMEs and increase the SME contribution to employment and value-added (OECD 2009f). Five policy pillars guide the strategy: (1) improvement of entrepreneurship; (2) enterprise development; (3) integration of SMEs into the international market; (4) improvement of the business environment; and (5) development of technological and innovative capacity. The primary objectives of the SME Technical Committee Action Plan are to improve the systems of credit guarantee and venture capital companies; improve cluster policy for SMEs; encourage SMEs to conform to environmental laws and regulations; and prepare a development strategy to develop the services sector (OECD 2009f).

The Turkish Grand Assembly has an SME Working Group that studies the problems of SMEs for discussion at the National Grand Assembly. A SME Advisory Committee, represented by government and private sector bodies, provides guidance to the government and to KOSGEB on the design and delivery of SME policies and support initiatives. KOSGEB works with other ministries and agencies, financial bodies and business organizations in the implementation of SME strategies and support mechanisms and has built an extensive network of SME support organizations and mechanisms: Enterprise Development Centres (IGEMs), Technology Development Centres (TEKMERs) and Synergy Centres (nodes for partnering organizations at the local and regional level) with links to financial institutions and programmes (Tezyetiş 2007).

Some progress has been reported on access to finance. Since 2003 a certain amount of KOSGEB's budget has been allocated to the SME Credit Support System, through which approved SMEs can obtain low- or zero-interest rate loans from intermediary banks. In 2004 KOSGEB launched a microcredit mechanism to support the establishment of new businesses. The EU in cooperation with the Turkish Credit Guarantee Fund (KGF) initiated a credit guarantee service for SMEs, and public and private banks have launched new SME loan facilities.[36] However SMEs continue to have difficulties meeting the collateral requirements of banks without loan guarantees, and existing start-up, risk capital and credit guarantee, supports are not sufficient to meet the demand (MIT 2007; SPO 2008).

Microcredit applications are rather new in Turkey with market dominance by state-owned banking institutions. A pending Draft Law on the Microfinance Institutions, if approved, will set up the legal framework permitting foundations, associations and non-governmental organizations (NGOs) to provide microfinance services, thus considerably increasing the number of microcredit programmes for SMEs. In the meantime more research is needed on microenterprises and microenterprise and microfinance support schemes (Karatas and Helvacioglu 2008).

Innovation policies

The R&D base in Turkey still needs development, an issue that has been gaining in importance. Turkey is a net importer of technology and in 2006 spent only 0.76 per cent of GDP on R&D (OECD 2008c). As part of its preparation for EU accession, the government has adopted a National Science, Technology and Innovation Strategy with a target to increase research intensity to 2 per cent of GDP. National technology platforms have been established to increase the R&D and innovation capacity of industry, and other initiatives are under way to support an increase in R&D capacity and to boost the capacity of SMEs to access knowledge from global suppliers. The greater awareness of private enterprises, particularly SMEs, regarding their role in R&D and innovation is a high priority in the government's national development plans. Through the 2001 Law on Technology Development Zones, the government provides support to technology-based enterprises, fosters cooperation between universities and industry and facilitates the diffusion of technology. Several technoparks have been set up in universities and research centres managed by the TEKMERs.

Conclusions

Turkey is more developed in many respects than the rest of the MENA-12 countries. It is the most economically developed country with the highest per capita GDP. Private sector and SME development have been the focus for a longer period of time than in most of the MENA-12. It has the advantage of being an OECD member and having a close alignment with the European communities. This has given Turkey the opportunity to learn good practices from developed countries, to be part of peer review processes for its policy and programme initiatives, and to participate in the EU Framework Programmes on entrepreneurship and SMEs and R&D and innovation.

However the high level of informality, low level of SME competitiveness, low labour force utilization, weak gender performance and poor performance on key regulatory and reform indicators are concerns.

NOTES

1. The existing bankruptcy law is outdated. Bankruptcy is treated as a criminal activity, personal belongings are seized, the principle of punishment rather than recovery is applied, recovery rates are low and procedures lengthy and costly (MoET 2005).
2. The 'Economic Vision for Enterprise Development' presents the SME policy framework and strategy to guide the public and private sectors for the next six years and a series of initiatives and programme concepts. This strategy is the result of two years of research and consultations and was developed on a consensus basis with stakeholders. See:http://www.economy.gov.lb/sme/newsletter/-%20DynaMesh%20For%20SME-newsletter4.2.htm.
3. The SME has to have fewer than 40 employees to qualify.
4. See http://www.baderlebanon.com. Bader is a private sector led initiative in partnership with the SME Support Unit, the Investment Development Authority, Kafalat and other business support organizations and associations.
5. FDI was down from 3.7 per cent of GDP in 2007 and 4.1 per cent in 2006, but up from 0.20 per cent of GDP in 2002 (WDI). The FDI inflow from 2000 to 2007 averaged 4.6 per cent of GDP (KOM 2008).
6. World Bank Enterprise Survey 2007, available at http://www.enterprisesurveys.org/ExploreEconomies/?economyid=132&year=2007 (accessed 13 September 2009).
7. Formal sector tax rates have been estimated at between 30 to 41 per cent.
8. 'Morocco announces relaunch of Moukawalati Programme', *Magharebia*, 18 February 2009.
9. JCPPR (2006) questions whether QIZs have contributed substantially to reducing unemployment or producing high-skilled jobs for Jordanians, reporting that 65 per cent of the QIZ workforce are guest workers, most jobs are low-skilled and exports from the QIZs are low-value-added. In August 2008 there were 44000 migrant workers and only 12000 Jordanians employed in the QIZs (ITUC 2008).
10. The level of ODA has declined from US$242 per capita in 2004.

11. The unofficial unemployment rate is estimated to be closer to 30 per cent (WFB).
12. More jobs than this will have to be created for Jordanians to reduce the unemployment rate.
13. World Bank Enterprise Survey 2006, available at http://www.enterprisesurveys.org/ExploreEconomies/?economyid=99&year=2006 (accessed 13 September 2009).
14. The costs of maternity leave benefits are now borne by the social security administration rather than solely by the employer.
15. The JLGC is owned by the Central Bank of Jordan, the banking sector and other public and private sector organizations.
16. The average term of Jordanian governments over the last 15 years has been less than two years. Between 2005 and 2007 there were three different Prime Ministers and five different Cabinets (Bertelsmann Stiftung 2008b).
17. Remittances in 2007 reached 5.9 per cent of GDP (WDI).
18. Small and medium enterprises with between a minimum capital of EGP500 000 and a ceiling of EGP25 million can apply for listing if they meet other requirements (see www.nilex.egyptse.com). In 2008 only three enterprises were listed (Bank Audi 2009a).
19. Property titles are difficult to search due to historically complex property ownership arrangements.
20. Data from the 2006 Egyptian Labor Market Survey Panel (ELMPS06).
21. World Bank Enterprise Survey 2008, available at http://www.enterprisesurveys.org/ExploreEconomies/?economyid=61&year=2008 (accessed 9 November 2009).
22. Exports in 2006 grew 12.6 per cent, while imports grew by 15.6 per cent (AfDB and OECD 2008d, p. 592).
23. The weakness in private investment is largely in domestic investment rather than in FDI (World Bank 2008j).
24. The source for sector composition of GDP is the WFB, 2009 estimates; sector employment figures from the Tunisian Institute of National Statistics for 2006.
25. There were 15 OSSs in the country in 2008.
26. *Pépinères* are equipped spaces to incubate entrepreneurs with innovative and promising ideas and provide support to help them launch their businesses. Cyber-parks are equipped spaces to help entrepreneurs launch enterprises based on technological services and ICT.
27. A series of national forums at which the issues of unemployment among university graduates and business start-up options are discussed (see http://www.salondelacreation.com.tn). The *salon* is a new tool of the Tunisian government's national strategy to promote entrepreneurship and business creation.
28. The national business incubator network is made up of up to 21 business incubators or *pépinères d'entreprises* located at Higher Institutes of Technological Studies, engineering schools, universities and technopoles.
29. Online discussion forums hosted by the Ministry of Industry and Technology to provide information on the business creation process and support programmes and services.
30. The unemployment rate for youth was over 19 per cent in 2008, rising to over 30 per cent for educated youth (Turkstat 2008a).
31. State control refers to the extent to which the government influences the decisions of firms through public ownership, price controls or forms of coercive rather than incentives-based regulation.
32. Barriers to entrepreneurship are measured by the ease of access to information on existing regulations, administrative burden for start-ups and other regulations that hinder the entry of new firms.
33. Trade and investment indicators look at barriers to foreign ownership of firms, tariffs and non-tariff barriers to trade.
34. The 12 Technical Committees focus on: (a) company establishment; (b) intellectual property rights; (c) investment promotion; (d) FDI legislation; (e) SMEs; (f) corporate governance; (g) R&D; (h) employment; (i) taxes and incentives; (j) licensing; (k) location of investment; and (l) foreign trade and customs.

35. The European Charter for Small Enterprise requires reporting against ten priority actions: (a) education and training for entrepreneurship; (b) cheaper and faster start-up; (c) better legislation and regulation; (d) availability of skills adapted to the needs of SMEs; (e) improving online access; (f) getting more out of the single market; (g) taxation and financial matters; (h) strengthen the technological capacity of small enterprises; (i) successful e-business models and top-class small business support; and (j) develop stronger, more effective representation of small enterprises' interests at Union and national level. These are slightly different than the ten areas under the Euro-Mediterranean Charter for Enterprise that is followed by nine of the other MENA-12 countries.
36. The government offers loan loss reserves to banks for their SME lending (OECD 2004c).

9. Profiles of less dynamic PSD environments

This chapter includes brief profiles of the six MENA-12 countries with below-average levels of private sector dynamism based on the categorization in Chapter 5. These are presented in the following order: Yemen, Sudan, the West Bank & Gaza, Syria, Algeria and Iraq.

THE CASE OF YEMEN

Context for Private Sector Development

Yemen is a low-income country with an estimated population of 22.8 million, growing at almost 3 per cent a year, and 2009 per capita gross domestic product (GDP) purchasing power parity, (PPP) of US$2458.[1] It is one of the least-developed countries in the world. Over 46 per cent of the population is under the age of 15, making Yemen the youngest population country of the MENA-12 countries. It also has the least urbanized population; only 31 per cent of the total population lives in urban areas. Owing to the uprising of fundamentalist groups in 2004, threat of Al-Qaeda and piracy incidents in the Red Sea, the government continues to face security challenges.

The Republic of Yemen was formed in 1990 by the unification merger of the socialist regime of South Yemen and the capitalist regime of North Yemen. The new republic adopted a liberal economic, democratic system based on free market principles. The country accepted a Structural Adjustment Programme in 1995 and began reform efforts to increase private investment and liberalize trade. Accession to the World Trade Organization (WTO) was requested in 2000 and Yemen continues to work on meeting the requirements for full membership.

The Yemeni government started privatization of its large number of state-owned enterprises (SOEs) in 1998 but continues to be heavily involved in the ownership and management of enterprises in a wide range of industrial sectors. Between 2004 and 2006 the government redirected its focus to improving the investment climate for foreign direct investment

(FDI) attraction. This was triggered by the opportunity to join the Gulf Cooperation Council (GCC). FDI amounted to 5.8 per cent of GDP in 2008 (up from 4.1 per cent in 2007), which places Yemen above the MENA-average. Yemen has liberalized trade, dismantled quantitative trade restrictions and simplified and reduced import tariffs. The country has a surplus trade balance, with exports amounting to 38 per cent of GDP in 2007 (mostly from oil) and imports totalling 41 per cent (World Development Indicators, WDI).

Yemen's GDP growth is slower than in most MENA-12 countries. The average annual growth in real GDP from 2000 to 2008 was 4 per cent (WDI), dropping slightly in 2009 (*World Factbook*, WFB), largely due to dwindling oil revenues. GDP per capita has been growing at a slower rate than GDP and is currently below the level reached before the 1990 Gulf War.[2] Remittances, at 5.3 per cent of GDP in 2008 (close to the volume of FDI inflows), are another major contributor to the economy (WDI).

Crude oil is the mainstay of the economy, contributing 70 per cent of government revenue, 90 per cent of exports and 30 per cent of GDP (World Bank 2008l). However the oil industry is not labour-intensive, employing less than 1 per cent of the workforce, and oil reserves are expected to be depleted by 2020. Agriculture is the main employer in the country, accounting for over half of the active labour force and creating livelihoods for at least two-thirds of the population, although it contributes less than 10 per cent to sector GDP (WFB). Manufacturing value-added compromises less than 5 per cent of GDP, and accounts for only about 12 per cent of the industrial sector contribution (WDI). The services sector, dominated by government services and transport, produces 51 per cent of GDP. Given declining oil resources, an unproductive agricultural sector and a weak industrial base, there is an urgent need for economic diversification.

Although Yemen has improved its ranking on the World Bank ease of doing business indicators from 123rd place in 2007 to 99th place in 2009 (now third among the MENA-12), the cost of starting a business is the highest in the MENA-12. Yemen performs poorly on the Knowledge Economy Index (WBI 2008) and is assessed as being a 'mostly unfree' economy on the Index of Economic Freedom (IEF) (Heritage Foundation 2010). It performs better on the business, trade, fiscal and labour freedoms than the average for the nine MENA-12 countries that are included in the 2010 IEF; but is considered a 'repressed economy' on investment and financial freedoms, freedom from corruption and property rights.

The country has a low level of human capital. Its literary rate is the lowest in the MENA-12 (only 56 per cent) and its female literacy gap the largest (a spread of 38 points). School enrolment, education quality and educational qualifications are low by international standards. Significant parts of the population do not have access to education and training facilities. In 2007 the gross enrolment rate at the secondary education level was only 46 per cent (WDI), much lower than the 71 per cent average for the MENA-12. Poverty levels are the highest in the MENA region. Over 17.5 per cent of the population in 2005 was living on under US$1.25 a day, and 46.6 per cent on under US$2 a day (UNDP 2009). Donor assistance in Yemen represents only 1 per cent of GDP and in 2007 aid per capita did not exceed US$10 (WDI). This is very low for a country at Yemen's level of development.

The overall labour force participation rate is about 47 per cent; 66 per cent for men, the lowest in the MENA-12, and 20 per cent for women (WDI). Women's share of the labour force and employment in 2007 was less than a quarter, with a higher rate in rural areas (CSO 2007), likely due to their role in subsistence farming activity. Cultural traditions limit women's access to education and workforce participation. Yemen is placed last among 130 countries on the 2008 WEF Global Gender Gap Index, with large gender gaps on women's economic participation, political empowerment and education (WEF 2008b).

The official unemployment rate is over 16 per cent (CSO 2007), but the unofficial rate could be as high as 35 per cent (WFB). The unemployment rate for women is four times higher than for men. Sixty to 70 per cent of youth are unemployed and unskilled. Labour demand exceeds labour supply and the public sector does not have the capacity to absorb the new labour force entrants. Reducing unemployment requires the creation of a large number of jobs, which will have to be generated through private sector growth. This will require significant investments in vocational training to upgrade labour force skills and a much stronger culture of entrepreneurship.

Yemen has a weak private sector base. The private sector is responsible for only about 58 per cent of domestic investment, amounting to 13.4 per cent of GDP in 2007[3] (World Bank 2008l). In principle, private companies can act freely, but they face many economic, political and social obstacles to development. These include infrastructural deficiencies, a shortage of literate and skilled labour, corruption, an inefficient judicial system and state domination in strategic business sectors (Bertelsmann Stiftung 2008a). Rule of law is weakly enforced and property rights are complicated by the lack of a land registry and prior claim of tribal groups. Market competition operates under a weak institutional framework, and the formation of monopolies and oligopolies is rarely regulated. The private sector is dominated by the interests of a few large families and businesses with close links to the government. Smaller enterprises have difficulty entering markets frequently dominated by these ruling elites.

Poor road transportation systems and unstable electrical supply cause significant losses for private enterprises in production, sales and productivity. Geographical terrain characteristics and scarce water are impediments to agricultural expansion and growth. Research and development facilities are almost non-existent.

The private sector is seriously credit-constrained. The level of domestic credit to the private sector is very low (7.8 per cent of GDP in 2008) and domestic credit provided by the banking system is only 11.4 per cent of GDP (WDI). These levels are among the lowest in MENA-12 countries. The Yemeni banking sector is underdeveloped, undercapitalized and largely urban-based. A number of the banks are owned by a few large businesses that are directly involved in their operations and use them as a source of self-borrowing. These banks are responsible for a large share of non-performing loans (UNDP 2006a). Restrictions in the Bank Act make the entry of new banks difficult. The state-controlled banks control a third of commercial bank assets. Commercial lending is characterized by limited competition, weaknesses in the legal and judicial framework, a lack of proper accounting and auditing standards, and a dearth of banking and financial skills (UNDP 2006a). The World Bank and the International Monetary Fund (IMF) continue to pressure the government for banking sector reforms. There are no capital markets in Yemen.

A large part of economic activity is informal although not much policy attention is paid to the issue. The informal sector amounted to over 27 per cent of gross national income (GNI) in 2006 (Schneider and Buehn 2009), lower than might be expected for a country at its level of development. Over half of non-agricultural employment is informal (OECD 2009d). A lack of transparency in government procedures, a complex regulatory environment, high costs of starting a business and weak administration of the tax system have been largely accountable for high informal activity rates.

The private sector share of employment in Yemen is about 77 per cent, higher than for half of the MENA-12 countries; however private non-agricultural establishments account for only about 20 per cent of employed workers[4] (CSO 2004). Less than 5 per cent of these workers are female. Not only is the private sector underdeveloped and poorly diversified, but it is also predominantly male. Although women are not very active in the formal private sector, they perform over 70 per cent of the agricultural work, mostly as unpaid labour (European Community 2006). Integrating women into the private sector labour market could have a significant impact on both poverty reduction and economic growth.

There are no recent statistics on the number of micro, small and medium enterprises (SMEs) in Yemen. The Small and Micro Enterprise

Promotion Service (SMEPS) estimates that there are close to 500 000, of which only 10 000–15 000 are believed to be medium enterprises.[5] Enterprises in Yemen are extremely small. Only 1.2 per cent of enterprises in 2004 employed more than 24 workers (CSO 2004). Microenterprises (less than five employees) are responsible for 83.5 per cent of employment in establishments. SMEs in Yemen have to overcome many challenges. Characterized by a low education level, entrepreneurs are crowded in low-entry-barrier activities, serving local markets, with low productivity and limited diversification tendencies. The biggest SME operating constraints are a bureaucratic legal and regulatory framework, high taxes, tough competition, small market size and lack of financing (IFC 2007). SMEs have weak entrepreneurship and management skills (El-Meehy 2009), weak marketing knowledge and insufficient labour skills (SFD 2008).

Only about 6 per cent of Yemeni MSEs have ever obtained a loan from a formal financial institution, but close to 60 per cent participate in some sort of informal financing, mostly on a non-interest basis. The demand for Islamic financing is high. Microfinance is in its early stages of development in Yemen and less than 6 per cent of the potential microfinance market is being served (IFC 2007). Business associations in Yemen are generally weak and very few SMEs are members of organizations that could advocate their interests or provide them with needed services. SMEs are largely excluded from active participation in decision and policymaking, an issue that has been identified as a major impediment to SME development (El-Meehy 2009).

The self-employment rate is 29.4 per cent; 30.3 per cent for men and 17 per cent for women (CSO 2004). The self-employment rate declined since the 1994 census due to a drop in male self-employment rates.[6] Self-employment grew at a slower rate than total employment during the 1999–2004 period: 3 per cent compared to 20 per cent. However the employer portion of self-employment more than doubled. Although women play a very small role in business ownership activity, their self-employment numbers from 1999 to 2004 increased by more than 80 per cent versus less than 1 per cent for men. Women's share of the self-employed and employers in 2004 was 5.1 per cent (CSO 2004). This is one of the lowest rates of female entrepreneurship in the MENA region. Women entrepreneurs in Yemen face many barriers: access to finance, markets, information and social networks; lack of capacity; absence of women business associations; and constraining cultural norms and mobility restrictions that limit their access to training, employment opportunities and markets (IFC 2005).

The density of entrepreneurs in the adult population is very low. Results from the 2009 Global Entrepreneurship Monitor (GEM) reveal that only 4.1 per cent of Yemeni adults own their own enterprise, the lowest entrepreneur density of 54 GEM countries (Bosma and Levie 2010). On the other hand almost 25 per cent of adults were actively trying to start a business in 2009, one of the highest nascent entrepreneur rates. This is an unusual set of metrics and suggests that Yemeni adults, many of whom do not have employment options, are out of necessity developing business ideas, but have difficulties actually getting businesses started. Lack of skills, know-how, confidence and finance could be contributing factors, as well as the bureaucratic complexity and costs. Yemen is also a country where there is a high preference for work in the public sector. Sixty per cent of 15–29-year-old Yemenis would prefer to work for the government (Silatech 2009), and 56 per cent of adults (IDRC 2010). Obviously the culture of public sector employment is very strong, likely requiring dramatic efforts to unleash the entrepreneurial spirit.

Government Priorities and Recent Policy Developments

Poverty and job creation are two of the key issues to address in Yemen. Objectives of the government's priorities, as laid out in the Third Five-Year Socio-Economic Development Plan for Poverty Reduction 2006–10 (DPPR), the 2006 National Reform Agenda and the Public Investment Program, are to create jobs; reduce poverty; diversify private sector-led economic and export-related activity out of oil;[7] develop human resource capacity (including gender equality measures); attract investment; develop the private sector; strengthen the poorly developed financial system; and undertake the governance and regulatory reforms to meet the requirements for accession to the WTO and membership in the GCC. The government has set targets to move Yemen from the low to the middle human development group of countries by 2025, to sustain GDP growth of 7 per cent and to halve poverty by 2015 (MPIC 2005).

Business environment and regulatory reforms

A one-stop shop (OSS) for investors was launched in 2008 by the General Investment Authority (GIA), and efforts were undertaken to make it easier to obtain municipal licences and register with the Chamber of Commerce and the tax office. A new procurement law (based on international good practices) was passed and reviews of the company law and labour law initiated (IMF 2009a). Business procedures have been simplified to reduce the time and cost of starting a business; a Tax Simplification Project was launched in 2009 to eliminate tax exemptions in the customs, income tax and investment laws, and reduce corporate and personal income tax rates; and efforts are under way to improve functioning of the commercial courts and apply the rule of law. An anti-corruption law was passed in 2007 and a Supreme National Anti-Corruption Authority created to design and implement an anti-corruption strategy (WBG 2008).

Substantial investments are planned to increase access to and reliability of electric power, develop renewable sources of energy, expand transmission and distribution networks in rural areas, expand and upgrade transportation systems, extend access to water and sanitation services, and enhance urban infrastructure and services to attract private investors (World Bank 2009d). The government is also preparing a new law to establish the legal framework for public–private partnerships (PPPs) in infrastructure projects to boost the role of the private sector in these activities (WBG 2009). Reforms to address the problems of insecure property titles, creditor rights protection and the structural and institutional weaknesses of the underdeveloped banking system are under way.

Education and training policies

Improving the level of education and skills of the Yemeni population and upgrading the quality of the education system are prerequisites for promoting accelerated pro-poor growth (UN 2006b). The government is implementing the National Basic Education Development Strategy and National General Secondary Education Strategy to increase enrolment rates, improve the quality and relevance of education offerings, develop teacher training, strengthen overall quality management and reduce regional and gender disparities. The strategy being implemented by the Ministry of Technical Education and Vocational Training (MTEVT) is focused on: (1) creating labour market linkages by engaging private enterprises in labour demand profiling, apprenticeships and qualifications accreditation; (2) expanding training centres, improving organizational structures and developing skills of educators and administrators; (3) integrating women students more fully into the vocational education and training (VET) system; and (4) adapting programmes to respond to demands of both the traditional and new economy. The goal is to have 300 technical institutes by 2012 with 15 per cent of secondary students[8] going on to vocational training. These targets will create huge capacity development challenges. The government adopted a strategic plan for the reform of higher education in 2006 with the goal of improving the overall quality of higher education and its emphasis on research and development (R&D) (ILO 2008a).

SME and entrepreneurship policies and programmes

Due to its dominance in private sector activity and employment, SME development is also a priority of the government (although it does not warrant much of a headline in the DPPR). The SFD, established in 1997 with the objective to reduce poverty, has the main responsibility for micro and small enterprise (MSE) development. The main focus of the SFD's Small and Microenterprise Development (SMED) Unit is microfinance.

The Council of Ministers approved the government's first national strategy for MSE development in January 2005 (SFD 2004). The updated strategy (El-Meehy 2009) is pending submission to Parliament as of late 2009. In 2007 the government announced a US$1 billion investment to support MSEs, mainly as a vehicle to facilitate employment creation.

The Small and Micro Enterprise Promotion Service (SMEPS) was set up in 2006 as a subsidiary of the SFD to direct and coordinate activities to stimulate growth, diversification and competitiveness of the MSE sector by facilitating access to improved non-financial services. It focuses primarily on existing MSEs with growth potential and promoting an entrepreneurial culture. It has established Technical Advisory Stations in different regions of Yemen to provide information on markets and advice. SMEPS partners with the International Labour Organization (ILO) to deliver Know About Business training modules in some vocational institutes, and cooperates with the International Finance Corporation (IFC) on delivery of the Business Edge training programme. Over 20000 Yemeni SME owners and managers have participated in the Business Edge training since its introduction in 2005 (IMF 2009a). Private sector training businesses and consultants have been trained to deliver the product on a commercial basis. There are a number of independent BDS providers in Yemen, but the industry is nascent and there are no coordinated efforts to promote these services to MSEs, a gap that SMEPS attempts to fill. The donor community has supported activities to build capacity of non-financial service providers in the delivery of BDS to entrepreneurs.

Creating a vibrant financial system is also a high priority of the government. A number of MFIs have been started to fill the gap left by lack of access to the formal financial sector. The Al-Amal Microfinance Bank, the country's first microfinance bank for the poor, became operational in 2008. Yemen adopted a National Microfinance Policy in August 2007, which aims to gradually integrate the microfinance industry into the formal financial sector. Legislation has been prepared for a microfinance law that will provide an enabling policy environment and legal and regulatory framework for the sector (WBG 2008). The Central Bank of Yemen, with German Technical Cooperation (GTZ) support, has been offering training to build capacity in microfinance lending.

There is not yet a credit bureau in Yemen and no mechanism for microfinance institutions (MFIs) to share credit information, an issue that the SMED Unit is working on. Recent changes to banking laws have eased entry conditions for foreign banks and a leasing law was introduced in 2007. These initiatives are likely to improve access to finance for SMEs.

There are about 2500 civil society organizations (CSOs) in Yemen, but only a few of them function in the economic development area. The 2001 NGO law gave more freedom to non-governmental organizations (NGOs) than in the past, but association formation is a very new concept in Yemen and the Ministry of Social Affairs (MSA) is cautious. Most NGOs have weak capacity and are poorly resourced.

Conclusions

Yemen stands out among the MENA-12 countries in a number of ways. It has the highest rate of population growth, highest fertility rate, highest poverty rate, lowest literary rate, lowest share of women in employment, largest gender gap, most rural population and one of the highest levels of unemployment. Its biggest threats are dwindling oil reserves, limited domestic investment opportunities and macroeconomic instability (IMF 2009a). Past growth has not been pro-poor (Republic of Yemen 2007). The focus on capital-intensive oil sector investments has not countered high youth unemployment rates or been inclusive of the role of women in development strategies.

Radical policies to liberalize and reform trade regimes have resulted in little evidence of the emergence of a dynamic private sector. Yemen lacks the organizations and institutions, human capital and enforcement mechanisms essential for the efficient functioning of a liberal open economy (UNDP 2006a). Weak capacity of the government to manage the aggressive list of reforms is compounded by overlapping ministerial jurisdictions, competing objectives and limited interministerial coordination. Consultations with stakeholders are not a normal part of the policy development process, a situation exacerbated by the weak capacity and fragmentation of CSOs and NGOs and the absence of strong associations representing the views of SMEs. There is no comprehensive approach to data collection and analysis of the private sector, SMEs and entrepreneurial activity, and a need for trained researchers and analysts to assist in the development of sound policies based on accurate statistical data.

THE CASE OF SUDAN

Context for Private Sector Development

Sudan is a lower-middle-income country with an estimated population of 41 million, a population growth rate of 2.1 per cent, and 2009 GDP per capita (PPP) of US$2380. Until the mid-1980s Sudan functioned as a centrally planned economy with a high level of state control and intervention. The government started to implement self-imposed economic policies in 1992 and embarked on structural reform in 1997. The major emphasis of these reforms was on liberalization of the economy, privatization and private sector development (PSD). Early privatization efforts contributed to increasing government revenues and reducing debt, but were largely unsuccessful due to corruption, lack of democratic accountability and substantial increases in unemployment (Suliman 2007).

For decades Sudan has been engaged in a series of civil wars. The toll of these conflicts has left many parts of the country with a daunting legacy of low human development, very limited capacity, inadequate and decaying physical infrastructure, displaced populations and shattered social structures. Peace agreements signed in 2005 and 2006 led to the formation of the Government of National Unity (GONU) and the Government of Southern Sudan (GOSS). The agreement provided for fiscal decentralization and equal sharing of oil revenues with Southern Sudan, the main issue behind the recent conflicts (World Bank 2008h). Despite these agreements, unrest and civil war are ongoing and security arrangements uncertain.

Sudan has been doing well in terms of economic growth. Annual GDP growth averaged over 7 per cent over the 2000–2008 period (WDI), the highest among the MENA-12, although it dropped to 3.8 per cent in 2009 (WFB). Oil exports and FDI inflows have been largely responsible for growth. Sharp drops in FDI, remittances and private sector credit in 2007 led to a slowdown in non-oil growth (IMF 2008a). Agriculture plays an important role in the economy, contributing one-third of GDP, employing about 60 per cent of the population and providing the main source of income for 80 per cent of Sudan's population (UNDP 2006b). The service sector is relatively small, contributing only 38 per cent of GDP, one of the lowest levels in the MENA-12. Exports and imports to GDP in 2008 amounted to 24 per cent and 23 per cent respectively (WDI), the lowest level of trade openness reported for the MENA-12 countries.

The country is highly indebted, with public debt to GDP of 104.5 per cent in 2009 (WFB), and financial sector indicators have deteriorated in recent years. Gross capital investment to GDP (20 per cent in 2008) is below the MENA-12 average; private investment accounts for about two-thirds of the total contribution. The level of private sector credit to GDP is low (10.9 per cent of GDP in 2008 compared to the MENA average of 35.8 per cent), affected by the large domestic arrears of the government. The ratio of non-performing loans to assets is increasing[9] and private sector credit growth declined from 60 per cent in 2005 to 16 per cent in 2007 (World Bank 2008f). The level of domestic credit being provided by the banking system reached 17 per cent in 2008, a big improvement over earlier years. Sudan is a low performer on the World Bank ease of doing business indicators, ranking 154 out of 183 countries (World Bank 2009b), the lowest position among the MENA-12.

There are widespread disparities in economic and social development. Health conditions are poor and infrastructure (roads, power, water and telecommunications) is either inadequate or non-existent. Literacy rates and education levels are among the lowest in the MENA-12, indicating a limited human capital base. An estimated 40 per cent of the population was living below the poverty line in 2004 (WFB) and there are large wealth distribution disparities between rural and urban areas (World Bank 2008f). Rural–urban migration is becoming a problem, with a rapid decline in the rural population from 64 per cent in 2000 to 57 per cent in 2008. Sudanese women face serious legal impediments and inequalities of basic rights, social services and representation in decision making (ADF 2006).

Sudan has very high unemployment, estimated at close to 20 per cent (WFB). The labour force participation rate is 52 per cent – 72 per cent for women and 31 per cent for women; and the employment to population ratio is 47 per cent (WDI). Although women's share of employment, at 27.5 per cent, is the highest among the MENA-12, women make up only 17 per cent of employees and account for more than 60 per cent of unpaid workers. Almost 41 per cent of the population is younger than 15 years of age (WFB) and massive job creation efforts will be needed to absorb large numbers of new labour force entrants over the next several years, as well as to reduce unemployment levels and integrate more women into the paid workforce. The private sector is responsible for about 84 per cent of employment (CBS 2006), above the MENA-12 average, but economic activities are concentrated in major centres in Northern Sudan. Private enterprises are almost non-existent in Southern Sudan except for small-holder subsistence level agriculture (Bior 2000).

There are no consolidated data on the size, characteristics and dynamics of the SME sector or the scale of the informal sector. According to the 2001 Industrial Census, small-scale industries, defined as those employing fewer than ten workers, accounted for 93 per cent of the industrial base and about 40 per cent of manufacturing employment. A large number of families are engaged in home-based microenterprise activities (UNDP 2006b). Self-employment and employer activity accounts for almost half of the employment status of the economically active population (CBS 2006). Only about 11 per cent of the self-employed have employees. Women represent 36 per cent of the self-employed. Apart from security and market access issues, SME development is hindered by weak management capabilities, lack of specific know-how and training, and difficulties in accessing financing and BDS.

Government Priorities and Recent Policy Developments

The post-conflict challenges and tasks are daunting. To achieve a united, peaceful and modern Sudan, the World Bank (2008f) outlines three interrelated challenges that will need to be addressed: improving governance; increasing access to basic services; and ensuring sustainable, diversified and pro-poor growth with primary attention to war-affected and marginalized areas.

Privatization and private sector development were emphasized as priorities in the government's Comprehensive National Strategy 1992–2002. Within the framework of the strategy key commitments were made to simplify the Encouragement of Investment Act; enhance entrepreneurship, particularly among women; build linkages between FDI and the local private sector; strengthen business support services; and improve the statistical and information base of the country (Bior 2000). The 1992–2002 National Plan gave a lot of attention to microenterprises, given their role in poverty alleviation, and set a target to provide 2 million poor with the means of production (Badr-El-Din 2002). The priorities of the government's Five-Year Plan 2007–11 (NCSP 2007) are to: (1) encourage a competitive private sector; (2) reduce poverty and expand services in health, education, water and sanitation; (3) strengthen governance and the rule of law; (4) build capacity of public institutions and CSOs; and (5) sustain peace and stability.

The government's objectives are to facilitate private sector investment in agriculture, industry, infrastructure and services, particularly in underdeveloped regions; double non-oil exports by upgrading production and management processes in the agricultural and industry sectors; expand foreign trade; update transportation systems; build the capacity of vocational and education institutions to meet labour market needs; and double efforts in scientific research and higher education (NCSP 2007). To achieve these objectives the government is planning reforms to simplify administrative and legal procedures, eliminate any form of monopoly, decrease the role of the government in commercial activities, encourage the establishment of financial investment funds, strengthen financial institutions and meet the WTO accession requirements. The Sudan government has established a PSD Steering Committee to lead this initiative, composed of the Central Bank of Sudan, the Minister of Finance, the Minister of Investment and other relevant ministries and agencies (Mutwakil and Magdi 2006) working in cooperation with a Multi-Donor Trust Fund (MDTF). A number of committees have been formed to oversee the development of specific action plans, involving a wide range of stakeholders. The Sudanese government is also preparing a national Poverty Reduction Strategy with heavy emphasis on policies to address post-conflict challenges, decentralization, an enabling environment for private sector growth, and capacity and institution building (Central Bank of Sudan 2008). The country is currently under a staff-monitored IMF programme.

SME and entrepreneurship policies and programmes

Sudan was one of the earliest countries in the MENA region to create a unit in government with responsibility for SMEs. The Small Scale Industries Department was established in the Ministry of Industry in 1988 to oversee development of the sector. The Supreme Authority to Promote Small-Scale Enterprises was established in 1995 by the Ministry of Social Planning, in cooperation with the Ministry of Industry, to coordinate efforts for small enterprise development (Badr-El-Din 2002). Although there does not appear to be a vision or strategy towards SME development in Sudan at the present time, the Ministry of Industry has outlined an overall strategy for developing small-scale industries. The strategy consists of planning, managerial and financial services; specialized training programmes to improve product designs and standards; support for industrial clusters; and facilitation of FDI linkages for technology transfer to local enterprises.

The focus on entrepreneurship as a development tool is emerging. An Entrepreneurship Development Unit has been established in the Ministry of Industry, supported by the United Nations Industrial Development Organization (UNIDO), to train young male and female entrepreneurs to take the lead in developing the private sector. A United Nations Development Programme (UNDP)-led project in East Sudan is providing business training and incubation to ex-combatants as a vehicle for reintegration into economic life. In January 2009 the Southern Sudan Ministry of Commerce and Industry launched a US$20.2 million project to stimulate the growth of the private sector in Southern Sudan, jointly financed by the GOSS and the MDTF for Southern Sudan. An integral part of this PSD project is development of an Entrepreneurship Development Strategy that will include the wide promotion of entrepreneurship; education of potential and existing entrepreneurs on how to start businesses and comply with regulations; business skills training; capacity building for business service providers and banks; and community mobilization.

Microfinance is an emerging, but early-stage industry in the country. In 2003 the United States Agency for International Development (USAID) supported creation of the Sudan Micro Finance Institute and in 2008 the Sudan Microfinance Development Facility was established by the Bank of Sudan with capital of US$20 million. Banks are required by the Central Bank of Sudan to channel at least 10 per cent of their total loans for microfinance. Although this is not well enforced, there are a number of specialized banks that cater to the SME sector[10] (Badr-El-Din 2002). To contribute to the economic rebuilding of Southern Sudan, USAID has launched a three-year, US$11 million to support development of the microfinance sector.

Conclusions

Since the comprehensive 2005 Peace Agreement the government has renewed its efforts to stimulate private sector activity by focusing on FDI, market access, development and educating Sudanese youth (World Bank 2006e). The imperatives are broad-based employment, absorption of demobilized soldiers into the labour force, investment generation and reduction of high poverty levels. To prepare for sustainable growth during the rehabilitation and recovery period, the government's priority is to redress the destruction of physical and human resources and the erosion of institutions and social capital over two decades of conflict. The promotion of microenterprises, establishment of a microfinance fund, SME investment and capacity building, entrepreneurship development and self-help housing are major components of this strategy.

Settling the conflicting situation in Sudan is a prerequisite to PSD and SME development. Much of the policy attention is directed towards political and macroeconomic stability, but there is interesting progress on a policy level to improve the business environment and boost economic activities, evidenced by the establishment of institutions and specialized organizations and the passing of laws. Increasing human resource capacity, combating corruption and installing transparency are essential for successful implementation of a PSD strategy. Concerted efforts to build a base of data and information on development of the private sector, particularly the SME component, are also needed.

THE CASE OF THE WEST BANK & GAZA

Context for Private Sector Development

The West Bank & Gaza (interchangeably used with 'Palestine' in this profile) is a small, lower-middle-income country with a population of 4 million, growing in excess of 2.7 per cent a year, and 2008 GDP per capita (PPP) of US$2900 (WFB). Forty per cent of the population lives in the Gaza Strip, which has lower-performing social and economic indicators than in the West Bank, largely due to the closure of Gaza borders.

In 2001 the West Bank & Gaza was described by the IMF as one of the most open economies in the Middle East (MNE 2005), but by 2007 it could be best described as a fragile economy sustained by government and private consumption, donor aid and remittances,[11] rather than one driven by investment and private sector productivity (World Bank 2007d). The Palestinian economy has been in unprecedented decline since the outbreak of the 2000 Intifada. Despite various peace agreements and interventions by third parties, conflicts are ongoing between Palestine and Israel.

The Israeli closure policy led to a collapse of tourism, the inability of Palestinians to work in Israel, and the suspension or closure of many enterprises, resulting in extremely high levels of unemployment and poverty. Losses generated by the destruction of private and public infrastructure, including establishments, equipment and utilities was estimated to cost the economy at least US$1.1 billion by the end of 2002. The Palestinian economy lost all of the growth it had achieved in the preceding 15 years and the standard of living of a large proportion of the population fell dramatically. Real GDP in 2002 was below its 1986 level, per capita GDP fell to 55 per cent of its 1999 level, and GNI per capita (which includes workers' remittances from abroad) fell by around 26 per cent.

The GDP growth rate between 2000 and 2008 averaged minus 1 per cent, tumbling to minus 15 per cent in 2002. GDP growth of 2.3 per cent in 2008 (WFB) was one of the lowest in the MENA-12, but a rebound to 7 per cent growth in 2009 was the highest for this group of countries (WFB). Economic recovery is very slow due to restrictions on the movement of people and goods imposed by Israel. The Palestinian National Authority (PNA) has compensated for the lack of capacity in private sector enterprises and the loss of employment opportunities in Israel by increasing social benefits and becoming the employer of last resort. Public sector employment grew by almost a third between 2000 and 2007, increasing the wage bill by 80 per cent and producing a negative impact on the budget (World Bank 2007d). The public sector share of employment in 2008 was estimated at 24.7 per cent – 16.7 per cent in the West Bank and 46.8 per cent in the Gaza Strip (PCBS 2009b). Before the 2000 Infitada the public share of employment was only 17.4 per cent. An estimated 46 per cent of the population in the West Bank lives under the poverty line, rising to as high as 80 per cent in Gaza (WFB).

Gross capital formation, at 17.8 per cent of GDP (WDI), is among the lowest in the MENA-12, and the level of private capital formation to GDP below the MENA-12 average (14.8 per cent compared to an average of 16.3 per cent), but the private share of gross investment is 80 per cent, one of the highest in the MENA-12. Private sector investment in R&D is almost non-existent.

Palestine has a large trade deficit. In 2007 exports were only 14 per cent of GDP and imports were up to 68 per cent of GDP (WDI). Trading activities are directed primarily towards Israeli markets and remain restricted. The existing trade regime (the 'separation wall') is a major impediment to sustained economic growth because it generates a huge bilateral trade deficit with the Israeli economy.[12] Reorienting the economy away from its heavy dependence on Israel through regional and global integration is an important priority. Palestine has signed trade and cooperation agreements with several Arab and other countries, but these agreements are hard to take advantage of. Very little FDI is attracted into the country – less than 1 per cent of GDP.

The banking sector has been largely liberalized, with low public ownership of bank assets. The number of banks and bank branches increased considerably from 1995 to 2007. In 2002 the level of private sector credit fell by 24 per cent from its 2000 level and very little domestic credit is now available to the private sector, amounting to only 7.5 per cent of GDP in 2007. The level of domestic credit provided by the banking system amounted to only 8.3 per cent of GDP (WDI), among the lowest in the MENA-12, along with Yemen and Algeria. The Palestine Securities Exchange was created in 1996, but it is very small with limited trading activity.

The Palestinian economy is heavily service-oriented. The services sector contributes 81 per cent of GDP, compared to 14 per cent by the industry sector and 5 per cent by agriculture (WFB). Agricultural products are one of the major sources of income in the Gaza Strip.

There is a small labour force of 872 000 persons (WFB). The employment to population ratio, at 30 per cent (WDI), is the lowest in the MENA-12. The labour force participation rate was 41.8 per cent in 2008 (PCBS 2009b), down from 43.5 per cent in June 2000 (ILO and CAWTAR 2008b). This drop reflects the slowdown in the economy caused by the Israeli occupation, and the withdrawal of part of the population from the labour force. Women's participation in economic activity remains very low. Their share of employment is only 18.6 per cent (PCBS 2009b). Unemployment rates are the highest among the MENA-12 countries – an average of 26 per cent in 2008; 19 per cent in the West Bank and over 40 per cent in the Gaza Strip (PCBS 2009b). With current rates of labour force growth (estimated at 3.4 per cent a year), the economy must generate 54 000 jobs annually to absorb new labour force entrants, even before considering reductions in the unemployment rate.

Indicators of literacy and education in Palestine are the highest in the MENA-12. The literacy rate in Palestine is 92.4 per cent (WFB), with a female literacy gap of only 8.6 points. Palestine also performs better than other MENA-12 countries on education indicators, but there is a lack of skilled labour. The technical and vocational education and training is designed to produce low-skilled workers for the Israeli labour market.

Given its underdeveloped industrial base, the private sector's contribution to job creation has been limited in recent years. One of the biggest hindrances to development of the private sector is mobility restrictions, but enterprises suffer from a number of deficiencies. The supply of raw materials and equipment to Palestinian companies is highly dependent on Israel. Inadequate infrastructure and the absence of an airport and national port system inhibit access to resources and markets and increase transactions costs for businesses (UNCTAD 2004). Access to credit is limited and firms have difficulty obtaining external financing to support their operations.

The legal framework governing economic activities remains weak. There are relatively cumbersome and lengthy procedures for setting up a business, especially if administered in local offices. Development and upgrading of key laws conducive to a more favourable business environment and improvements in the Palestinian court system are needed. The West Bank & Gaza was ranked 139 out of 183 countries in the *Doing Business 2010* report (World Bank 2009b), placed eighth among the MENA-12 countries. Palestine's performance was especially weak on the number of days to start a business, cost to deal with construction permits, number of days to register property and the number of documents required to import goods.

The Palestinian economy is highly dependent on its micro and small enterprises. Enterprises with fewer than ten employees account for over 72 per cent of private sector employment (PCBS 2008). Only 3 per cent of enterprises have more than ten workers, although this group accounts for over a quarter of enterprise employment. As a result of downsizings and closures due to shrinking economic opportunities, the average firm size has dropped by about a third in enterprises with 1–50 workers and by 20 per cent in enterprises with more than 100 workers (UNCTAD 2004). SMEs function largely with outdated or obsolete technology. Research institutions and labs necessary for testing product quality are almost nonexistent. Opportunities for industrial subcontracting relationships with medium-sized Israeli enterprises, which provided an important point of access to more advanced technology and industrial management knowledge, have been curtailed. These factors affect the quality and innovation of SMEs' products and their access to technology and global markets. One of the most pressing issues is the lack of skills and knowledge of workers. Other obstacles more related to the regulatory environment hinder the performance of SMEs, including: high transportation costs; high taxes imposed on establishments; high customs duties and taxes; complex export and import laws and high costs; and difficulties in obtaining loans to finance import and export activities (MAS 2005). Many of the existing Palestinian laws and legal frameworks do not address the needs of the SME sector or serve it well (Khalifa and Abu Hantash 2009).

Although informality does not appear to be a huge policy priority, about 40 per cent of private enterprises are informal, and informal employment equals about 30 per cent of the formal private sector employment (MAS and PCBS 2005).

Self-employment in Palestine averaged 24.8 per cent in 2008 (PCBS 2009a). The proportion of employers among the self-employed (about a quarter) is one of the highest in the MENA-12. Self-employment activity was reported to take a big jump between 1999 and 2002, increasing from 19 per cent to 26 per cent. During this time the number of paid workers in the labour force dropped from 68 to 50 per cent. Starting a small subsistence enterprise was the only survival option available (UNCTAD 2004). Women make up only 10.3 per cent of the self-employed, and the female employer rate (1.4 per cent) is among the lowest in the MENA-12. Although attitudes towards women's role in economic life are changing, women struggle to obtain access to the resources and skills to start and manage their own businesses. The Palestinian Businesswomen Association plays an important role in fostering entrepreneurial activity among women and developing their skills.

The density of entrepreneurs in the Palestine Territories is above average for the MENA-12. About 12.5 per cent of adults own a business, between the levels in Syria and Egypt (IDRC 2010). However, the proportion of adults actively trying to start a new business is only 3 per cent, lower than in all MENA-12 countries except Tunisia. Promoting an entrepreneurship culture is seen as a necessary condition for Palestine's future prosperity. Although the majority of 15–29-year-olds would prefer to work for the work government (30 per cent) or to have a paid job in the private sector (18 per cent), 27 per cent of Palestine youth would prefer to be self-employed, one of the highest levels in the MENA-12 (Silatech 2009). However the education system is not seen as promoting an entrepreneurial culture. Teaching methods do not emphasize creativity and independent input, secondary education focuses on preparing students for paid employment in the job market, and Palestinian universities are not offering courses or modules on entrepreneurship and associated skills (MAS 2007b). The Palestinian Economic Policy Research Institute (MAS) recommends the adoption of policies to nurture entrepreneurship skills throughout the education system, introduction of schemes to encourage banks to finance the business projects of young people, and new legislation that would offer incentives for young entrepreneurs and tackle some of the obstacles they face.

Government Priorities and Recent Policy Developments

The PNA's Medium Term Development Plan 2005–07 prioritized two main objectives: (1) to address poverty through a framework in support of job creation, recovery, and social and economic development; and (2) to improve the effectiveness of the governance system by building institutional capacity and accelerating reforms (MOP 2005). Several laws were drafted to create a more conducive environment for private sector growth, but progress on the reform agenda, including implementation of the Palestinian Education Initiative and the opening of OSSs, was deterred.

The PNA subsequently prepared a three-year Palestinian Reform and Development Plan (PRDP) 2008–10 (PNA 2007), signalling the government's intention to redouble its efforts to promote PSD as the engine of sustainable growth and path to financial sustainability. The plan was developed through a consensus process with input from government representatives, CSOs and the international donor community. Donors pledged US$7.7 billion to support implementation of the PRDP at the Paris Donor's Conference in December 2007.

Regulatory and administrative reforms

Reform has been a priority of every Palestinian Cabinet since 2002. The reform process has been led by a National Reform Committee represented by government, the private sector and CSOs. It started with a complete review of ministerial structures and legal frameworks governing and regulating the work of each ministry and the judiciary system (PMO 2003). Since 2008 the PNA has adopted a new income tax law, drafted a new company law, simplified company procedures, unified regulations between the West Bank and the Gaza Strip, and initiated reforms to the competition law and the investment promotion law. The Institutional Reform for Enterprise programme aims to create a more coherent legal framework for the private sector and to spend US$16 million on improving land administration policy and legislation.

SME and entrepreneurship policies and programmes

Palestine adopted the Euro-Mediterranean Charter for Enterprise in 2004, but the development of SMEs is only recently attracting a higher level of attention on the PNA's policy agenda. An SME law has been drafted and a report prepared by the Prime Minister's Office has recommended the creation of a Palestinian SME Development Agency that would develop a vision, plan and efforts to coordinate and unify actions of the various stakeholders trying to support SMEs (Shunnar 2008). The development of an actual SME policy has not yet emerged. Atyani and Al Haj Ali (2009) outline a number of necessary public sector actions to provide the necessary framework for the operation of SMEs, specifically: the adoption of a clear-cut SME definition; developing and upscaling SMEs by creating business incubators and industrial zones; guiding SMEs in the process of exporting; establishing an SME fund to improve access to financing; and improving licensing requirements.

Only a few SMEs are aware of the provision of business development services (BDS). Low take-up levels are associated with the mismatch between what is demanded by SMEs and what is supplied by the market, and the lack of access to these services outside of certain cities (MAS 2007a; SEC 2007a, 2007b). SMEs have limited resources to cover the cost of BDS and training, so BDS providers, mostly in the private sector, are dependent on donor funding to finance programme and service delivery. Hamid et al. (2009) recommend that technical support centres be set up at the national level (with subsidiary offices and branches in all provinces, smaller towns and villages) to provide business development assistance and guidance to SMEs at all levels of their development from inception to production to entry into the market place. They also recommend the implementation of OSSs to facilitate business registration procedures.

Developments have taken place on the issue of private sector financing. A US$160 million Loan Guarantee Program,[13] established in 2007 through a partnership between the Palestine Investment Fund and US investment corporations and foundations, has started to attract the participation of Palestinian banks. The PNA also launched the Enterprise Investment and Development Program to improve credit services for export-oriented businesses and those in trade services and logistics. The IFC and the Capital Markets Authority signed an agreement in 2008 to develop the leasing market, and actions are under way. With an 18-year history in Palestine, the microfinance industry is well established. A number of microcredit organizations facilitate access to credit to SMEs and several donors are involved in funding microfinance programmes.

Within the framework of the Euro-Med Charter for Enterprise, efforts to address private sector and SME weaknesses are ongoing. Several initiatives have been undertaken within the scope of the ten policy areas, such as simplifying business procedures for enterprises, but according to the 2008 assessment, progress has been constrained by curtailed administrative powers, security restrictions applied by Israel, lack of budgetary resources and political instability (European Communities and OECD 2008).

Innovation policies

Investments in R&D and related infrastructure are seen as critical for strengthening the competitiveness of the Palestinian private sector (El-

Jafari et al. 2008). The Palestine Academy for Science and Technology has been given the mandate to promote and coordinate the development of science, technology and innovation. However, Palestine does not have an R&D and innovation strategy and innovation policy is not well-developed. Legislation on intellectual property rights, on the other hand, has been prepared but not enforced. Some innovation centres and incubators have been set up, but mostly on an ad hoc or pilot basis and funded by donors.

The role of civil society

Civil society organizations play an important role in the Palestinian society, often being the only organizations capable of delivering basic services to the population in areas such as health, education, vocational training, water and small business support (World Bank 2007d). A number of public organizations and professional and sector associations are involved directly and indirectly in PSD. Many of the business and sector associations have formed the Coordination Council for Palestinian Private Sector Organizations to represent the views of the private sector to government and to facilitate dialogue regarding the reform agenda. A law on NGOs came into force in 2000 (amended in 2003) to regulate the establishment of unions and rights of association, but new NGOs often face excessive delays in registration and their activities are closely monitored by the PNA.

Structures have been put into place under the PNA to facilitate progressive, consensus-based public–private sector dialogue. This was done through creation of the National Economic Dialogue Project (NEDP). Through the National Dialogue process, private sector institutions reach consensus and formulate evidence-based White Papers with specific policy recommendations on key policy issues that should receive priority treatment by the government. These papers are then discussed with representatives of the PNA and line ministries during workshops before being published for public dissemination.

Conclusions

Palestine has relatively high levels of human capital, but private sector and SME development is seriously hampered by the political situation. The weak market economy legal framework and the uncertain business environment are making it difficult to attract sufficient local and foreign investment to create jobs and reduce poverty. Little progress has been made to accelerate the necessary reforms to revitalize the private sector. Corruption continues to be a serious problem due to the weak legal framework and lack of enforcement measures.

Reorienting the economy will require regional and global integration to reduce dependence on Israel. But this must be done within the context of a cohesive development strategy to restructure the industrial base to create jobs and allow for increased specialization in higher value-added products. The development of SMEs is critical to achieving these objectives. Considerable efforts will be needed to build the expertise and capacity of Palestinian institutions to formulate and implement long-term strategies for promoting private sector and SME growth.

THE CASE OF SYRIA

Context for Private Sector Development

The Syrian Arab Republic is a middle-income country with an estimated population of 21.7 million, growing at a rate of about 2 per cent, and 2009 GDP per capita (PPP) of US$4887. Although Syria has not been directly involved in conflict in recent years, its relationship with Lebanon and its alliance with Iran make it a target for political isolation.

The country is managed under a planned economic system with a high degree of state control and public ownership of companies. The collapse of the Soviet Union in the early 1990s, its major trading partner, and increasing competitive pressures forced the government into an economic reform programme to attract foreign and domestic investment. This initially led to the lifting of tariff barriers, simplification of customs procedures, establishment of Free Trade Zones (FTZs) and abolition of public sector monopolies on commodities imports, but general progress on reforms has been slow.

The government is heavily involved in economic activity. Public sector monopolies exist in oil and gas, electricity, transportation systems, heavy industry, telecommunications and several commodity markets. The government made the strategic decision not to pursue a privatization programme, but to 'corporatize' the SOEs, particularly the loss-making ones. The government is gradually opening up to private investment by offering foreign ownership incentives in areas of manufacturing previously monopolized by the government.

Syria attracts very low levels of FDI, estimated at 3.1 per cent of GDP in 2008, among the lowest in the MENA-12, and below the MENA region average of 4.6 per cent (WDI). Foreign investors are deterred by the uncertain legal climate, high business costs and an unconducive regime for competitive performance. The oil sector is the main recipient of foreign capital.

Reforms to liberalize the trade regime have only really started since

2001 when Syria submitted its request to the WTO to begin the accession process. Negotiations were initiated for an EU Association Agreement in 2004 and Syria gained entry to the Greater Arab Free Trade Area (GAFTA) in 2005. Exports and imports each accounted for about 43 per cent of GDP in 2008, below the average for all MENA countries (WDI), and a sharp decline from levels in 2006.

From 2000 to 2008 Syria's annual GDP growth averaged 4.4 per cent (WDI), but dropped to 1.8 per cent in 2009 (WFB). Growth is largely dependent on the petroleum and agricultural sectors, which together account for almost half of GDP. Agriculture, responsible for 19 per cent of GDP and almost 20 per cent of the labour force (WFB), is very important to the Syrian economy. The sector is perceived by policymakers as crucial in absorbing the growing working-age population, meeting the government goals for food self-sufficiency, enhancing export earnings and stemming rural migration. The manufacturing sector, which is dominated by large, inefficient SOEs and relatively small family-owned firms, accounts for about 13 per cent of GDP, well under half of the industry sector share. The oil industry is the largest component of the industry sector, contributing 22 per cent of GDP, almost a quarter of government revenues and 20 per cent of exports (OBG 2009). Syria is projected to run out of oil by 2015, which will result in a decelerated rate of annual real GDP growth, contraction of trade activity and increasing pressure on the tax base. The service sector accounts for almost half of GDP and absorbs two-thirds of the labour force, but very little policy attention has been paid to developing the sector.

The Syrian financial sector is not well developed or highly competitive. The government did not legalize private banking until 2001. Although this has considerably changed the competitive landscape and range of product offerings, branch coverage and human resources are lagging (OBG 2009). By 2007 the public banks still owned over 94 per cent of total assets. Syria has a low level of domestic credit to the private sector, measured at 15.6 per cent of GDP in 2008 (well below the average for MENA-12 countries), and the scale of domestic credit provided by the banking sector is only 37 per cent of GDP (WDI), again below the MENA-12 average. Faster growth depends on reform of the financial sector, which currently favours public enterprises and agriculture at the expense of manufacturing, private enterprises and SMEs (UN 2006a).

Syria's business environment is not highly favourable. It ranked 143 among 183 countries in the *Doing Business 2010* report (World Bank 2009b), third to last among the MENA-12 (followed by Sudan and Iraq). Its relative performance on *Doing Business* indicators is poor on the cost of starting a business, the cost of registering property, enforcing contracts and hours spent dealing with tax payments. Syria is categorized as a 'repressed' economy on the Index of Economic Freedom (Heritage Foundation 2010). It has very low performance on investment and financial freedoms, freedom from corruption and property rights; although fiscal freedom and government size are assessed as being high, and labour and monetary freedoms as 'moderately free'. Syria also performs poorly on the Knowledge Economy Index (WBI 2008). These indicators suggest that in spite of many reforms considerably more needs to be done to move to a market economy and dcvclop the potential for PSD and investment.

Although the private sector accounts for about 62 per cent of GDP (SEBC 2007) – up from 50 per cent in the 1980s (EC 2005b) – and 72 per cent of employment (CBS 2008), the state retains a high degree of control over the economy. Open competition has been limited and there are substantial barriers to entry in many economic sectors. The government has indicated that it plans to be less tolerant of monopolies by public sector companies, but competition legislation is yet to be passed. The private sector industrial base is small.[14] Public sector enterprises were responsible for 80 per cent of net domestic product in the industrial sector in 2007 (CBS 2008). Along with Algeria and Sudan, Syria has the lowest private gross capital formation to GDP of the MENA-12 countries (about 16 per cent in 2008); just a little more than half of capital investment is contributed by the private sector.

The population literacy rate, at almost 80 per cent, is mid-range for the MENA-12 countries, and the female literacy gap one of the smallest: 86 per cent for men and 74 per cent for women (WFB). Syria has the second-lowest poverty rate of the MENA-12 countries. Just over 11 per cent of the population was living under the poverty line of US$2 a day in 2004 (El Laithy and Abu-Ismail 2005). Syria has the lowest aid per capita among the MENA-12 – US$7 per capita, owing mainly to political issues.

The labour force participation rate is about 50 per cent: 78 per cent for men and 21 per cent for women (WDI). The employment rate is 45 per cent, about average for MENA countries. However reducing the level of unemployment, estimated at 9.2 per cent in 2009[15] (WFB), combined with pressure to absorb upwards of 240 000 new entrants into the labour market annually (Zaman 2007), makes job creation one of the biggest challenges for Syria. Women's share of employment is the lowest of the MENA-12 – only 14 per cent (CBS 2009). Women's share of private sector employment is only 8.5 per cent, although it is about a quarter of public sector employment. Syrian women have equal rights under most laws, but social codes discourage women from entering public and economic spheres and often impede their access to equal rights. Research is needed on the barriers women face in securing employment and social protection, particularly in the informal economy (RWEL 2008b).

Syrian workers have a low average level of education. Only around 5 per cent of manufacturing workers have more than 12 years of schooling (World Bank 2005e). Only 6.2 per cent of working individuals in 2006 had university degrees (UNDP 2007b). High drop-out rates from vocational institutes and universities has led to a poorly educated workforce that is not in line with improving productivity, technology development or competitiveness (UNDP 2005). Syria has a large network of publicly operated vocational training schools, but they respond poorly to labour market needs and the system for retraining adult workers is incoherent (World Bank 2005e). A vast improvement in public and private education and training institutions is needed.

The size of the informal sector is estimated to approach 20 per cent of GDP (Schneider and Buehn 2009), the lowest in the MENA-12, but it accounts for up to 40 per cent of private sector employment. Bureaucratic over-regulation in the form of licensing, certification and registration; restrictive labour laws regarding private sector hiring and lay-offs; a burdensome and inequitable tax regime that is inconsistently applied; and numerous other administrative procedures are the major causes of the large informal sector (ERF and L'institut de la Méditerranée 2005).

Statistics on the SME sector are limited, but most enterprises are very small. Only 0.04 per cent of enterprises have more than 50 employees (SEBC 2007). The majority of SMEs are enterprises with no employees, or family-owned enterprises with weak corporate governance structures ill-equipped to support growth. Entrepreneurs face high transaction costs in doing business, including an unpredictable system that lacks transparency in the implementation of administrative procedures. SMEs lack management capacities and marketing skills, adequate internal financial and accounting systems, quality control mechanisms and proper business planning. Low SME productivity levels are due to the low quality of labour and the lack of access to technology. Only a small percentage of SMEs can access bank financing for working capital (World Bank 2005e).

The total self-employment rate reached 32.3 per cent in 2008 (CBS 2009), the third-highest rate among the MENA-12 countries. Almost a quarter of the self-employed create jobs for others, comparing very favourably against the other MENA-12 countries. Women's share of self-employment is only 4.8 per cent, the second-lowest in the MENA-12, and there are few initiatives to promote the development of women entrepreneurs.

Due to Syria's history of socialism and its centrally planned system of governance, which did not encourage a dynamic entrepreneurial culture, private sector entrepreneurial activity is low and still embryonic. Until 2001 the government mandated five years of public service for all graduates (Huitfeldt and Kabbani 2005), effectively guaranteeing them a government job. Despite a slowdown in government hiring since the early 2000s, many Syrians still prefer to secure a job in the government system. Fifty-five per cent of 15–29-year-olds report that they would prefer to work for the government (Silatech 2009), and almost 40 per cent of Syrian adults (IDRC 2010). The public sector offers more security, higher wage rates and more attractive non-wage benefits than the private sector, creating unfair competition for private sector employers in the labour market, especially for educated workers (Kabbani 2009).

In 2009 a Syrian team led by the Syria Trust for Development (STD) joined the Global Entrepreneurship Monitor project. Preliminary results from this research indicate that almost 12 per cent of Syrians are already entrepreneurs with operational businesses, a slightly lower density than in Egypt and the West Bank & Gaza, but higher than in Algeria, Jordan, Turkey and Yemen (IDRC 2010). Over 11 per cent of Syrians were actively trying to start a business in 2009, a higher percentage than in most of the GEM-MENA countries. Annual GEM-Syria surveys will provide a clearer picture of entrepreneurial dynamics and provide important baseline information for the government as well as guidance on policy actions to improve the environment for entrepreneurship.

Government Priorities and Recent Policy Developments

The first stage of aggressive economic reforms in Syria was initiated by the new government in 2000. The first Economic Reform Programme (ERP) was drafted in 2002. The 10th Five Year Plan (FYP) 2006–10 (SPC 2005) was the first to state the importance of the role of the private sector in the economy and the government's commitment to becoming a 'social market economy' (combining the stability of social protection with the dynamism of a free market). The plan laid out the government's key medium- and long-term objectives for the economy: to boost economic growth to 7 per cent by 2010,[16] reduce unemployment to 8 per cent by accelerating job creation, reduce poverty to 10 per cent of the population and ensure social justice. Public–private partnerships (PPPs) and other forms of investment systems are being explored by the government to stimulate private sector investment in development and infrastructure projects. A legislative framework is being prepared to facilitate PPPs. The FYP also emphasized reducing regional disparities and improving living conditions in rural areas, focusing on vulnerable groups, pro-poor policies and gender empowerment; transitioning to a knowledge-based society with an emphasis on R&D incentives and an upgraded education system; implementing regulatory simplification and economic reforms related to the private sector; and reducing government spending from 31 per cent to 20.5–25 per cent of GDP.

Regulatory and administrative reforms

The government started an initiative in 2002 to implement OSS services at its ministries to streamline licensing procedures, but they are only applied in industrial cities with limited geographic scope in the country. A new tax law was passed in 2004 reducing the highest corporate tax bracket from 65 per cent to 35 per cent, and legislation was introduced to reform the country's rigid labour laws (Kabbani and Kamel 2007). Measures have been taken to improve the investment climate by reducing red tape and undertaking reforms in the judicial system. In 2003 the government opened up its FTZs for all types of services. The National Quality Program launched in 2007 has the objective to align Syrian legislation, national standards and conformity assessment systems with international practice.

In 2007 the State Planning Commission (SPC) carried out a comprehensive analysis of the national competitiveness of the economy. This report presented a series of recommendations for the key priorities to improve the country's competitiveness performance (UNDP and SPC 2007). These include: upgrading of physical infrastructure; speeding up the preparation of up-to-date laws for protecting various kinds of intellectual property; improving macroeconomic stability; improving the quality of the education system and level of involvement of the private sector; finalizing legislation to simplify the processes of starting, operating and closing a business; creating more flexibility in the labour law; improving the financial intermediation role of the banking sector; and increasing the level of public and private investment in research and development (R&D) (UNDP and SPC 2007). One of the planned initiatives is a National Competitiveness Observatory that will monitor the economy's competitiveness, suggest good practices and disseminate information.

Formalizing informal enterprises is a priority of the government. In 2008 the government engaged Hernando de Soto to oversee a systematic and comprehensive survey of the informal sector, in cooperation with the Central Bureau of Statistics, which will lead to a national strategy for regulating the informal sector.

The 10th FYP also outlines plans to prepare decrees and laws to allow formation of associations in all sectors including SMEs, and mechanisms to involve the private sector in decision-making. The Ministry of Industry has invested considerable effort in promoting the formation of sector associations and more open consultative dialogue processes.

SME and entrepreneurship policies and programmes

The Syrian government is a late entry on the matter of formal SME policy. The Ministry of Economy and Trade (MoET) only created an SME Directorate in 2007. The major issues on the directorate's agenda are reform of the legal and regulatory framework, financing, competitiveness and innovation. It has been assessing laws that are likely to affect SMEs and mapping business procedures to determine the main business bottlenecks. The plan is to apply the Guillotine Review methodology to eliminate unnecessary laws and simplify business procedures (MoET 2009).

The MoET started a process in 2008 to develop a formal government-wide SME policy and strategy. A National Committee on SMEs, chaired by the Minister of the MoET, was formed to act as a coordination mechanism between the different ministries. The committee is supported by a Technical Committee consisting of public and private sector officials. A new SME definition was adopted at the end of 2008 and the SME Strategy was completed at the end of 2009 (MoET 2009). The three pillars of the strategy are: (1) Improvement to the SME environment; (2) SME intermediary capacity building; and (3) SME competitiveness. A new SME Agency is to be formed to coordinate the strategy's management and implementation.

The Syrian Enterprise and Business Centre (SEBC), an independent NGO under the supervision of the MoET, is the national SME support institution. It plays the major role in assisting private sector businesses to access international markets; encouraging a friendly regulatory and administrative framework for the private sector; and facilitating the development of a framework for effective business support organizations. The SEBC has one person in each Chamber of Commerce and Industry working with it on SME initiatives. The Public Commission for Employment and Enterprise Development (PCEED), established under Law 71/2001 to Combat Unemployment in 2006, provides employment training and loans to family businesses and MSEs in an effort to create jobs and supplement the social safety net system.

Since the focus on SME development in Syria is very recent, the institutional landscape for SME support is relatively weak. This is partially due to the limited presence of NGOs. Since 2000 the Associations and Private Institutions Law governing NGOs and associations has become more flexible, but the culture of civil society is not strong, which impedes the emergence of independent business associations.

The most prominent NGO supporting entrepreneurship is the Syria Young Entrepreneurs Association (SYEA). Its mission is to inspire an entrepreneurial mindset among young people and to enhance their competencies and networks. The SYEA has an entrepreneurship centre project that offers information and workshops, organizes job fairs and provides linkages to a network of angel investors. In 2007 the SYEA launched a Ventures project to support start-up companies by providing advice and funding. BIDAYA, a youth business programme, registered as an NGO in 2006, provides financial support and mentoring to unemployed and underemployed youth in an effort to deepen the pool of potential entrepreneurs and to create jobs. The STD, established as an NGO in early 2007, also provides support to develop enterprises, mostly in rural areas, and performs research of interest to policymakers. SHABAB, an NGO started in 2007 under the umbrella of the STD, targets 15–24-year-olds with awareness, advice and training on how to become successful employees and entrepreneurs. SHABAB has introduced the ILO Know About Business curriculum in public secondary schools and universities, evaluated as being very effective in orienting students to entrepreneurship and enhancing their skills (Al-Habash et al. 2007a, 2007b). The Ministry of Social Affairs and Labour has launched a Youth Employment Strategy that also focuses on building an entrepreneurial and business-oriented young workforce prepared to enter the SME sector.

To improve access to financing, the government has taken steps to establish loan guarantees and bank insurance policies. The European Investment Bank (EIB) extended a €40 million loan to the Syrian government in 2003 to provide a state credit guarantee system for SME bank loans and a further €80 million in 2008. The Ministry of Finance established a special SME Fund to manage the EIB funds and sought local and foreign expert assistance to transfer knowledge to Syrian bankers regarding assessing risks and appraising loan requests.

The microfinance sector is young and underdeveloped relative to an estimated market demand of over 1 million potential clients (CGAP 2008). Few microfinance facilities exist and most of these operate as pilot projects. The government issued a General Microfinance Decree in 2007 to permit the licensing of Social Financial Banking Institutions to provide microlending, deposit-taking and micro-insurance to the unbanked poor. Under the new Microfinance Decree, the Aga Khan Development Network established the First Microfinance Institution-Syria. In order to develop the microfinance sector, a commitment is needed to develop capacity of regulators, policymakers and microfinance providers.

Provisions for credit guarantee schemes and lease financing are in early stages of development. There are no equity funds in the country, although the government has recently licensed a number of holding companies to mobilize equity funds from private investors. A Capital Markets Authority was established in 2006 and the Syria Stock Exchange approved in 2007 (although not operational until 2009).

Education and training policies

The government has undertaken reforms in the education system, although there is much to be done. The 10th FYP states the objectives to introduce new vocational trades, upgrade existing ones, amend curriculum in consultation with the private sector to match the needs of employers better, establish entrepreneurship training centres in all governorates, and encourage the business community to establish associations to nurture entrepreneurship.

The 2002 Basic Education Law extended compulsory education to the end of the ninth grade (15-year-olds) and initiated changes to the curriculum system (UN 2005). Education and training centres have been established to improve the skills of trainers and teachers, and new training centres have been created to provide management training (Ministry of Industry 2006). Implementation of the EU-funded Modernization of Vocational Education and Training Programme has been ongoing since 2006. Based on the success of the SHABAB Know About Business pilots, the Minister of Education has approved the incorporation of entrepreneurship curriculum into all Syrian vocational education institutions (Nehlawi 2007).

In 2001 the government removed restrictions to the entry of private educational institutions and allowed private universities for the first time. This has increased the capacity for university enrolments, while the lifting of restrictions on university entrance requirements has increased the demand. The EU-supported Higher Institute of Business Administration (HIBA) has been established to offer Master of Business Administration (MBA) and Executive MBA programmes in an effort to meet the market need for skilled executives and managers.

Innovation policies

Policies to foster innovation are nascent. The Higher Commission for Scientific Research, established in 2005, is in the process of elaborating a framework for innovation policy with a focus on scientific research and technological development and improving linkages between R&D mechanisms and public and private industry (European Communities and OECD 2008). New technology facilities have been established at a number of universities, pilot incubators are in place, and the Ministry of Telecommunications and Technology is planning a Technology Park. The Syrian Network of Innovation and Entrepreneurship was launched in August 2008 as a forum for NGOs and government organizations working in the field.

Conclusions

Syria is in need of a higher level of investment and jobs from an expanding private sector, invigoration of the entrepreneurial spirit and potential of

Syrians, more trade openness, a better business and investment climate, major efforts to restructure and build capacity of the SME sector to enable its growth, a more elaborate system of institutional support for SME development, and more independent NGOs and business associations to help develop entrepreneurship and SMEs. In most of these areas, Syria is not as advanced as other MENA-12 countries. Making the transition to a market economy will continue to require firm political commitment at the highest level of government, and effective civil society participation.

THE CASE OF ALGERIA

Context for Private Sector Development

The People's Democratic Republic of Algeria is an upper-middle-income country with an estimated population of 34.2 million growing at about 1.2 per cent, and 2009 per capita GDP (PPP) of US$6869 (IMF 2010). The government initiated a series of structural adjustment reforms in 1994 to set up the foundation for transition from the central planning system to a market economy with a pivotal role for the private sector. Due to the turmoil caused by civil war during the 1990s, economic liberalization and privatization made little headway.

The legal framework for privatization was adopted in 2001, but only a few SOEs had been privatized by 2004. Restrictive rules regarding the terms of ownership and retention of workers, and the lack of an active capital market, have been constraining factors. Algeria's history in attracting FDI is recent. Between 2001 and 2006 significant achievements were made in improving the situation. The first foreign investment law was passed in 2001 offering incentives and guarantees for investors, but the level of FDI remains very low, amounting to only 1.6 per cent of GDP in 2008 (WDI). This is the lowest among the MENA-12 countries.

Algeria has been more successful with its trade liberalization efforts. In 2008 exports to GDP totalled 47 per cent and imports amounted to 23 per cent of GDP (WDI), resulting in a sizeable trade surplus, mostly due to oil exports. Algeria has signed several Free Trade Agreements (FTAs) and agreements with other countries and has been undertaking reforms towards full compliance with the EU–Algeria Association Agreement that came into effect in 2005, but export growth has been relatively static. More work is needed before Algeria is able to meet the legislative and regulatory requirements of accession to the WTO.

From 2000 to 2008 Algeria's annual average GDP growth was 4.3 per cent (WDI), although dropped to 2.8 per cent in 2008 and to 2.6 per cent in 2009 (WFB). Much of the improved economic environment in Algeria since 2000 can be attributed to the oil and gas sector and has had little impact on reducing unemployment and improving living standards. The industry sector is by the largest contributor to GDP in Algeria – 62.9 per cent of GDP, compared to just over 8 per cent for agriculture and 29 per cent for services (WFB). The hydrocarbons sector is the main backbone of the economy, accounting for 46 per cent of GDP (AfDB and OECD 2008b), nearly 80 per cent of budget revenues (World Bank 2009a) and 95 per cent of exports. Manufacturing contributes less than 5 per cent of GDP. About 14 per cent of the workforce is employed in the agriculture sector, 30 per cent in the industry sector and 57 per cent in services (ONS 2008).

The majority of banks in Algeria are private, but the state-owned banks dominate the sector, holding more than 90 per cent of the deposits and credits (World Bank 2009a). They are also responsible for a large volume of non-performing loans. The government started banking reform in 2004, but regional and international integration of the banking system has been progressing slowly. The level of domestic credit to the private sector is very low, amounting to only 13.5 per cent of GDP in 2008, much lower than the MENA region average of 35.8 per cent of GDP; domestic credit provided by the banking sector was reported as −13 per cent of GDP (WDI). Banks are slowly coming around to the idea of financing productive investments and commercial enterprises, but the collapse of three banks between 2003 and 2005 damaged public confidence and support for the privatization of public banks (World Bank 2005a).

Algeria ranked 83 out of 133 countries on the 2009–10 Global Competitiveness Index, one of the weakest competitiveness performer in the MENA region, notwithstanding its reasonable economic growth and relative macroeconomic stability (WEF 2009b). Its performance is weakest on goods and labour market efficiency, financial market sophistication, the sophistication of firms' operations, strategy and networks, and innovation capacity. Algeria is assessed as a 'moderately unfree' economy on the 2010 Index of Economic Freedom (IEF); although it achieved scores in the 'high degree' of freedom category on fiscal freedom, and the 'mostly free' category on business, trade and monetary freedoms (Heritage Foundation 2010). Its lowest performance was on investment freedom, freedom from corruption and property rights (a 'repressed' economy). Algeria's IEF score has risen slightly since 2005, with the largest improvement on trade freedom. On the *Doing Business 2010* survey, Algeria ranked 136 out of 183 countries (World Bank 2009b), dropping slightly in the rankings from the previous year. It ranked eighth among the MENA-12, showing its weakest relative performance on the number of procedures to start a business and to register property, the time required to deal with permits, the number of tax payments per year, the number of hours spent dealing with tax payments, rigidity of employment, labour tax and contributions, and total tax rate. The implication of these rankings is that Algeria's business climate is less favourable than most of the countries in the MENA region, which results in barriers to the economy's competitiveness.

The adult literacy rate is 74 per cent: 83 per cent for men and 64 per cent for women. The education of the population is quite low. Of the employed population, more than a third has only primary education, more than two-thirds did not complete a secondary education and only 10.7 per cent has a higher education level (RWEL 2008a).[17] Participation rates in higher education are lower than in countries with similar income levels and graduates of the system are not well prepared for working life. The technical and vocational education and training (TVET) sector suffers from a high student attrition rate, a low level of teachers' qualifications and a deteriorating teacher–student ratio (AfDB and OECD 2008b). The poverty level in Algeria is quite high. Almost a quarter of the population lives on less than US$2 per day and about 7 per cent on less than US$1.25 per day (UNDP 2009). Donor assistance to Algeria constitutes less than 0.5 per cent of GDP. Aid per capita in 2007, at US$12, is significantly lower than the average for the region or for low- and middle-income countries (WDI), but higher than it has been in recent years. Remittances amounted to only 1.3 per cent of GDP in 2008, the second-lowest in the MENA-12.

Algeria has the highest employment-to-population ratio of the MENA-12: 49 per cent in 2008 (WDI). The overall labour force participation rate of 58 per cent is also the highest: 77 per cent for men and 37 per cent for women (WDI). Women's share of formal employment is only 15.2 per cent (ONS 2009), one of the lowest in the MENA-12. The unemployment rate in 2009 was 9.2 per cent (WFB) with slightly higher unemployment rates for women than men. Nearly three-quarters of the unemployed are under the age of 30, many of them with higher education levels (ONS 2009). An estimated 250000 new entrants are entering the labour market each year to compete for 100000 jobs.[18] Addressing the job deficit is one of the major priorities for the Algerian government.

The private sector is competing with the public sector in many areas of economic activity. The government owns a large number of industrial enterprises and most of the construction companies. The public sector is the largest employer, with 34.4 per cent of the total workforce (ONS 2008). The private sector share of gross capital formation in 2008 was only 39 per cent, amounting to about 10.5 per cent of GDP (WDI), the lowest in the MENA-12. Slow privatization efforts have not allowed the private sector to emerge fully. In the late 2000s the government opened 20 key sectors for growth that had previously been closed to the private sector. This will create more industrial and service sector opportunities for private engagement and investment. However other challenges must be overcome. There is over-regulation, corruption, and complexity in commercial laws, hurdles to starting a business, customs barriers, low liquidity in the banking system, a lack of innovation infrastructure and risk capital, and high taxes. Labour regulations are rigid, with high non-wage labour costs and strict lay-off rules. There is a lack of qualified workers due to a gap between the skills output of the education system and labour market needs. Access to industrial land and business premises, inadequate titling and property rights are also major challenges for Algerian entrepreneurs (EC 2006b).

There is a high level of informality in the enterprise sector. Schneider and Buehn (2009) estimated this to be as high as 35.6 per cent of GDP in 2006. Unofficial country-level estimates suggest informal activity may be closer to 50 per cent of GDP.[19] Fifty to 75 per cent of private sector enterprises employing 1–20 employees operate on an informal basis, and up to 50 per cent of the labour force is informal.

SMEs are very important to Algeria's future growth, but the sector is underdeveloped. The density of registered enterprises is only 10.1 per 1000 population (MPMEA 2008). Private SMEs (with up to 250 workers) account for 99.8 per cent of all enterprises but for only about 16 per cent of total employment[20] (MPMEA 2008). The number of private SMEs and SME workers has been growing at an annual rate of 9–10 per cent since 2002, which is a faster rate than in most countries. Algeria is rather unique among the MENA-12 countries for the large role played by the construction sector. Compared to other countries, the commercial and retail sector is underdeveloped. More than 42400 new SMEs and artisans entered the market in 2008, producing a business entry rate of 10.3 per cent. The exit rate was very low at 1.8 per cent (MPMEA 2009).

SMEs in Algeria face a number of challenges. Similar to other MENA countries, Algerian enterprises are mostly family-run MSEs with weak management structures and low capitalization. SMEs face high costs and compliance burden in dealing with start-up and operational procedures; have a low level of competitiveness; lack standardization, management and capital to meet the quality requirements of production in a globalized and highly competitive market; and will have difficulty competing under the graduated tariff reductions within the framework of the European Union (EU) FTA. SMEs are largely excluded from the formal credit market and have little access to bank credit (Boumghar 2006a, 2006b). Private sector BDS services are largely unavailable to Algerian SMEs, although advisory and consultancy services are provided through government SME-support programmes. Some donor efforts are under way to create a BDS market.

The self-employment rate (own-account and employers) is 29.2 per cent: 29 per cent for men and 30.1 per cent for women (ONS 2009). Algeria stands out among the MENA-12 countries for its high female self-employment rate. Self-employment rates fluctuate from year to year, but have been generally climbing since 1989 (Hammouda and Assassi 2008).

Due to its socialist history, the phenomenon of entrepreneurship in Algeria is relatively recent. Although Algerian adults see entrepreneurship as a less desirable career choice than adults in other MENA countries (IDRC 2010), Algeria is one of the few Arab countries where the majority of 15–29-year-olds state that they would prefer to be self-employed than to work for the government (46 per cent versus 32 per cent) (Silatech 2009). The density of existing entrepreneurs is below average for the ten MENA-12 countries involved in the 2009 Global Entrepreneurship Monitor. About 9.6 per cent of adults own a business (IDRC 2010). The proportion of adults trying to start a business is 11.3 per cent, the third-highest level for the ten GEM-MENA countries. There is very little published research on entrepreneurship in Algeria, so not much is known about the profile and performance of Algerian entrepreneurs (exceptions are Hammouda and Assassi 2007, 2008).

Algeria has only a few business associations.[21] While some of these organizations were established in the 1990s, most were established in the last few years and are in need of capacity building and technical assistance to improve their reach, range of services and advocacy efforts.

Necessary steps to improve Algeria's performance in SME and entrepreneurship development include: administrative simplification; entrepreneurship education in the school system; modernization of SMEs; adoption of information and communication technology (ICT); a total quality certification system for SMEs to improve the quality of their products and management systems; strengthening of SME support centres (training institutions, consultancy and technical support); and development of the role of sector associations (EC 2007b).

Government Priorities and Recent Policy Developments

The government's priorities are to accelerate the transition to a market economy through increased openness, international trade and private sector participation, while at the same time reducing unemployment (especially among young people), alleviating poverty and ensuring social stability. The first major reform programme to achieve this was presented in the Plan for Economic Revitalization 2001–04, supported by a €6 billion budget. This was followed by the Complementary Plan for Growth Support 2005–09, a public investment programme to promote economic activity, expand housing (to deal with the country's massive housing shortage), fund infrastructure projects, invest in education and training, and modernize and enhance public services. One of the growth targets of this growth plan was to create 100 000 new enterprises by the end of 2009. Job creation for educated yet unemployed people is seen as one of the priorities, which would also contribute to improved security.

The government has a 10–20-year plan to attract more FDI, and several ministries and agencies have been created to achieve this. The plan outlines various investment incentive regimes and maps out industrial zones with support services that are in the process of being converted to competitiveness nodes, technopoles for ICT and technoparks.

Regulatory and administrative reforms

In 2006 the government adopted a package of laws to ease the creation of private enterprises and, in accordance with the EU Association Agreement, reduced numerous tariff and non-tariff barriers (Bertelsmann Stiftung 2008a). The government has set up 13 OSSs for investors and entrepreneurs to simplify the business entry and investment process and has plans to expand nationwide. Tax reforms have led to a reduction of taxes on business profit from 30 to 25 per cent and a single fixed tax for businesses with a turnover of less than DZD3 million (AfDB and OECD 2008b). The Labour Code was reformed in 2005 to increase flexibility in firing and contract terms, but social security taxes remain high. Further reforms to the Labour Code are being considered (World Bank 2009a). In an attempt to deal with the shortage of land for private sector development, Algeria has made progress in establishing an economic real estate market and issued four executive decrees in 2007 to define an operational framework for its proper functioning (AfDB and OECD 2008b).

Education policies

Active education reform has been a priority of the government since 2003. The ultimate objectives are to raise the education level of the population, improve the quality of education and respond to the needs of the modern economy. Reform of the TVET system is focused on designing new occupational programmes to meet the needs of a knowledge-based economy better. Efforts emphasize residential and apprenticeship training, revival of traditional craft and manual trades, new training courses on ICT, training for teachers and administrators, and partnerships with the private sector that will assist in targeting the occupations and skills in most demand. A TVET framework bill passed in 2006 lays out the legal and institutional framework for improving coordination of the various bodies involved in the TVET system. At the higher education level, the government's aims are to improve the performance of the system, expand its capacity, improve country-wide access, introduce masters and doctorate programmes and build research capacity. A criticism of the educational reform programme is that it has focused too much on enrolment rates, completion rates and expanding capacity, and not enough on reforming curricula, improving quality and dealing with the inadequacy of the institutional framework (AfBD and OECD 2008b).

SME and entrepreneurship policies and programmes

In line with efforts to diversify the economy away from its dependence on the petroleum industry, SME competitiveness and entrepreneurship development have become more important in the Algerian government's list of priorities. The main responsibility for SME development rests with the Ministère de la Petite et Moyenne Entreprise et de l'Artisanat (MPMEA) established in 1992. Algeria is the only MENA-12 country with an SME ministry and the first to create one. It is also one of only three of the countries, and the first, to have an SME law (RADP 2001) and one of the few MENA-12 countries to have an SME advisory council. The Conseil National Consultatif pour la Promotion des Petites et Moyennes Entreprises (CNC PME) was launched in 2004 as a public–private sector body to promote regular dialogue between the government, SMEs and SME professional associations on strategies for SME development. The CNC PME was also given the role of conducting studies to inform SME policies and programmes.

The SME law was followed in 2004 with the release of a government White Paper on SMEs (MPMEA 2004) and adoption of the Euro-Mediterranean Charter for Enterprise. As a result of these events, the MPMEA funded the creation of several incubators (*pépinières d'entreprise*[22]), a cross-country network of 'single window' facilitation centres to respond to the needs of SMEs and entrepreneurs, and Technical Centres for SMEs to provide skills training. It has also been encouraging universities to offer technical entrepreneurship courses. The MPMEA is in charge of the DZD4 billion National Programme for SME Promotion launched in 2005 to upgrade the innovation and technological capacity of SMEs. This programme is dedicated primarily to implementing the Mise à Niveau SME upgrading scheme to improve the capacity of SMEs to compete under an FTA with the EU.

Algeria has an elaborate system of government support for SME and entrepreneurship development. The Mise à Niveau scheme is being implemented by the Agence Nationale de Développement de la Petite et Moyenne Entreprise (ANDPME), which became operational in 2007 as the coordinating body for SME support programmes and services. The

Agence Nationale de Soutien à l'Emploi des Jeunes (ANSEJ), established under the Ministry of Labour and Employment in 1996 to combat youth unemployment, promotes the creation of microenterprises by young Algerians between the ages of 19 and 35 who have graduated from universities or technical institutes. ANSEJ was tasked with contributing to the government's objective of creating 100 000 new enterprises and helps young entrepreneurs develop their business ideas, navigate the start-up process and acquire financing through a government-backed loan guarantee program. To the end of 2008 ANSEJ had assisted in the creation of 97 015 enterprises employing 274 741 people; 18 per cent of the enterprises were led by young women (MPMEA 2009).

The government established two guarantee funds in 2004 to help address the collateral needs of SMEs: the SME Guarantee Fund (FGAR) to provide mutual guarantees to banks as an incentive for making loans to new MSEs and financing the upgrading and expansion activities of existing SMEs; and the Investment Credit Guarantee Fund (CGGI) as an instrument of bank guarantee for investment credits to SMEs. The government issued a decree at the beginning of 2004 to define microcredit activities and procedures, but few microfinance programmes exist and most of these are based on government-run social services.[23] The National Microcredit Management Agency (ANGEM) was created in 2004 to deliver the National Microcredit Support Fund to borrowers starting income-generating activities. Although NGOs have been offering microfinance to MSEs, their reach and capacity are very limited. Leasing is a new concept in Algeria, and although regulations are in place, significant weaknesses constrain development of the leasing industry.

The risk capital investment society, FINALEP, was created by the government in 1991 in an effort to stimulate private investment. FINALEP takes a minority equity position in companies. Apart from FINALEP, the private sector venture capital industry in Algeria is weak and underdeveloped with only a handful of private venture capital companies.

Innovation policies

The Agence de Valorisation de la Recherche et du Développement Technologique (ANVREDET) is the primary agency for R&D for SMEs and has a wide network of researchers, research institutes and labs. ANVREDET provides assistance to researchers with ideas by helping them with the assessment and registration of patents, preparation of business plans and linkages to investors. Although there appears to be a strong research emphasis in Algeria, success with the commercialization of R&D has been limited due to the underdevelopment of commercialization infrastructure, such as risk capital and venture capital funds, and commercialization expertise. There is no apparent policy seeking to address these gaps.

Conclusions

Algeria has a number of socio-economic challenges to overcome: high unemployment, especially among young people; an annual deficit of approximately 150 000 jobs; low participation of women in formal, private sector employment; a high level of poverty; a low level of private investment, both foreign and domestic; overdependence on the oil sector; a low density of formal private enterprises; and low competitiveness of SMEs. The private sector is underdeveloped and private sector reforms remain relatively marginal. Boukhari (2009) concludes that existing public policies are inadequate to realize a significant improvement in the level of entrepreneurship, innovation and SME development that is needed to create employment, grow the private sector and ensure the country's global competitiveness. He advocates stronger cooperation between the different public entities and a wide range of accelerated reforms to reduce informality and promote the emergence of innovative entrepreneurs.

THE CASE OF IRAQ

Context for Private Sector Development

Iraq is a lower-middle-income country with an estimated population of 28.9 million, growing at a rate of 2.5 per cent a year, and GDP per capita (PPP) of US$3570.[24] In the 1980s Iraq had per capita income levels comparable to South Korea, one of the best education systems in the Arab world, good standards of medical care (DfID 2004b), a vibrant private sector and an educated and skilled workforce. Since then it has deteriorated from being one of the most advanced nations in the Middle East to a country with among the lowest human development indicators.

Its poor economic performance has been attributed to territorial conflicts and wars, high public debt, a decade of United Nations-endorsed sanctions and oil wealth that has not trickled down to benefit the population (Desai 2007). War has resulted in the destruction of most of the country's social, economic and scientific institutions and facilities. Since 2003 more than 4 million people have been displaced or become refugees in neighbouring or other countries, depleting Iraq of talented professionals and expertise. The adverse effects of war reflected in a negative annual average GDP growth of −11.4 per cent in the 2000–2008 period (WDI), although GDP growth rebounded to 9.5 per cent in 2008, dropping in 2009 to 4.3 per cent (WFB). The country is currently in a reconstruction and reform phase and has been described by the World Bank (2004a) as a 'nascent market economy'.

Iraq has the second-largest oil reserves in the world, one of its biggest assets. The oil sector accounts for over 90 per cent of government revenues and foreign exchange earnings (WFB). The manufacturing sector share of industrial output is very weak – estimated at less than 2 per cent of GDP in 2006 (WDI). No more than 4 per cent of the labour force was employed in manufacturing in 2007 (MPDC 2007). The service sector, at 27.6 per cent of GDP, is the smallest in the MENA-12, although it absorbs almost 60 per cent of the Iraqi labour force. Almost 20 per cent of the labour force is in the agricultural sector, which generates about 10 per cent of GDP (WFB).

The public sector owns the majority of large enterprises in the country. There are close to 200 state-owned enterprises (SOEs) employing more than 500 000 workers,[25] although many of these SOEs are not commercially viable (MPDC 2007). Their idle and unproductive status due to security issues, infrastructure destruction and inefficient human capacity is an economic burden on the government. There is a pressing urgency to increase the efficiency of non-oil sectors in order to increase overall output and growth, including attention to agricultural production and rebuilding private sector industrial enterprises and facilities that were either completely destroyed during the Gulf wars or have remained idle for a long period of time (Abdel-Fadil 2003).

The banking industry is not well developed and modern banking practices and products are rare. Up to 90–95 per cent of banking assets are concentrated in the state-owned and specialty banks, there are restrictions on the lending activity of private banks and there is reluctance to lend to micro and small enterprises (MSEs) (IZDIHAR 2007a, 2007b). The banking sector was liberalized in 2004 and the Iraq Stock Exchange is operational, but capital markets are virtually non-existent.

Due to Iraq's reliance on oil revenues, not much attention was given to building private sector capacity in the past, and private sector growth is constrained by the absence of a base of competitive industries and local industrial experts (IZDIHAR 2006b). Besides security and stability issues, which are a prerequisite for any sustainable economic activity, the legal and regulatory framework and service infrastructure for private sector development are either missing or badly in need of development. Iraq's relatively unfavourable business environment is indicated by its rank of 150 out of 183 countries on the World Bank ease of doing business indicators (World Bank 2009b), the second-lowest among the MENA-12. Major barriers to revitalizing the economy include: absence of a long-term programmatic economic reform agenda; lack of dialogue with civil society; persistent unattractiveness of the Iraqi investment climate; low management capacity of private enterprises; absence of functional institutions and legislation; weak enforcement of existing laws; corruption; and lack of transparency (OECD 2009c).

At 37 per cent, the employment to population ratio in Iraq is the second-lowest in the MENA-12. The labour force participation rate is only 41 per cent (WDI), the lowest in the MENA-12. A third of wage workers are employed in the government or public sector (COSIT 2008). Women's share of employment is only 16 per cent (MPDC 2007, p. 52), at the low end along with Jordan, Algeria and Syria. An important dimension of private sector development will be integrating more women into the labour force, reducing the barriers they face in working in the private sector and building their entrepreneurial capacity (IFC 2004). Unemployment is a critical priority, with levels estimated at between 15 and 30 per cent (WFB). Individuals in over a quarter of Iraqi families were living on less than US$1 a day in 2005 (MPDC 2007).

Prior to 2003 there was virtually no private sector in Iraq. Private enterprises operated under restrictions on the type of activity and the size and movement of capital and investments, and were heavily reliant on government support. The private sector consists of a few large firms, a small number of SMEs and a large number of microenterprises (World Bank 2004a). The majority of private sector enterprises operate in the grey economy and the informal sector absorbs 75 per cent of the labour force (IZDIHAR 2007b).

A little over 30 per cent of Iraqis earn income from self-employment activity[26] (COSIT 2008). The culture of entrepreneurship is weak. In the 2009 Gallup survey of Arab youth, only 14 per cent of 15–29-year-old Iraqis stated that they would prefer to be self-employed, compared to 63 per cent who would prefer to work for the government (Silatech 2009). The share of youth interested in entrepreneurial activity was among the lowest in the MENA-12.

There is very little data on the composition of the SME sector in Iraq, however informal SMEs dominate the private sector. In addition to deficiencies in the institutional framework affecting PSD generally, SMEs in Iraq have difficulty accessing finance, information, business support services and capacity building (World Bank 2004a). Commercial lending to Iraqi SMEs is almost non-existent. The absence of modern business practices, the use of outdated bookkeeping and accounting systems, and the lack of office space and modern equipment are impeding SME growth (IZDIHAR 2006b).

The main challenges for SME development include: entrepreneurship development and enterprise creation; cheaper and faster business registration and start-up procedures; incentives to guide new businesses towards formalization; strengthening of microfinance networks to assist new entrepreneurs; a simplified regulatory environment; a simple and fair taxation system; programmes to improve the business skills of entrepreneurs; promotion of small business and entrepreneur associations; and removal of discrimination against small business entities in licensing, permits and public procurement (OECD 2009c).

Government Priorities and Recent Policy Developments

Apart from rebuilding the country's infrastructure, the main priorities for the Iraq government are alleviating unemployment, improving living standards, reducing the dependence on oil reserves and increasing the private sector contribution to GDP (Al-Saadi 2006). Since 2003 the Iraq government has embarked on efforts to diversify its sources of income, revive the private sector, develop an investment promotion strategy, liberalize foreign trade for export, open its market to foreign products and improve basic transportation and communication services to activate the economy's commercial abilities (MPDC 2005b, 2007). The government's vision is to transform Iraq into a peaceful, unified federal democracy and market-oriented economic powerhouse, with full integration into the global economy (MPDC 2005b).

Regulatory and administrative reforms

A commission has been set up to review options for the reform and privatization of SOEs and an Inter-Ministerial Committee for Reform of State-Owned Enterprises established to work on a 'best-practices' privatization law to guide private investment in the SOEs. The Rehabilitation of State-Owned Plants Program is geared to address the productivity challenge of ageing SOEs, use of antiquated technology and low productivity. Similar rehabilitation efforts are needed to 'jump re-start' private factories that either closed or deteriorated during the latest Iraq war.

Financial markets were liberalized in 2004, which opened up the banking sector to private competition; privatization of the banking sector is being encouraged. Several economic and commercial laws have recently been passed, including those related to securities, public financial management and public procurement. Since 2005 the government has passed a new investment law and created the National Investment Commission to promote and attract FDI and increase private sector employment. Iraq also signed an agreement with the Multilateral Investment Guarantee Agency (MIGA) providing for political insurance to investors in Iraq, a necessary element in its efforts to attract FDI.[27] The Iraq Investment Promotion Agency was created in 2006, and regional investment promotion commissions are to be set up in governorates and regions, including OSSs to facilitate licensing and registration processes. Free zones have been created to encourage industrial, commercial and service projects, and industrial zones have been built to accommodate foreign companies. Iraq has cancelled restrictions on trade, assigned a uniform customs tax on imports and signed numerous bilateral and multilateral agreements relating to foreign trade in goods and services. An Iraqi Trade Information Center has been created as an OSS to serve private firms seeking information about trade and investment opportunities.

Since 2007 the MENA-OECD Initiative on Governance and Investment has been directing efforts to promote PSD in Iraq (OECD 2008a). The Iraqi government has launched a Task Force on Economic Reforms and Private Sector Capacity (TFER) to conduct a broad assessment of legislative, institutional and sector needs. The aim is to guide the design of policy and legislation and regulatory and institutional reform that will diversify the economy through private enterprise promotion and investment (OECD 2009c). The TFER functions to provide coordination and support to the government and CSOs in the private sector reform process and to act as the main institutional counterpart of related donor programmes. Activities focus on developing a business climate development strategy to increase investment and competitiveness; quality drafting of laws to improve business regulations and create a business-friendly regulatory environment; public finance policy reform to improve taxation and revenue administration; corporatization of SOEs and pubic–private partnerships to address issues of overemployment and depleted capital equipment; and developing the building blocks of an effective policy to deal with the many inefficiencies of Iraqi SMEs. Measures are also being undertaken to combat corruption, including creation of a Commission on Public Integrity with Inspectors General in each ministry (MPDC 2005b).

Employment creation and poverty reduction are high on the list of government priorities. Several measures are being undertaken to improve the quality of human capital and social protection. Training and career development programmes, labour-intensive public works programmes, vocational training programmes, income-generating microcredit programmes, improved labour legislation and inclusive employment policy are all identified as possible solutions in the National Development Strategy 2007–10 (MPDC 2007). Included is a target to increase women's labour force participation to 35 per cent.

SME and entrepreneurship policies and programmes

The Ministry of Industry and Minerals (MIM) is responsible for industry development in the public sector, the private sector and the 'mixed'[28] sector, including foreign and local investment, and appears to have responsibility for SMEs. Although the MIM is committed to establishing industrial and technology incubators and industrial clusters to foster the private sector creation of SMEs, there is no evidence that an overall SME strategy has been adopted on the national level.

IZDIHAR,[29] a three-year USAID-funded project launched in 2004, worked with the Iraqi government to help promote a market-based economy and growth of the private sector. It commissioned a number of studies to underpin policy and programme directions and achieved a number of outcomes to improve the operating environment for SMEs, particularly in the area of financing. It facilitated the development of the Iraq Microfinance Strategy (IZDIHAR 2007b) and helped build the capacity of microfinance entities. By December 2008 there were 12 NGOs delivering donor-supported microfinance loans in all 19 governorates (Tijara 2009). Tijara has developed an MFI Performance Classification and Monitoring System, which has been in place since the end of 2007. IZDIHAR also developed SME lending programmes that were introduced to banks and implemented credit analysis training to banks to build their SME lending capacity. The intent of the IFC-approved US$170 million Iraq Small Business Financing Facility in 2003 was to encourage financing on a commercial basis through commercial banks. In 2006 12 privately owned Iraqi banks partnered in the creation of the Iraqi Company for Bank Guarantees (ICBG) to improve access to bank financing for smaller enterprises. USAID provided US$5 million to supplement the loan guarantee fund, which guarantees the lending banks for up to 75 per cent of the value of SME loans. The Iraqi Council of Ministers approved a SME lending programme in 2007 that would provide Ministry of Finance-backed loan guarantees to Iraqi banks for small projects.

IZDIHAR and Tijara have supported the development of 12 Small Business Development Centers (SBDCs) in partnership with existing business associations and business centres in 19 locations. Having received training on service delivery, the SBDCs offer business consulting, courses on how to start a business, computer training and a voucher-based system for BDS. The Center for International Private Enterprise (CIPE) is working with Iraqi universities and institutions to foster an entrepreneurship culture and offer entrepreneurship education and training. However the need for these types of services far outweighs the supply of institutions. The government has only recently passed an NGO law and there are many restrictions and difficulties to establish a new organization.

In 2003 the Iraqi Governing Council requested assistance from the World Bank in learning about best-practice policy environments for women entrepreneurs. The World Bank organized women's trade and capacity building missions and workshops to share international experience of women's business associations and to build capacity in how to engage women in linkages with FDI (IFC 2004).

Conclusions

Iraq's major economic development challenges are security, oil dependence, idle SOEs and the absence of a competitive private sector base. The amount of work required for the country's development is huge. It needs to cover the institutional framework that governs all activities, including laws, regulations, processes and procedures, public and private organizations, human resources capacity and informal rules, such as perceptions and corruption, as well as reconstruction and infrastructure development.

Critics suggest that the 2005–2007 National Development Plan did little to improve policies affecting Iraqis (Al-Saadi 2006) and that the neoliberal, Washington Consensus free market development strategy in Iraq has failed (Looney 2005). Al-Saadi (2006) holds the view that premature calls for economic liberalization and privatization of the oil industry, tight fiscal policy and non-productive reconstruction and occupation expenditures have actually damaged the drive for a free market and larger private sector role, and only benefited foreign businesses and Iraqi trade dealers. Al-Saadi further claims that, while free market forces are seen by economic planners as a necessary and sufficient condition for economic growth and employment, this is not sufficient to deal with the high unemployment, poverty and wide disparities in income and wealth. What is needed is a new political platform that appeals to the low-income groups and helps to produce a growing middle class in terms of income, education and entrepreneurial skill (Al-Saadi 2006).

For private sector and rapid job growth, industry, professional and business associations will need to play an active role in policy advocacy and provision of member services (World Bank 2004a). Concerted efforts to address the knowledge gap about the private sector and SMEs are also needed.

NOTES

1. Using the nominal method of calculation, the GDP per capita in 2009 was US$1061 (IMF 2010).

2. Almost 1 million Yemeni migrants returned to Yemen from Saudi Arabia and the Gulf States during the Gulf War, not only creating pressure on employment and government services, but also substantially lowering remittance income.
3. In 1998 the private share of domestic investment was over 70 per cent, amounting to almost 25 per cent of GDP.
4. According to the 2004 Census the total number of employed persons in 2004 was 3.55 million of which 719000 were employed in private establishments. Of course to be added to this are the self-employed, who represented 29.4 per cent of total employment, and workers in the agricultural sector.
5. Based on an interview with SMEPS officials who define medium enterprises as those with 10–24 workers.
6. The 1994 Census reported a self-employment rate of 35.8 per cent: 41.3 per cent for men and 14.8 per cent for women (Bielen and Aleryani 1997).
7. Strategies are being developed to stimulate investment in tourism and maritime activities, the natural gas sector and the mining sector.
8. It is noted that female students make up only about 3 per cent of vocational education and training (VET) students and are segregated into gendered technical programmes, such as sewing, hairdressing and weaving (ILO 2008a, p. 22)
9. Non-performing loans were up to 26 per cent in 2007 (IMF 2008a).
10. The whole banking system in Sudan has been converted into Islamic banks (Badr-El-Din 2003).
11. Donor aid in 2008 was valued at US$659 per capita and remittances amounted to about 14 per cent of GDP.
12. About 90 per cent of the Palestinian export business and 70 per cent of its import business is done with Israel.
13. Loan amounts are from US$10000 to US$500000 so are geared to the SME market.
14. At the end of 2003 there were 116720 manufacturing enterprises in Syria. Only 26000 of these (22 per cent) were privately owned SMEs (SEBC 2005, p. 15).
15. The official unemployment rate for youth in 2007 was 19 per cent and represented 57 per cent of total unemployment (Kabbani 2009).
16. To reach this target Syria needs investments of US$40 billion during the Five-Year Plan (FYP) period; half of this can be covered by the government budget and private sector investment flows must contribute the other half.
17. RWEL (2008a) noted that the number of students in higher education institutions doubled to almost a million from 2000–01 to 2006–07.
18. Information from key informant during country visit in August 2007.
19. Informal activity was inadvertently encouraged during the late 1980s as a means of overcoming the constraints of import restrictions and unemployment (Bertelsmann Stiftung 2008a).
20. Total employment in 2007 was 9.15 million (ONS 2008); 1.49 million were employed in private SMEs (MPMEA 2009).
21. For example, the Forum des Chefs d'Entreprises (FCE); the Club d'Action et de Réflexion (CARE), a private think-tank established in the 2000s by a group of entrepreneurs and lawyers to advocate private sector issues with the government; and the Association des Femme Chefs d'Entreprises (SEVE), an association of women entrepreneurs.
22. The objectives of the *pépinière* programme are to develop entrepreneurial skills for innovative enterprises, engage young graduates in setting up businesses and implement innovative projects developed by researchers. These are frequently located in technology parks and on university campuses.
23. The main institution providing microfinance services has been Algérie Post, which was set up in 2002 to provide both postal and financial services (CGAP 2006). However most of the financial services are for consumer spending rather than income-generating activities.

24. The nominal method of GDP conversion produces a value of only US $2108 (see IMF 2010).
25. See IZDIHAR (2006a) for discussion of the excess employment situation in SOEs.
26. A gender breakdown for self-employment and employer activity is not reported.
27. Data on FDI inflows into Iraq are not available from international agencies.
28. The 'mixed sector' refers to enterprises with minority public participation, particularly evident in engineering, food, chemicals and construction sectors.
29. IZDIHAR is the acronym for Iraq Private Sector Growth and Employment Generation. The IZDIHAR project ended in March 2008 and was replaced by the Tijara Provincial Economic Growth Program.

References

Abdel-Fadil, M. (2003), 'Issue of Economic Reconstruction of Iraq: The Larger View', Study presented to the ESCWA, Cairo, Egypt: Cairo University and American University in Cairo.

Acs, Z.J. (2006), 'How is Entrepreneurship Good for Economic Growth?' *Innovations*, Winter, 97–107.

Acs, Z.J., D. Audretsch, P. Braunerhjelm and B. Carlsson (2005), 'Growth and Entrepreneurship: An Empirical Assessment', Discussion Papers in Entrepreneurship, Growth and Public Policy # 3205, Jena, Germany: Max Planck Institute of Economics,

Acs, Z.J. and L. Szerb (2009), 'The Global Entrepreneurship Index (GEINDEX)', *Foundations and Trends in Entrepreneurship*, **5**(5), 341–435.

ADB (Asian Development Bank) (2004), 'Private Enterprise Formality and the Role of Local Government', Discussion Paper No. 02, Making Markets Work for the Poor project, November, Manila, Philippines: Asian Development Bank.

ADB (2006), *Private Sector Development: A Revised Strategic Framework*, February, Manila, Philippines: Asian Development Bank.

ADB (2007a), *Measuring Performance in Private Sector Development*, Regional and Sustainable Development Department, Manila, Philippines: Asian Development Bank.

ADB (2007b), 'Private Sector Development and Operations: Harnessing Synergies with the Public Sector', Reference Number: SST: REG 2006-06, May, Operations Evaluation Department, Manila, Philippines: Asian Development Bank.

ADE (Consulting and Advisory Services) (2005), 'Evaluation of European Community Support to Private Sector Development in Third Countries, Final Report', prepared for the European Commission, Belgium.

ADF (African Development Fund) (2006), 'Sudan: Capacity Building for Poverty Reduction and Good Governance, Appraisal Report', Tunis, Tunisia: African Development Bank Group.

AfDB (African Development Bank) (2007), 'Tunisia: Country Strategy Paper 2007–2011', Country Regional Department, Tunis, Tunisia.

AfDB and OECD (Organisation for Economic Co-operation and

Development) (2008a), *Africa Economic Outlook 2007/2008*, Paris: OECD Development Centre.
AfDB and OECD (2008b), 'Algeria', in *African Economic Outlook 2007/2008*, Paris: OECD Development Centre, pp. 107–20.
AfDB and OECD (2008c), 'Morocco', in *African Economic Outlook 2007/2008*, Paris: OECD Development Centre, pp. 447–57.
AfDB and OECD (2008d), 'Tunisia', in *African Economic Outlook 2007/2008*, Paris: OECD Development Centre, pp. 585–98.
AFII-ANIMA (Agence Française pour les Investissements Internationaux and Euro-Mediterranean Network of Investment Promotion Agencies) (2005), 'Innovation, Technology Centres and Investment Attraction in the Mediterranean: Mediterranean Intelligence', ANIMA Papers and Documents No. 9, Agence Française pour les Investissements Internationaux/Marseille Innovation, November.
Al-Anagreh, A., M. Al-Marouq and S. Al-Tayeb (2005), 'Non-Traditional Factors Influencing the Commercial Banks Lending to Small and Medium-Sized Enterprises (SMEs) in Jordan', Department of Economics, Mutah University and Department of Economics, Hashemite University, Amman, Jordan.
Al-Habash, L., D. Achi and N. Kabbani (2007a), 'Assessing the Effect of Know About Business (KAB) on the Knowledge and Attitudes of Secondary School Students', Research Division, August, Damascus, Syria: Syria Trust for Development.
Al-Habash, L., D. Achi and N. Kabbani (2007b), 'Assessing the Effect of Know About Business (KAB) on the Knowledge and Attitudes of University Students', Research Division, August, Damascus, Syria: Syria Trust for Development.
Al-Saadi, S.Z. (2006), 'Iraq's National Vision, Economic Strategy, and Policies', *Strategic Insights*, **5**(3), March, Monterey, CA, USA: Center for Contemporary Conflict, available at http://www.nps.edu/Academics/centers/ccc/publications/OnlineJournal/2006/Mar/saadiMar06.html.
Alissa, S. (2007a), 'Rethinking Economic Reform in Jordan: Confronting Socio-economic Realities', Carnegie Papers, Number 4, Carnegie Middle East Center, Beirut, Lebanon: Carnegie Endowment for International Peace.
Alissa, S. (2007b), 'The Political Economy of Reform in Egypt: Understanding the Role of Institutions', Carnegie Papers Number 5, October, Carnegie Middle East Center, Beirut, Lebanon: Carnegie Endowment for International Peace.
Amorós, J.E. (2009), 'Entrepreneurship and the Quality of Institutions:

A Developing-Country Approach', Research Paper No. 2009/07, February, UNI-WIDER, World Institute for Development Economics Research, Helsinki, Finland: United Nations University.

ANPME (Agence Nationale pour la Promotion de la Petite et Moyenne Entreprise) (2007), 'Objectif PME', Bulletin d'information de l'ANPME No. 14, Statistiques à fin juin, Rabat, Maroc.

Arab Republic of Egypt (2007), *The Sixth Five-Year Plan 2007/08–2011/12*, Cairo, Egypt.

Ardagna, S. and A. Lusardi (2008), 'Explaining International Differences in Entrepreneurship: The Role of Individual Characteristics and Regulatory Constraints', Working Paper 14012, May, Cambridge, MA, USA: National Bureau of Economic Research.

Assaad, R. (2006), 'Unemployment and Youth Insertion in the Labor Market in Egypt', Working Paper No. 118, December, Cairo, Egypt: Egyptian Center for Economic Studies.

Assaad, R. (2007), 'Labor Supply, Employment and Unemployment in the Egyptian Economy, 1988–2006', March, Cairo, Egypt: Population Council.

Assaad, R. and R. Roushdy (2006), 'Poverty and the Labor Market in Egypt: A Review of Developments in the 1998–2006 Period', prepared as a background paper for the Egypt Poverty Assessment Update, December, Cairo, Egypt: Population Council.

Aterido, R., M. Hallward-Driemeier and C. Pages (2008), 'Investment Climate and Employment Growth: The Impact of Access to Finance, Corruption and Regulations Across Firms', paper presented at the Comparative Enterprise Data Conference, 22–24 May, Central European University, Budapest, Hungary.

Atyani, A. and S. Al Haj Ali (2009), *Problems of Micro, Small and Medium Enterprises in Palestine*, Ramallah, Palestine: Palestine Economic Policy Research Institute (MAS).

Audretsch, D., R. van der Horst, T. Twaak and R. Thurik (2009). 'First Section of the Annual Report on EU Small and Medium-sized Enterprises', January, commissioned by the European Commission, Directorate General Enterprise and Industry, Zoetermeer, the Netherlands: EIM Business & Policy Research, available at http://ec.europa.eu/enterprise/entrepreneurship/craft/sme_perf_review/spr_main_en.htm (accessed 10 October 2009).

Ayadi, M., G. Boulila, M. Lahouel and P. Montigny (2005), 'Pro-Poor Growth in Tunisia', March, Paris: International Development & Strategies.

Ayyagari, M., T. Beck and A. Demirgüc-Kunt (2003), 'Small and Medium Enterprises across the Globe: A New Database', Policy Research

Working Group Working Paper 3127, August, Washington, DC, USA: World Bank.

Badr-El-Din, I.A. (2002), 'The Role of Home Based Enterprises (HBEs) in Alleviating Sudanese Urban Poverty and the Effectiveness of Policies and Programmes to Promote HBEs', Sudan Economy Research Group, Bremen, Germany: University of Bremen.

Badr-El-Din, I.A. (2003), 'Poverty Alleviation via Islamic Banking Finance to Micro-Enterprises (MEs) in Sudan: Some Lessons from Poor Countries', Discussion Paper No. 35, Sudan Economy Research Group, Bremen, Germany: University of Bremen.

Bank Audi (2008), 'Lebanon Economic Report', 1st Quarter 2008, Beirut, Lebanon.

Bank Audi (2009a), 'Egypt Economic Report', June, Cairo, Egypt.

Bank Audi (2009b), 'Jordan Economic Report', April, Amman, Jordan.

Barro, R.J. (1998), *Determinants of Economic Growth: A Cross-Country Empirical Study*, Cambridge, MA, USA: MIT Press.

Baumol, W. (1990), 'Entrepreneurship: Productive, Unproductive and Destructive', *Journal of Political Economy*, **98**(5), 893–921.

Bennett, J. (2009), 'Informal Firms in Developing Countries: Entrepreneurial Stepping Stone or Consolation Prize?' Research Paper No. 2009/19, March, UNI-WIDER World Institute for Development Economics Research, Helsinki, Finland: United Nations University.

Bertelsmann Stiftung (ed.) (2008a), *Bertelsmann Transformation Index 2008*, Gűtersloh, Germany: Verlag Bertelsmann Stiftung.

Bertelsmann Stiftung (2008b), 'BTI 2008 – Jordan Country Report', Gütersloh, Germany: Verlag Bertelsmann Stiftung.

Bertelsmann Stiftung (2008c), 'BTI 2008 – Morocco Country Report', Gütersloh, Germany: Verlag Bertelsmann Stiftung.

Berthélemy, J-C., S. Dessus and C. Nahas (2007), 'Exploring Lebanon's Growth Prospects', Policy Research Working Paper 4332, August, Social and Economic Development Group, Middle East and North Africa Region, Washington, DC, USA: World Bank.

Bibi, S. (2006), 'When is Economic Growth Pro-Poor? Evidence from Tunisia', Centre Interuniversitaire sur le Risque, les Politiques Économiques et l'Emploi (CIRPEE) and Faculté des Sciences Économiques et de Gestion de Tunis (FSEGT), Tunis, Tunisie.

Bibi, S. and M. Nabli (2010), 'Equity and Inequality in the Arab Region', ERF Policy Research Report, PRR No. 33, February, Cairo, Egypt: Economic Research Forum.

Bielen, R. and A. Aleryani (1997), *UNDP Microfinance Assessment Report for Yemen*, New York, USA: United Nations Development Programme.

Bior, I. (2000), 'Some Reflections on Economic Liberalization in the Sudan', Sudan Economy Research Group Discussion Papers, Bremen, Germany: University of Bremen.

Bjørnskov, C. and N.J. Foss (2008), 'Economic Freedom and Entrepreneurial Activity: Some Cross-Country Evidence', *Public Choice*, **134**(3–4), 307–28.

Blanc, F. and M. Louis (2007), 'The Challenge of Employment in the Mediterranean Countries', Research No.FEM3d-02, November, coordinated by A. Galal and J-L. Reiffers, FEMISE Research Programme 2006–2007, Marseilles, France: Institut de la Méditerranée.

Bosma, N., Z.J. Acs, E. Autio, A. Coduras and J. Levie (2009), *Global Entrepreneurship Monitor, 2008 Executive Report*, Wellesley, MA, USA: Babson College and Universidad del Desarrollo.

Bosma, N. and J. Levie (2010), *Global Entrepreneurship Monitor: 2009 Global Report*, Wellesley, MA, USA: Babson College, Universidad del Desarrollo and Reykjavik University.

Boukhari, M. (2009), 'Rôle de l'État vis-à-vis des TPE/PME dans un pays nouvellement adhérent à l'économie de marché: cas de l'Algérie', Colloque international, La vulnérabilité des TPE et des PME dans an environnement mondialisé, 11es Journées scientifiques du Réseau Entrepreneuriat, 27 au 29 mai, Université du Québec à Trois-Rivières, Trois-Rivières, Québec, Canada.

Boumghar, M.Y. (2006a), 'Distribution du crédit et croissance: un essai de mesure du lien pour l'Algérie', Document de travail n°01/2006, juin, Alger, Algérie: Centre de Recherche en Économie Appliquée pour le Développement (CREAD).

Boumghar, M.Y. (2006b), 'La relation PME-Banque: un essai de compréhension', Document de travail n°02/2006, octobre, Alger, Algérie: Centre de Recherche en Économie Appliquée pour le Développement (CREAD).

Carr, M. and M. Chen (2001), 'Globalization and the Informal Economy: How Global Trade and Investment Impact on the Working Poor', Working Paper on the Informal Economy, Employment Sector, Geneva: International Labour Organization.

Carree, M. A. and A.R. Thurik (2003), 'The Impact of Entrepreneurship on Economic Growth', in Acs, Z.J. and D.B. Audretsch (eds), *The Handbook of Entrepreneurship Research*, Boston, MA, USA, Dordrecht, Netherlands and London, UK: Kluwer Academic Publishers, pp. 437–71.

Carree, M.A., A. van Stel, A.R. Thurik and S. Wennekers (2002), 'Economic Development and Business Ownership: An Analysis using Data of 23 OECD Countries in the Period 1976–1996', *Small Business Economics*, **19**, 271–90.

CAS (Central Administration of Statistics) (2007), *Statistical Yearbook 2007*, Presidency of the Council of Ministers, Beirut, Lebanon: Lebanese Republic.

CBS (Central Bureau of Statistics) (2006), *Statistical Yearbook 2006*, Ministry of Council of Ministers, Khartoum, Sudan: Republic of the Sudan.

CBS (2008), *Statistical Abstract 2008*, Damascus, Syria: Syrian Arab Republic.

CBS (2009), *Statistical Abstract 2009*, Damascus, Syria: Syrian Arab Republic.

CEC (Commission of the European Communities) (1998), 'A European Community Strategy for Private Sector Development in ACP Countries', Communication from the Commission to the Council and the European Parliament, COM(1998) 667, Brussels.

CEC (2009), 'Implementation of the European Neighbourhood Policy in 2009 Progress Report Egypt', Commission Staff Working Document, SEC(2009)523/2, 23 April, Brussels: European Commission.

Central Bank of Sudan (2008), 'Memorandum of Economic and Financial Policies', Submitted to the IMF in letter of intent and technical memorandum of understanding, May, Khartoum, Sudan.

Çetindamar, D. and U.Y. Çetinkaya (2008), 'Turkey, as the EU candidate country', in *Strategies for the Development of Entrepreneurship and the SMS Sector in the Black Sea Economic Cooperation Region*, May, Çankaya-Ankara, Turkey: Konrad-Adenauer-Stiftung, pp. 269–87.

CGAP (Consultative Group to Assist the Poor) (2006), 'Microfinance in Algeria: Opportunities and Challenges', June, Joint CGAP and AFD Mission under the auspices of the Ministry of Finance Deputy Minister for Financial Reform, Washington, DC, USA: CGAP.

CGAP (2008), 'Policy and Regulatory Framework for Microfinance in Syria', January, Washington, DC, USA.

Chen, M. (2005), 'The Business Environment and the Informal Economy: Creating Conditions for Poverty Reduction', draft paper for the Committee of Donor Agencies for Small Enterprise Development Conference on 'Reforming the Business Environment', November, Cairo, Egypt.

Chen, M.A. (2007), 'Rethinking the Informal Economy: Linkages with the Formal Economy and the Formal Regulatory Environment', DESA Working Paper No. 46, ST/ESA/2007/DWP/46, July, Department of Economic and Social Affairs, New York, USA: United Nations.

CIDA (Canadian International Development Agency) (2005), 'Private Sector Development: Strategic Directions for CIDA', prepared by the Economic Policy Division, 20 July, Ottawa, Canada: CIDA Policy Branch.

CNRS (National Council for Scientific Research) (2006), 'Proposed Plan for Science, Technology and Innovation Policy (STIP) for Lebanon', Beirut, Lebanon.

COSIT (Central Organization for Statistics and Information Technology) (2008), *Iraq Household Socio-Economic Survey IHSES-2007*, Central Organization for Statistics and Information Technology of Iraq, Kurdistan Region Statistics Organization, and International Bank for Reconstruction and Development/World Bank, Baghdad, Iraq.

CRI (Consultation & Research Institute) (2003), 'Competition in the Lebanese Economy: A Background Report for a Competition Law for Lebanon', prepared for the Ministry of Economy and Trade, May, Beirut, Lebanon.

CSO (Central Statistical Organization) (2004), *Final Results: Population, Housing & Establishment Census 2004*, Sana'a, Yemen: Republic of Yemen.

CSO (2007), *Statistical Year-Book 2007*, Sana'a, Yemen: Republic of Yemen.

Davutyan, N. (2008), 'Estimating the Size of Turkey's Informal Sector: An Expenditure Based Approach', Working Paper 403, May, Cairo, Egypt: Economic Research Forum.

DCED (Donor Committee for Enterprise Development) (2008), *Supporting Business Environment Reforms: Practical Guidance for Development Agencies*, 2008 Edition, August, Business Environment Working Group, Cambridge, UK: DCED.

De Paula, A. and J.A. Scheinkman (2007), 'The Informal Sector', NBER Working Paper 10175, Cambridge, MA, USA: National Bureau for Economic Research.

de Soto, H. (2000), *The Mystery of Capital: Why Capitalism Triumphs in the West and Fails Everywhere Else*, New York, USA: Random House.

Desai, S. (2007), 'Post-conflict Microfinance: Assessment and Policy Notes for Iraq', JENA Economic Research Papers # 2007-060, Jena, Germany: Max Planck Institute of Economics.

DfID (Department for International Development) (2004a), *Accelerating Pro-Poor Growth through Support for Private Sector Development*, London, England: DfID.

DfID (2004b), *Iraq: Interim Country Assistance Plan*, February, London, England: DfID.

DfID (2004c), 'Making Markets Work Better for the Poor: A Framework Paper', London, England: DfID.

DfID (2007), *Governance, Development and Democratic Politics: DfID's Work in Building More Effective States*, London, England: DfID.

DfID (2008), *Private Sector Development Strategy, Prosperity for All: Making Markets Work*, London, England: DfID.

Di Tommaso, M.R., E. Lanzoni and L. Rubini (2001), *Support to SMEs in the Arab Region: The Case of Tunisia*, Geneva, Switzerland: UNIDO and UNDP.

Djankov, S. (2008), 'A Response to *Is Doing Business Damaging Business*', January, Washington, DC, USA: World Bank.

DOS (Department of Statistics) (2006), 'Employees and Enterprise by Economic Activity and Size Group by Employment (2006)', Amman, Jordan: Hashemite Kingdom of Jordan.

DOS (2008), 'Employment and Unemployment Survey, August 2008', Amman, Jordan: Hashemite Kingdom of Jordan.

EBI (Egyptian Banking Institute) and CBE (Central Bank of Egypt) (2005), *The National Strategy for Microfinance*, prepared in coordination with the Social Fund for Development and funded by KfW and USAID, Cairo, Egypt: Central Bank of Egypt.

EC (European Commission) (2004), 'Euro-Med Partnership – Lebanon: National Indicative Programme 2005–2006', Brussels: European Commission.

EC (2005a), 'Euro-Mediterranean Partnership: Country Report Lebanon', Brussels: European Commission.

EC (2005b), 'Final Report on Identification and Formulation of SME Support Programme in Syria', 31 March, Brussels: European Commission.

EC (2005c), 'Turkey 2005 Progress Report', COM(2005)561final, SEC(2005) 1426, November, Brussels: European Commission.

EC (2006a), 'Report on the Implementation of the Euro-Mediterranean Charter for Enterprise', Commission Staff Working Document (SEC(2006) 940), Enterprise and Industry Directorate-General, Luxembourg: Office for Official Publications of the European Communities.

EC (2006b), 'Strategy Paper 2007–2013 & National Indicative Programme 2007–2010, Algeria', European Neighbourhood and Partnership Instrument, Brussels: European Commission.

EC (2007a), 'Morocco 2007–2010 National Indicative Programme', European Neighbourhood and Partnership Instrument, Brussels: European Commission.

EC (2007b), 'Programme d'Appui aux PME/PMI des résultats et une expérience à transmettre', Brussels: European Commission

EC (2007c), 'Turkey 2007 Progress Report', Commission Staff Working Document, {COM(2007)663 final}, SEC(2007)1436, November, Brussels: European Commission.

EC (2008a), 'Document de Travail des Services de la Commission Accompagnant la Communication de la Commission au Conseil et au Parlement européen, 'Mise en Oeuvre de la Politique Européenne de Voisinage en 2007', Rapport de Suivi Tunisie, SEC(2008)401, Brussels: European Commission

EC (2008b), 'European Neighborhood Policy Implementation, Progress Report 2007', April, Brussels: European Commission.

EC (2008c), 'Implementation of the European Neighborhood Policy in 2007 Progress Report Lebanon', Commission Staff Working Document accompanying the Communication from the Commission to the Council and the European Parliament, COM(2008) 397, April, Brussels: European Commission.

EC (2008d), 'Turkey 2008 Progress Report', Commission Staff Working Document, {COM(2008)674 final}, SEC(2008)2699, November, Brussels: European Commission.

EC (2009), *European Charter for Small Enterprise: 2009 Good Practice Selection*, Enterprise and Industry, Brussels: European Commission.

ECA (Economic Commission for Africa) (2004), 'The Missing Link in Growth and Sustainable Development: Closing the Gender Gap', ADB/ECA Symposium on Gender, Growth and Sustainable Development, 24 May, Kampala, Uganda.

Ecevit, Y. (2007), 'A Critical Approach to Women's Entrepreneurship in Turkey', Ankara, Turkey: International Labour Office.

ECOSC (Economic and Social Council) (2003), 'PME/PMI: Situation Actuelle et Perspectives', Beirut, Lebanon: Lebanese Republic.

El-Jafari, M., I. Abu Hantash and S. Al Haj Ali (2008), *The Role of Research and Development in Enhancing the Competitiveness of the Palestinian Private Sector*, Ramallah, Palestine: Palestine Economic Policy Research Institute (MAS). [In Arabic]

El Laithy, H. and K. Abu-Ismail (2005), *Poverty in Syria: 1996–2004, Diagnosis and Pro-Poor Policy Considerations*, June, Damascus, Syria: United Nations Development Programme Syria.

El Mahdi, A. (2006), *MSEs Potentials and Success Determinants in Egypt 2003–2004: Special Reference to Gender Differentials*, FEMISE Research Report, Research no. FEM21-31, December, Cairo, Egypt: Economic Research Forum (ERF) and Marseilles, France: Institut de la Méditerranée.

El Mahdi, A. and A. Rashed (2007), 'The Changing Economic Environment and the Development of the Micro and Small Enterprises in Egypt 2006', Working Paper No. 0706, Working Paper Series, Cairo, Egypt: Economic Research Forum.

El-Meehy, T. (2009), 'National Micro, Small and Medium Enterprise

Development Strategy for Yemen, 2009–2019', prepared for GTZ Private Sector Development Programme and the Ministry of Planning and International Cooperation, January, Sana'a, Yemen: GTZ.

Enders, K. (2007), 'Egypt – Searching for Binding Constraints on Growth', IMF Working Paper WP/07/57, Middle East and Central Asia Department, Washington, DC, USA: International Monetary Fund.

ENCC (Egyptian National Competitiveness Council) (2007), *Taking the Next Big Step: The 4th Egyptian Competitiveness Report*, Cairo, Egypt: ENCC.

Entrust (Entrust: Development & Management Consultants) (2006), 'SME Mapping Survey', conducted for the Small Enterprise Development Organization/ Social Fund for Development (SEDO/SFD), Cairo, Egypt: Social Fund for Development.

ERF (Economic Research Forum) (2006), 'Policy Brief: Étude sur la micro et petite entreprise au Maroc', Cairo, Egypt: Economic Research Forum.

ERF and L'institut de la Méditerranée (2005), *The Road Ahead for Syria: Syria Country Profile*, FEMISE 2006 Network, February, Cairo, Egypt: Economic Research Forum.

ETF (European Training Foundation) (2009), 'ETF Country Plan 2009, Jordan', Torino, Italy.

European Community (2006), 'Yemen-European Community Strategy Paper for the period 2007–2013', Brussels: European Commission.

European Communities and OECD (2008), *Report on the Implementation of the Euro-Mediterranean Charter for Enterprise: 2008 Enterprise Policy Assessment*, prepared by the European Commission Directorate-General for Enterprise and Industry, the Private Sector Development Division of the OECD and the European Training Foundation, Luxembourg: Office of the Official Publications of the European Communities.

FEMISE (Forum Euroméditerranéen des Instituts Economiques) (2006a), *Micro and Small Enterprises in Lebanon*, Research Report Series No. 0417, Research No. FEM21-31, December, directed by K. Hamdan, FEMISE Research Programme 2002–2004, Marseilles, France: Institut de la Méditerranée.

FEMISE (2006b), *Women and Economic Development in the Mediterranean*, coordinated by S. Radwan and J-L. Reiffers, April, Marseilles, France: Institut de la Méditerranée.

FEMISE (2008), *Analysis and Proposals of the Euro-Mediterranean Forum of Economic Institutes*, FEMISE Report on the Euro-Mediterranean Partnership, Marseilles, France: Institut de la Méditerranée.

FEMISE (2009), *Les Pays Partenaires Méditerranéens Face à la Crise*, Rapport du FEMISE sur le partenariat Euro-Méditerranéen, Marseilles, France: Institut de la Méditerranée.

FSAP (Financial Sector Assessment Program) (2004), 'Algeria FSA/ Financial Sector Assessment', Washington, DC, USA: World Bank and International Monetary Fund.

Furman, J.J., M.E. Porter and S. Stern (2001), 'The Determinants of National Innovative Capacity', Washington, DC, USA: National Bureau of Economic Research.

Gabr, H. and A. Hoffman (2006), 'A General Policy Framework for Entrepreneurship,' FORA, Division for Research and Analysis, Copenhagen, Denmark: Ministry of Business and Economic Affairs.

Galal, A. (2004), 'The Economics of Formalization: Potential Winners and Losers from Business Formalization', Working Paper No. 95, March, Cairo, Egypt: The Egyptian Center for Economic Studies.

GAFI (General Authority for Investment) (2008), 'Small and Medium Investment (SMI): a window of opportunity for Egypt', November, Cairo, Egypt: Ministry of Investment.

Gallup Organization (2007), 'Entrepreneurship Survey of the EU (25 Member States), United States, Iceland and Norway, Analytical Report', Flash Barometer, Brussels: European Commission.

Goheer, N. (2008), 'Reforming the Business Environment for Small Enterprises in Syria: Challenges and Recommendations', prepared for the International Labour Office (ILO), Regional Office for Arab States.

GONU (Government of National Unity) (2006), 'Proposal to National Multi-Donor Trust Fund: Sudan Microenterprise Development', presented by the Central Bank of Sudan, the Ministry of Finance and National Economy and the Ministry of Investment, August, Khartoum, Sudan.

Gries, T. and W. Naudé (2008), 'Entrepreneurship and Structural Economic Transformation', Research Paper No. 2008/62, June, UNI-WIDER, World Institute for Development Economics Research, Helsinki, Finland: United Nations University.

Habib, M. and S. White (2007), 'UNDP Private Sector Benchmark Study', prepared for the UNDP's Private Sector Division, New York, USA: UNDP.

Hall, J.C. and R.S. Sobel (2008), 'Institutions, Entrepreneurship, and Regional Differences in Economic Growth', *Southern Journal of Entrepreneurship*, **1**(1), 69–96.

Hamid, M., I. Abu Hantash, M. Khalifa and O. Salah (2009), *International Experiences in Supporting MSMEs: Lessons for Palestine*, Ramallah, Palestine: Palestine Economic Policy Research Institute (MAS).

Hammouda, N-E. and M. Assassi (2007), 'Essai sur le potentiel entrepreneurial en Algérie', ERF 14th Annual Conference, 28–30 December, Cairo, Egypt.

Hammouda, N-E. and M. Assassi (2008), 'Potentiel entrepreneurial en Algérie: Entre capital humain et informalité, quelle croissance?' Working Paper No. 433, Cairo, Egypt: Economic Research Forum.

Harberger, A.C. (2005), 'On the Process of Growth and Economic Policy in Developing Countries', PPC Issue Paper No. 13, December, Washington, DC, USA: USAID.

Hattab, H. (2009), *Global Entrepreneurship Monitor: Egypt Entrepreneurship Report 2008*, Cairo, Egypt: British University in Egypt and Industrial Modernisation Centre.

HCP (Haut-Commissariat au Plan) (2009), *Activité, Emploi et Chômage Année 2008*, Premiers résultats, Division des enquêtes sur l'emploi, Direction de la statistique, Rabat, Maroc: Royaume du Maroc.

HCST (Higher Council for Science and Technology) (2004), *Strategy of The Higher Council for Science and Technology 2005–2010*, prepared by the General Secretariat, August, Amman, Jordan: Hashemite Kingdom of Jordan.

Henrekson, M. (2007), 'Entrepreneurship and Institutions', IFN Working Paper No. 707, Stockholm, Sweden: Research Institute of Industrial Economics.

Heritage Foundation (2009), *2009 Index of Economic Freedom*, Washington, DC, USA: Heritage Foundation, and New York, USA: Dow Jones & Company.

Heritage Foundation (2010), *2010 Index of Economic Freedom, The Link Between Economic Opportunity and Prosperity,* Washington, DC, USA: Heritage Foundation and Dow Jones & Company.

HKJ (Hashemite Kingdom of Jordan) (2008), *Jordan in Figures 2007*, Issue 10, May, Amman, Jordan.

Holmes, K., E. Feulner and M.A. O'Grady (2008), *2008 Index of Economic Freedom*, Washington, DC, USA: Heritage Foundation and Dow Jones & Company.

Huitfeldt, H. and N. Kabbani (2005), 'Labour force participation, employment and returns to education in Syria', 12th Annual Conference of the Economic Research Forum, 19–20 December, Cairo, Egypt.

Husrieh, A. (2005), 'Public Policy Research and Studies Program', University of Kalamoon, 4 June, Damasus, Syria: University of Kalamoon.

IDRC (International Development Research Centre) (2004), 'The Private Sector and Development: Scan of Activities and Research', prepared for the Private Sector Development Task Force by K. McKague, Schulich School of Business, York University, 18 October, Ottawa, Canada: IDRC.

IDRC (2006), 'In Focus: A Mapping Study of Current and Future Private

Sector Development (PSD) Research at IDRC', Working Draft for internal IDRC use only, October, prepared by L.N. Semeluk, Ottawa, Canada: IDRC.

IDRC (2008a), 'Final Workshop Report: Regional Workshop on Project to Support Private Sector Development and SME Development Efforts in MENA Countries, November 20–21, 2007', February, Cairo, Egypt: IDRC.

IDRC (2008b), 'Roundtable Proceedings Report', MENA Region Roundtable to Discuss the MENA SME Observatory and Entrepreneurship Monitor Project, October 13–14, 2008', November, Cairo, Egypt: IDRC.

IDRC (2010), *Global Entrepreneurship Monitor: GEM-MENA Regional Report 2009*, Middle East/North Africa Regional Office, Cairo, Egypt: IDRC.

IFC (International Finance Corporation) (2004), *PSD Gender Notes*, Vol. 1, Issue 1, May, Washington, DC, USA.

IFC (2005), *Yemen Gender Entrepreneurship Markets (GEM) Study*, Washington, DC, USA.

IFC (2007), *Assessment of MSE Financial Needs in Yemen, Final Report*, December, Washington, DC, USA: International Bank for Reconstruction and Development/World Bank.

IFC and CAWTAR (Center of Arab Women for Training and Research) (2007), *Women Entrepreneurs in the Middle East and North Africa: Characteristics, Contributions and Challenges*, IFC Gender Entrepreneurship Markets and the Center of Arab Women for Training and Research (CAWTAR), June, Washington, DC, USA: International Finance Corporation/World Bank Group.

ILO (International Labour Organization) (n.d.), 'Economically-Active Population Estimates and Projections 1980–2020', Geneva, Switzerland, available at http://laborsta-ilo.org (accessed 4 February 2010).

ILO (2006), *Decent Work Country Programme, Jordan*, August, Geneva, Switzerland: ILO.

ILO (2008a), *Decent Work Country Programme 2008–2010, Republic of Yemen*, July, Geneva, Switzerland: ILO.

ILO (2008b), *Global Employment Trends for Youth*, Employment and Labour Market Analysis Department, October, Geneva: International Labour Office.

ILO and CAWTAR (2008a), *Gender Equality and Workers' Rights in the Informal Economies of the Arab States: A Regional Overview*, July, ILO Regional Office of the Arab States and Center of Arab Women for Training and Research (CAWTAR).

ILO and CAWTAR (2008b), 'Unprotected Employment in the West Bank

and Gaza Strip: A Gender Equality and Workers' Rights Perspective', Geneva, Switzerland: International Labour Organization.
IMD International (2009), *World Competitiveness Yearbook 2009*, Lausanne, Switzerland: IMD International.
IMF (International Monetary Fund) (2008a), 'First Review of Performance under the 2007–2008 Staff-Monitored Program', prepared by the Middle East and Central Asia Department, 15 May, Washington, DC, USA: IMF.
IMF (2008b), 'Tunisia – Concluding Statement of the Article IV Consultation Mission June 9', Washington, DC, USA: IMF.
IMF (2009a), *IMF Country Report No. 09/100*, Washington, DC, USA: IMF.
IMF (2009b), *Regional Economic Outlook, Middle East and Central Asia*, World Economic and Financial Surveys, October, Washington, DC, USA: IMF.
IMF (2010), 'World Economic Outlook Database', April 2010 edition, World Economic and Financial Surveys, Washington, DC, USA: IMF.
ITUC (International Trade Union Confederation) (2008), 'Internationally Recognised Core Labour Standards in Jordan', report for the WTO General Council Review of the Trade Policies in Jordan, Geneva, 10–12 November, Amman, Jordan.
IZDIHAR (Iraq Private Sector Growth and Employment Generation) (2006a), 'Excess Employment in State Owned Enterprises in Iraq', produced for review by USAID, June, Baghdad, Iraq.
IZDIHAR (2006b), 'Iraq Competitiveness Analysis', Final Report, produced for review by USAID, May, Baghdad, Iraq.
IZDIHAR (2007a), 'An Overview of the Iraqi Banking System', produced for review by USAID, March, Baghdad, Iraq.
IZDIHAR (2007b), 'The Iraq Microfinance Strategy', produced for review by USAID, February, Baghdad, Iraq.
JCPPR (Jordan Centre for Public Policy Research and Dialogue) (2006), *The Jordanian Economy into the Third Millennium*, prepared in conjunction with Capital Investments, Amman, Jordan: Capital Bank of Jordan.
JEDCO (Jordan Enterprise Development Corporation) (2009), 'The Jordan Enterprise Venture Capital Programme: Early Stage Fund – Capital-for-Growth Fund. Revised Call for Proposals', 20 May, Amman, Jordan.
JNCT (Jordan National Competitiveness Team) (2007), *Jordan's Competitiveness Report 2007*, Amman, Jordan: Ministry of Planning and International Cooperation.

Joekes, S. and P. Evans (2008), *Competition and Development: The Power of Competitive Markets*, Ottawa, Canada: International Development Research Centre.

Kabbani, N. (2009), 'Why Young Syrians Prefer Public Sector Jobs. Policy Outlook', Middle East Youth Initiative, March, Dubai: Wolfensohn Center for Development at Brookings, Dubai School of Government.

Kabbani, N. and N. Kamel (2007), 'Youth Exclusion in Syria: Social, Economic, and Institutional Determinants', Middle East Youth Initiative Working Paper Number 4, September, Dubai: Wolfensohn Center for Development, Dubai School of Government.

Karadeniz, E. and O. Ozdemir (2009), 'Entrepreneurship in Turkey and Developing Countries: A Comparison of Activities, Characteristics, Motivation and Environment for Entrepreneurship', *MIBES Transactions*, **3**(1), 30–45.

Karatas, A. and A.D. Helvacioglu (2008), 'The Microcredit Strategies for SMEs in Turkey in the EU Harmonization Process', presented at the Eighth Global Conference on Business and Economics, 18–19 October, Florence, Italy.

Khalifa, M. and I. Abu Hantash (2009), *Evaluation of the Legal Environment of Micro, Small and Medium Enterprises in Palestine*, Ramallah, Palestine: Palestine Economic Policy Research Institute (MAS).

Kheir-El-Din, H. and H. El-Laithy (2006), 'An Assessment of Growth, Distribution and Poverty in Egypt: 1990–91 to 2004–05', Working Paper No. 115, Cairo, Egypt: The Egyptian Center for Economic Studies (ECES).

Kirzner, I.M. (1980), *The Prime Mover of Progress: The Entrepreneur in Capitalism and Socialism*, London, UK: Institute of Economic Affairs.

Klapper, L. (2007), 'New Data on Business Creation and How to Promote It', *Viewpoint Entrepreneurship*, Financial and Private Sector Development Vice Presidency, Note Number 316, August, Washington, DC, USA: World Bank Group.

Klapper, L., R. Amit and M.F. Guillén (2009), 'Entrepreneurship and Firm Formation Across Countries', June, Washington, DC, USA: World Bank. (Forthcoming in Lerner, J. and A. Schoar (eds), *International Differences in Entrepreneurship*, Cambridge, MA, USA: National Bureau of Economic Research.)

Klein, M. and B. Hadjimichael (2003), *The Private Sector in Development: Entrepreneurship, Regulation and Competitive Disciplines*, Report No. 26290, May, Washington, DC, USA: World Bank.

KOM (Kingdom of Morocco) (2008), *Millennium Development Goals, National Report 2007*, September, Rabat, Morocco.

Kraay, A. (2004), 'When is Growth Pro-Poor? Cross-Country Evidence',

IMF Working Papers WP/04/07, March, Washington, DC, USA: International Monetary Fund.
Kuchta-Helbling, C. (2000), 'Background Paper – Barriers to Participation: The Informal Sector in Emerging Democracies', prepared for the workshop, Barriers to Participation: The Informal Economy in Emerging Democracies', November, World Movement for Democracy, Second Global Assembly, Sao Paulo, Brazil, Washington, DC, USA: Centre for International Private Enterprise (CIPE).
LaPorta, R. and A. Shleifer (2008), 'The Unofficial Economy and Economic Development', Working Paper 14520, December, Cambridge, MA, USA: National Bureau of Economic Research.
Lazonick, W. (2008), 'Entrepreneurial Ventures and the Developmental State: Lessons from the Advanced Economies', Discussion Paper No. 2008/01, January, UNI-WIDER, Helsinki, Finland: United Nations University.
Levie, J. and E. Autio (2008), 'A Theoretical Grounding and Test of the GEM Model', *Small Business Economics*, **31**(3), 235–63.
Lingelbach, D. and L. de la Viña (2005), 'What's Distinctive About Growth-Oriented Entrepreneurship in Developing Countries?' Center for Global Entrepreneurship, Working Paper 1, San Antonio, TX, USA: University of Texas San Antonio College of Business.
Looney, R. (2005), 'A Plan for Revitalizing the Iraqi Economy', *Strategic Insights,* **6**(8), National Security Affairs Department, Center for Contemporary Conflict, Monterey, California, USA: Naval Postgraduate School.
Lundström, A. and L. Stevenson (2005), *Entrepreneurship Policy: Theory and Practice,* New York, USA: Springer.
Lyman, T.R. and K. Lauer (2005), 'Diagnostic Report on the Legal and Regulatory Environment for Microfinance in Jordan', June, Washington, DC, USA: Consultative Group to Assist the Poor (CGAP).
Lynch, M.M. (2003), 'Evaluation of the Small, Medium and Micro Enterprise Policy Development Project', prepared for the International Development Research Centre, November, Ottawa, Canada: International Development Research Centre.
MAGG (Ministère des Affaires Générale du Gouvernement) (1999), *Le Livre Blanc: La Petite et Moyenne Entreprise, Moteur de la Croissance Économique*, Rabat, Maroc: Royaume du Maroc.
Mallat, G. (2006), 'Review of Business and Commercial Legislation to Enhance Business Development in Lebanon', prepared for the SME Support Programme, May, Beirut, Lebanon.
MAS (Palestine Economic Policy Research Institute) (2005), *Report: Financing Palestinian SMEs*, Ramallah, Palestine.

MAS (2007a), *Business Development Services in the Palestinian Territory: Analysis of Demand and Supply Conditions*, Ramallah, Palestine.

MAS (2007b), *Policies to Promote Entrepreneurship Among Young People in the West Bank and Gaza Strip*, Ramallah, Palestine.

MAS and PCBS (Palestinian Central Bureau of Statistics) (2005), *Structure and Characteristics of the Palestinian Informal Economic Sector*, Ramallah, Palestine.

MBRF (Mohammed bin Rashid Al Maktoum Foundation) and the UNDP/RBAS (United Nations Development Programme/Regional Bureau for the Arab States) (2009), *Arab Knowledge Report: Towards Productive Intercommunication for Knowledge*, Dubai, United Arab Emirates.

MCIT (Ministry of Communications and Information Technology) (2007), 'The Egyptian Vision Towards Building R&D Strategy for Innovative ICT', IST Africa 2007, 9–11 May, Maputo, Mozambique.

MDIC (Ministry of Development and International Cooperation) (2007), *Towards a New Level of Growth: 11th Five-year Economic and Social Development Plan 2007–2011*, June, Tunis, Tunisia: Republic of Tunisia.

MICMANE (Ministère de l'Industrie, du Commerce et de la Mise à Niveau de l'Économie) (2005), 'Rapport national sur la mise en œuvre de la Chartre Euro-méditerranéenne pour l'Entreprise au Maroc', Juin, Rabat, Maroc: Royaume du Maroc.

MICNT (Ministry of Industry, Commerce and New Technologies) and DPTIT (Department of Post, Telecommunications, and Information Technologies) (2007), *E-Morocco 2010 Strategy: Accomplishments, Perspectives and Action Plans*, Reference Book (summary version), October, Rabat, Morocco: Kingdom of Morocco.

MIEPME (Ministère de l'Industrie, de l'Energie et des Petites et Moyennes Entreprises) (2005), 'Mise en Œuvre par la Tunisie de la Chartre Euro-Méditerranéenne Pour l'Entreprise', Octobre, Tunis, Tunisie: Republique Tunisienne.

Migliorisi, S. and M. Galmarini (2004), 'Donor Assistance for Investment Climate Reforms and Direct Support to Firms: An Overview of Available Data', background paper for the World Development Report 2005, July, Washington, DC, USA: World Bank.

Ministry of Industry (2006), 'Euro-Mediterranean Charter for Enterprise Country Report, Syria', June, Damascus, Syria: Syrian Arab Republic.

Ministry of National Education (2007), *National Education Statistics: Formal Education 2006–2007*, Ankarat, Turkey: Republic of Turkey.

MIT (Ministry of Industry and Trade) (2007), 'Regional Competitiveness Operational Programme (CCI no. 2007 TR 16 1 PO 003)', November, Ankara, Turkey.

MNE (Ministry of National Economy) (2005), 'National Report–Implementation of the Euro-Mediterranean Charter for Enterprises Palestine 2005', Ramallah, Palestine.

MoE (Ministry of Economy) (1998), *A Draft National Policy on Small and Medium Enterprise Development in Egypt*, Cairo, Egypt: Ministry of Economy.

MoET (Ministry of Economy and Trade) (2005), 'Charter Process in Lebanon: Country Report 2005', SME Support Unit, December, Beirut, Lebanon: Ministry of Economy and Trade.

MoET (2006a), 'SMEs Business and Market Review', Final Report, SME Support Programme, August, prepared by Consultation & Research Institute, Beirut, Lebanon.

MoET (2006b), 'SMEs Business and Market Review, Wave 2 – Post War', Final Report, SME Support Programme, November, Beirut, Lebanon.

MoET (2008), 'The Integrated SME Support Programme (Outline of an SME Strategy)', Beirut, Lebanon, available at http://www.economy.gov.lb/NR/rdonlyres/C94D11AC-64F8-42DC-A2CB-B04FB18B2F4E/0/TowardssettinganSMEstrategyinlebanonpresentedonAug22008.pdf (accessed 3 January 2009).

MoET (2009), 'First Syrian SME Strategy: SME Strategy 2010–2014', SME Secretariat, October, Damascus, Syria: Ministry of Economy and Trade.

MoF (Ministry of Finance) (2004), *Enhancing Competitiveness for SMEs in Egypt: General Framework and Action Plan*, Cairo, Egypt: Ministry of Finance.

Ministry of National Education (2007), *National Education Statistics: Formal Education 2006–2007*, Ankara: Republic of Turkey.

MOP (Ministry of Planning) (2005), *Medium Term Development Plan 2005–2007*, Ramallah, Palestine: Palestinian National Authority.

Morrison, A., D. Raju and N. Sinha (2007), 'Gender Equality, Poverty and Economic Growth', Policy Research Working Paper 4349, September, Gender and Development Group, Poverty Reduction and Economic Management Network, Washington, DC, USA: World Bank.

Moulin, H. (1988), *Axioms of Cooperative Decision Making*,' Cambridge, UK, New York, USA, and Melbourne, AU: Cambridge University Press.

MPDC (Ministry of Planning and Development Cooperation) (2005a), *Iraq Living Conditions Survey 2004*, May, Baghdad, Iraq.

MPDC (2005b), *The National Development Strategy 2005–2007*, Iraqi Strategic Review Board, June, Baghdad, Iraq: Republic of Iraq.

MPDC (2007), *The National Development Strategy 2007–2010*, March, Baghdad, Iraq: Republic of Iraq.

MPIC (Ministry of Planning and International Cooperation) (2004), *The*

National Social and Economic Development Plan (2004–2006), Amman, Jordan: Hashemite Kingdom of Jordan.

MPIC (2005), *Yemen's Strategic Vision 2025*, Sana'a, Yemen: Republic of Yemen.

MPIC (2006), *The National Agenda 2006–2015, the Jordan We Strive For*, Amman, Jordan: Hashemite Kingdom of Jordan.

MPIC (2008), *National Strategy for Microfinance*, Amman, Jordan: Hashemite Kingdom of Jordan.

MPMEA (Ministère de la Petite et Moyenne Entreprise et de l'Artisanat) (2004), *ACTES des assises Nationale de la PME*, Janvier, Alger, Algérie: République Algérienne Démocratique et Populaire.

MPMEA (2008), 'Bulletin d'information économique N° 12, indicateurs pour l'année 2007', Direction des systèmes d'information et des statistiques, Alger, Algérie: République Algérienne Démocratique et Populaire.

MPMEA (2009), 'Bulletin d'information statistique N° 14, indicateurs pour l'année 2008', Direction des systèmes d'information et des statistiques, Alger, Algérie: République Algérienne Démocratique et Populaire.

Muasher, M. (2008), *The Arab Center: The Promise of Moderation*, New Haven, CT, USA and London, UK: Yale University Press.

Mutwakil, M.A.A. and A. Magdi (2006), 'Private Sector Development in Sudan: Investing in Peace', presentation to Sudan Development Program, Dubai, United Arab Emirates, February, Washington, DC, USA: World Bank.

Nasnas, R. (2007), *Emerging Lebanon: Towards an Economic and Social Vision*, January, Beirut, Lebanon: Éditions Dar An-Nahar.

Naudé, W. (2008), 'Entrepreneurship in Economic Development', Discussion Paper No. 2008/20, UNI-WIDER, World Institute for Development Economics Research, March, Helsinki, Finland: United Nations University.

Naudé, W. (2009), 'Out with the Sleaze, In with the Ease: Insufficient for Entrepreneurship Development?' Discussion Paper No. 2009/01, UNI-WIDER, World Institute for Development Economics Research, January, Helsinki, Finland: United Nations University.

NCSP (National Council for Strategic Planning) (2007), *The Five-Year Plan (2007–2011)*, Khartoum, Sudan: Republic of Sudan.

Nehlawi, Z (2007), 'SHABAB: Marching into the Private Sector', *Forward Magazine,* September, Damascus, Syria.

Noland, M. and H. Pack (2007), *The Arab Economies in a Changing World*, April, Washington, DC, USA: Peterson Institute for International Economics.

Noutary, E. (2008), *Funding Start-ups and SME Innovation: A Guide throughout MENA Countries, Medibtikar Guidebook*, ANIMA Investment Network, April, ANIMA-Medibtikar.

Nyström, K. (2008), 'The institutions of economic freedom and entrepreneurship: evidence from panel data', *Public Choice*, **136**(3–4), 269–82.

OBG (Oxford Business Group) (2009), 'The Report: Syria', London, UK.

ODI (Overseas Development Institute) (2006), 'Independent Evaluation of the SMEPOL Project: Impact, Lessons and Options for Replication', prepared by J. Court and D. Osborne for the International Development Research Centre, Regional Office for the Middle East and North Africa, Cairo, Egypt: International Development Research Centre.

OECD (Organisation for Economic Co-operation and Development) (1994), 'DAC Orientations for Development Co-operation in Support of Private Sector Development', Paris: OECD.

OECD (1995), *Support of Private Sector Development*, Development Co-operation Guidelines Series, Development Assistance Committee, Paris: OECD.

OECD (2002), *Handbook on Measuring the Non-observed Economy*, Paris: OECD.

OECD (2004a), *Accelerating Pro-Poor Growth through Support for Private Sector Development: An Analytical Framework*, DAC Network on Poverty Reduction, Paris: OECD.

OECD (2004b), 'Economic Survey of Turkey, 2004, Policy Brief', *OECD Observer*, Paris: OECD.

OECD (2004c), *Small and Medium Enterprises in Turkey, Issues and Policies*, Paris: OECD.

OECD (2005a), 'MENA-OECD Investment Programme: Fostering an Entrepreneurial Business Environment for Firm Creation and SME Growth in the MENA Region: Background Report, Conclusions and Recommendations', CFE/SME(2005)19, Working Party on SMEs and Entrepreneurship, 28 October, Paris: OECD.

OECD (2005b), *Mobilising Private Investment for Development: Policy Lessons on the Role of ODA*, Paris: OECD.

OECD (2006), *Promoting Pro-Poor Growth: Policy Guidance to Donors on Supporting Private Sector Development*, Development Cooperation Directorate Development Assistance Committee, Paris: OECD.

OECD (2007a), *Business for Development: Fostering the Private Sector*, Development Centre, Paris: OECD.

OECD (2007b), 'Lebanon National Investment Reform Agenda Workshop, Background Paper for Session IV, Improving the Entrepreneurial Finance: Venture Capital and Access to Credit for SMEs', prepared

by A. Kolderstova, Financial Sector, MENA-OECD Investment Programme, Paris: OECD.
OECD (2007c), 'MENA-OECD Women Business Forum, Concept Note', MENA-OECD Investment Programme, Paris: OECD.
OECD (2008a), *Making Reforms Succeed: Moving Forward with the MENA Investment Policy Agenda*, Private Sector Development in the Middle East and North Africa, Paris: OECD.
OECD (2008b), *OECD Economic Outlook – Preliminary Edition*, Paris: OECD.
OECD (2008c), *OECD Science, Technology and Industry Outlook 2008*, Paris: OECD.
OECD (2009a), *Economic Policy Reforms: Going for Growth*, Structural Policy Indicators, Priorities and Analysis, Paris: OECD.
OECD (2009b), 'Evaluation of Programmes Concerning Education for Entrepreneurship', OECD Working Party on SMEs and Entrepreneurship, Paris: OECD.
OECD (2009c), 'High-level Meeting of the Task Force on Economic Reforms and Private Sector Capacity – Summary', 20–21 January, MENA-OECD Initiative on Governance and Investment for Development, Middle East and North Africa, Paris: OECD.
OECD (2009d), *Is Informal Normal? Towards More and Better Jobs in Developing Countries*, Paris: OECD.
OECD (2009e), *Measuring Entrepreneurship: A Collection of Indicators 2009 Edition*, OECD-Eurostat Entrepreneurship Indicators Project, Paris: OECD Statistics Directorate.
OECD (2009f), 'SMEs in Turkey and SME Support Mechanism of the Small and Medium Industry Development Organisation (KOSGEB)', 35th Session of the Working Party on SMEs and Entrepreneurship (WPSMEE), 4–5 June, Room Document No 1, Warsaw, Poland, Paris: OECD.
ONEQ (Observatoire National de l'Emploi et des Qualifications) (2008), 'Statistiques de l'emploi 2008', Décembre, Ministère de l'Emploi et de l'Insertion des Professionnelles des Jeunes, Tunis, Tunisie: République Tunisienne.
ONS (Office National des Statistiques) (2008), 'Emploi et chômage (au quatrième trimestre 2008)', Statistiques Sociales, Alger, Algérie: République Algérienne Démocratique et Populaire.
ONS (2009), 'Emploi et chômage au 4ème trimestre 2009', Statistiques Sociales, Alger, Algérie: République Algérienne Démocratique et Populaire.
Ovaska, T. and R.S. Sobel (2005), 'Entrepreneurship in Post-Socialist Economies', *Journal of Private Enterprise*, **21**, 8–28.

Özar, S. (2004), *Micro and Small Enterprises in Turkey: Uneasy Development*, Research Report Series No. 0420, Cairo, Egypt: Economic Research Forum.

Palmade, V. (2005), 'Industry-Level Analysis: The Way to Identify the Binding Constraints to Economic Growth', *Small Enterprise Journal*, **16**(4), 19–31.

Papps, K.l. (2008), 'The Effect of Social Security Taxes and Minimum Wages on Employment Growth in Turkey', presented at the Third IZA/World Bank Conference on Employment and Development, 5–6 May, Rabat, Morocco.

PCBS (Palestinian Central Bureau of Statistics) (2007), *Labor Force Survey Database 2000–2006*, Ramallah, Palestine: Palestinian National Authority.

PCBS (2008), *Economic Establishments, Main Findings: Population, Housing and Establishment Census 2007*, May, Ramallah, Palestine: Palestinian National Authority.

PCBS (2009a), 'Labour Force Survey (April–June, 2009) Round (Q2/2009)', 17 August, Ramallah, Palestine: Palestinian National Authority.

PCBS (2009b), 'On the occasion of May 1, International Workers' Day the Palestinian Central Bureau of Statistics (PCBS) issues a Press Release: The Labour Force in the Palestinian Territory', available at http://www.pcbs.gov.ps/DesktopDefault.aspx?tabID=3355&lang=en (accessed 7 February 2010).

Perry, G.E., O. Arias, P. Fajnzylber, W.F. Maloney, A. Mason and J. Saavedra-Chanduvi (2007), *Informality: Exit and Exclusion, Building Effective and Legitimate Institutions*, World Bank Latin American and Caribbean Studies, May, Washington, DC, USA: World Bank.

PlaNet Finance (2007), 'National Impact and Market Study of Microfinance in Jordan', presented to the Ministry of Planning and International Cooperation and the Agence Française de Développement, Paris.

PlaNet Finance (2008), *National Impact Survey of Microfinance in Egypt*, prepared with support from the Small and Medium Enterprise Policy (SMEPol) Development Project; the Egyptian Ministry of Finance; the Canadian International Development Agency (CIDA); the International Development Research Centre (IDRC); the German Technical Cooperation (GTZ); the Social Fund for Development (SFD)/the United Nations Development Programme (UNDP); First Microfinance Foundation (FMF)/Aga Khan Agency for Microfinance (AKAM); and PlaNet Finance Egypt, Cairo, Egypt.

PMO (Prime Minister's Office) (2003), *Report on Palestinian Reform*, Reform Coordination and Technical Support Unit (RCSU), Cabinet

of the Prime Minister, 8 December, Ramallah, Palestine: Palestinian National Authority.
PNA (Palestinian National Authority) (2007), *Building a Palestinian State: Towards Peace and Prosperity, Palestinian Reform and Development Plan 2008–2010,* Ramallah, Palestine.
Porter, M.E. (1990), *The Competitive Advantage of Nations*, New York, USA: Free Press.
Pratap, S. and E. Quintin (2006), 'The Informal Sector in Developing Countries: Outputs, Assets and Employment', Research Paper No. 2006/130, November, World Institute for Development Economics Research (UNU-WIDER), Helsinki, Finland: United Nations University.
RADP (République Algérienne Démocratique et Populaire) (2001), *Loi N° 01-18 du 12 décembre 2001 portant sur la loi d'orientation sur la promotion des PMEs*, Alger, Algérie.
Razzaz, S. and F. Iqbal (2008), *Job Growth Without Unemployment Reduction: The Experience of Jordan*, 10 April, Washington, DC, USA: World Bank.
Republic of Yemen (2007), *Yemen Poverty Assessment, Vol 1: Main Report*, November, Joint publication with the UNDP and the World Bank, Sana'a, Yemen.
République Tunisienne (2007), 'Loi relative à l'Initiative Economique: Loi n° 2007-69 du décembre 2007', *Journal officiel de la République Tunisienne*, 28–31 décembre, Tunis, Tunisie.
Reynolds, P.D., W.D. Bygrave, E. Autio, L.W. Cox and M. Hay (2003), *Global Entrepreneurship Monitor: 2002 Executive Report*, Wellesley, MA, USA: Babson College and London, UK: London Business School.
Richards, A. and J. Waterbury (2008), *A Political Economy of the Middle East*, 3rd edition, Boulder, CO: Westview Press.
Royaume du Maroc (2002), 'Dahir No 1–2–188 du jourmada I 1423 (23 juiliet 2002) portant promulgation de la loi no 53–00 formant charte de la Petite et Moyenne Entreprise', Bulletin Official no 5036 du Dimanche 5 Septembre, Rabat, Maroc.
RWEL (Role of Women in Economic Life) (2007), Euromed Programme 'Role of Women in Economic Life', *Quarterly Newsletter*, **1**(3).
RWEL (2008a), *Analysis of the Economic Situation of Women in Algeria*, Role of Women in Economic Life Programme, Brussels: Euromed Information Centre.
RWEL (2008b), *Analysis of the Economic Situation of Women in Syria*, Role of Women in Economic Life Programme, Brussels: Euromed Information Centre.
RWEL (2008c), *Comparative Analysis of Economic Situation in Ten South*

Mediterranean Countries, Euromed Role of Women in Economic Life Programme, Brussels: Euromed Information Centre.

RWEL (2008d), *Women's Economic Rights in the South Mediterranean Region: A Comparative Analysis of Law, Regulations, and Practice*, prepared by C.F. El-Solh and N. Hijab for the Euromed Role of Women in Economic Life Programme, Brussels: Euromed Information Centre.

Sala-i-Martin, X., J. Blanke, M. Drzeniek Hanouz, T. Geiger, I. Mia and F. Paua (2008), 'The Global Competitiveness Index: Prioritizing the Economic Policy Agenda', in *The Global Competitiveness Report 2008–2009*, Geneva, Switzerland: World Economic Forum, pp. 3–63.

Saif, I. and Y. Tabbaa (2008), 'Economic Growth, Income Distribution and the Middle Class in Jordan (2002–2006)', Center for Strategic Studies, Amman, Jordan: University of Jordan.

Schmidt, R. (2008), 'Enough Foreign Direct Investment quickens economic growth everywhere', October, Ottawa, Canada: North–South Institute.

Schneider, F. (2005), 'Shadow Economies of 145 Countries all over the World: Estimation Results over the Period 1999 to 2003', Washington, DC, USA: World Bank.

Schneider, F. and A. Buehn (2009), 'Shadow Economies and Corruption all Over the World: Revised Estimates for 120 Countries', Version 2, 27 October, *Economics, the Open-Access-Assessment E-journal*, available at http://economics-ejournal.org/economics/journalarticles/2007-9 (accessed 22 November 2009).

Schneider, F. and F. Savaşan (2005), 'The Size of Shadow Economies of Turkey (and of her Neighbouring Countries) Including an Informal Hiring and Sectoral Analysis of the Turkish Shadow Economy', Department of Economics, Linz-Auhof, Austria: Johannes Kepler Universitat.

Schulpen, L. and P. Gibbon (2002), 'Private Sector Development: Policies, Practices and Problems', *World Development*, **30**(1) 1–15.

SEBC (Syrian Enterprise and Business Centre) (2005), 'Overall Policy Framework for Industrial Private Sector Development', SEBCII/2004/006/PF, May, Damascus, Syria.

SEBC (2007), 'SME Policy Paper Update', Project No. MEDA/2005/17542, SME Support Programme in Syria, Damascus, Syria.

SEBC (2008), 'SME Support Programme, Work Plan 3, 1st September 2008–30th June 2010', Damascus, Syria.

SEC (Small Enterprise Center) (2007a), 'Business Development Services – BDS: Market Analysis in Gaza', Ramallah, Palestine.

SEC (2007b), 'Demands of Micro and Small Enterprises for Business Development Services (BDS) in Gaza', Ramallah, Palestine.

Sekkat, K. (ed.) (2008), *Competition and Efficiency in the Arab World*, New York, USA: Palgrave Macmillan.

Sekkat, K. (2010), 'Economic Policies, Firms' Entry and Exit and Economic Performance: A Cross Country Analysis', in K. Sekkat (ed.), *Market Dynamics and Productivity in Developing Countries: Economic Reforms in the Middle East and North Africa*, a co-publication with the International Development Research Centre, New York, USA, Dordrecht, Netherlands, Heidelberg, Germany and London, UK: Springer, pp. 145–66.

SFD (Social Fund for Development) (2004), *Small and Micro Enterprise Development in Yemen: Strategy and Proposed Action Plan*, Small & Micro Enterprise Development Unit, Sana'a, Yemen.

SFD (2008), *Small & Micro Enterprise Development in Yemen*, Small & Micro Enterprise Development Unit, Sana'a, Yemen.

SFD (2009), 'Mobilizing Egyptian Micro and Small Enterprises in Egypt 2009–2013: National Strategy for Micro and Small Enterprise Development and Blueprint for Initiatives', prepared for the Social Fund for Development with technical assistance from the Canadian International Development Agency (CIDA), Cairo, Egypt.

Shunnar, H. (2008), 'Project for Establishment of SMEs Development Agency in Palestine', presented at meeting of the MENA-OECD Working Group on SME Policy, Entrepreneurship and Human Capital Development, 18 November, Manana, Bahrain.

Sida (Swedish International Development Cooperation Agency) (2004), *Policy Guidelines for Sida's Support to Private Sector Development*, Department of Infrastructure and Economic Co-operation, October, Stockholm, Sweden: Swedish International Development Cooperation Agency.

Silatech (2009), *The Silatech Index: Voices of Young Arabs*, June, Washington, DC, USA: Gallup.

Snodgrass, D. and J.P. Winkler (2004), 'Enterprise Growth Initiatives: Strategic Directions and Options', Final Report, prepared for the US Agency for International Development, Bureau of Economic Growth, Agriculture, and Trade, February, Maryland, USA: Development Alternatives.

Sobel, R.S., J.R. Clark and D.R. Lee (2007), 'Freedom, barriers to entry, entrepreneurship, and economic progress', *Review of Austrian Economics*, **20**, 221–36.

SPC (State Planning Commission) (2005), *The 10th Five Year Plan 2006–2010*, Damascus, Syria: Syrian Arab Republic.

SPO (State Planning Organization) (2004), *SME Strategy and Action Plan*, January, Prime Ministry, Ankara, Turkey: Republic of Turkey.

SPO (2006), *Ninth Development Plan 2007–2013*, Prime Ministry, Ankara, Turkey: Republic of Turkey.

SPO (2008), *2008 Annual Programme (Ninth Development Plan 2007–2013)*, Ankara, Turkey: Prime Ministry, Republic of Turkey.

Stevenson, L. and A. Lundström (2002), *Beyond the Rhetoric: Defining Entrepreneurship Policy and its Best Practice Components*, Stockholm, Sweden: Swedish Foundation for Small Business Research.

Stevenson, L. and A. Lundström (2007), 'Dressing the emperor: the fabric of entrepreneurship policy', in D.B. Audretsch, I. Grilo and A.R. Thurik (eds), *Handbook of Research on Entrepreneurship Policy*, Cheltenham, UK and Northampton, MA, USA: Edward Elgar Publishing, pp. 94–129.

Storey, D. (1994), *Understanding the Small Business Sector*, London, UK and New York, USA: Routledge.

Suliman, O. (2007), 'Current Privatization Policy in Sudan', Policy Brief #52, April, The William Davidson Institute, Ann Arbor, MI, USA: University of Michigan.

Syrquin, M. (1988), 'Patterns of Structural Change', in H. Chenery and T.N. Srinivasan (eds), *Handbook of Development Economics*, Amsterdam, Holland and New York, USA: North-Holland, pp. 203–73.

Tezyetiş, S. (2007), 'SMEs in Turkey & Vision and Supports of KOSGEB', PowerPoint slides, November, available at http://www.dpt.gov.tr/bgyu/abbp/italya/docs/4.Study_Visits/2.Study-visit-II_November_2007.3.materials/8.KOSGEB.pdf (accessed 10 December 2008).

Thurik, A.R., A.R.M. Wennekers and M. Carree (2008), 'The relationship between entrepreneurship and economic development: Is it U-shaped?' Zoetermeer, the Netherlands: EIM Business & Policy Research.

Thurik, R. (2009), 'Entrepreneurship, Economic Growth and Policy in Emerging Economies', Research Paper No. 2009/12, March, UNI-WIDER World Institute for Development Economics Research, Helsinki, Finland: United Nations University.

Tijara (2009), 'The Iraq Microfinance Industry Performance Report Dec 2008', produced for review by USAID, Baghdad, Iraq.

Turan, M. and A. Kara (2007), 'An Exploratory Study of the Characteristics and Attributes of Turkish Entrepreneurs: A Cross-country Comparison to Irish Entrepreneurs', *Journal of International Entrepreneurship*, **5**, 25–46.

Turkstat (Turkish Statistical Institute) (2008a), 'Household Labor Force Survey for the Period of August 2008 (July, August, November 2008)', Press Release No. 181, 17 November, Prime Ministry, Ankara, Turkey: Republic of Turkey.

Turkstat (2008b), *Turkey's Statistical Yearbook 2008*, Ankara, Turkey: Turkish Statistical Institute.

Turkstat (2009), *Turkey in Statistics 2009*, Ankara, Turkey: Turkish Statistical Institute.

UN (United Nations) (1997), 'Enabling Private Sector Development: Characteristics of the Ideal Policy Environment', Report prepared by the Secretariat, Group of Experts on the United Nations Programme on Public Administration and Finance, Meeting of 27 May – 4 June, New York, USA: United Nations.

UN (2005), *Common Country Assessment 2005, Syrian Arab Republic*, Damascus, Syria: United Nations Country Team in Syria.

UN (2006a), *Country Development Assistance Framework 2007–2011*, New York, USA. [Syria]

UN (2006b), *United Nations Development Assistance Framework, Republic of Yemen, 2007–2011*, New York, USA.

UN (2007), *World Population Prospects: The 2006 Revision*, Department of Economic and Social Affairs, Population Division, New York, USA: United Nations.

UN (2008), 'United Nations Development Assistance Framework: Jordan 2008–2012', UN Resident Coordinator Jordan, Amman, Jordan.

UN-ESCWA (United Nations Economic and Social Commission for Western Asia) (2006), 'Lebanon's Rebuilding and Revival: A Policy Paper with Initiatives', Beirut, Lebanon.

UNCTAD (United Nations Conference on Trade and Development) (2004), *Palestinian Small and Medium Enterprises: Dynamics and Contribution to Development*, UNCTAD/GDS/APP/2004/1, New York, USA and Geneva, Switzerland: United Nations.

UNCTAD (2007), *Investment Policy Review of Morocco*, TD/B/COM.2/76, 6 February, Geneva, Switzerland.

UNDP (United Nations Development Programme) (2004), *Unleashing Entrepreneurship: Making Business Work for the Poor*, Report to the Secretary-General of the United Nations, Commission on the Private Sector & Development, March, New York, USA: United Nations Development Programme.

UNDP (2005), 'National Human Development Report 2005: Education and Human Development in Syria, Executive Summary', Damascus, Syria: United Nation Development Programme and the Prime Minister's Office.

UNDP (2006a), *Macroeconomic Policies for Growth, Employment and Poverty Reduction in Yemen*, Sub-Regional Resource Facility for Arab States (SURF-AS), Beirut, Lebanon.

UNDP (2006b), *Macroeconomic Policies for Poverty Reduction: The Case of Sudan*, Khartoum, Sudan: United Nations Development Programme in Sudan.

UNDP (2007a), *Promoting Inclusive Market Development, UNDP Private Sector Development Strategy*, September, New York, USA: United Nations Development Programme.

UNDP (2007b), 'The Economic Status of Syria: A focus on Women's Economic Participation', Office of the Resident Coordinator, Damascus, Syria: United Nations Development Programme in Syria.

UNDP (2008), *Turkey 2008 Human Development Report: Youth in Turkey*, Ankara, Turkey: United Nations Development Programme in Turkey.

UNDP (2009), *Human Development Report 2009, Overcoming Barriers: Human Mobility and Development*, New York, USA: United Nations Development Programme.

UNDP and AFESD (Arab Fund for Economic and Social Development) (2002), *Arab Human Development Report 2002: Creating Opportunities for Future Generations*, Regional Bureau for Arab States, New York: USA: United Nations Development Programme.

UNDP and AFESD (2003), *Arab Human Development Report 2003: Building a Knowledge Society*, Regional Bureau for Arab States, New York, USA: United Nations Publications.

UNDP and AFESD (2006), *The Arab Human Development Report 2005: Towards the Rise of Women in the Arab World*, Regional Bureau for Arab States, New York, USA: United Nations Development Programme.

UNDP and SPC (2007), *The First National Competitiveness Report on the Syrian Economy 2007*, Damascus, Syria.

UNECE (United Nations Economic Commission for Europe) (2008a), *Developing Entrepreneurship in the UNECE Region: Country experience in reducing barriers to enterprise development*, New York, USA and Geneva, Switzerland: United Nations.

UNECE (2008b), *Non-observed Economy in National Accounts: Survey of Country Practices*, New York, USA and Geneva, Switzerland: United Nations.

UNESCO (United Nations Educational, Scientific and Cultural Organization) (2008), 'UNESCO National Education Support Strategy UNESS Jordan', LB/2008/ED/PI/28, Beirut, Lebanon: UNESCO Office.

US Department of State (2009), '2009 Investment Climate Statement – Tunisia', Bureau of Economic, Energy and Business Affairs, Washington, DC, USA.

USAID (United States Agency for International Development) (2005), *Removing Barriers to Formalization: The Case for Reform and Emerging Best Practices*, prepared by Development Alternatives Inc. and Bannock Consulting, Washington, DC, USA: USAID.

USAID (2006), 'The New Generation of Private Sector Development Programming: The Emerging Path to Economic Growth with Poverty Reduction', microREPORT #44, prepared by Development Alternatives, Inc., March, Washington, DC, USA: USAID.

USAID (2007), 'Regulatory Quality and Competitiveness in Morocco', IBCM Report 07-04, prepared by the Improving the Business Climate in Morocco Program, Rabat, Morocco.

USAID (2008a), 'Egypt Economic Performance Assessment', April, Bureau of Economic Growth, Agriculture and Trade, Washington, DC, USA: USAID.

USAID (2008b), 'Morocco's Economic Performance Assessment', Bureau of Economic Growth, Agriculture and Trade, May, Washington, DC, USA: USAID.

USAID (2008c), *Shaping the Future: A Strategy for Economic Growth*, Washington, DC, USA: USAID.

USAID and EMFN (Egyptian Microfinance Network) (2008), *Microfinance Programs Map: Map of Egyptian Microfinance Programs on Governorate/District Level*, April, Cairo, Egypt: USAID.

van Stel, A., D. Storey and A.R. Thurik (2007), 'The Effect of Business Regulations on Nascent and Young Business Entrepreneurship', *Small Business Economics*, **28**(2–3), 171–86.

Verheul, I., S. Wennekers, D. Audretsch and R. Thurik (2001), *An Eclectic Theory of Entrepreneurship: Policies, Institutions and Culture*, EIM Research Report 0012/E, Zoetermeer, Netherlands: EIM Business & Policy Research.

WBG (World Bank Group) (2008), 'Yemen Economic Update', Spring, Sana'a, Yemen: World Bank Office.

WBG (2009), 'Yemen Economic Update', Spring, Sana'a, Yemen: World Bank Office.

WBI (World Bank Institute) (2008), *Measuring Knowledge in the World's Economies, Knowledge Assessment Methodology and Knowledge Economy Index*, Knowledge for Development Program, Washington, DC, USA: World Bank.

WEF (World Economic Forum) (2008a), *The Global Competitiveness Report 2008–2009*, Geneva, Switzerland: WEF.

WEF (2008b), *The Global Gender Gap Report 2008*, authored by R. Hausmann, L. Tyson and S. Zahidi, Geneva, Switzerland: WEF.

WEF (2009a), 'Educating the Next Wave of Entrepreneurs: Unlocking Entrepreneurial Capabilities to Meet the Global Challenge of the 21st Century', A Report of the Global Education Initiative, Geneva: Switzerland: WEF.

WEF (2009b), *The Global Competitiveness Report 2009–2010*, September, Geneva, Switzerland: WEF.

Wennekers, A.R.M. (2006), *Entrepreneurship at Country Level: Economic and Non-Economic Determinants*, ERIM PhD Series in Research in Management, Erasmus Research Institute of Management, Rotterdam, the Netherlands: Erasmus University.

Wennekers, S. and R. Thurik (1999), 'Linking Entrepreneurship and Economic Growth', *Small Business Economics*, **13**, 27–55.

Wennekers, S., A. van Stel, M. Caree and A.R. Thurik (2008), 'The Relationship between Entrepreneurship and Economic Development: Is it U-shaped?' EIM Research Reports H200824, December, SCALES (Scientific Analysis of Entrepreneurship and SMEs), Zoetermeer, the Netherlands: EIM Business & Policy Research.

WFB *(The World Factbook),* Washington, DC, USA: Central Intelligence Agency, available at http://www. cia.gov/library/publications/the-world-factbook/.

White, S. (2008), 'A Conceptual Framework to Guide Research on Private Sector Development in Developing Countries', IDRC Working Papers on Globalization, Growth and Poverty, No 6, August, Ottawa, Canada: International Development Research Centre.

Williamson, J. (2002), 'Did the Washington Consensus Fail?' Outline of the speech at the Center for Strategic and International Studies, 6 November, Washington, DC, USA, available at http://www.peterson-institute.org/publications/papers/paper.cfm?ResearchID=488 (accessed 7 August 2008).

World Bank (2001), 'Engendering Development Through Gender Equality in Rights, Resources and Voice', World Bank Policy Research Report No. 21776, Washington, DC, USA: World Bank.

World Bank (2002), 'Private Sector Development Strategy – Directions for the World Bank Group', 9 April, Washington, DC, USA: World Bank.

World Bank (2003), 'World Bank Group Private Sector Development Strategy Implementation Progress Report', Washington, DC, USA: World Bank.

World Bank (2004a), 'Building a Sustainable Investment Climate in Iraq', Reconstructing Iraq Working Paper No. 1, September, Finance, Private Sector and Infrastructure Development, Middle East and North Africa Region, Washington, DC, USA: World Bank.

World Bank (2004b), 'Gender and Development in the Middle East and North Africa: Women in the Public Sphere', MENA Development Report, Washington, DC, USA: World Bank.

World Bank (2004c), *Republic of Tunisia Development Policy Review:*

Making Deeper Trade Integration Work for Growth and Jobs, Social and Economic Development Group, Middle East and North Africa, Washington, DC, USA: World Bank.
World Bank (2004d), *Unlocking the Employment Potential in the Middle East and North Africa: Towards a New Social Contract*, Washington, DC, USA: International Bank for Reconstruction and Development/ World Bank.
World Bank (2005a), 'Country Assistance Strategy Progress Report for People's Democratic Republic of Algeria for the Period 2004–2006', Report No. 32956-DZ, 27 July, Washington, DC, USA: World Bank.
World Bank (2005b), 'The Economic Advancement of Women in Jordan: A Country Gender Assessment', Social and Economic Development Group, Middle East and North Africa Region (MENA), Washington, DC, USA: World Bank.
World Bank (2005c), 'Economic Growth in the 1990s: Lessons Learned from a Decade of Reform', Poverty Reduction and Economic Management (PREM) Network, Washington, DC, USA: World Bank.
World Bank (2005d), *The Status and Progress of Women in the Middle East and North Africa*, June, World Bank Middle East and North Africa Social & Economic Development Group, Washington, DC, USA: World Bank.
World Bank (2005e), *Syrian Investment Climate Assessment: Unlocking the Potential of the Private Sector*, Middle East and North Africa Region, 8 June, Washington, DC, USA: World Bank.
World Bank (2005f), *World Development Report 2005: A Better Investment Climate for Everyone*, Washington, DC, USA: World Bank and Oxford University Press.
World Bank (2006a), 'Entrepreneurship', in *Viewpoint*, Note Number 313, November. Financial and Private Sector Development Vice Presidency, Washington, DC, USA: World Bank Group.
World Bank (2006b), *Fostering Higher Growth and Employment in the Kingdom of Morocco*, A World Bank Country Study, No. 37100, Washington, DC, USA: World Bank.
World Bank (2006c), *Is There a New Vision for Maghreb Economic Integration*? Social and Economic Development Group, Middle East and North Africa, Washington, DC, USA: World Bank.
World Bank (2006d), 'Private Sector in MENA', Sector Brief, September, Washington, DC, USA: World Bank.
World Bank (2006e), 'Sudan Multi Donor Trust Funds, First Progress Report, Reporting Period July 1 – December 31, 2005', Multi Donor Trust Fund – National, Technical Secretariat, Khartoum, Sudan: World Bank.

World Bank (2006f), 'Turkey Labor Market Survey', Report No. 33254-TR, April, Poverty Reduction and Economic Management Unit, Europe and Central Asia Region, Washington, DC, USA: World Bank.

World Bank (2007a), *Doing Business 2008 Middle East and North Africa (MENA)*, Washington, DC, USA: International Bank for Reconstruction and Development/ World Bank.

World Bank (2007b), *2007 Economic Development and Prospects: Job Creation in an Era of High Growth*, Middle East and North Africa Region, Washington, DC, USA: World Bank.

World Bank (2007c), *The Environment for Women's Entrepreneurship in the Middle East and North Africa Region*, Washington, DC, USA: World Bank.

World Bank (2007d), 'Investing in Palestinian Economic Reform and Development', Report for the Pledging Conference, 17 December, Paris, Washington, DC, USA: World Bank.

World Bank (2007e), *Turkey Investment Climate Assessment*, (2 vols), Report No. 41611-TR, Finance and Private Sector Development Department, Europe and Central Asia Region, Washington, DC, USA: World Bank.

World Bank (2008a), '*Access to Finance and Economic Growth in Egypt*, a study led by S. Nasr, Middle East and North Africa Region, Washington, DC, USA: World Bank.

World Bank (2008b), *Doing Business 2009: Comparing Regulations in 181 Countries*, Washington, DC, USA: International Bank for Reconstruction and Development/ World Bank.

World Bank (2008c), *Doing Business 2009 Middle East & North Africa: Comparing Regulations in 181 Countries*, Washington, DC, USA: International Bank for Reconstruction and Development/World Bank.

World Bank (2008d), *2008 Economic Developments and Prospects: Regional Integration for Global Competitiveness*, Middle East and North Africa Region, June, Washington, DC, USA: World Bank.

World Bank (2008e), *Global Development Prospects 2009: Commodity Markets at the Crossroads*, Washington, DC, USA: World Bank.

World Bank (2008f), 'International Development Association Interim Strategy Note for the Republic of Sudan', Report No. 43036-SD, March, Sudan Country Management Unit, Africa Region, Khartoum, Sudan: World Bank.

World Bank (2008g), *The Road Not Traveled: Education Reform in the Middle East and North Africa*, MENA Development Report, Washington, DC, USA: World Bank.

World Bank (2008h), 'Third Sudan Consortium: Joint Staff Assessment Report', May 2008, Oslo.

World Bank (2008i), 'Top 10 Reformers from Doing Business 2009', Washington, DC, USA: World Bank Group.

World Bank (2008j), 'Tunisia's Global Integration: Second Generation of Reforms to Boost Growth and Employment', Draft Report No. 40129-TN, Social and Economic Development Sector Unit, Middle East and North Africa Region, May, Washington, DC, USA.

World Bank (2008k), 'Turkey Country Economic Memorandum: Sustaining High Growth, Selected Issues', 10 April, Washington, DC, USA: World Bank.

World Bank (2008l), 'Yemen Development Policy Review', Report No. 35393-RY, Social and Economic Development Sector Unit, Middle East and North Africa Region, Washington, DC, USA: World Bank.

World Bank (2009a), 'Country Brief, Algeria', April, Washington, DC, USA, available at http://go.worldbank.org/T2K4PW3270 (accessed 16 July 2009).

World Bank (2009b), *Doing Business 2010: Reforming through Difficult Times*, September, New York, USA: Palgrave Macmillan.

World Bank (2009c), *From Privilege to Competition: Unlocking Private-Led Growth in the Middle East and North Africa*, MENA Development Report, November, Washington, DC, USA: International Bank for Reconstruction and Development/ World Bank.

World Bank (2009d), 'International Development Association and International Finance Corporation Country Assistance Strategy for the Republic of Yemen for the Period FY 2010–2013', Yemen Country Management Unit, Middle East and North Africa, Report No: 47562-YE, April 29, Washington, DC, USA: World Bank.

World Bank (2009e), 'The Status and Progress of Women in the Middle East and North Africa', World Bank Middle East and North Africa Social and Economic Development Group, Washington, DC, USA: World Bank.

World Bank (2009f), 'What is Inclusive Growth?' PRMED Knowledge Brief, 10 February, Washington, DC, USA: World Bank.

World Bank (2009g), *World Development Indicators 2009*, Washington, DC, USA: International Bank for Reconstruction and Development/ World Bank.

World Bank (2010), *World Development Indicators 2010*, Washington, DC, USA: International Bank for Reconstruction and Development/ World Bank.

YEA (Young Entrepreneurs Association) (2004a), *Global Entrepreneurship Monitor, Jordan's National Report 2004*, Amman, Jordan.

YEA (2004b), *Mindset, Environment, Conditions and Possibilities for Jordan to Flourish as a Hub for Entrepreneurship,* Amman, Jordan.

YEA (2009), 'Public Policy Advocacy Project: Towards Effective Advocacy in Jordan, Request for Proposals', 5 January, Amman, Jordan.

Zaman, C. (2007), 'Quantifying the excess supply of labor in the Syrian economy', January, Warsaw, Poland: Center for Social and Economic Research, available at http://ssrn.com/abstract=959967 (accessed 8 June 2009).

Zinnes, C.F. (2009), 'Business Environment Reforms and the Informal Economy,' discussion paper prepared for the International Finance Corporation, 20 October, IRIS Center, MD, USA: University of Maryland.

Index